Staked Plains Refugee

Staked Plains Refugee

How Texas Conservatives Grew a Liberal
and Didn't Know It

LITERARY PRESS
LAMAR UNIVERSITY

ISBN: 978-1-942956-70-9
Library of Congress Control Number: 2019940921

Manufactured in the United States

Lamar University Literary Press
Beaumont, Texas

For my life partner, Lynda, tenacious in her support of social justice, equality for all, and my many jousts with windmills.

Other Nonfiction from Lamar University Literary Press

Jean Andrews, *High Tides, Low Tides*
Robert Murray Davis, *Levels of Incompetence: An Academic Life*
Ted L. Estess, *Fishing Spirit Lake*
William Guest, *Places You Want to Go*
Dominique Inge, *A Garden on the Brazos*
Terry C. Maxwell, *Tales of a Journeyman Naturalist*
Jim McJunkin, *Deep Sleep*
Jeanetta Calhoun Mish, *Oklahomeland*
Jim Sanderson, *Sanderson's Fiction Writing Manual*
Steven Schroeder, *What's Love Got to Do With It? A city out of thin air*

For Information on these and other books, go to
www.lamar.edu/literarypress

Acknowledgments

Without question, the most enduring and valuable relationship in my journey as a writer has been my friendship with Jerry Craven, who was my thesis adviser and mentor in the graduate English program at what was then West Texas State University. I owe him much more than a mere thank-you for years of help, including much time spent with the development of this book. Another major influence on me as a journalist and writer was the late Buck Ramsey, cowboy, reporter, writer and poet, who introduced me to everything from how to write a proper feature story to how to properly react to injustice. Others who have given me support when it was most needed include the late Mark Robertson-Baker, Larry Statser, the late Archie Pool, Jeanne Bookout Marosis, Suzanne Thompson Turner, the late Bill Lee, Francis Tate, Darrell Coleman, Bill Gulledge, Buddy Grace, Eddie Barker, Deanna Watson, the Rev. Hector Medina, Tom Dawson, the late Neil Hawkins, the late Iris Matney, the late Leon Gibbs and Ida Lee Cope.

Introduction

When I first began reading Carroll Wilson's memoir, I was struck by a number of coincidences. I describe some of the details of my life by way of introduction to this memoir. Before reading it, I thought I had followed an odd, idiosyncratic route to becoming a liberal Democrat.

I grew up poor in the small North Texas town of Ennis, 20 miles south of Dallas. I was a B student at Ennis High, threw the *Dallas Morning News*, went to East Texas State University in Commerce, planning to teach high school English. My family and friends were racist, mainly good ol' boys and girls. I thought little about Texas politics until November 22, 1963, when the Kennedy Assassination awakened me to the world of politics. My college years were spent looking over my shoulder at Vietnam.

When I was drafted in 1969, I became politicized—a left wing, Texas liberal opposing the war, which in Ennis seemed at first an act of treason. I thought I was alone. To buy time trying to avoid going to Vietnam, I applied for and was accepted for U.S. Army Infantry Officer Candidate School at Fort Benning, Georgia. I completed OCS by avoiding talking politics and was about to be commissioned an Infantry 2nd lieutenant eventually bound for the Vietnam boonies. Instead I was designated an honor graduate in OCS and got to choose my assignment to the Adjutant General Corps, the paperworks branch of the Army. With Nixon's drawdown through his secret Vietnamization plan, I finished my time teaching new AG officers how to write at Fort Benjamin Harrison, Indiana and got an early out. Then the GI Bill was my lifeline and carried me to the Ph.D. program at the University of Colorado, Boulder.

I've been teaching English at Texas State University in San Marcos for the last 28 years. When my old friend Jerry Craven, publisher of Lamar University Literary Press, asked me to read Carroll Wilson's manuscript, I looked at the title and read the first few pages. Then I began to feel odd because this memoir by someone I'd never met smashed my general belief that I had traveled a singular trail. I discovered that Wilson grew up in Amarillo but spent much time with his grandfather in East Texas, near where I'd gone to school (and Carroll's father). In West Texas, he worked in publishing, went through ROTC in college, and was commissioned a U.S. Army second lieutenant by spending training days at Fort Benning. Like me, he was an honor graduate and also chose to stay out of the infantry by transferring into the Adjutant General Corps. He too ended up doing his time at Fort Benjamin Harrison, just north of the city of Indianapolis. Wilson and I got to Fort Harrison by similar paths at about the same time, worked on different sides of Fort Harrison, and were both involved in different aspects of communications and received early discharges. Oddly, we never met, although he may have been in one of my classes. These aspects of Wilson's life connect with much of mine, culminating in our ending up in Wimberley, Texas, with our wives (both of whom are named Linda/Lynda), where we finally met earlier this year.

While reading Wilson's manuscript and seeing our similar experiences, I noted that Wilson made it clear that one of his purposes was to explain how someone like him—and me—could grow up in the strict narrowness of right-wing Texas. We each became a committed lefty—anathema to our parents and to most of friends and people in the towns where we grew up. Carefully, he clearly explains how he's "become what you'd probably call a flaming liberal. I belong to the Democratic Socialists of America. And yet I grew up and lived for more than 30 years in the most conservative city in the most conservative state in the country."

One result of the political trail that Wilson found himself following was deciding to write a daily response to the events of 2017 (the year that he turned 70), chronologically recording the personal and professional activities and the public events he noted. Among the strange and upsetting daily events were the puzzling paths of the man who had somehow become the President of the United States of America: Donald J. Trump. Wilson's concentration on 2017 holds in relief the effect of the trampling of norms that ironically has become habitual in the wake of Trump's presidency.

But he is not consumed by Trump. He reads the Sunday *New York Times* and the *New Yorker* and reflects on the varied subjects on which they focus, including the books he discovers such as *Back Home* by Mort Rosenblum, *Hillbilly Elegy* by J.D. Vance, and others. He also recalls some of his varied experiences over the years, including his opposition to the Pantex nuclear weapons assembly plant northeast of Amarillo off Interstate 40, and the various Texas newspapers he worked for.

But beyond Wilson's reactions to the political events, he discusses his own personal activities, which provide a guidepost for how a committed, interesting man in his 70s moves into this stage of his life with energy and the belief that someone approaching old age need not give up the recognition of the values of keeping sharp. After gently accepting retirement status, Wilson became antsy, began taking online courses through Duke, the University of Virginia, and one offered by Coursera called "Transmedia Storytelling." He ran for and was elected to the CARD steering committee. (CARD stands for Citizens Alliance for Responsible Development, and it oversees development in the Wimberley Valley.) He also is a member of the board of the Wimberley Valley Dark Sky Alliance and is on the vestry at St. Stephen's Episcopal Church. He expanded his volunteer work at the Wimberley library to a paid position with more weekly hours when a coworker left.

Those among the Trump stalwarts may think such a book is not for them. But the larger matters Wilson addresses transcend the topical issues of Trump's presidency. This book will lead you to consider the larger concerns of a life: how do you pursue and accomplish a life well-lived as issues of the world cloud our understanding and as our bodies and minds irrevocably and inevitably lose their strength and sharpness? Living and thinking well are the best revenge.

Mark Busby
President, Texas Institute of Letters, 2004-05

Preface

In the year 2017, my 70th on the planet, my worst nightmare in a lifetime of bad dreams came true: Donald Trump took over as president of the United States.

This confluence set me to thinking about where I'd been and what I'd done to deserve this particular slap on the butt. But even before the election of 2016 I had been planning to write a journal in '17.

I'd done some family history research that left me wondering about what life was really like on a day-to-day basis for my ancestors. Here I had a chance to set out some details for my own great-grandchildren.

I admit right up-front that this version of personal history they read will need to be placed into a context they probably won't know anything about. That's because I've become what you'd probably call a flaming liberal. I belong to the Democratic Socialists of America. And yet I grew up and lived for more than 30 years in the most conservative city in the most conservative state in the country. I grew up in Amarillo, center of the Texas Panhandle.

Few who actually know anything about the history of Amarillo will argue with me about its political nature. But, let me bolster my contention with some comments from scholars and other observers.

This statement comes from H.M. Baggerly, editor and publisher of *The Tulia Herald*, who was well-known nationally in the '60s for being a radical leftist among radical rightists: "Probably no other city in the 50 states is more ultra-conservative than Amarillo, Texas. ... Most Amarillo Democrats have to go underground to survive, socially or economically. Last fall it was hardly safe to wear a Kennedy button to a public meeting in Amarillo. People eyed you as if you were wearing a hammer and sickle." (From Texas Country Editor: *H.M. Baggerly Takes a Grass-Roots Look at National Politics*, edited by Eugene W. Jones, The World Publishing Co. of Cleveland and New York, 1966, page 223)

A somewhat more recent outside observer, A.G. Mojtabai, writes in her book called *Blessed Assurance: At Home With the Bomb in Amarillo, Texas*, about how Gene Howe, publisher and editor of the Amarillo papers in the '30s and '40s, mirrored the opinions of his readers: "Howe opposed the income tax, along with any programs and policies which, he felt, relied too much on outside control or assistance. Dependence was weakening; he reminded his readers of what the pioneers had struggled through. When people softened up, he warned, they perished." (*Blessed Assurance* was published by Houghton-Mifflin Co., Boston, 1986)

Terry Isaacs, writing about one of the most conservative groups to emerge in the '60s, contended that Amarillo enthusiastically and wholly embraced the John Birch Society. In his 1996 article in the *New Mexico Historical Review* about the Birchers, he enumerates several efforts undertaken by Birchers in the county courthouse to ban books from stores and libraries because they were "Communistic."

And in *Cowboy Conservatism: Texas and the Rise of the Modern Right*, Sean P. Cunningham takes it to an even more personal level in his discussion of J. Evetts Haley:

"Among Texas's most outspoken idealogues, Haley was a rancher, historian, proud member of the John Birch Society, and longtime thorn in liberal Democrats' sides ... He is most famous for his scathing indictment of Lyndon Johnson in a book entitled *A Texan Looks at Lyndon: A Study in Illegitimate Power*, published in 1964."

Too, Cunningham also cites what other authors have illuminated about Amarillo and the Panhandle: "... white dispensational Protestantism in Texas has long reinforced notions of independence, self-determination, free will, and a resistance to change and reform."

I can personally vouch for the descriptions of all writers who call Amarillo the most conservative place in America. I knew Evetts Haley. I knew H.M. Baggarly. I grew up Protestant. I grew up knowing about Birchers and got my own copy of Haley's book from two Birchers at Amarillo College who were handing them out from the trunk of their car.

So, how did I make it out of all this alive and well and in complete opposition to what Amarillo stood for?

I hope this book, a diary and a memoir and a running commentary, explains that well enough to keep a reader who is not just a curious great-grandchild entertained and intrigued.

Jan.1: In May of this year, I will turn 70, and one of my keenest hopes is that I not blindly stumble into that den where hide the Furies that manage Ironic Destiny. By that I mean I want to avoid what They just brazenly visited upon the hapless Debbie Reynolds, who died just one day after the death of her daughter Carrie Fisher, an ironic development if there ever were one. To be a little more explicit about it, I don't want either of these things to be said about me in 2017: "Alas, poor fellow, how ironic that he was hit by that train just a day (a week, a month) *before* he celebrated his 70th birthday!" or "Poor Wilson, how ironic that he choked to death on a chunk of prime beef just a day (a week, a month) *after* he turned 70 years of age!" I want to live in a place where irony cannot touch me.

I also want to live in a place not ruled by Donald J. Trump. I have told many people since the November 2016 election that were I a young man, were I single and were I wealthier, I would be heading out the door for Costa Rica, a lovely place, I am told, and a place not yet ruled by Donald J. Trump or his lackeys. As it is, ironies notwithstanding, I shall continue to live in Wimberley this year with my wife Lynda and my dog Chi-Chi. If I am allowed more than one keen hope for 2017 it would be that Donald J. Trump would wake up one morning and realize he would hate being president of the United States and would walk away from the job. But, he will not, and so this is bound to be a year of heartbreak and anger and pissiness.

Too, I want to live a day at a time. That is, I want to follow the advice of all those hundreds of authors of feel-good best-sellers and approach each day as if it is my last (not yet victimized by Irony!) and make the best of things, and live for the present, and meditate, and give thanks for the simple gifts, and ha-ha-ho-ho-hee-hee-ta-da-ta-dum. Not, as they say, gonna happen. What famous advisors might want my life to be like is not going to eventuate. It will be what it will be, and if history is any indication I will do my best to get in some intense walking, eat well but not lavishly, abstain from drinking and smoking and love my wife and dog and other family members who make themselves available.

The year is off to a good start. A very pleasant morning after a good night's sleep, thanks to the fact that the neighbors who live in the cul-de-sac behind us for some reason decided not to shoot off fireworks all night long like they did last year. Chi-Chi was, thus, not a trembling wreck. So, neither were we. I did my 30 minutes of interval walking, something I do four days each week, then read the Sunday edition of *The New York Times* as delivered to my driveway. (I read the *Times* four days a week online and three days a week at the dining room table while I have my very strong Cubano coffee, which may or may not taste like something from the island in the Caribbean; I would love to find out by taking a trip down there!) *The Times Sunday Review* section is filled, as it has been since November, with mea culpas and strained observations about the Trump triumph. It is not so much tedious as pathetic. Where were these blithering assholes back in March, or August, or November?

After a nice shower, I took off for church, to be there by 10 a.m. so that I

13

could do some sound checks with the pastors. Even after doing a sound check with the guy who was to do preaching his mic started acting up mid-sermon, and I had to go right up there to the altar and give him a new mic setup.

Jan. 2: After a beautiful 70-degree Sunday, last night turned nasty. Storms started rolling in after midnight, and they kept Chi-Chi from getting any sleep and, thus, me from getting any sleep. During a thunderstorm, Chi-Chi doesn't shiver like many dogs; instead, she just mopes around under the covers. She can't get still. I try to quieten her down, but she moves constantly. At least she is not trying to get out of bed and howling and barking. Today the sun rose to a wet ground but completely cloudless skies. I did my 30-minute sustained walk circuit that takes me by the golf course.

Brother John sent me another in a long, long series of whacky emails yesterday. Actually, he stopped sending me far-right emails back during the campaign when it dawned on him that we were not supporting Donald Trump. He was, of course. Yesterday's email gave a completely political spin to the reason why we eat black-eyed peas on New Year's Day, which we do. According to the author of the email, the custom came into being during Sherman's march to the sea during the late part of the Civil War. I did not read the whole thing because I just don't need to stay in a constant state of upset by something John has forwarded. It surprises me somewhat that John seems to be turning into, not only a Trumpite, but a Southern sympathizer and slavery-as-inhumane denier. I did not reply. I just deleted.

Jan. 3: Over the weekend, I read somewhere – perhaps in *The New York Times*, perhaps in the AARP magazine, maybe online – that new research results show that to keep mentally and physically fit as you age you need to do more than simply work a few more Sudoku puzzles every day or add another 15 minutes to your morning walk. You have to push yourself until what you're doing is painful. No pain, no gain. I understand the concept when it comes to trying to build up endurance or muscles like your heart. I'm not sure I know what to do to get to the pain level mentally that will keep me going well past 70. To me, trying to figure out how to finish a Sudoku borders on the painful. What am I supposed to do? Read "Ulysses?" Try to learn Mandarin Chinese? Start a degree program in particle physics? I wonder, too, how this research deals with other approaches, like the practice of Zen Buddhism or Tai Chi, where there is no pain at all. I did do my 30-minute walk this morning in 43-degree weather (another beautiful day after Monday's perfection), and as usual I pushed myself to a certain uncomfortable level of pain trying to get up that darn hill that's west of our house.

I see in today's *Times* that the Republicans in Congress have dismantled the office that was created to make sure people in their positions and others at the higher echelons of government act ethically. The decision was made in secret, an ethical breach in and of itself. As a nation we will pay dearly for the election of Donald Trump and the validation of his worldview.

Today I must mail off a parcel to John containing a book called *My Combat Diary with Eighth Air Force B-17s 390th Bomb Group* by Andrew Anzanos. I found the book last week on Amazon after, just for the heck of it, doing a search on Google for the name "Liberty Bell-E." The Liberty Bell-E was a B-17G Flying Fortress that was shot down over Germany in February 1944. It is significant to John and to me because Mom's only brother Edmund was the ball turret gunner on that airplane and died in the crash. I was unaware of the Anzanos book. Back 25 years ago or more I tracked down crew members who survived that catastrophe and did a story about Edmund and Mother and the Liberty Bell-E. The story of Mother and her brother is a poignant and sad one, and I hoped to get some insight about Edmund from the Anzanos book, which is basically a publication of his daily journal. Unfortunately, it does not contain much that is new; it simply reaffirms that the Liberty Bell-E was, in the author's words, a lemon. John will appreciate the book. I am sure he has not heard of it or he would have alerted me to it.

Jan. 4: I went to the post office early yesterday to mail the book package to John. I was fifth or sixth in line, and there was one postal work at the counter. Two people ahead of me in line was a fairly big older guy wearing a gimme cap with TRUMP stitched on the back. As I leaned against the rail for the wait, an older gentleman came in and took up his position right behind me in the queue. After only a few moments, he said to me, "Well, d'ya think they're gonna unscramble this Obama care mess?"

"I believe they will," I said.
"What d'ya think'll happen then?" he asked.
"I'm not sure," I said, "but it will surely be a disaster, whatever it is."
I kept an eye on the TRUMP man. He didn't seem to hear or notice.
"My son's got Obama care, and he has to pay $100 a month, and it's got a $6,000 deductible," the old man said.
"That doesn't sound too bad," I said. "What he's got is catastrophic care. I guess his option will be to go to the emergency room."

I looked away and kind of twisted toward the counter. He got the message.
The TRUMP man stepped to the slot with the clerk and got embroiled in a conversation about his transaction that soon involved two clerks and had him moving to a different slot. I hoped he would be trapped till noon in a briar patch that people in Congress just like him created by gutting the postal service.
On our patio out in the backyard we have a black Weber grill that has two side platforms that you can fold up to hold plates or utensils while you cook. I just leave them up all the time. For the past week or so I've watched a male cardinal out the back door. He stands underneath one of the platforms and jumps straight up flat-footed until his head bangs against the metal, then he falls to the patio and jumps straight up again. He does this over and over. I'm thinking of him as the mascot of America's angry white males.

Jan. 5: The Seguin library is awe-inspiring, I must say. We got there at mid-morning and had a tour. The building is located on a beautiful creekside, shaded by giant trees, and is almost all glass. It is a place where I could just install a bedroom and live, although it would be a pretty big house at 48,000 square feet. The Tye Preston Library in Canyon Lake was a little less impressive and downright

15

shabby/dark when compared to the new facility in Seguin. I will write up some reports on our visits.

A week or so ago, the book review section of The *New York Times* published short pieces by famous people I'd never heard of about their favorite books, and one of them mentioned *Zen and the Art of Motorcycle Maintenance*. This favorable citation kind of surprised me because even though I have read *Zen and the Art ...* several times over the years I guess I supposed that it would be looked down upon by the la-ti-da literati as sophomoric, something along the lines of *Atlas Shrugged* by Ayn Rand or *The Glass Bead Game* by Hermann Hesse. I never put it in that category myself, but I'm not a la-ti-da literati, either. I decided I need to read *Zen* again, so I found a new copy on Amazon and ordered it. It arrived yesterday in such pristine condition I almost hate to open it up and ruin the back. I will read it, though. I remember the last time I read it, I was editor of the newspaper in Canyon, so it was in the '70s, probably after I got out of the Army. *Zen* is about defining quality. Right now, I'm trying to define what it is about this country that makes it seem that everything is way off kilter or out of whack. Maybe re-reading *Zen* will help me define what I feel so I can put it into words.

Jan. 6: Someone posted an item on Facebook that John picked up on and forwarded to Lynda and me. It's a photocopy of the front-page segment of a story I wrote back in 1966 or 1967 when I was working as a reporter at the Amarillo newspaper. The story is about the Amarillo teen ritual of "dragging Polk Street." I graduated from high school in 1965, at what was probably the peak of interest in packing your car with friends and driving back and forth, north to south to north on Polk Street, the main street in Amarillo. This was kind of a mindless exercise in a town where there wasn't much else to do. On a typical weekend night, Amarillo High kids would drive over to The Ranger drive-in restaurant on the Canyon Expressway, get a Coke, and then drive to Polk and go back and forth. Tascosa kids did the same thing starting at Stanley's drive-in on Georgia Street. And Palo Duro kids started the ritual at Twing's drive-in on the north side of Amarillo. Dragging Polk allowed for arms-length interaction, but it also involved the high drama of light-to-light drag racing.

At some point not long after I wrote this story, Amarillo Air Force Base was closed down, and almost overnight downtown Amarillo, which had been a bustling retail center for the entire Texas Panhandle, turned into a ghost town. The shops just shut their doors. In a sad effort to try to entice customers back to the city's center, the chamber of commerce coaxed the City Council into closing off Polk Street to all traffic one Christmas in that time frame, and they set up Christmas trees and tinsel and people stayed away in droves. So much for dragging Polk.

The closing of the base was just the last straw, though, and not the entire cause of the demise of downtown Amarillo. The opening of a couple of big shopping malls in south Amarillo had more to do with dooming Polk Street than anything else. Big retailers like Sears and J.C. Penney and Dillard's and Montgomery Wards were all in the malls, not downtown. Like most Amarilloans, I liked the malls better than I did downtown. The weather in that part of Texas is unpredictable and can be truly horrible in the wintertime. Inside a mall is the place to be if you need to shop. I loved going to the bookstores at the mall, maybe doing some shopping, mainly just people watching.

In an odd episode of cosmic coincidence, I picked up *The New York Times* today to learn that Macy's is laying off 10,000 workers and closing stores in malls all across America. Sears is doing the same thing. The *Times* story puts these events in context:

"Green Street Advisors, which tracks the mall industry, said in a report last year that more department store closures 'should ultimately result in a larger number of malls becoming irrelevant retail destinations'."

Everyone is shopping online, not going to big department stores or malls. I haven't been to a mall in five years. Lynda did all of her Christmas shopping mainly by using Amazon. I guess I don't miss the mall experience too much or I would make an effort to go to one.

I received an email from WimDems this morning seeking people to go on a bus to the women's march in Austin on Jan. 21. I want to go, and going by bus would be far preferable to driving by myself.

Donald Trump has his intelligence briefing today on the Russian hacking of our elections, something he says didn't happen. We will see how stupid he really is when he comes out of the meeting and talks with the press. Can you impeach a president before he takes office?

Jan. 7: We woke up to an outside temperature of 22 degrees. That's the lowest temperature we've experienced since we moved to the Hill Country in 2011. I put on the warmest gear I could find and headed out around 8 o'clock. There was no wind, so it was more than bearable. I've found this winter that when it's colder my legs don't hurt so much when I push myself on my slow-fast interval walks. So, I didn't mind this at all. When I think about getting freaked out about being cold outside I put it in perspective. I grew up in Amarillo and spent 10 years in Canyon, so I know about low temperatures, blizzards, drought and searing heat. I remember being really cold when I was a kid throwing my paper route on early Sunday mornings. Usually, if it had snowed the temperatures were more bearable than if a cold front moved through with winds and very low temperatures and no moisture at all. But, no particular day stands out as so brutally cold I couldn't stand it. I must pause a moment to recall Mrs. Helm, a wonderful lady who lived on Fannin Street. She was Malcolm Helm's mother, and Malcolm was my best friend. On those really cold Sunday mornings when I was throwing papers, Mrs. Helm would meet me at her front door and invite me in for a cup of hot cocoa. It was such a nice thing to do that I'll be forever grateful for her kindness. Still, those mornings were not the coldest I've ever seen. The worst cold I've personally experienced was one day in February in 1981 or 1982. I was working as a reporter for KFDA-TV, which had its station north of Amarillo. From the front door of the station you could see all the way to the North Pole and there was nothing to stop the frigid wind when it started howling in from the Arctic Circle. On this particular morning, I was dispatched with a partner to a home in North Amarillo where a body had been found inside a car that was in the driveway. Our assignment was to get video of the car and, if possible, the body, and the cops, ambulances, etc., and to wait to get more video when the body was removed and more video with sound when the cops decided to tell us whether foul play had been involved. This turned into a marathon ordeal with us waiting outside our van to keep tabs on the cops. At that point in my life I had one heavy winter coat, a leather bomber jacket that was actually worn more for the macho looks of it than for comfort in cold weather. No hat or cap. No gloves. No long johns. The wind was blowing sleet horizontally straight out of Alaska, and the temperature had to be in the 20s, and I couldn't get warm. I felt as if I were facing the winter gods with no clothes on at all. Of course, I should have been better prepared.

Donald Trump got his briefing yesterday from the CIA and other intelligence sources. Their report is stunning. So is Trump's reaction: *Let's just move on because I really don't believe what the CIA has to say.*

Jan. 8: I spent probably four hours yesterday researching and writing the devotionals that people will receive to read every day during the one week I am assigned later in January. Eight or nine of us at the church write the daily devotionals on a regular schedule. I seem to always put off the task until the last minute, which is what I did this weekend. I am assigned to write six devotionals based on passages from Isaiah, Mark or the letter of Paul to the Galatians. I looked at the passages from Mark and from Isaiah and decided on Galatians. I just couldn't figure out how to make something with an episodic quality out of Isaiah. He seems to be all of one fabric and one message, and I don't know how to vary that enough to carry through six days of daily thoughts. Mark I skipped because Mark's passages describe what Jesus was doing, and you don't need a commentary to figure that out on your own. It's not like there is some hidden meaning there, although a lot of TV preachers and big-church preachers would like to make it seem so. The parts of Galatians I was assigned are in Chapters 5 and 6, and they are crystal clear about Paul's message to the audience. In particular, and as an example, let me pull up what I wrote about one passage:

Galatians 5:1-15
For in Christ Jesus, neither circumcision nor noncircumcision counts for anything, but only faith working through love.

To be more specific about his emphasis on the need to abandon Mosaic law and adopt love as the standard for behavior, Paul uses the practice of circumcision in these passages. But, he wants the Galatians to understand that this business about circumcision involves a rule that deflects their attention from what should be the real focus of their lives – exercising their faith by loving their fellow human beings. Faith is what counts, not blind adherence to regulations that have little or nothing to do with the human spirit. If faith is what counts, and this is a lesson that reaches to us from across the eons, then how does one make faith count here in the 21st Century? The answer is right here in Verse 14: "For the whole law is fulfilled in one statement, namely, 'You shall love your neighbor as yourself.' " In this entire letter, in the entirety of the works of Paul, in the entirety of the preaching of Jesus Christ, that is the bottom line: Love your neighbor as yourself. It is unequivocal. But, like our counterparts of centuries past, we are very good at arguing the finer points here. Who, exactly, is our neighbor? What does it mean to actually love your neighbor? Love? Is that a noun? Or a verb?

Let us hear about one Cedric Herrou, 37, described recently by *The New York Times* as "a slightly built olive farmer" in France. Cedric Herrou was the subject of a front-page story in The *Times* on January 6. He was on trial in southern France. He stood charged with helping smuggle illegal immigrants into his country. "Why did you do all this?" the judge asked him one day during the trial, and Mr. Herrou "turned the tables and questioned the humanity of France's practice of rounding up and turning back Africans entering illegally from Italy in search of work and a better life. It was "ignoble," he said. "There are people dying on the side of the road," Mr. Herrou replied. "It's not right. There are children who are not safe. It is enraging to see children, at 2 in the morning, completely dehydrated. I am a Frenchman," Mr. Herrou declared. Mr. Herrou saw a moral dilemma where the state did not. Mr. Herrou loved his neighbor. The state did not. We are Americans. How blind must we be not to see the children, dehydrated and dying, as they and their families make their way to this country for better lives? Why do we choose not to see? How easy it is to pass regulations that have no cosmic meaning while we neglect universal laws that require us to express our true humanity.

I am inspired by Mr. Herrou, who held to his beliefs even in the face of the pressure of the state. We in the United States will need the backbone of Mr. Herrou to stand up and say to Mr. Trump and his allies: "No. You will not treat immigrants and their children like bricks! No. You will not make the rich richer and poor poorer! No. You will not dismantle our public schools! No. You will not enrich yourself on the taxpayers' dollars! No. You will not get in bed with Vladimir Putin! No. You will not send us to war in the Middle East or anywhere else! No. Mr. Trump! No."

Jan 9: We were watching Anthony Bourdaine last night during supper, and one of his comments prompted Lynda to ask me if I'd ever hitch-hiked. Just once, I told her. It had to be about this time of year in 1965. A group of us guys had piled into a couple of cars and headed to my best friend David Woodburn's cabin in Eagle's Nest, N.M., for a long weekend. I remember riding with Woodburn in his 1954 two-toned green Mercury. We were almost to the cabin, driving on snowy roads, when the car developed a leak in the gas line, I think it was. We stumbled into the cabin, and I guess Woodburn headed out the next day to get the car fixed; I don't remember. I went up there with the promise from the guys that one of them with a car was going to return to Amarillo in time for me to get ready to be in George Pulley's wedding. GG was a good friend who had startled all of us by announcing during our senior year in high school that he was going to get married before graduation. So, I just figured I would hitch-hike; it was my only real option.

On the morning I needed to leave, I got a ride into town and waited around the country store hoping to get someone to agree to take me somewhere close to Amarillo. Finally, the mailman said he'd take me as far as Cimarron, which was a good piece up the road. I figured once I got to Cimarron, a picturesque and touristy kind of place, it would be no problem to get a ride on toward home. The mailman took his sweet time, and he let me off in Cimarron in mid-afternoon. As the afternoon began to turn to dusk, I noticed a carload of teen-age boys were driving past me in one direction and then turning around and coming back, and they were all looking at me like I was fresh meat. So, I trudged into the St. James Hotel and asked the clerk to use the phone and got hold of Dad. After some discussion, he agreed to pick up the tab on the hotel and to come the next morning to pick me up. I was so relieved. I even got a good night's sleep, even though I went to bed hungry. The ghosts left me alone.

I'm now a card-bearing member of the Democratic Socialists of America. Got the card in the mail yesterday, along with some things to read through. We want to watch Bernie Sanders tomorrow evening on TV. We will be boycotting anything having to do with Donald Trump this week, and Lynda is going to find a list of official corporate sponsors of any Trump event so we can boycott those people, too. I'm dead serious when I say the only appropriate response to Trump on ANYTHING is NO!

This is the week during which network television people will prepare us for the coronation as if this were a normal transition of power from one stable person to another stable person. This may be an ordinary series of events and an ordinary schedule of coverage, but this has all the feel of the regal crowning of an emperor anointed by the Almighty himself, without the acknowledgement of such by the subject despot. It is maddening to watch the Matt Lauers of the world slobber all over themselves as they get token access to the Great Man and his entourage. Donald Trump holds them in contempt, and who can wonder why. There's not a handful of courageous journalists among them.

It is stunning that White Trash Nation has elected a narcissist, racist, know-it-all bully to be their leader. It is remarkable that the checks and balances that one hoped would be in effect in the media and in the system of governance itself would keep someone like Donald Trump out of the top office in the land. But no one has had the guts, including members of the Electoral College, who adhered to the letter of their agreements while ignoring the spirit of the Constitution. The White Trash Nation will pay one way or another and potentially in many ways.

We are in the second week of the new Congress, and there has been no bill passed to repeal Obamacare. The Republicans promised this would happen instantly as soon as the new Congress was sworn in. After all, they voted to repeal Obama care more than 60 times in the last four years of his presidency.

Jan. 10: For many years, KGNC-TV in Amarillo had a very early morning farm show whose host was Cotton John, a skinny old guy who had a nasal twang that perfectly fit into the Panhandle motif. Cotton John was proud of proclaiming on a daily basis that sunrise was the very best part of a Golden Spread Day! It could be freezing outside, and Cotton John would be just proud as peaches of the sun rising over the drivers suffering the misery of getting to work. We do not live in the Golden Spread, an apt phrase, by the way, to describe the Panhandle. This morning, though, Cotton John would have been beaming. I hit the street at 7:15, and the temperature was 59 degrees.

The New Yorker reports that celebrities and big-name groups are staying away from the Trump inauguration. One performer who refused an invitation said accepting it and performing would be like tossing roses at Hitler. The Rockettes will perform, but the individuals will be volunteers. In my dreams, Trump will mount the scaffolding to take the oath of office and will peer out on an empty Capitol vista. Donald Trump *must* find the next four years so frustrating and terrible that he will never seek election again.

Jan. 11: Like the inestimable man of class that he is, President Obama gave his last official speech to the American people last night, and I was impressed by the fact that he managed to tiptoe around the elephant in the living room. He only tangentially talked about what the future might hold for this country under the dictatorship of Donald Trump. Obama warned us to get involved, to be vigilant and to take it to the streets if we couldn't make our voices heard. He urged us to get organized at the grassroots level. This must happen. Late last year, some very smart young former Washington staffers circulated a memo that told liberals how to fight Trump just like conservatives fought Obama. And we have to do that. We have to start that fight at the courthouse and in the Legislature so we can undo the horrendous gerrymandering that has given Republicans such a stranglehold on this state. Obama, in very brief form, outlined the major accomplishments of his administration, and they have been numerous—from health-care reform to a complete uprighting of an economy that was on the very edge of depression. These things were done with absolute 100-percent Republican opposition, which makes them all the more remarkable.

True to his own form, Donald Trump had his first press conference in six months today and blamed everything on the media. He did admit that the Russians might have hacked our elections on 2016, but from there he went into a rant about how the media had fabricated a memo that was leaked saying that the Russians had an embarrassing dossier on Trump that they could hold over his head. He continues to play to his White Trash constituency, forgetting that he lost the popular vote by almost 3 million. Another take-away from the speech: He will not divest himself of his many properties. His lawyers argue that the Constitution does not include the presidency in its prohibition of accepting gifts or favors from foreign powers, even though every president since Ben Franklin's time has been advised that the Constitution does intend that the presidency be included in the ban. It is to be fervently hoped that he will stick to his guns and we will very soon have an impeachment trial and a vote that will strip him of power. At the very least, he needs to be tied up in court and in Congressional hearings until the cows come home.

This morning we started up the Reading Buddies program again at Jacob's Well Elementary School. Every Wednesday last fall and again now that the holidays are over, several of us have met with second-grade students who need help learning to read. I have three students, M., T. and H. M. is a cute girl, and H. and T. are boys. The two boys were at about the same reading level— below the second grade—before Christmas. M. was still struggling. Today, the two guys whipped through their books. They did well, stumbling only on certain words. T. did the best. He told me he'd been reading over the break, and it shows. M. was actually behind where she was three weeks ago. She has some catching up to do before she is back even. This is an excellent program, but I wonder if waiting to try to help these kids until second grade is a little too late. I volunteered as a reading tutor for some first-graders a couple of years ago over at Scudder Primary School, and they were doing very well by the end of that first year. Not that it matters. This is what the teachers have designed, and I am happy to go with it. No child should get out of second grade without being able to read at a level beyond that.

Jan. 12: Donald Trump's press conference yesterday compared to the president's final speech the night before really helped to show the difference between a man who is petulant, narcissistic, ignorant of the facts and combative and a man who is confident in his power to do good and improve the lot of his people. One man wants it all his way; the other wants it the way that will be the best for the United States.

Russia and Putin continue to dominate media conversations about Trump. Putin and Russia have truly taken on an outsize role in defining international relationships. I was reminded of this the other day when The *New York Times* printed a story about Russia pulling an aircraft carrier back to home port from action around Syria. The carrier happens to be the only one that Russia has. And it's got a history of maintenance problems. It's not much of a weapons system anyway: It carries 15 aircraft. I wanted to see how much of a threat Russia truly poses to western democracies in military terms, so I looked it up on the web, going to a site that aggregates military force information called GFP. GFP data for 2016 show that while Russia has one aircraft carrier, the United States has 19. They have 60 submarines; we have 75. They have 751 fighter jets; we have 2,308. They have an annual military budget of $46.6 billion; we have a budget of $581 billion. It truly is no contest. Russia is a sad big Third World country. Putin must be laughing his ass off.

We watched "Blue Collar Millionaire" for the first time last night, and one of the segments involved a guy in Fort Worth who ran an automotive junk yard and turned it into a million-dollar business and more. Certainly, he was not the first to turn abandoned acreage into a grungy parts supply business. But he was among the first to actually pull together an inventory of what he had and where to actually put things where you could find them if you wanted to buy them. I have had experience with junkyards, and the staff at every junkyard I've ever visited had a general idea of what kinds of vehicles they had but no idea what parts could be salvaged from those vehicles. "Oh," they'd say, pointing abstractly to the South Forty, "we might have one of them out there somewhere. You're welcome to look around." It was like a treasure hunt that you really didn't want to make because you could spend hours looking through the wrecks and never find anything you could use. And the pricing was completely arbitrary. I got the impression that guys ran junkyards, not to make money, but to have some place to go every day where they could tear stuff up, smoke, drink some beer and get away from the women.

Jan. 13: Good news arrived with The *Times* this morning. The Justice Department is going to see if there is sufficient evidence to charge James Comey, the FBI director, with the crime of trying to fix a federal election. Most certainly he did. Just days before the Nov. 6 election Comey announced he was reopening an investigation into Hillary Clinton's emails. Then a couple of days later, after the damage was done, he said, Oh well, never mind. This man needs to go to jail. I don't know why President Obama has not fired his sorry ass.

22

Fiat Chrysler is being accused of programming its diesel vehicles to pass emissions tests while dirtying up the air at illegal levels. This is the same thing VW did, but, of course, Fiat Chrysler said they did nothing of the sort. It's sobering to consider how many of our corporate citizens act so badly. Apple has its headquarters in Ireland so it can avoid corporate taxes in America. VW engineers its cars to pollute. So does Fiat Chrysler. And the list goes on and on. By the way, no support coming from this quarter for AT&T, Chevron and Boeing, all of whom are corporate sponsors of the Trump inaugural. I will be looking for other businesses to boycott because they are supporting the man. I can have little impact on Boeing or Chevron. I don't buy Chevron gasoline, anyway, and I'm probably not going to be buying a jet anytime soon. But, over the long haul I might do a little damage to L.L. Bean, which The *Times* reports today has been a big supporter of Trump. They are not going to sell me one more item. And I will be out bad-mouthing them as much as possible.

I got an email today that I am, in fact, on the bus for the Women's rally in Austin next Saturday.

I presented an update to the library district board yesterday on the activities so far of the committee I'm heading up to look at expansion possibilities. I was surprised to learn that the board has no plan to build or build on, even though they just bought three acres of land north of the library for that purpose. I was equally surprised to learn the board had no clue how to finance a construction project.

Jan. 14: Overcast and 57 this morning when I went for my interval walk. The only other person out there was the little lady who supported Trump. I avoid her.

For the last week, the TV stations out of Austin have been running a commercial for the Shrine Circus, which is having shows in Cedar Park this weekend. One clip shows an elephant act, and another shows a tiger act. A crawler seems to suggest that the elephants may be disappearing from the circus at some point, kind of the way Shamu and his brethren have gone the way of the dodo in water world acts. I hope so. In fact, I can't believe that the circus still has elephants. I am not completely aware of the status of elephants in the wild, but I am aware that these creatures are acutely in tune with their environments. They are smart. They feel pain. They have preferences. In today's always-plugged-in world, I simply cannot see why anyone would pay to see elephants mistreated. I feel the same way about tigers. You don't need to even go to a zoo to see tigers. Just Google them. If you Google the word "elephants," you pull up 103 million hits. Google the term "tigers," and you get 133 million hits. I rest my case.

Maybe 25 years ago now, when I was editor of the newspaper in Wichita Falls, we got wind of a huge event at our local mall, Sikes Senter. On a school day morning, it seemed, a particular shoe store was being mobbed. Our reporters learned that the phenomenon was one of national proportions. A new sneaker endorsed by some basketball superstar was going on sale that morning, and every kid in the school system had to have a pair to be cool. At the time, as I recall, the shoes were going for something like $65 a pair, which was a ridiculous price to pay. I had the feeling that moms and dads were shelling out that kind of money for sneakers when they were sending their kids to school with no lunch money. To this day, I've not understood this craze, and it has not abated one iota. We were watching a show about the rich and famous the other night, and one of the guys had a closet full of celebrity endorsed sneakers worth thousands of dollars. I see in today's *Times* that Michael Jordan sneakers are still outselling those endorsed by LeBron James. Jordan, after all, helped lead his team to six NBA titles; James has led for only three. Nike released 23 pairs of James shoes today. They will bring from $3,000 to $25,000 a pair. But, that's nothing compared to what Michael Jordan sneakers bring. One guy quoted by the *Times* said he had spent $75,000 last year on 300 pairs of shoes "and had not bought a single pair of LeBron sneakers." I am stunned.

The *Times* reports today that performers from the fourth and fifth tiers have signed up for his inaugural parties. Bless their little pointy heads.

Jan. 15: One of those keynote performers at the inaugural backed out yesterday. Seems that she had made her name by developing a fan base in the LGBT community. When they found out she was going to perform for the Emperor of White Trash Nation, they went ballistic and she withdrew. She said she just didn't realize that people would interpret her performance as support of His Liege. What in the world was she thinking, then?

Last evening was our third annual Wimberley Film Festival, and it was a smash hit. SRO. We showed 20 movies, and the Traveling Murphys, my kids and granddaughters, performed after the movies and while the judges deliberated. The girls were great. After the show, we all went to Kate's for dinner. While we were waiting, D'Arcy and Rosy started talking about a black friend she has made at Pearland High School. He's a big football player who never has had and never imagined having a white friend. She said it's been interesting watching him open up a little.

From there the conversation turned to what school was like when Lynda and I were in elementary, junior high and high school. Our schools were all segregated. The black kids had their own schools in their own part of town, both in Amarillo, where I grew up, and in Wichita Falls, where Lynda grew up. Lynda actually had a lot more contact with blacks than I did because her grandparents had maids and a man-servant whose name was Eli. Her parents also had maids, and maids looked after most of Lynda's cousins. I never ran into black folks anywhere in my world.

But, then, I had to tell Rosy about the most embarrassing moment of my life, even up to this moment. It was the summer of 1963 or 1964, when I was 16 or 17 years old and working at Uncle Zeke's Pancake House in Wolflin Village. On this particular evening about dusk I was working the front counter as the host of the evening. My job was to seat guests, get them menus, water and silverware and then get a waitress. On their way out, I worked the cash register. During a lull that evening, I heard a knock at the front door. Nobody ever knocks on the front door of a restaurant. So, at first I thought it might be a prank. The knock persisted, so I finally went to the front door and opened it up so I could look out. Standing there was a black man in a brown suit with his hat in his hands. Beside him was his wife and in front of them his daughter, about 12 or 13. "Excuse me," the man said, "but do you all serve Negroes in this establishment?" I was well aware of the Civil

Rights movement and the changing laws about public accommodations. But nobody in authority had ever told me our policy on serving Negroes. That meant, to me, that there was no policy against it, and I invited them in and showed them to a table. After giving them menus and ice water and silverware, I headed to the back to find M., the waitress responsible for that table. She peered around the corner, then jerked back, her face as red as her hair. "We do not serve niggers in this restaurant," she hissed at me. Her contempt was instant. "You go tell them they have to leave. We will not serve them here." And she just stood there. I had no idea what to say or do. Finally, I had to go to the family's table and tell them quietly that they would have to leave. I had been wrong. We couldn't serve them. Without a word, they left the table and went out the front door. They never looked back.

Over the years, I have looked back many times.

Today at church I forgot to record the pastor's sermon. No excuses. I just flat forgot.

Jan. 16: The Barnum & Bailey circus has announced it is going out of business this spring. They have seen steep declines in ticket sales. People don't want to watch animals being abused. So, instead of trying to go on and put together a show without elephants and tigers, the owners are closing up shop. They may be victims of an advanced consciousness on the part of audiences about the nature of our relationship with animals. But they are more clearly victims of their own lack of imagination. For the Shrine Circus, the show does go on, or at least it did this weekend. No reports of protests that I'm aware of, which is too bad. Austin is better than that.

Donald Trump feels beyond entitled. The man is also beyond stupid. Over the weekend he has gotten into a feud with one John Lewis, a congressman who had his head literally cracked open back during the Civil Rights marches of the mid-1960s. Lewis is the real thing. He took the risks. He fought. He bled. He survived. Trump did nothing, as Paul Krugman points out in a column in The *Times* this morning. Trump tweeted against Lewis because Lewis said on TV that he thought Trump's presidency was not legitimate. Russian hacking and the FBI director's illegal meddling in the election tainted the Trump win. Trump continues to pretend that he won by a landslide, and he is outraged that his primacy should be challenged by a mere black man. Let's be clear: The Russians did hack the election. The FBI director did intervene illegally. Both of these actions, if not others, call into question the fealty we owe to the new emperor of White Trash Nation. Those "others" include the obviously unconstitutional gerrymandering of thousands of congressional districts. The emperor doesn't care whether he ticks off the nation's blacks. He never had them in his corner anyway. His White Trash constituency is just as racist as it's ever been.

Three names to add to my list of those who I will boycott because of their mega-dollar donations to Donald Trump: AT&T, UPS and Toby Keith. It will be easy to boycott Keith and AT&T. I'll have to figure out how to keep UPS from getting my business.

The *Times* has an interesting story this morning about how President Obama found strength and solace during his eight years in office from reading.

Michiko Kakutani interviewed the president about his reading habits. He read a lot of history.

Has Donald Trump ever read a book?

I remember one day back when Ronald Reagan was running for president. I was editor of *The Canyon News*. Dr. Pat Sullivan, head of the English Department at West Texas State, came into the office all lathered up and red-faced. "Reagan has never read a book!" he declared. Pressed for his source, he said he'd read it in *The Christian Science Monitor*. Regardless of whether it was literally true, the notion was demonstrably true based on Reagan's view of government.

Jan. 17: I did some art work yesterday for Julia and Mel, postcards with my new theme about "The Gods." One I will send this week and another next week. I anticipate having some inauguration crowd shots to work with this weekend for a new one. (I send them a postcard every week. Julia is my middle daughter, a professor of art history at the University of California at Berkeley, and Mel, her partner, is also a professor there.)

I see in *The New Yorker* that at least some of Donald Trump's appointees are making a good-faith effort to have their ethical situations vetted by the proper authorities. The Exxon executive who will be secretary of state seems to have taken this seriously. And Trump's choice for his speech-writing staff, a serial plagiarist, withdrew herself from nomination rather than go through the process. The main person NOT taking it seriously and refusing to acknowledge there is a process? Donald Trump, emperor-in-waiting. I fervently hope this comes back to bite him in his big ass.

Lynda broke into tears yesterday watching video replays from the inaugural festivities held for the Clintons and for Obama. So many of the talented people who were there are gone now: Michael Jackson, Ray Charles. Is Harry Belafonte still with us?

I contacted L.L. Bean yesterday to tell them I will never ever buy from them again because of their pro-Trump stance. They wrote me back saying they had not taken a political stand and would not. Why, then, are they associated with backers of Trump? They have some stuff to take care of before they get me back. I also contacted Roger Williams, our congressman, urging him to keep hands off Social Security and Medicare. I have not heard from him.

Jan 18: I drove to San Marcos this morning with Clay Ewing, a local Realtor, to look at the public library there so we could take some notes for possible use in our committee about future space for our library. Clay drives a Prius, so I told him the story about trying to change out Mel's battery three years ago in Oakland—a process that ended in stalemate when I didn't have the proper tool. (Mel is my middle daughter Julia's spouse.) Clay is an avid bike rider and promoter of safer venues for bicyclists in the Hill Country. This is no place for people who have to use a bike to go from Point A to Point B. There are no shoulders on our roads, so bicycle riders compete with cars and dump trucks and 18-wheelers for the roadbed. It's a game loaded against the two-wheelers. Clay tried to make the point that the indifference toward bikers starts in the courthouse and filters out to the rest of us. I don't think so. I think when these roads were built and right-of-way was established there were no bikes and, thus, no bike lanes or shoulders. The courthouse may be indifferent or even hostile. I wouldn't know. Clay is also a yellow-dog Democrat just as Lynda and I are. He, too, believes that Trump must be opposed at every turn just as the Republicans opposed Obama for eight solid years. No ground must be given. For example, there were hearings yesterday and today on Trump's selection for secretary of education. This woman is a billionaire who never went to public school and who sends her own kids to private schools. She is completely dedicated to vouchers and charter schools and the dismantling of public schools. Democrats must oppose her absolutely.

Jan. 19: The president had his last press conference as the president yesterday, and I was proud of him for saying he will not step out of public life when Donald Trump takes office. The president said this, according to *The New York Times*:

"There's a difference between that normal functioning of politics and certain issues or certain moments where I think our core values may be at stake. I put in that category if I saw systematic discrimination being ratified in some fashion. I put in that category explicit or functional obstacles to people being able to vote, to exercise their franchise. I'd put in that category institutional efforts to silence dissent or the press. And for me at least, I would put in that category efforts to round up kids who have grown up here and for all practical purposes are American kids, and send them someplace else, when they love this country."

No other president I'm aware of has sent that kind of warning shot over the bow of the incoming ship of state. Now, let's see if Obama will carry through when the new president does, in fact, cross those lines in the sand. I fear that he won't. He has used "line-in-the-sand" language before in describing certain international threats, and the rhetoric has been empty.

Still, Obama will have the bully pulpit as long as he wants to have it, and he must use it to focus this country on what are the right things to do—not in every instance, but enough and strongly enough that he can make a difference in policies that would harm this nation and its people.

Talking with Clay Ewing yesterday, the talk didn't take long before turning to newspapers. Clay had written some op-ed pieces for the *Corpus-Christi Caller Times* when he lived there, and I knew the editorial page editor, Nick Jimenez. Clay had the impression that when Nick took over, the editorial pages became less provocative and less interesting. That was not all Nick's fault, I told him. The *Caller Times* was a big sister to the *Wichita Falls Times Record News* (and the San Angelo, Abilene and Albuquerque newspapers, too). We were all owned by Harte-Hanks and then purchased as a group by the E.W. Scripps Co. out of Cincinnati. Somewhere along about the time that the *Caller Times* editorial pages were becoming bland and predictable the same thing was happening all across America. Very subtle pressures were put on editors to adopt no attitudes that did not reflect their communities. By "communities," the powers-that-be meant "constituencies," and by "constituencies," they meant the tight-ass, white, middle-class, well-educated folks who shopped at Dillard's and J.C. Penney's and high-end jewelry stores, the kinds of businesses that bought ads in newspapers. And the bosses needed to make sure we locked onto those people because it was those very people who were most at risk of leaving newspaperdom for that new thing called The Internet. Don't piss people off, was the unwritten coda. It made newspapering less fun and newspapers less important, thus helping to doom them over the long haul.

Newspapers are still around, of course. When we first moved here I subscribed to the American Statesman in Austin for seven-day-a-week delivery. Some time back, I quit. The Statesman adopted early deadlines so as to be printed in San Antonio. That meant no Saturday morning scores from Friday night football. In Texas! That was unprecedented.

What else would they give up to make sure they kept that extra dollar in their pockets? Last year before the presidential campaign really heated up, the Statesman announced it would no longer publish editorials. That's probably not an unprecedented decision, but for a newspaper in a state capital? How chicken-shit could you get? Again, this was all about the money. If you piss people off, they just have too many options, and they don't mind dropping the paper. Which is what I did. They did piss me off by turning into spineless stenographers shilling for the money boys back in Atlanta.

Jan. 20: Today is Donald Trump's triumphant elevation to the nation's highest office. I refuse to watch anything having to do with it. I hope that the hoopla over Trump and his family as the New Royals will not herald in a "honeymoon" normalization of their behavior and beliefs and those of their cronies and buddies. Creeping normalization is something to be closely guarded against.

I have referred many times over the years to a book called "Back Home" written by Mort Rosenblum, who was the Associated Press correspondent in Europe based in Paris, at the time of its writing. Rosenblum was the keynote speaker at a Texas AP Managing Editors convention in El Paso back in the early 1990s. I don't remember the year, but that was the AP convention I drove to with Don James, then editor of the *Times Record News*. So, it was before I was named editor after Don's death. The book has a copyright date of 1989. What Rosenblum did was chronicle, on a trip around the country, how it had changed over the 20-plus years he was based in Paris. He returned just about every summer to Tucson, where his parents lived. And over time, he noticed how much America had been altered, and not necessarily for the better. During that two-decade period, he saw us become more antagonistic toward foreigners, more willing to do anything to make sure we were secure on our island nation. For his final chapter, Rosenblum visited Washington, D.C., and, among other things, looked up an old friend, a former diplomat named Wayne Smith, then teaching at Johns Hopkins. Smith told him that in terms of foreign policy, the American government had none: "The degree of imprecision is enormous. Decisions are made on the basis of no information. It's all there, but the higher the level, the more it is hermetically sealed." In Washington, Rosenblum concluded, "you got to be an expert on the world by talking about it, not by understanding it."

We are so, so much worse off today because of the advent of cable news and the 24-hour news cycle. Everyone shouts and few listen, and fewer still truly understand, and that is not going to get better. It will only get worse. Our perverse obsession with our own security got worse as Rosenblum experienced it over time, and it will get worse in the future. Back then, "With little thought to consequences, Americans were prepared to toy with their most fundamental freedoms." And what of today and tomorrow, after the Trump propaganda machine gets well-oiled and fully operational? What is wacko today will be normal in White Trash America.

In 1989, Mort Rosenblum looked at our government and concluded: "We need to elect people on the basis of their good sense, solid character, world experience and courage to do what is best within a broad philosophy. We have to let them apply painful, costly, slow-acting remedies. We have to accept contradictions. But we have to watch them as if our lives depended on it."

Jan. 21: Today, I am off to Austin with two busloads of people from the Wimberley-San Marcos area for the Women's March in Austin. As many as 30,000 people are expected. It is to be a bright, sun-shiny day, in all ways.

Jan. 22: We returned about 5 o'clock from the Austin march last evening, and I was tired but very satisfied. The estimates are that 50,000 people took part in the Women's March. Fifty thousand! I was very proud and humbled to be part of such a group of people willing to stand up against Trump and his minions who want to remake America as a place where the wealthy have their choices of women to feel up or rape without recourse. This morning, I wrote this email to my daughters and to Bryan:

"Resolve was in the air, a resolve not to let this era pass without clear opposition, fearless refusal to follow along with the normalizing of abnormal, dangerous behavior on the part of the president. Some of you may have participated in your own cities. I hope so. We cannot sit by and do nothing. When good people do nothing, you will recall, evil prevails."

Today's edition of *The New York Times* notes that protest marches took place throughout the world yesterday. There were record crowds in Washington and New York City and Los Angeles and Chicago. They didn't mention other places, but Lynda read online that yesterday saw the largest single-purpose demonstration worldwide that has ever been staged. This will not humble a man for whom humility is a word from outer space.

After yesterday, I feel somewhat better, but I am still wary and will remain so for four long years. This morning at church, I greeted Tom J., a retired junior college president and longtime academic and, by the way, a jazz musician. He's very conservative and voted for Trump, without apologies—at the time. I told him I'd missed him at the Women's March, and he said, laughing, that I'd just missed him. "Right," I said. Well, he said, "it's out of our hands. It's all up to God." "No," I countered. "It's in our hands and it's up to us and there is much we can do and much we will do." We left it at that.

Two articles in today's *Times* set me to wondering what that great conservative William F. Buckley Jr. would say about Trump and the White Trash Nation. My guess is that Buckley would have begun handling Trump with utter contempt long ago when the man first decided to run for president. Buckley did not suffer fools, and Trump would have headed his list. If there are any true conservatives cast in the Buckley mold left, they, too, must worry over the fate of the Republic just as much as liberals do.

29

Trump is no conservative. And he is no leader of the sort required for the highest job in the land. He is amoral. He is ego-driven. He must win at all costs. He is dangerous. And he is now loose on the land. Peter Wehner, a Republican and senior fellow at the Ethics and Public Policy Center, wrote on the op-ed page in today's *Times* about why he did not vote for or support Trump even though Wehner counts himself a conservative: "Donald Trump has not only spent much of his life stepping outside of traditional morality," Wehner writes, "he seems to delight in doing so. ... Because Republicans control Congress, they have the unique ability and the institutional responsibility to confront President Trump. What this means is that Republican leaders in Congress need to be ready to call Mr. Trump on his abuses and excesses, now that he is actually in office. It is a variation of the Golden Rule, in this case treating others, including a Republican president, as they deserve to be treated. They need to ask themselves a simple, searching question: 'If Barack Obama did this very thing, what would I be saying and doing now?'—and then say and do it."

In the book review section of the newspaper, an essay by Beverly Gage, who teaches history at Yale, applies some of the lessons from a book by Sinclair Lewis published in 1936 called "It Can't Happen Here." I read the book years ago and had completely forgotten about it. In the book, an American nominee sweeps into the office of president by offering thousands of dollars to every American family. He sells himself as the champion of "forgotten men." He attacks newspapers. He talks about the great national decline and what he will do to fix it. After becoming president he has members of Congress arrested. He becomes a dictator. And with the military and most of the police forces in his corner, there is not much to be done about it.

I wonder if there is a take-away there.

Jan. 23: I was struck by the total absence on Saturday at the Women's March of clergy leadership. Religious collars were nowhere to be seen. There were no speakers representing people of faith. Perhaps I make too much of it, but it seems to me that other big protest movements have had at their core an element of moral authority, an appeal to a higher law. The Civil Rights movement had Martin Luther King Jr., among many others. The Vietnam antiwar movement had the Berrigan Brothers, among many others. Mahatma Gandhi was a religious leader in his own country. Priests and nuns and men and women of cloth were at the forefront, making arguments based on the eternal values of freedom and justice embodied so eloquently in our Declaration of Independence and in the inter-national Declaration of Human Rights. Why are these people absent or why have they made themselves invisible?

In truth, the entirety of organized religion around the modern world has been marginalized. The practice of Christianity has been hijacked by the far-right elements who would have you believe that the Christian faith is only about abortion. That issue alone has taken such precedence and provoked such virulence that everyone who might otherwise be attracted to the faith is put off by the odor of a rotting cause. That is a factor, but a larger factor is that on the ground where it needs to be viable, Christianity just doesn't work anymore. Thanks to modern communications, only a hermit in the backest of back country could not see the pathetic efforts made by "Christian" peoples in the face of mass disasters, unending wars and rampant injustice. In terms of alleviating human suffering, it is hard to see that Christianity has moved the needle one bit. We are a practical people. We want to believe in something that can have an impact. So, a growing number of Americans have joined their European cousins in walking away from the practice of Christianity as a quaint remnant from other times and other places.

At the church I attend, St. Stephen's Episcopal Church of Wimberley, the rector studiously avoids sermonizing about current events. Her focus is generally on how much God loves us, blah, blah, blah. The content is so irrelevant that I tune out most of the sermons and spend 20 minutes just contemplating other things.

Also absent from the Saturday parades: A good, solid slogan and good music relevant to the cause. Remember, "Hell No We Won't Go"? Or "Hey Hey LBJ How Many Kids Did You Kill Today?"? There were many songs that grabbed people and had them humming, helping them keep focused on the tasks of peace-making at hand. "Down by the Riverside" was one. "Draft Dodger Blues" was another. And, of course, "We Shall Overcome."

Jan. 24: I found out via email this morning that Becca, my youngest daughter, was in Austin for the Women's March. She never said a word. Maybe we could have met up; maybe not. She's obviously mad at me about something, and I don't know what it is.

The New York Times had an article yesterday about the great rush to buy up leases in the Permian Basin. Exxon has millions of acres leased, and other majors are not far behind. According to one expert quoted in the article, that area of Texas is attractive again for two reasons: multiple shales that can be mined at one time, and the price to drill makes $40 a barrel feasible. Coincidentally, I talked to one of the library's regular patrons last Friday about the property John and I have out in that part of the state. The man, Bubba L., said he's not a landman, but he does that kind of work. He may be a retired oil and gas lawyer. He said he knew people who might be interested in leasing our properties. So, yesterday I took him copies of the paperwork from the last group that leased those two sections (at $34,000 per section for John and $34,000 per section for me). He said he thought he could get the sections leased out again. We'll see.

The mineral rights on those sections once belonged to Mom's aunt Sadie. I never met Aunt Sadie. But, when I was growing up, Mother used to tell me that when Aunt Sadie died we'd be rich and she would buy me a Porsche. At that time, a Porsche was about $6,000, I think, a huge amount of money back then. When Aunt Sadie actually did die, about the time I was a senior in high school, Mom gave me a Porsche—a little Matchbox version. It's been lost along the way.

On the bus going to Austin on Saturday, I sat by a woman in colorful garb who turned to me as we were leaving San Marcos and declared that the trip reminded her of a bus ride she took with her parents from Wilmington, Del., to Washington, D.C., in 1969 to protest the war in Vietnam. I didn't know exactly how to respond, so I told her I was in the Army in 1969 and rode on a different kind of bus. She didn't say another word.

Being a journalist all those years kept me away from protests as a participant. I was almost always an observer or the guy directing the observers. I recall seeing the Civil Rights protesters blasted by water hoses and attacked by dogs back in the '50s, on our black-and-white television set. And I suppose I was aware of all the anti-Vietnam War protests in the '60s, but I don't recall watching them. By 1966, I was a reporter anyway. I was stunned, though, by the protests in Chicago during the Democratic Convention of 1968. I remember going over to Buck Ramsey's house, and he was sitting up in his bed watching reports about those kids being beaten and gassed, and he was outraged, red in the face, bouncing up and down as he hollered at the TV. Buck was my idol in the reporting/writing world. He grew up in the Panhandle and was a cowboy for the Bivins Ranch. At some point as a young man he was thrown from his horse in a ravine and suffered a back injury that left him permanently disabled and in a wheelchair. But, the man could write and do so beautifully. I read everything he wrote two or three times to see how he did what he did, and then I tried to do it myself. So, when Buck was outraged, I was outraged, and I began to examine my political views and question what I believed, and *right on that very day I became a liberal just like Buck Ramsey*.

After I got out of the Army in 1972, Susan and I decided it was time to get into a church, and we joined First Presbyterian in Canyon. I was editor of The Canyon News. About the same time, we were desperate for money. My job didn't pay enough for the three of us to get by and before long there were four of us. My only real option was to go back to college and pick up $350 a month, tax-free, from the GI Bill. I didn't need another degree and didn't want another degree, but I couldn't pass up the money. I chose a path to a master's in political science, and among the professors in that department there were two who went to First Presbyterian and only a single conservative in the entire bunch. In both arenas, church and university, I began to become more and more liberal. The support and nurturing were there for the strong development of the superstructure of an outlook on life that found sturdy roots in socialism.

Jan. 25: Our preacher at First Presbyterian was Baldwin Stribling, who was one of the best preachers I have ever heard. Strib preached many sermons from the letters of Paul, and he focused on the importance of fostering development of a Christian community and the importance of living a life envisioned by Paul that would be in service to others. Strib's messages seemed to mesh nicely with what I was reading and studying at West Texas in my political science classes, and they just reinforced in me the idea that faith without works was dead, in the words of the writer of the Book of James. The editorials and columns I wrote once a week for The Canyon News took on a clearly left-wing political tone with a radical Christ at the center.

In the mid-1970s, perhaps about the time I finished up my political science master's degree, Susan and I became aware of and got involved in a political action group in Amarillo that was meeting at the law offices of Betty Wheeler and her partner. They were immigration lawyers but also committed environmentalists and liberals. This small group included several folks from the Unitarian Fellowship and other mainly Protestant congregations.

The formation of this group was compelled by three political situations that

32

involved the Panhandle of Texas but that were national in scope. The most challenging threat came from the Reagan administration, which wanted to build a multiple-warhead nuclear missile system on rails on a large swath of American territory. The theory was that if the Soviets wanted to knock out the system, that would be as physically impossible as whacking all the moles in the board game at the same time. Promoters of Amarillo wanted the so-called MX Missile system to be based in the Panhandle.

The second threat came from the planned expansion of the Pantex nuclear weapons assembly plant northeast of Amarillo off Interstate 40. Pantex was the final assembly point for every nuke in the American arsenal.

The third threat came in the form of a plan by the U.S. Atomic Energy Commission to bury all of the nuclear waste from all of the country's nuclear power plants in salt formations that flowed underground from Randall County southward. None of these were idle threats. Government officials were already mapping out and surveying MX Missile platform and rail sites. Pantex was drawing up plans. And holes were being drilled in the salt formations in Randall County to assess their viability as waste repositories.

Our small group meeting at the Wheeler law offices opposed all these measures on environmental grounds, first. For many in the group, protection of the environment was of primary importance. There seemed to be little question that a massive, multiple-tentacled rail system would disturb wildlife habitats and breeding grounds all across the Panhandle. There were rumors that over the years the Pantex plant had polluted the air and soil for miles around the facility. An expansion, desired by the Reagan administration to up the ante against the Soviets, would simply amplify the possibilities for pollution. And the idea of putting spent nuclear fuel rods anywhere in the United States was, well, explosive. Nuclear waste was the most toxic man-made substance in the history of our species, and it would not become benign for millions of years.

But, for Susan and for me the issue was bound up with the morality of preparing for nuclear warfare, and our role as participants in those preparations. On moral grounds, we objected to all three projects. *To be continued.*

The news media report that Donald Trump has issued gag orders for scientists in the Agriculture Department and some other departments. They are no longer to have access to the media. This is part of his war on the media. Ultimately, the war will backfire on Trump. But in the meantime, serious damage will be done to the nation's ability to know what's going on. When the president cracks down on media access, bureaucrats at other levels who harbor grudges with the news media or who want to do their business in the dark jump on the band wagon and impose their own gag orders. I have seen this first-hand in Wichita Falls and, worse, in Temple, following the tightening up of security in the wake of the 9-11 attacks on the World Trade Center buildings. Trying to pry news out of police departments in those cities and others became just so much harder when city officials came to believe that they could clamp a lid on what the public could be made aware of.

Jan. 26: The two second-grade boys who read to me every Wednesday morning continue to do well. I'm not sure they need my help anymore. But sweet little M., the girl, is struggling still. Even the easiest words stump her. I don't know whether she's just not paying attention or can't remember the words she has seen before many times. I wrote their teacher and reported on their progress, but this poor woman has something like 25 kids to worry over. That is way too many in a second-grade classroom.

Trump signed orders yesterday to keep Muslims and Syrians out of the country for three or four months while the immigration authorities "tighten up" security. The process for people to settle in this country from others is already about as "tight" as you can imagine. It takes months to resettle a family. Trump is playing to his hysterical White Trash Nation residents. Likewise, he ordered the wall built between the United States and Mexico. He continues to assert that Mexico will pay for the wall, while the Mexican president says he won't do it. This is a billion-dollar project. Surely Congress will make certain this doesn't get funded. And Mexico won't pay for it anyway. It's more racist blather.

Chuck Todd of "Meet the Press" got into it over the weekend with Trump's official press advisor, a woman whose very presence reminds me of fingernails on a chalkboard. She had used the term "alternative facts" to describe the deliberate misstatements of the White House press secretary when he was talking about the crowd at Trump's inauguration. Todd basically called her out: "alternative facts" are "lies," he pointed out. Now, I read in *The Times* that sales for the old science fiction work called "1984" are rising quickly as people scurry to find out about Doublespeak. Chuck Todd and others in his profession simply must keep the Trump people honest. They must call a spade a spade—every time.

Peter Baker of *The Times* wrote a piece this morning that began with this second paragraph about Trump:

"He sits in the White House at night, watching television or reading social media, and through Twitter issues instant judgments on what he sees. He channels fringe ideas and gives them as much weight as carefully researched reports. He denigrates the conclusions of intelligence professionals and then later denies having done so. He thrives on conflict and chaos."

I ran into a couple of guys yesterday who predicted Trump will be impeached and tossed out of office within a year. They think that even solid Republicans are looking for ways to get rid of him so Pence can be president.

Let me return now to my growing opposition to the expansion of the Pantex nuclear weapons plant outside Amarillo, the location of the MX Missile System in the Panhandle and the possible burial of the nation's nuclear wastes in salt formations under Randall County, where I lived. While there were clear environmental reasons to oppose these three projects, for Susan and me the moral grounds for opposition were taking precedence as we continued meeting with our small group at the Amarillo law offices and with small groups of parishioners at First Presbyterian in Canyon. Planning for and building with the goal in mind of conducting a nuclear war was the most morally objectionable undertaking our nation had attempted, ever. While we might have been forced into a MAD game with the Soviets, a sane approach would have been to try every measure short of nuclear buildup to sustain a reasonable peace. We were not at all convinced that American leaders had truly made that effort. To wit: the proposal to put a sleight-of-hand missile system on railroad tracks in the middle of the Panhandle, a wildly expensive proposal that we opposed because it simply made the idea of war with the Soviets more palatable. And war of any sort with the Soviets could not be justified on any kind of moral basis (unlike, say, the war on the Germans, who were in the process of putting millions of people under the jackboot of pure evil). The use of nuclear power to provide electricity to the nation's cities was a folly based on the guilt felt by the scientific establishment that had harnessed nuclear power to kill thousands of people to end World War II in the Pacific. To continue to pursue the development of nuclear power in the face of known facts about the dangers of nuclear waste—forever—was morally reprehensible, particularly when there were safer alternatives available right at hand and others that could be developed with a little financial resolve—such as solar power and wind power and battery technology. We rooted our moral outrage in the many teachings of Jesus and of Paul. How could we call ourselves a Christian nation while spending vast sums on preparations for war and far less on peace and peace among our own people?

Early in 1980, our small group of concerned citizens in Amarillo learned that plans were being developed for the expansion of Pantex. This was part of President Reagan's program to paint the Soviets into a corner. The government plan did not include the production of an environmental impact statement, something every other large government (or nongovernment) project had to come up with to satisfy relatively new regulations from the EPA. Betty Wheeler, our lawyer, put together a lawsuit pitting our small group as plaintiffs against the federal government and their contractor/operator of Pantex asking a federal judge to delay construction until an environmental impact statement had been properly put together. Even though I was a resident of Canyon and, thus, very far physically from the plant, I signed onto the lawsuit seeking standing as a plaintiff based on my interest in ensuring the public had access to information that should be made available to the public.

For the several years leading up to the summer of 1980, Troy Martin, the owner and publisher of The *Canyon News*, had been almost completely absent. He had no interest in the newspaper other than the profits it made for him. And he rarely if ever showed up at the office. I was in charge of everything, for all practical purposes. During his absence, I had absolutely turned the editorial pages on Sunday into windows on liberal thought. Every Sunday, I wrote an editorial, a column and a separate column under a pseudonym. Many of them attacked the conservative dogma of the day, as well as local issues, of course. Unquestionably, though, I had turned the News into a "liberal rag." That summer, Troy remarried, and the woman he married took a sudden interest in the operation of The *Canyon News*. She had one son become the circulation manager, for example. She never came around, but Troy started showing up, and I think he slowly realized that he'd lost control. *To be continued.*

Jan. 27: The *Times* reports this morning on Page One that Trump's resident Joseph Goebbels, Stephen Bannon, who used to run a neo-Nazi website, called out the media as "the opposition party." I hope this does not set off the usual hand-wringing among button-downs who sit in publishers' offices across the land. It could. They are not the bravest souls and haven't been for quite some time. Joseph Pulitzer once famously bragged that the newspaper's role was to "comfort the afflicted and afflict the comforted." When I learned about that comment when I was a young reporter, it lit a fire under me like nothing else I was told. That's what I wanted to do!

Somewhere along the line between the 1960s and 2011, when I left journalism, the Pulitzer quote was long forgotten. The *Washington Post* and The *New York Times*, however, have their own cherished traditions of never cowering before power. It is my fervent hope that they, and perhaps others, will stand together and give Bannon and Trump the finger as they forge ahead to make sure White Trash Nation learns the truth about his cabal of government amateurs and professional liars.

Whatever sense of ethics and practical morality I got from my parents and teachers was intensified by my experiences as a young journalist and reinforced over time. My bosses were strictly correct, and they expected no less of me.

We will soon not be able to find mangos, tomatoes, avocadoes and who knows what else on our store shelves because Trump and his lackeys in the House and Senate are proposing a 20 percent tariff on imports. The idea is to use that money to give rich folks a tax break. Did you read that sentence right? Yes, you did.

Following up on my story about The *Canyon News*: At some point in the fall of 1980, Troy started reading his own newspaper, and it hit him hard that it was no longer a conservative voice among so many others in the Panhandle. At that time, there were three liberal weeklies or semi-weeklies in that 25-county area: the Canadian Record published in a little town north of Amarillo on the Canadian River breaks, and The Tulia Herald published by H.M. Baggerly in a town about 30 miles south of Canyon—and The *Canyon News*. Right about then, my marriage with Susan was falling apart for a variety of reasons, not the least of which because I had fallen in love with Lynda, then advertising manager of the newspaper.

Around Thanksgiving the citizen action committee's lawsuit against Pantex was set for trial in federal district court in Amarillo, and we sent out a press release about that. On the morning the press picked up the story, Troy heard about it and stormed into the office to confront me about my role. For something less than an hour, we went back and forth about whether I had a right to be a plaintiff in the suit, what my participation was doing to The *Canyon News* and its credibility and, finally, of course, to the liberalization of the newspaper while he was sleeping. In our final exchange, I quit. Or Troy fired me. I don't remember exactly right now, and it probably depends on who's telling the story which version you believe.

Right then and there, I knew that was definitely the end of my career at The *Canyon News*. There was no going back. But, I had no other job, and no prospects of getting one. I couldn't go to the Amarillo newspaper because over the years I had deliberately crapped on their shoes as spineless conservatives. In fact, they'd be happy to see me go.

And almost at the same time, Susan and I had that one final great blow-up that sent me packing with nothing but the clothes on my back and a few dollars. I stayed for a few nights at the home of Jerry and Linda Craven, who were out of town but left me the key. I spent another few nights at the apartment of Bill Melin, a buddy from elementary school who was trying to finish a master's at WT and lived not far from campus. Then, I moved in with Mike Keller, our newspaper photographer and a nursing student at WT, and his roommate, a big guy who was an electrician. They let me put up a small bed in the living room of their dinky cottage just off campus. When the folks at the citizen action committee heard I'd lost my job, they rallied to my side. First, they quickly obtained a $3,000 grant from the Libra Foundation to pay for a part-timer to coordinate the lawsuit and other activities on their behalf. So, I went to work at the Wheeler law office, showing up most of every day to expand our scope and raise our collective voice against the MX-Missile program, the nuclear waste disposal plan and the expansion of Pantex. I could do this job, which paid $300 a month, because my dad bought me a 1976 Toyota Celica off a used-car lot in Amarillo. It was most generous of him to do so, especially because he knew of my involvement with the anti-war people and strongly disapproved. *To be continued.*

Jan. 28: We have only one copy of "1984" at the library, and I checked it out yesterday afternoon to a young lady. "Nice choice," I said. She smiled. The *New York Times* has a story on its business page this morning about the boom in "dystopian classics" like "1984" and Sinclair Lewis's "It Can't Happen Here." I need to re-read that one. Demand for those two books and Margaret Atwood's "The Handmaid's Tale," also set in a bleak future, has risen to such a level that publishers are firing up their presses for large runs again. I take this as a good sign. It means people can and do make connections between what's happening now in Washington and what can happen as envisioned by novelists if our base tendencies as a race are allowed to play out in the public arena. I wonder if there is a spike in sales of "The Rise and Fall of the Third Reich" or "Man's Search for Meaning" because I think while we can learn a lot from science fiction we can also learn a lot from history. It can happen here.

Lynda hollered at me while I was reading the newspaper at the dining room table (I receive it in actual newsprint form three days a week) to tell me that the chief psychotherapist at Johns Hopkins had completed a study of Donald Trump's personality and declared him a malignant narcissist. What a surprise.

Picking up where I left off on the story of my experience with protests, my first efforts at the Wheeler law office in the employ of the environmental committee were to put together a brochure explaining our stands on the three outstanding issues and to pull together a body of information for if and when the district judge ruled on our lawsuit. We felt the judge, Mary Lou Robinson, would side with Pantex, the government and the contractor operating the plant for the government, Mason & Hanger Silas Mason and Co. That would mean expansion could take place without the benefit of an environmental impact statement. So, we needed to be ready to present our case to the public in that event.

Judge Robinson did not wait for long. Either late in 1980 or early in 1981, she ordered the government to do the environmental study required by law. We won! For our small group, this was a major development, and it gave us instant credibility in our fights on the other two fronts we faced.

One January afternoon, I was working away at the law office, and a guy came in who I'd never seen before. He was tallish, maybe six feet, and was not overweight, although it was hard to tell because he had on a heavy wool shirt covered by a heavy wool jacket. He wore faded jeans and those bulky, clunky work boots you see on crews that frame houses for a living. He had longish hair, parted and combed over so that sometimes it fell in his face when he really got to talking. He introduced himself as Ladon Sheats. As he spoke, I detected an accent I couldn't exactly place—maybe Michigan filtered through Manhattan, but certainly not West Texan. Ladon said he was not just passing through, although his father lived in Lubbock and he had a brother in the Dallas area. He was intending to stick around Amarillo for a while because he had a job to do. *To be continued.*

Jan. 29: I write this after church, so it is almost 1 p.m., and all across the country protesters are in the streets and congregating at airports to speak out against Trump's off-the-wall immigration ban. Governors are berating him, as are many, many others, excluding, of course, House and Senate Republicans, who may not like what Trump is doing but who are going to give him his head because they, of all the people in the world, can benefit the most from a crazy, out-of-control president. Today's issue of *The New York Times* has a front page almost entirely devoted to the phantasmagoric tragedy unfolding in the White House, from the immigration disaster to his and his aides' persistent and deliberate unwillingness to tell the truth. I would say about the man what Troy Martin used to say about Dr. James C. Cornet, then president of West Texas State University: The man would climb a tree to tell a lie if he could tell the truth standing on the ground. Elsewhere in *The Times* we have a variety of commentators who are, in general, absolutely aghast at the first week of the Trump administration.

A story on an entirely separate issue gets above-the-fold treatment in *The Times* this morning, and it is simple coincidence that it helps make a point by way of concrete example that I have been alluding to in my running commentary on my opposition to the three nuclear-central initiatives undertaken by the government in the late 1970s in the Texas Panhandle. This story bears the headline, "Veterans Feel Cost of U.S. Nuclear Tests." No, this story is not about the GIs who were forced to watch the atomic bomb tests in New Mexico and Nevada during World War II, without proper protective gear. Nor is it about the soldiers and sailors who were forced to participate when this nation set off hydrogen bomb explosions in the Pacific Ocean after the war as the Cold War ramped up. This story is just another cut from that same cloth, though. This time, the abused veterans were put onto islands rendered uninhabitable by the H-bomb explosions in the late 1970s to see how things were going. They didn't have protection. Now, they suffer the consequences. The subhead: "Troops Who Cleaned Up Radioactive Islands Can't Get Care."

The examples are precisely why we did not for one minute trust the government to tell us the truth about what was going on at Pantex or what would be the real threat of burying radioactive waste under our soil in salt deposits. The government simply was not trustworthy on these matters. I had the feeling then and continue to have it today that if the government says and then believes that something horrible is "in the national interest," then, come hell or high water, that horrible thing is going to happen, innocent people be damned. So, we sued to get Pantex to do the absolute minimum as it planned an expansion—to tell the public

38

and taxpayers how that would affect the environment. To be honest, we did not expect to win, and we certainly did not expect the government to tell the truth if forced to produce an impact statement.

When Ladon arrived at the Wheeler law office in Amarillo, we had made our case to Judge Robinson and she had ruled in our favor and we were waiting for the other shoe to drop. We thought we would see the government appeal the order, and so we would be in for another go-round. Ladon explained to me on that first day that he had landed at the law office because he had heard of the lawsuit and had heard of our challenges to the status quo. We could be his allies, he said, in an action he and friends were planning for the following August. Ladon came to Amarillo by bus from Detroit. Over the next few hours, I learned that he was living and working in Detroit in a mission set up to serve the homeless. It was an organization not affiliated with any particular religious group. It was just addressing a need in a very human way. I sensed, though, that Ladon had a religious background, and perhaps a religious motive, even if he was not officially a member of any formal faith group.

What Ladon and his compatriots wanted to do was gather together in August, on roughly the anniversary date of the bombing of Hiroshima and Nagasaki, at the gates to Pantex. Together, they would join arms and cross the fence into Pantex itself and there they would kneel and pray until arrested. "You do understand that the guards out there carry automatic rifles?" I asked him. He smiled. They wouldn't fire a shot; he and his friends would simply be arrested and jailed and then tried and then imprisoned. Clearly, this was not Ladon's first rodeo, as he later told me.

For the week he would be in Amarillo that winter of 1981, he wanted to call on the preachers of each of the big churches in town and ask them to join his small group of protesters in the Pantex action in August. I guess I probably laughed out loud. No way in hell pastors of ANY church in Amarillo, Texas, were going to protest Pantex or any other thing the Reagan Administration wanted to do, up to and including going to war on Russia right then and there. "Would you go with me to call on them?" he asked me. I shrugged and told him "OK" even though I knew it was a lost cause. That evening, I invited Ladon to Lynda's house after giving her fair warning, and when we showed up she had dinner ready and Bryan and Sarah were there, too. Ladon charmed Bryan, just as he intrigued and mesmerized Lynda. At the end of the evening, which went way into the wee hours as we talked about Reagan and war and nuclear weapons, Lynda pulled me aside and confided, "You know, he's more like Jesus than anyone I've ever met." She was right. He made that first and lasting impression.

During our talks, Ladon told us that he had grown up in Lubbock, the son of a Pentecostal preacher, and had graduated with an MBA from Texas Tech. Soon, he found himself working for IBM in a tower in New York City. And from that lofty perch he watched wave after wave of anti-Vietnam War demonstrations. The more he thought about the war and those who opposed it, the more he came to believe that what he was doing was not only aiding and abetting the prosecutors of an unjust war but directly contributing to the death of hundreds if not thousands of people in a faraway world he'd never heard of until the protests began in earnest. After long and sober reflection, he quit IBM and found his way to the

Maryland outpost of the Berrigan Brothers, Catholic religious who were at the forefront of the anti-war movement. With the Berrigans he participated in protests large and small, and many times he was jailed for his actions. After that war ended, Ladon went to Arkansas or Alabama to help out the guy who founded Habitat for Humanity, and he worked there awhile before heading for Detroit. In Detroit, his small group, which included some Catholic religious, focused again on the rising militarism of America under Ronald Reagan. At one point, they made a protest pilgrimage to Rocky Flats in Colorado, where nuclear triggers for weapons were manufactured for shipment to Amarillo's Pantex plant, and final assembly. They were arrested and spent time in a federal penitentiary.

I did not understand Ladon's insistence on doing things that would land him in prison, but he felt that was his calling and he intended to follow that voice. So, over the course of the week that followed we made appointments with the pastors of the First Baptist Church, First Methodist Church, First Presbyterian Church and the bishop of the Catholic Diocese of Amarillo. Each pastor was cordial. Each heard our message and our invitation. Each heard Ladon explain this rationale for direct opposition to Pantex: "What if you had lived outside the gates of Dachau or Buchenwald and had chosen to say nothing when you knew everything?" None of them laughed at us. Of course, none agreed to join up. Except Bishop Leroy Matthieson of the Catholic Diocese. Bishop Matthieson declined to participate, but he was the most sympathetic and listened the most closely when we reiterated what was by then our belief that when one is confronted by evil one is compelled by conscience to stand up and say, "NO."

Ladon left Amarillo at the end of the week promising to return with friends. He was not disappointed, not dejected, not resentful. He had given the good preachers of Amarillo their chance to show what they believed in, and they had taken the opportunity.

Jan. 30: Today, it was 36 degrees when I went walking. Yesterday, 33. There's no wind, though, so those temperatures are pretty moderate.

Yesterday, Christian leaders across the land blasted Trump for his ban of Muslims. Turns out that's not what they wanted after all. Who knew? Certainly nobody who carefully watched the Trump campaign unfold over the last 14 months. Careful what you wish for, Christian leaders!

Speaking of Christian leadership, our rector preached yesterday out of the Matthew version of the Sermon on the Mount. The message she wanted to get across is that all of us at St. Stephen's Episcopal Church are blessed. And, being blessed, we are to visit blessings on others. She never got into specifics, which would have been a nice thing to do given the present situation. Are we blessed so that we can ban others from our wonderful country? How did we become blessed? Is the blessing exclusively for us? A writer in Sunday's edition of *The New York Times* wrote briefly about the problem with feeling blessed. Obviously, to be blessed is to have been chosen. And if one is chosen, why? What for? And who says? It is not too far down the road when you follow this reasoning that you end up with the obvious answers. The proof of my blessing is that I do not suffer and I do not want. I am rich. The fact that I am rich shows I am blessed and thus chosen, and if you are poor you are clearly not chosen and thus not blessed. What a tangle. I'm not sure she thought this through.

Jan. 31: Trump is to name his candidate for Supreme Court justice today. Whomever it is, he or she will be approved by the Senate, so we are stuck with his choice. We can only hope that, in this case anyway, the job will make the man or woman. He or she will understand the gravity of the task and will take the job seriously enough to think about the impact of rulings on the future. Justice Scalia, bless his little pea-pickin' heart, never got it, and neither has Uncle Tom Clarence Thomas.

The Trump ban of Muslims has not set well with many folks. My prediction is that what he has done will stick. People who are not citizens of this country do not have constitutional rights. They may have human rights, but they are not privileged to share our safety net. And Trump has broad discretion in this particular area. So, all these people coming out of the woodwork now, where were you when Donald Trump was promising to do what he just did back last year? And this is only the beginning. Maybe we need to go back now and look at all those other promises he made.

I have read and re-read the column written by the Bishop Coadjutor of the Diocese of West Texas in the latest church newspaper. The Rt. Rev. David Reed seems to do a nice dance around the elephant in the room, the clear immorality of the present administration and its malignant, unChristian application of the laws of the land. In the face of the clear and present danger posed by Trump and his White Trash Nation, Reed writes that "perhaps in 2017, we (individually and in our churches) may be renewed by the Spirit in Christian practices of prayer, forbearance and patience. Maybe humility, graciousness and generosity of spirit will flourish among us and be like cool, clean water for our society. Maybe we'll receive grace to give each other a break (even those least likely to give us a break), and maybe we'll be brave and wise enough to be quiet when we're tempted to dehumanize and diminish."

He goes on in the same vein in his concluding paragraph:

"This is a chance for you, and for your church, to offer yourselves as peacemakers, reconcilers, evangelists, healers, teachers, light-bearers, truth-tellers, lovers and forgivers. You can, by grace, offer yourselves as servants and friends of the Lord who bring the Kingdom, the new polis, and says, 'Behold, I make all things new.' "

Bishop Reed's sentiment echoes those spoken by hundreds of church leaders through the ages who want to confront evil, if at all, with a wet noodle. The use of the word "maybe" in the passages above are a dead giveaway that the Bishop won't take a stand on anything substantially meaningful in terms of confronting the bad things that will be forthcoming from the Trumpists and White Trash Nation. "Maybe" waters everything down, even the puny attributes Reed recommends. It is a weasel word, to quote my dad.

In the final paragraph, Reed completely skirts the idea that Christians can be aggressive in opposition to evil, even if only aggressively passive. Recall that Martin Luther King Jr. and Mahatma Gandhi counseled nonviolence. But, they also counseled resistance. Without resisting, we will all be led to the gas chambers or we will continue to sing away in the cotton patch, and everyone will believe it is going to be OK. Of course, Bishop Reed, like the Rev. Sandy, must live in the real world, right? The world where if you speak out you might lose some from your congregation. The world where you might lose your job. The world where you might suffer a little because of your faith. Heaven forbid that we must move out of our comfort zones. Justice and peace are not the natural state of human affairs. To have them in this country required force and resistance. To keep them will require the same efforts. Bishop Reed would have us be lambs. It is time we roared like lions.

Feb. 1: Almost as an afterthought yesterday morning, I emailed our rector and asked her when the bishop of our Episcopal diocese planned to make a statement about the ban on immigration. I have not heard back from her yet. I guess I will send another email today asking the same question. I have an uneasy feeling that the bishop(s) are going to do nothing, which is simply unacceptable. If he or they don't speak out on this issue, what issue would prompt them to try to be heard? Catholic leaders across the country have made their views known. I haven't checked on leaders of other denominations, such as the Presbyterians, but I'd be surprised if they were silent. At times like these, silence is tantamount to fellow traveling.

I read up yesterday afternoon on a Catholic bishops' statement about what the Bible says about "the stranger." There can be no doubt that, particularly for a rich first-world country, it is required of us to welcome the stranger, clothe and feed him. We aren't called to be overrun by immigrants, but that is hardly the situation, even along the border with Mexico. Immigration is a Straw Man. A ban on immigrants, especially Muslims, is simply a straightforward way to demonize an "other," in much the same way Hitler and his crew demonized Jews. This kind of thing appeals to the haters in our midst, the professional victims like the West Virginia coal miners who blame everyone but themselves for their lack of a good job and insurance. Trump appeals to this bitter core of people who have been displaced from what they consider their rightful seat at the dinner table because they haven't changed or won't change or fear change so much they are immobile. They resent anyone else getting a place setting, because they fear there won't be enough to go around—in the richest nation in the history of humankind.

So, do we, as Christians, speak truth to power? Of course we do. Jesus' entire ministry was about dealing with Rome and the wealthy and powerful Jewish leadership. Recall his reaction to the money-changers. Recall his power lunch with the Jewish hierarchy.

I was disappointed to hear on NPR yesterday that several Democratic Senators have voted to approve the nominations of some of Trump's Cabinet appointees. I believe that the Democrats in both House and Senate should give to Trump and the Republicans what Mitch McConnell and the Republicans gave President Obama for eight years: nothing, nada. Zero. Or better, utter contempt.

Feb. 2: Trump has announced his pick for the Supreme Court. I tried to do some digging around yesterday into his background, and read through parts of the hearings he was involved in when he was named to the circuit court in Denver. He is said to be a strict constructionist, like Scalia, of the Constitution. I guess I no longer really understand what that phrase means. It used to mean that a person who was a strict constructionist would look at the mandates in the Constitution in the way the makers of the document looked at it. The original intent would not be seen as having fallen out of synch with modern times. Everything else around us might change, but the way the framers dotted their i's and crossed their t's would remain sacrosanct.

We talked about this a lot when I was taking constitutional law in graduate school, and there were several reasons why we concluded that this was kind of a wrong-headed way to look at the Constitution. One was simply the matter of judicial review. The Constitution as framed does not say a word about judicial review, which is the power of the courts to overturn laws that are in conflict with the Constitution itself. The court, in Marbury vs. Madison in 1803, declared that the right of judicial review existed. So, what would our strict constructionists have us do? Well, of course, they would say that's not a good example of judicial activism. OK, what about giving us an interpretation of the Ninth Amendment? It states: "The enumeration in the Constitution, of certain rights, shall not be construed to deny or disparage others retained by the people." Now, there is a snake pit, one that no justice wants to touch. But, there it is. Why not bring it into play? (Back when I was trying to find a good topic for a master's thesis in my political science program, I proposed to my thesis director that I be allowed to pursue a full explanation of why the Ninth Amendment is off limits. He declined, so I went another direction.) It seems very likely that the Democrats in the Senate will go along with Trump's appointee. They won't act like Republicans. Instead, they will conclude that this guy is probably the best that Trump will ever come up with, and they will just decide to live with him.

The people around Plymouth, Mass., have risen up against the continued use of a nuclear power plant there after a report that it was in bad shape. The *Times* had a report on it this morning. The protesters fear bad things will happen when new fuel rods are loaded into the plant this spring. I fear what will happen to the rods. There is still no good waste site for the long-term disposal of nuclear materials like these rods. The fact that there might never be a good solution for storing nuclear waste and related contaminants was at the core of our protest movement back in the late 1970s and early 1980s in Amarillo when our small group sued Pantex and opposed dumping nuclear materials in salt deposits under Randall County.

During the short period of time I worked for the group out of the Wheeler law office, I spent hours studying the issues having to do with nuclear arms and nuclear power and became something of a regional expert. I appeared on some television interview programs, and I actually led some protests. The first was in Carlsbad, N.M., where the government intended to use underground rock formations to pile up low-level nuclear waste items like gloves and hammers and pliers and similar products that couldn't just be tossed into a regular landfill. I drove over to Carlsbad and was keynote speaker at a rally against the project. I don't remember much of a crowd, but the small group there did get on TV and into the newspaper. Ultimately, the government got what it wanted over there. Back in Amarillo, not long after that, I led a rally in Memorial Park against the triad of lurking nuclear evils. Somehow, Dad found out about this event and my role in it, and he showed up in a tree line not far from the site of the rally. I saw him out there and went over to see what he was doing. He asked me not to be involved. But, I was far more than merely involved. He walked away looking very sad and very upset.

Feb. 3: Dad was a longtime conservative in the mold of William F. Buckley Jr., a man I admired myself when I was growing up and reading *The National Review*, his magazine. I'm not exactly sure what turned Dad in that direction. All of his siblings and his mother were Democrats. In fact, his brother Basil was a state senator in Oklahoma and a staunch Democrat. As I recall, Mama Jo's main reason for being a Democrat was because President Abe Lincoln was a Republican. She had no use for Republicans, and I trace that to her father's ill treatment as a Confederate soldier and then as a refugee forced to flee with his family to East Texas after the Civil War and to start over as a share-cropper. Their lives from 1865 on must have been very hard. I sensed bitterness in her voice when she talked about her father's life in the army of Gen. Joseph E. Johnston and then as a cotton farmer in one spot or another in East Texas trying to eke a living out of the Blackland Prairie. Dad was the youngest of four sons, and I think he was just naturally a little rebellious, so maybe his embrace of conservatism had something to do with that. Over time, though, I know that he came to accept Republican ideas about the economy and about the War in Vietnam, etc.

Dad, though, was thoroughly devoted to "reason," and he taught a high-school course on Critical Thinking. We talked about the class and what he was teaching, and he simply reinforced in me the idea that reason should take precedent over emotion, and that ethics should certainly be primary of social norms.

Today, I go to a church retreat at Mustang Island down near Corpus Christi.

Deep inside its business section this morning, The *New York Times* has an item about its annual earnings report, delivered yesterday to investors. The news was not good, just as it has not been good for a long, long time. Print advertising revenue fell 16 percent last year. Total ad revenue dropped 9 percent, which means the company made up a little of the shortfall with ad revenue from online products. Worse, for the last quarter, ad revenue fell 20 percent. That is the quarter that includes Christmas, and should not see this level of decline ever, ever. The story says that the *Times* will make adjustments in its editorial department, meaning it will cut, cut, cut right on into the bone. This has been the standard response by publishers to inadequate ad sales ever since the Internet came along in 2000 or so. When ad revenue drops, you just cut news staff. The editorial product inevitably suffers, so readers fall away and ad revenue drops again. It is the most vicious of cycles, but one I have watched play out all across the industry and, first-hand, in Wichita Falls, Temple and Austin. This process is insane, and leaders in no other industry I know of would follow this practice right down the sinkhole.

I became editor of *The Times Record News* in Wichita Falls in 1995. At the time, I felt we were pretty lean and mean as a newsroom staff, but had enough quality people to put out a good newspaper. Still, big changes were on the horizon, and I was well aware of them. Along about 1993, when I was managing editor, I

44

found out from some of my copy editors about "bulletin boards" that were being established around the country to facilitate communication. The police chief in Wichita Falls had a cops bulletin board where he posted information for his people, and we knew how to tap into that. At some point in 1993 or 1994, I attended the national meeting of managing editors in Dallas. The program was absolutely full of presentations about "the internet" and "America Online" and "HTML" and predictions about how emerging technologies would have bots driving our cars, answering our phones, delivering our packages and giving the news. I was astonished. But I was also very much aware of the threat. If newspapers did not co-opt this new platform for information delivery, we could find ourselves completely obsolete and out of business.

As soon as I got back to the office, I brought together my four brightest young reporters and put together a Skunk Works right then and there to help us figure out how to compete in the new environment. One thing we did right away was put together a Thursday night chatroom on AOL. Every Thursday at 8 o'clock I would log on, and we would have a no-holds-barred conversation about anything anybody wanted to bring up. (Two things of interest came out of that AOL chatroom experience. One: Richard Mize, my farm editor, met his wife-to-be in the chatroom. Two: The city's head librarian was a frequent participant, and one night we devoted the time to the horrible damage done to the library by a recent downpour. The back walls of the old library, built in 1917, had nearly collapsed, and the entire World War II book collection had been damaged beyond repair. I suggested she and I and others who might be interested in exploring another library location get together the following Tuesday at the newspaper conference room. That Tuesday, more than 100 people showed up, including the city manager and mayor. As a result of that chatroom conversation, Wichita Falls got a wonderful library in a different location and the city got a building that was repurposed as an arts center.) Another immediate adventure had us hooking up an audio feed through AOL to give live election results on the night of voting. I did the bulletins. We got no good feedback on that attempt, but at least we were trying.

Of course, anything we could come up with required money, and I lobbied the publisher as hard as I could to get an IT person dedicated to our online presence, to building a web page, to keeping it updated, and so on. Right about then, in 1995, I was named editor of the newspaper. Bill Gulledge was publisher. He was a pretty savvy guy, an engineer by training. He'd been brought into the *Times Record News* from the Harte-Hanks newspapers in Boston. He was a Texan and wanted to get back home, and he'd done a good job of combining operations of the newspapers up there. Coming home was his reward, although not a good one as it turned out. I remember the day Gulledge was plugged into the internet by our IT guy, David. Dave sat Gulledge down at his computer and fiddled with the mouse, and before long Gulledge was online. "Is this what you call 'surfing the 'net?' " he asked. Bill saw the potential as well, but other publishers in our newspaper group, which by then included Abilene, San Angelo, Corpus Christi, us and Albuquerque, weren't so quick to jump on the wagon. I think the newspaper group president, a guy who'd grown up East Texas, figured that out pretty quickly. All the publishers and editors convened in Abilene in 1995 or 1996 to discuss our strategy about how to leverage our websites to make money and keep our news franchises. Each publisher was supposed to give a presentation on one piece of the puzzle. During these talks, the group president paced back and forth at the back of the room, running his hands through his hair. At one point, I heard him mutter, "paradigm shift." Not long after that meeting, Harte-Hanks sold the newspapers—all of them—to E.W. Scripps.

Feb. 4: Last evening at the vestry retreat I think I drank about a glass too much red wine. We had a round-table discussion with Charlie Cook, the leader of our talks this weekend and a retired Episcopalian priest and professor, and we quite naturally got off on the president. Through it all, I said a lot about Trump and the failure of our church to oppose him on the immigration ban. But, I completely forgot to bring up what I believe to be THE salient point about church membership across the spectrum in America: a failure of nerve, a fear of making people mad, of challenging their long-held prejudices. I will bring that up today if I have the chance, even though it will not go over well. It is absolutely what I believe is driving a decline in enthusiasm for the American church. We don't walk the walk.

Feb. 5: Just as I thought, I was sick all day yesterday, miserable, actually, with a cough, constantly dripping nose and general achy feeling. I pretty much kept my mouth shut and took some notes and tried to be pleasant. I ate a half sandwich for lunch, about all I could force down, and kept Kleenex at my side all day long. The ride home was especially awful because I felt so bad, had to sit the backseat so I couldn't hear anything, it was cold and rainy out—and we got lost right out of the chute. I had hoped to be in the car for about three hours. It ended up being four and a half. I skipped dinner and went to bed at 9:15.

In today's edition of The *New York Times*, the public editor has a short piece in the Review section about changes that are under way in the editorial department. I mentioned previously that the *Times* is losing money in its print product and not regaining it in the electronic version. The discussion by the public editor had to do with eliminating line editors and streamlining the editing process. Well, good luck with that! For more than 20 years newspapers of lesser repute and style have cut and cut in their editorial staffs to the point that they're not particularly accurate or careful about catching errors, and I mean errors like typos and errors like lousy or wrong tone and errors like omitting key information or taking a bad point of view.

My first newspaper job was as a night reporter for the *Amarillo Daily News*. Before any item went into the morning newspaper, it went through this gauntlet: The reporter gathered information and wrote the story with some upfront guidance from the city editor about things like sourcing and length of finished product. The story in hard copy form went to the city editor, who edited it. That included fixing typos, double-checking facts, correcting for tone, ensuring proper sourcing and attribution, and so on. The city editor passed the story to the news editor, or "slot man," on the copy desk, and he would give the story a cursory glance to assign it to a page editor and to make sure it was suitable for publication in an overall sense. The slot man passed the story to a rimmer or page editor. Here, the real copy editing took place. These rim men had seen it all; they were seasoned

46

veterans. You could not get anything past them, from a misspelled name to an untrustworthy source. They were smart, they were experienced and they were uniformly pissy. They hated mistakes. The rim men would edit the story, write a headline, assign the story to a page and send it to the back shop via pneumatic tube. There, the story was set in type by a typesetter who was literate, so the story could actually be fixed or flagged at that point. Once in type, the story, if important enough, might be sent back to the newsroom in proof form for another review. A proof would also be pulled for an honest-to-God little old lady with green eyeshade proofreader. Obviously, her job was to be final arbiter on the story's accuracy and value in print. When it was ready to go, the type would be set up in a chase, which meant that if you wanted to read the story in type you had to be able to read upside down and backwards, which is what the guys who performed this function could do. Conceivably, this guy could catch errors himself, so that was another check, although rarely significant. So, a story would be looked at with a critical eye by as many as six or seven people.

The computerization of the newsroom and the pressure to increase profitability starting in about 1970 led to the streamlining that I refer to above. I will call it "streamlining" because the noun is useful in a visual sense. "Slashing and burning" might be a less charitable way to put it. With every passing year, the pressure mounted to cut, cut, cut in newsrooms across the country. Mechanization eliminated entire layers of the safety net. National Public Media's On the Media program this morning highlighted the depth and breadth of the problem. Since 1990 newspapers have lost 60 percent of their workforce and revenues are off 72 percent in that time. Half of statehouse bureaus have closed and there are virtually no foreign bureaus at all.

The cuts in most newspapers have come in the editorial departments (after certain production cuts because of technological advances). And a great many of those reductions have been in copy and line editors. After all, publishers thought, don't we have SpellCheck? Well, no, you don't. Thanks to SpellCheck you have an excuse to feel better about getting worse because you can tell yourself you're actually getting better! Of course, readers know the difference, and that's one reason they are leaving newspapers for something else. It's always true that when you misspell a person's name or title or his hometown or something either dear to him or known to him by its correct spelling, you suffer erosion in trust. It happens so often now everywhere that I'm just ready to throw up my hands and call it quits. The Wimberley View is an absolute disaster in this regard. Not a single article is published without an error in spelling, a typo, some kind of mistake. It would be funny if it weren't so sad. Don't these people give a shit? No. And neither, ultimately, do the people who are going to cut the newsroom at *The New York Times*. They may "rethink" their processes in the editorial department to save money but in the end all they will do is save money at the expense of accuracy and trust.

Feb. 6: I finished the book *Hillbilly Elegy* yesterday. It's been at the top of the best-seller list for months. The author, J.D. Vance, is a Yale-educated lawyer who lives in San Francisco with his wife and kids. He's not an old guy, so it seemed odd he'd feel compelled to write a memoir, but the timing probably seemed right. And, boy, was it. The book came out well before the presidential election, and it is about the white folks who proved to be instrumental to the Donald's win—white trash. Vance had a pretty lousy childhood. His mom was a drug addict who went through seven or eight men before Vance left home to live with his grandmother, a certified redneck hick who loved him like nothing else in this world. The boy took more hard knocks than a busted fender. Ultimately, he went into the Marines, they straightened him out and then he got into Ohio State and then Yale. He's a smart guy, and he endured, overcame his circumstances. But, the book is really not about J.D. Vance as Howard Roark. It's more about the horrifying decay of a large swath of middle America where people don't have and don't want good jobs, do have drugs and do have very shitty attitudes about everything. They are pissed off at the world. No wonder Trump was their man.

I can't really relate to those folks and their kind. My grandparents migrated to East Texas from Alabama and Georgia after the Civil War. They might have been hillbillies back in the Deep South, but I don't think so. For one thing, they did pick up and move to a better place, and the hillbillies in J.D. Vance's book couldn't muster the strength of character to go to Wal-Mart in the next town over, much less move across the country just in case they might better themselves and their kids. Then, when the Wilsons and the Boswells got to East Texas they took up residence on the Blackland Prairie, a soil type they were familiar with for the farming of cotton, and they set out to make a living. For the Wilsons, anyway, the going was pretty rough. They moved from one tenant farm to another before finally settling on some rented farmland outside Greenville in Hopkins County. When my granddad was old enough, he married a Boswell from a neighboring property and went to work to raise kids and crops. He was lucky on the kids part, not on the crops part, and went to work in early marriage as a clerk at the country store in Cumby, but kept on farming as well. At some point, he figured it was all not going to work out, so he started studying by correspondence on how to be an accountant. When he finished that coursework, he got a job with the Internal Revenue Service in Greenville and moved his family of seven kids into town in 1912, when my dad was 4 years old.

After reading through *Hillbilly Elegy* I can't help thinking that, given what little I know about my family's climb out of abject poverty, there's something about those people's upbringing that fails to instill in them the will to better their own lives. It is easy to be facile about making judgments. I know that. But, I also look at the thousands of refugees who have risked their lives to get themselves and their children out of, for example, Syria, across treacherous waters and through ugly regimes to a better place. If they can do that what's so hard about getting off your ass and moving out of a coal mining town that's dying to a place that's thriving when all you have to do is put gas in your pickup and find the interstate? I mean, the Okies did that, right? So, maybe White Trash Nation will look up in four years out of the lap of luxury that they anticipate coming their way and re-elect the Donald to another four.

Feb. 7: The worst Trump appointee ever will probably be confirmed by the Senate today after Democrats staged an all-night talk-a-thon. She is Betsy DeVoss, a very rich woman who never had a public education, never sent children to public schools and, in fact, hates the very idea of governmental support for educating kids, unless that government support goes exclusively to private schools. Her hearings in the Senate have shown she has little to no knowledge about public education, which is a likely outcome of her lack of acquaintance with it. Yet, she may skate right on through. It tells you how cynical Trump is about our country that he would nominate someone so obviously wrong as a candidate to head up the Department of Education, someone not just wrong but stupefyingly wrong. That he will get what he wants anyway tells you a lot about the lapdogs in the Senate.

Remember, the overarching goal of conservatives in government is to make public education so awful that it produces Betas who are too dumb for self-government and thus are completely subservient to a ruling class with superior smarts paid for by the hicks at the bottom. Vis a vis: White Trash Nation.

Trump said something late last week about undoing the so-called Johnson Amendment, a rule of law that prohibits preachers from endorsing political candidates from the pulpit, among other things similar in nature. Frankly, I had never heard of the Johnson Amendment and had always wondered why so few pastors spoke out on political campaigns, other than, of course, pastors of Black churches. I brought up the subject at breakfast Saturday at the Vestry retreat, mainly because our rector was sitting right next to me and I wanted to get her reaction. She said she would never endorse a candidate from the pulpit and would never allow any clergy working under her to do so. Why, I asked. Essentially, she said that she did not and would not focus her sermons on issues of the day because there were too many of them. Instead, she wanted her homilies to change the hearts of her parishioners. If their hearts changed, their attitudes about issues of the day would change.

This sounded reasonable—until I started thinking about it. How long, I wonder, would it take to change the heart of an adult in the White Trash Nation until that heart became compassionate toward the refugee, the poverty stricken, the victim of a system rigged against her?

Our esteemed governor did announce last week that he wants cuts in every agency budget, including those of higher education. The fact is that cuts happen every time the Legislature convenes. Nothing seems to ever get added to the budget even as Texas continues to be among the fastest growing states. That's just one reason that Texas students graduate from college with huge amounts of loan debt: The state no longer feels it has an obligation to educate its children. This is a massive change from when I was a student. I made the decision to attend Amarillo College in 1965 mainly because I had terrible high-school grades and because I couldn't afford to go anywhere else. Each semester's tuition at AC cost me $78. Fees and books added another $22, so total cost per term was $100. If you adjust that figure for inflation, using a Bureau of Labor Statistics calculator, you find that it would now be $762. Kids today would absolutely jump at the chance to attend college that cost only $762 a semester. That tuition/fee price is non-existent. Even when I went to West Texas State, the per-semester cost was something like $350.

Today, young people graduate from college with $20,000, $30,000, $40,000 in student loan debt because the price of tuition, books and fees has risen far beyond what inflation would dictate. And that rise has come because the states have backed out of subsidizing college educations. The amount of subsidy has gone from almost 100 percent to almost zero percent, and our friends in the Texas Legislature and in the governor's mansion would like to drive it into negative territory. In Texas, they have shifted some public education funds to private schools already, and others they have just cut.

I would like to think that this long-term, deliberate dismantling of public support for education will eventually bite them on the ass, but I'm thinking now that Trump is in the White House thanks to White Trash Nation that it won't. Still, there are a lot of guns out there in the hands of increasingly ignorant people. Who knows.

Feb. 8: I emailed Senator John Cornyn of Texas yesterday to urge him to vote against Betsy DeVoss as secretary of education. Of course, he voted for her. Back when John Cornyn was a candidate for various offices in Texas, he would come around *The Canyon News* and the Wichita Falls paper looking for editorial endorsements, and I always liked him. I thought he was a brilliant lawyer and a man you could trust. Something happened to him in Washington. He is now just another political lackey sucking up whatever dollars he can from the right wing and voting, without fail, for whatever the Koch Brothers want. He is at least as bad as Ted Cruz, whom I did not write, but at least I can harbor a tiny hope that Cornyn might change. Cruz will not, except for the worse.

While Texas legislators yak back and forth about the importance of restroom regulations, it appears they will again refuse to outlaw the act of texting while driving. Texas is one of only a handful of states that has not banned this dangerous practice. Gov. Rick Perry and now Gov. Greg Abbott strongly oppose a ban, and I can't for the life of me figure out why. There must be some hidden financial interest associated with continuing to allow texting while driving. Someone must win monetarily from that stance. But, who?

Earlier this week, *The New Yorker*'s George Prochnik wrote a story about Stefan Zweig, a German I never heard of. Zweig was an intellectual in the '20s who wrote a book called *The World of Yesterday*. His primary concern was the overwhelming victories of the Nazis over their own peoples and those in nearby countries leading up to and during World War II. Zweig watched with clear vision as the Nazis came to power, and he was appalled by their effective use of propaganda to move the masses to their cause. Prochnik notes that Zweig warned that once the propaganda machine starts winning and really gets rolling, it is very hard to stop: "The excruciating power of Zweig's memoir lies in the pain of looking back and seeing that there was a small window in which it was possible to act *(in opposition, or to resist)*, and then discovering how suddenly and irrevocably that window can be slammed shut." (emphasis added) In the same issue Adam Gopnik reminds us: "Dissent is not courageous or exceptional. It is normal—it's Madison-ian, it's Hamiltonian. It's what we're supposed to do." But, it is so hard for a lot of people to push themselves to do anything beyond the normal routine. We can only hope that those we have elected and selected to protect our Constitution and our way of life recognize their solemn obligations to be loyal nay-sayers.

The Ninth Circuit Court will decide in the next several days whether Trump crossed the line with his immigration ban. I'm truly not up on the law as it relates to the president's powers on immigration regulation, so I'm not sure where the court will land. I will say that just on human-rights grounds, they should unanimously toss the case into the Atlantic without a life raft. The judiciary may be the only thing that stands against rising Trumpism. That and the media with guts to continue to refuse to submit to the jackboots of Bannon and Conway.

Feb. 9: I will say that Trump's pick for the Supreme Court, Gorshum, at least has a set of balls. He told a Senator yesterday that Trump's chiding of the Ninth Circuit Court was embarrassing and demoralizing and disheartening. So, the guy is at least not a Clarence Thomas so intent on getting the position that he'll go along with absolutely anything. This makes me think better of him, even though it befuddles me how a smart man can go through law school and come out believing that the Constitution should be interpreted as if this were 1778.

Elizabeth Warren likewise has guts. She stood up to the Senate leadership by reading from a letter from Coretta Scott King about the suitability of Senator Jeff Sessions to be Attorney General of the United States. Mitch McConnell, the jellyfish who runs the Senate, cut her off, saying, "She persisted," after being warned repeatedly to shut up and sit down. Sessions has now been confirmed, so we have a racist in charge of U.S. justice.

Right out of the clear blue sky, there's a legislator in Texas who is showing an extraordinary amount of good sense for a person in her position. I'm going to have to do some research about a legislator named Burton, who became the subject of a Trump outburst the other day because she has introduced a bill that would eliminate the longstanding right of law-enforcement officials to seize and keep and sell or use property that is used in the commission of a crime BEFORE the property owner is found guilty or innocent of a single thing. We can thank the war on drugs launched under Reagan for this thoroughly unconstitutional law that has enriched police departments and sheriff's offices and the offices of district attorneys nationwide since the 1970s. Here is what happens: A guy has a drug-running operation. You arrest him. You take his boats, his cars, his guns, his bank accounts—everything you can link to drug money. Then you sell all that stuff, or you keep it to use, and he goes to jail and then he goes to court. He may or may not be guilty. But he still loses his stuff even if found innocent. This is so wrong it's hard to see how it has stayed on the books.

I remember that the first time I encountered this law was when I was covering the federal courthouse in Amarillo as a reporter for KFDA-TV. A former state legislator had a son who was arrested on federal drug charges. All his stuff was seized by the feds, including a new black SUV that his dad had bought him. Dad wanted the truck; under the law it was no longer his son's, even though the boy had never been convicted of so much as a parking ticket. Since the man was a former legislator upset with a law it made a pretty good story for TV. But the wrong never got righted. Besides the fact this is patently unfair, the more practical effect of the law was for cops to go shopping for something they wanted—nice boat, nice car, nice guns—and then trump up charges so they could have what they desired without a crime having been committed.

Feb. 10: KXAN-TV is continuing a series that it launched last fall about the effectiveness of the surge in Texas highway patrol troopers on the border with Mexico. You won't find a DPS trooper up around Dallas anymore, because they are all in Brownsville, Juarez and Laredo. Yesterday, the DPS superintendent asked legislators to approve another $1 billion (with a "b") for more troopers to go to the border. So far, an investigation by KXAN shows that the surge has made NO, Zero, NADA impact on drug trafficking in Texas. Almost 60 percent of the arrests made by troopers in the last year on the border have been for misdemeanors. The surge is a failure, but border "security" is such a hot-button issue for Republicans that the DPS will get the $1 billion and might have to duck out the door while even more dollar bills are flung at them. When KXAN asked the lieutenant governor about why the surge should be supplemented when it was so clearly a failure, he blamed the "mainstream media" for something I couldn't even discern from his conversation. The man is a fucking lunatic, all chewing gum and butch wax and well-rehearsed hokum about motherhood and apple pie, blah, blah, blah. He and Kellyann Conway must have gone to the School of Completely Empty Rhetoric. They're like skunks who spray us, but we've lost our sense of smell.

Speaking of Ms. Conway, she got her ass in a crack yesterday by encouraging Americans to buy all things Ivanka because that big, bad Nordstrom's said it would no longer carry the little darling's line of clothing. Oops, said some Republicans, naughty, naughty. Not supposed to endorse Ivanka's stuff on White House time. Oh, said the stupefyingly obtuse Ms. Conway, sorry! So, without even a hand slap she gets a free pass on something that would have launched a multi-million dollar, months-long House investigation under Obama.

It appears that some among the American farm gentry have figured out that Donald Trump's ideas of immigration reform, which involves booting every single illegal immigrant out of the country and letting no new ones in, might suddenly leave them without anyone to tend their crops. They voted for Trump, after all, thinking … thinking what? That he would NOT deport millions of immigrants and close the door to further new-comers? He promised to do just that! So, today The *Times* reports they are worried. But, come on, guys, listen to the reformists' assurances like the one from one Dan Stein, president of the Federation for American Immigration Reform, who told The *Times*: "Limiting the use of foreign labor would push more Americans into jobs that had primarily been performed by immigrants." Has this nut job ever even been on an American farm? Mexicans are out there picking and chopping because no American will do that job. What about the whiney-butts in coal mine country? Will they go into the tobacco fields or corn fields to work or will they sit there in the holler and smoke dope and bitch about not finding meaningful work? Clearly they will do the latter all day long while some Mexican with his kids in diapers is out there at dawn chopping cotton and picking peaches. Give me a fucking break.

In the early 1980s when I was working for Channel 10 in Amarillo as a reporter, Larry Statser and I went one day to Hereford, which is west of Amarillo in Deaf Smith County. That county has most always been one of the most productive in terms of agricultural products, not even counting hogs and cattle. You plant something in Deaf Smith County and, for some reason, it grows. Big farms have been the norm in that county, and farmers grow acres upon acres of onions and peppers and corn and soybeans and sun flowers.

Hereford is the big town and county seat, so over the years migrant laborers have gathered there during growing and harvesting seasons. In general, they would find housing in filthy, rundown shack-like apartments that I guess were owned by growers and operated by overseers. Every morning before dawn, flatbed trucks would pull into the apartment complexes and load entire families for the short trip to the acreage to be worked that day. At sundown, the families returned.

Statser and I were in Hereford after being alerted to the sorry way migrants were treated by staff lawyers of the Texas Rural Legal Aid office in Hereford. These three or four lawyers had been trained at Harvard, and they had come to Texas because they wanted to help. They worked for very low wages, lived in horrible housing and worked long, long hours. When we got to Hereford we were greeted by the Harvard guys and by Jesus, a labor organizer who had come to town to try to get the migrants to understand their situation and try to do something about it.

At the same time, Jesus and the TRLA team were about to file a federal suit against one of the biggest growers in Deaf Smith County, a guy named Max Brand. The suit would contend that the workers were not being paid federal minimum wage and that the court needed to take steps to make sure the law on wages was followed. The growers argued that they did pay the minimum wage, just not the way an ordinary business might do so. I never really understood the growers' logic, because here is the way the compensation system worked: As a worker, you were required to fill a brown burlap bag with X number of onions in a certain amount of time. Each onion had to be pulled from the ground. The stalk end had to be clipped with scissor-like utensils, the roughage had to be sloughed off the onion, and the relatively clean onion plopped into the bag. At the end of the day you would be paid for the bags you filled up to the quota and for the bags you filled over the quota. It was physically impossible for a grown man to fill enough bags by himself to meet the quota, much less hit the bonus number. So, his wife and children worked alongside him, and altogether the family might be able to fill all the bags required by the end of the day. This system meant no one took breaks, and there were no portable facilities in these fields, anyway. No one sat down for lunch. I saw two-year-olds in diapers carrying scissor utensils that were almost as big as they were. Kids pulled onions, they clipped tops, they pulled bags.

At the end of the growing season in Texas, they moved on, and at the end of their trip across the United States, they got to go back to Mexico with a little money, not enough for a car or a house. In these vegetable forced-labor camps, which is what they were, no health insurance was provided, no medical care was available. The grower had no responsibilities other than to make sure the overseer put you into the rodent hotel at night and fetched you at daybreak. This all made stunning video: the kids pulling onions, the hot sun of summer, Jesus in full outrage, the TRLA boys at their broken-down desks.

We did tell their story, and the lawsuit was filed, and the Brands of Texas did lose. They were supposed to fix the wage payment system. I don't know that they did that. I don't think that to this day any grower anywhere provides health and life insurance for migrants or good housing or suitable breaks. Or a living wage, for that matter. For migrants, the deck is just stacked against them. They are completely vulnerable. Come on, White Trash Nation: Take them jobs, boys!

I emailed Konnie Burton, a state senator from Fort Worth, yesterday telling her to hang in there on the asset forfeiture law she wants to see passed. She's the senator singled about by Trump this week as someone who must be destroyed because of her bill.

Feb. 11: Trump is vulnerable in so many ways that it is really hard to see why the Democrats cannot get ahold of him like vicious bulldogs and refuse to let go until he is appropriately run out of office. I don't get it. The elephant in the room is his business dealings.

The images that stick with me from my time as a reporter at Channel 10 in Amarillo in the early 1980s are from our trips to Hereford during the TRLA lawsuit against Max Brand and other growers to try to get a decent wage for migrant workers.

While I was at KFDA-TV that spring of 1981, two events of significance occurred.

One, the federal judge in Amarillo ordered Pantex and the government to produce an environmental impact statement before expanding the plant. So, we won the lawsuit. Within a few months, the government did, in fact, provide an environmental impact statement, something that in most governmental hands would have taken years. This slim volume answered none of the questions people would normally have about such a project: Will it increase the amount of nuclear material in air or water or soil? Will it threaten any species of animal or plant? Will it cause any environmental damage whatever? No. It was all just hunky-dory. As a group we Amarillo peaceniks had to be satisfied with the fact that we had raised awareness about the plant and its mission and its place in the American arsenal. Nothing we could have done would have shut the plant down. Nothing, as it turned out, could have stopped expansion. We did have a small impact in the moral realm. The bishop of the Diocese of Amarillo, Bishop Matthiesen, did issue a letter to the Catholics in the Panhandle telling them that working at Pantex—preparing for nuclear war—was immoral, and if they worked there they should quit. He offered to pay their salaries and help them find new jobs. As you might expect— this being Amarillo—exactly one person quit. He was an ordained deacon in the Catholic church and, thus, had little real choice.

The other event of significance was a federal court order telling Max Brand and other growers they had to pay minimum wage, and the wage had to have a reasonable basis in time worked, not bags filled. At the time I called this a victory. But, of course, it wasn't really, because there was no one around to enforce the order and the law. Nothing much changed. Ultimately, Republicans defunded the TRLA and other rural legal aid organizations around the country so that outrages like the successful lawsuit against Max Brand could not be filed. Poor people could not get legal help for divorces. They had no recourse when screwed by businesses. (Some time much later the American lawmakers had a hiccup of conscience toward migrants and enacted a law that said that the owners of U.S. companies that HIRED illegal immigrants could be prosecuted. You can imagine how well that went over even though, of course, that was exactly the best way to stop the flow of immigrants out of Mexico. If they couldn't find work, they would not come. But, this was such a threat to businessmen that they soon had the law undone, giving them the right to continue to exploit frightened migrants, who themselves were then the criminals for trying to find jobs in a place of perpetual sunshine and fresh air.)

Feb. 12: Lynda is antsy about what to do when we can no longer afford to live in this house. We met a couple of weeks ago with Laura and Scott to broach the subject that we build an addition to their place at Canyon Lake. They were very cool to the idea, partly because—or mainly because—they have five or six dogs and the dogs are boisterous. They will not get rid of any dogs, and they will not put the dogs where they cannot be heard at all hours of the day and night. I don't want to live out my final days listening to dogs bark. So, we will move on down the road. I have at least 10 years left before I'm a complete physical and mental wreck, and I will take care of Lynda, so she need not worry about it.

Feb. 13: We drove up to see our daughter Sarah's new house in north Austin yesterday. It's about an hour and a half to get there. The little house is in a tightly orchestrated subdivision. The houses are very close together with tiny yards in front and back. The house itself is 1,300 square feet in two stories, not a bad size for her. I think it's a very livable space with not much upkeep required. A good choice. It cost $150,000, which I guess is reasonable for Austin. She thinks that is a good price for the product. Her dad paid for it, doesn't like it and wants to sell it immediately, putting her back in limbo. He always has to make himself feel smarter than anyone else, so his assessment is far less about the value of the house than his exertion of power and demand for fealty.

So, $150,000 is on the low end in Austin. That's still a bargain when you compare that to prices on the coasts. Lynda and I regularly see shows where home values are approaching three-quarters of a million dollars, and those are fixer-uppers. By the time the buyers are through, they've spent almost $1 million.

Now the interesting thing here is that most of them, I think, are in their 20s and 30s. They are hardly at their peak in terms of earning power. Our question, then, is, What kind of salaries do these kids draw that allow them to buy million-dollar starter homes? In our wildest imaginations we never thought we could afford a million-dollar house at the very top of our games. And this is all post-2008 when the nation's lenders never qualified anyone for a home and just loaned out money willy-nilly.

We did not watch the Grammys. We don't listen to popular music. In the car, I listen to NPR exclusively. We don't have a radio on at home, and actually own only one, an emergency radio that has multiple electrical inputs for use when the lights go out. Even if I lived all by myself, I would not listen to music stations. Country music isn't anymore. It's all over-produced pop. And rap and hip-hop just aren't my genres. I'm aware that I could probably hear some of my favorites by plugging into Pandora or a similar music service, but I relish having a quiet place.

Feb. 14: I have been reading here and there about the posturing that's taking place in advance of the late-April White House Correspondents Dinner. It seems some reporters are saying they might boycott the event if Trump is invited and accepts. The whole unseemly affair should be cancelled regardless of Trump's presence. The dinner has become a celebrity do-dah of the first order, with men in black ties and tails and women in long dresses and jewels. Big names attend, and reporters rub elbows with people the rest of us worship from afar. It is an evening of fawning and preening, as if reporters and editors were rock stars. It's kind of sickening when you think about it. No wonder the national news media completely missed the Trump landswell in the heartland of America. They wouldn't know the people of the heartland if these poor yokels bit them on the ankle.

By participating in a whingding like this one, these journalists show the rest of us that they are not like us at all. They are celebrities in their own right, rich people enjoying a rich people's game. Jimmy Breslin, Ernie Pyle, and a host of other journalists: What would they think of this display of avarice and conceit? I wrote a letter to the White House Correspondents yesterday telling them to cancel the dinner and get to work. I found out a guy from the Dallas Morning News is secretary of the group and wrote him, too. I reminded him of the role of a journalist in America: to comfort the afflicted and to afflict the comforted. I just wonder how these people can actually contemplate playing host to a man who hates their guts and laughing and smiling like everything is just hunky-dory.

Feb. 15: I got a form letter from John Cornyn yesterday by email in response to my own letter to him urging him to vote against Betsy DeVoss. In his letter he says she is so concerned about public education, especially for the poor. Right. She's so concerned about education for the poor that she wants to kill their schools and make them go to some inferior version paid for with government vouchers where they can learn about Jesus and not about science. Cornyn has completely squandered his intellect and sold out just like another Texas senator I knew named Phil Gramm. Gramm also chose money over conscience. He's a wealthy man now living out there somewhere. I have no idea how he looks at himself in the morning when he shaves.

Every day of the week if you need to hire day labor you can find men standing around and sitting in old green plastic chairs out in front of St. Mary's Catholic Church on Ranch Road 12. They get there before daybreak and stay until they're picked up for odd jobs around the valley. Linda Eagleton told me yesterday that these guys are no longer showing up. They worry that ICE will pick them up and deport them. These are not idle or frivolous worries. ICE has stepped up its activities in Austin and appears to be rounding up people at random. They even lie about what they're doing, which is no surprise. These thugs have been given license to do as they please by the Trump White House, where rules don't matter so long as you get the job done, and that job can include telling the Russians to calm down about sanctions after meddling with our presidential election—and don't get caught.

It's pretty clear at this point that I am in the camp with those who believe that Trump and his fellow travelers must be actively resisted on every move they make. I want them to face "No" on every proposal and initiative. I want it to be so hard to govern that they hate what they are doing even more than they hate the government they are leading—and get the hell out and never come back. So, I concede that I look for opinions that mirror or bolster my own, although I am willing to entertain different views. For example, David Brooks, an op-ed writer for The New York Times, penned what I'm sure he viewed as a reasonably argued column for yesterday's editions. It begins with the simple question, "How should one resist the Trump administration?"

I'm not entirely sure where Brooks is coming from. I think he pretty conservative, but I have read columns by him that I thought were rational and realistic. So, I'll give him the benefit of the doubt. He answers his own question by saying that the response depends on what kind of threat we believe the Trump administration poses. He lists three possibilities: Authoritarianism or fascism; stagnation and corruption; or incompetence and anarchy. Brooks believes the last offers the best explanation, and that the remedy is the election of someone stable and bland like Gerald Ford, who followed Dick Nixon into the White House.

The problem, to restate it from the Brooks perspective, is incompetence, incoherence and stupidity. The solution is the stability of a Ford.

I would say Brooks' choice is too pat and simple. Yes, the administration is incompetent, the atmosphere is circus-like. But, it is also an advocate for authoritarianism and it is as corrupt as any that's ever taken up residence on Pennsylvania Avenue. A Ford will hardly be able to deal with all those issues, because we may not ever get to a Ford if the insidious erosion of reality and rights continues at its present speed of light.

Adam Gopnik, a regular writer for The New Yorker, is much closer to the truth in his front-of-magazine piece in the February 13 & 20 edition that we got in the mail yesterday. What Gopnik sees is far more sinister than what Brooks divines: "... the special cocktail of oafish incompetence and radical anti-Ameri-canism ..." Gopnik writes, "Some choose to find comfort in the belief that the incompetence will undermine the anti-Americanism. ..." It won't happen. What should Americans do?

"With the near-complete abdication of even minimal moral courage in the Republican Party, and the strategic confusion of Democrats, all that Americans can turn to is the instinct for shared defiance, and a coalition of conscience, the broader the better, to counter the chaotic cruelty." Gopnik likes the various marches; he wants to avoid the use of the term "resistance" as too over the edge. So, he stops short of embracing the nascent movement that will have everyone of like values saying over and over again, "NO, NO, NO!" until our voices are heard over the squeals of delight of the pigs at the government trough at the White House.

Brooks calls that reaction taking a page from the works of Dietrich Bonhoeffer. A Lutheran pastor before the during World War II, Bonhoeffer was arrested for his views as an anti-Nazi and killed by Hitler's boys. "In the face of fascism, he wrote, it is not enough to simply 'bandage the victims under the wheels of injustice, but jam a spoke into the wheel itself,' " Brooks writes. "If we are in a Bonhoeffer moment, the aggressive nonviolent action makes sense: marching in the streets, blocking traffic, disrupting town halls, vehement rhetoric to mobilize mass opposition."

One wonders what it would take for Brooks to come to believe that we are in a Bonhoeffer moment? Wasn't that a Bonhoeffer moment when civil rights leaders said, "Enough," and took to the streets because that was the only venue available? Wasn't that a Bonhoeffer moment when anti-war protesters swarmed Washington and New York City to get us out of Vietnam? How were those injustices more important to resist than the present threat of a complete theft of our government by the Trumpites? The very least we can do is rise up as one and say, NO. The very least.

A first-of-its-kind email arrived in my inbox at work yesterday. It was from daughter Julia, and in it she urged me to go to Standing Rock to show solidarity with the veterans and Native Americans who are opposing the construction of an oil pipeline across sacred Indian lands. She even said she would help pay for transportation and expenses. I was very surprised. Not long after that I got a similar email from my youngest daughter Rebecca. My goodness.

I have fired off some emails to Veterans for Peace in Austin to see if they can help connect me up with people on the ground in the Dakotas. I need to figure out how to get there, where to stay, how I can help, etc. Last fall I thought about trying to go up there, but without even checking I knew a trip would cost too much. Julia's offer opens a door, and I do have some friends here in Wimberley who have cold-weather gear I might borrow. One lady I know pretty well takes regular trips to Antarctica, so I'm pretty sure she might put me in touch with people who can help me out. I spent $1,000 or more on stuff to get me to Honduras and make me comfortable while I was there last April, and I can't really spend that much again this year.

I think I'm so critical of the White House Correspondents Dinner because I saw first-hand and right up-close how removed from the common people journalists became the closer they came to an elite education. When I started as a young reporter in 1966 at the Amarillo newspaper, I was on my way to a college education, but I was not there yet. I would say there were 70 people in the editorial department, and I would guess that maybe a third or less of them had a baccalaureate degree from any college. One or two of the copy editors may have graduated with a degree, but the guy who ran the desk, Max Vanderveer didn't, at least as far as I know. My first city editor, Don Williams, had a degree from somewhere, and while he was working in Amarillo he was pursuing advanced degrees at Texas Tech.

The general attitude of just about everyone around me was anti-college. I got the distinct feeling that they believed that the more educated you became the less you wanted to get down in the trenches and advocate for the real people out there who were struggling to get by against some powerful forces in the economy and in government. (Those were not college boys who were coming home from Vietnam in body bags.) I liked the grit of Jimmy Breslin and some of the other nationally syndicated columnists who were just down-to-earth guys. I admired Ernie Pyle, who most famously did not rub elbows with the generals, but mucked through the hedgerows beside the grunts. Starting with my generation of young journalists, managing editors began to see the real value of a college degree, and the value was not in the knowledge gained or wisdom accrued from coursework.

The value of the degree to the hiring editors was that it gave them a blunt instrument to use to cull the employment applications. If you only accepted resumes from the degreed, you didn't have so many people to deal with, and you had some assurance that if nothing else at least those who had degrees had learned to put up with a certain amount of bullshit. They had a certain higher level of tolerance for pain. When I became a hiring editor myself, I strictly enforced this rule: no degree, no interview.

In reality what we were creating was a kind of elite that was completely out of touch with the problems faced by people who earned an hourly wage or who were out of work or who had to fight for every little thing they got. The degreed perceived themselves as somehow better than the great unwashed. And so, over the years, the focus of our coverage shifted to reflect those elitist attitudes. We began to publish newspapers almost exclusively for the Dillard's and Lord & Taylor shoppers, not for those who could barely afford to shop at Wal-Mart or Target. Our prices began to rise. Maybe the New York and Washington media have always considered themselves better than the rest of us (and I do have stories about encountering *New York Times* reporters out here in the hinterlands). But the worst example is this celebration of elitism called the Correspondents Dinner. It is not merely about elitism, it is about the worst part of elitism—the tendency to want to rub other people's noses in it.

I don't think the *Times Record News* was better over time because we hired only college graduates. Eventually, in fact, it caught up with us as we tried to appeal to readers in minority communities. We had no real clue how to do that. And we couldn't hire minority kids to help us figure it out. We were just too small a place to afford the kinds of salaries black and Hispanic graduates could command from the Dallas Morning News or Houston Chronicle right out of college. I could pay a newly minted college-educated journalist somewhere in the range of $25,000 to $27,000 a year. They could start at the *Morning News* or *Chronicle* for far more than that. So, at jobs fairs, absolutely nobody of color would line up at my table. Why should they?

Feb. 17: I did some more online research yesterday about how to get to Standing Rock and what I could do to help out there. I found a couple of articles in yesterday's newspapers from that area. The Spokane newspaper said the camp was breaking up and people were leaving. It was all finished.

So, my window of opportunity has slammed shut. I sent the above to Julia and have not heard back from her. It was so sweet and generous of her to offer to send me there.

The president had a press conference all by his bigself yesterday, and acted like a lunatic on Prozac, from what I hear. David Brooks, not the wildest commentator out there, said Trump was seriously unhinged. He doesn't think the administration will last a full year. But, as *Times* editorial writers and Paul Krugman note this morning, if it implodes it will not be because the Republicans have done one damn thing to hold the administration accountable for sins that would have gotten any Democrat tossed into jail long ago. It seems clear right now that Trump's boys assured Russia there would be no sanctions for hacking our elections if they'd back off and wait for Trump to take office. This is treason, friends.

In my musings of yesterday, I wrote about how hard it was for me to hire minority journalists at the *Times Record News*. It was impossible. For one thing,

I couldn't pay them what they could earn at bigger newspapers—ever. For another, they did not want to live in Wichita Falls. Women reporters who were single and black knew the pool of good black men for them to marry was small, to begin with. It was almost non-existent in Wichita Falls. And there were just darn few black men in journalism programs, period. There were fewer Hispanics of either gender.

I did try, nevertheless. I tried to grow my own minority journalists right there in Wichita Falls. At first this was simply an idea I stumbled over by accident. One day when I was city editor of the afternoon paper and in charge of the weekend arts and entertainment section, I had a visit from a lanky young black man who barely spoke above a whisper. He was a high-school sophomore, he told me, and he wanted to be a playwright and author. He was dead serious. He had with him a Macintosh disc that he'd written something on over at the library, and he wanted me to look at it. I asked him a lot of questions, and the idea came to me that I might hire this kid for minimum wage and help him along and he might turn out to be something special. So, I told him to do some interviews and to write something up and bring it back to me by 5 o'clock the following Friday. I figured he'd never come back. But, he did return with a story and it wasn't all that bad. It was hand-written, but that was OK. So, I gave him another assignment. He came back again with the story, again not that badly written. I told him then that I wanted him to be a regular columnist for the arts and entertainment section. We'd run his mugshot and his column every Friday morning, so he always had a deadline to meet, and I would pay him by the column. I forget how much I offered. He accepted, and through that school year, he did what he said he would do, and so did I. As I began to see that he had some talent and that he had a lot of drive and that he would stick with it, I began to see we might be able to keep Michael Hines and turn him into a journalist who would stick around after college.

Thus was born my grow-your-own program. At some point during that year, I got Michael to sit down and learn how to write stories on the computer—he had to learn to type, which he did in our newsroom. We taught him how to write obituaries from the forms dropped off every day by the funeral homes. And at the end of the year, I offered him a 20-hour-a-week job writing obituaries five nights a week during the summer vacation months. He did well. I never met Michael's parents. I never met his grandmother. I believe he lived with her in the "projects" near downtown. I just worked with Michael.

At the start of his senior year at Wichita Falls High School I made him an offer that I had cleared with my bosses: I would continue to have a job for him after school and would employ him full-time the following summer as a reporter. If he would go to Midwestern State University and major in journalism and promise to come back and work full-time for me for two full years after graduation, I would pay all his tuition, fees and books. He agreed. (When the newspaper editor Don James learned that Michael was on board for this program, he wanted to take Michael and the managing editor and me out to lunch to celebrate and formally seal the deal. And thus unfolded one of my most embarrassing moments. Don decided we should have lunch at the Wichita Club at the top of one of the bank buildings in downtown Wichita Falls. The Wichita Club's main clientele was older white oilmen and their wives and a smattering of doctors and lawyers and petroleum accountants. If there was a single black member I'm not aware of it. The members, and thus those who lunched at the Club, were, then, all white. The staff, on the other hand, was all black. Every single waiter, cook, server, hostess and busboy was black. So, there we were at our nice table with a white tablecloth and fine china and black people serving us and little old Michael the only black person in the whole building being allowed to eat with the white folks. He never said a word about it to me.)

At the end of his senior year, Michael came into my office and told me in a very sheepish voice that he had accepted a scholarship in drama to attend the University of Texas at Arlington. I knew that all his expenses would not be paid, and that he was turning down my offer after a lot of soul-searching. I figured he knew that if he took my deal he'd never escape Wichita Falls and he'd never be more than a skinny black kid in the eyes of his peers. I wished him only the best.

The following fall, I headed over to Hirschi High School and found Kimberley Ponder, a black girl who wanted to be a journalist and who was willing to sign up for my program. I talked with her parents. Her dad was in the Air Force, and her mother was a secretary at one of the junior high schools. They accepted the offer with the understanding that it would ultimately be up to Kimberley. She worked as an obituary clerk for more than a year, and then announced she was going to Atlanta, Ga., to attend an historically black college there. I didn't blame her, either. (One notable black man who grew up in Wichita Falls and made something great of himself was the mayor of Kansas City and then a congressman from that area. A reporter asked him one time when he returned home how his upbringing in Wichita Falls had prepared him for such achievements. He told her that he did everything in his power to get out of Wichita Falls and to be so successful he'd never have to come back.)

Feb. 18: Kimberley's departure left me with no black journalists, and I could not find another one in the high schools to try to train and persuade to stay with us.

At some point in the early 2000s (I'm guessing here), I got a phone call out of the blue from someone at the Society of Professional Journalists and/or the Managing Editors Association asking me to come—at the end of that week—to a quickly called conference on how to deal with the lack of minorities in the nation's newsrooms. I had never been to San Francisco, and I had never been asked my opinion on this subject, so I went, all expenses paid. Over the course of a couple of days, we participants came to the conclusion that we would have to "grow our own" as a profession. We would have to recruit our own folks and train them and place them and subsidize their salaries until newspapers could catch up. My contribution was to suggest that these folks be trained as I was when I was in officers basic at Fort Benjamin Harrison. There, everything was hands-on, and we worked a subject until we had mastered it and then moved on. We did not go to classes on MWF or TT. We were in class eight hours every day and had homework at night. The course was eight weeks in duration, which sounded about right for our new journalism training program.

This idea was adopted and the school opened in Nashville, I think. The *Times Record News* had help recruiting a mature black woman, a single mom, who was a secretary or something like that down in the Dallas-Fort Worth area.

61

Under our auspices and with some financial help, she attended the course, graduated and then moved to Wichita Falls to work on the copy desk. She was a nice lady.

Along about 2005, I went to Atlanta or Kansas City to be a judge of the Scripps-Howard national journalism awards program. Along with two other editors, I was to pick the best opinion column published in a newspaper in the previous year. These awards were very prestigious and came with cash prizes. Winning one would be a game-changer. The woman on our three-person team was right then in charge of the minority recruitment/training program in Nashville, and during a lunch break she asked me my opinion about it. I told her that our candidate was very pleasant and tried very hard but just wasn't ready to go to work when she came aboard. She did not do well and soon moved on to something else.

The *Times* today has a brief item about Donald Trump's late-evening tweet calling the news media the enemy of the American people. "SICK!" he wrote. The tweet is sick all right. It reflects Trump's complete narcissism, his inability to take criticism of any kind, his total self-absorption. The real threat here is that this kind of statement from the president, repeated over and over again, will absolutely scare publishers and station managers to death. They are not the strongest proponents of democracy to begin with; their allegiance, like Trump's, is to cash. So, even a tiny threat sends them head-hunting, lopping at the crania of journalists who might be telling true stories. Truth be damned when what matters is money.

Think I'm being cynical? Check out another story in today's *Times*: "In Trump Era, Newsrooms Face Risk of Self-Censorship." This is the story of a San Antonio radio station that has a 70-year-old commentator and DJ who said in an on-air editorial that the region's congressman, Lamar Smith, was being utterly foolish by telling constituents that the only source they could trust for news was Donald Trump. Smith's people called the station manager, who went to shiverin' and vacillatin' and hunkerin' down. Ultimately he got the radio comment killed because it offended Lamar Smith. Then, when he was roundly criticized for being a man with no balls at all, he changed course. Then, he told The *Times* that he had to protect the neutrality of the station because somebody might have considered the commentary to be "slander." What? I guess he never learned that you can't slander a publicly elected official. Too dumb, this guy, to be anything but a DJ on a teeny station out in Marathon, Texas.

I got this email from Rebecca this a.m., in reference to the Standing Rock situation:

"Go dad go!!!!! I remember being 3 or 4 and waking up way before dawn, being loaded into Fred and whisked away to the edge of Amarillo. I was so sleepy but I couldn't resist the energy that I felt from you and Mom. We hobbled out of the car and held up our handmade banner that mom had sewn together and we all helped to paint. I will NEVER forget the moment that LaDon jumped the wall of Pantex. Dad....you have to do this. It's time."

What Becca remembers there is the actual morning of the protest at the fence of Pantex staged by LaDon Sheats and some others from a Detroit cooperative. Over Christmas in 1980-81, LaDon had visited with me when I was working as a $300-a-month coordinator for a Panhandle protest group. Together, we talked with almost all of the mainstream church pastors about going over the fence with LaDon at Pantex to protest its expansion and its very existence as the final assembly point for the nation's nuclear arsenal. None agreed to join him, and only Bishop Matthiesen of the Catholic Diocese of Amarillo encouraged his flocks to avoid contact with Pantex for moral reasons. After the bishop's newsletter call for Catholics not to work at Pantex, several Amarillo groups, including the Chamber of Commerce, condemned him for taking an anti-jobs stance. These Amarillo leaders pulled their funding from things like Catholic Family Services. Of course, at TV-10 we aired story after story about this clash of values.

The Amarillo leaders never got the moral parallel between their willful acceptance of a moral wrong and that of the community leaders going about their business just outside the gates of Buchenwald and Dachau.

On the evening before the day LaDon and his friends went over the fence, we had a prayer service at the Wheeler law firm in Amarillo. Then at dawn they went over, and I was there as a KFDA reporter. We filmed the whole thing, then filmed the hearings, and I attended the hearings before federal Judge Mary Lou Robinson. She asked them for statements, and LaDon and the others gave eloquent defenses of their moral positions. She set bail and sent them to the Armstrong County Jail. Ultimately, LaDon wound up doing his time in the Potter County Jail, and Lynda and I went out to see him several times until he was released and headed for Colorado.

(A.G. Mojtabai, a woman author, wrote a book about Amarillo's refusal to face its moral dilemma called "Blessed Assurance: At Home with the Bomb in Amarillo, Texas." The book came out in 1986, and I was already in Wichita Falls. Lynda and I had married. Pantex was far behind me. I did read the book. I thought it was basically correct in pointing out Amarillo's moral lapses. She wouldn't go far enough to say the community leaders were gutless opportunists. I say that.)

Feb. 19: Netanyahu is in a pickle. He should have learned to be careful what you wish for. He and his supporters have always wanted to have one state in the Middle East for Jews: Israel. Everything they claim, including the West Bank and the Golan Heights and all of Jerusalem would be Israeli. America, among other nations, has most consistently pushed for two states, one for Palestinians and one for Israelis. When Netanyahu visited with the president last week, Trump told him he liked the idea of just one state, not two states. I'm sure Netanyahu was flabbergasted. Oh my! What would he do with one state that included both Palestinians and Jews? Is that really even possible? Do you just kill off the Palestinians or do you load them into buses and move them to, say, Syria? If you get your one state, you will have hell to pay from Arabs all over the world. Does Netanyahu really want to live in Hell? And, more ethereally, what does someone like Netanyahu do without a sworn enemy at his door step? How do you deal with a people who have been completely deprived of hope?

I was startled to see a commercial on TV the other evening run by Academy sporting goods store. The spot is selling a baseball bat for children: **FOR** $159.99. You read that right: almost $160 for a baseball bat. How many little poor kids have parents who can afford a $160 bat? And, it's not made from wood; it's metal. Bats and gloves must not have cost very much when I was a kid on Bowie Street in Amarillo because my dad never griped about buying them, and I had a very nice glove. I don't remember bats, but I recall the glove because one afternoon I got it signed out at the Amarillo ballpark by every single member of the Gold Sox team.

I was trying to think about whether any advertiser or business owner ever pressured my bosses to come down on me for a story, column or editorial we'd printed at Amarillo, Canyon, Wichita Falls, Temple or in my very short television on-air career. Only one time was I aware of pressure, and that was to kill a story before it was published. It did *not* arise out of any concern for loss of advertising or revenue.

Feb. 20: I regularly worked Sunday evenings at the Amarillo paper (a shift was from 2 p.m. to 11 or 3 p.m. to midnight, depending on what the weekend city editor wanted). This was spring or summer of 1968, when terrible riots were happening in big cities all across the country, when Martin Luther King Jr. was assassinated, when Robert Kennedy was assassinated, when peace marches were bringing down a White House, when thousands of draftees were dying in Vietnam and Laos and Cambodia.

The Sunday evening crew was very small, because the Monday paper was the smallest of the week, and not much happened around Amarillo on Sundays, what with most people being in church for two services. The night city editor on Sundays was a guy named H. M. He was an older reporter who filled in on the city desk, but he was no great editor. He just made sure assignments were covered, if there was anything to cover on Sundays, and that the obituaries were taken over the phone and typed up correctly.

The official night city editor was Bob Kerr, a guy who was an OK editor but a huge jokester and implementer of torture for young "cub" reporters. One of the ways Kerr had dreamed up to make my life miserable had to do with race in Amarillo. At that time, the races were completely separate. Blacks lived in The Heights and The Flats. The Heights were in north Amarillo, and The Flats were right off downtown. They had their own schools, their own teams, their own civic lives. Hispanics lived in the Barrio which was east and south of downtown. They had their own elementary schools. I literally never crossed paths with black or Hispanic people all the time I was growing up in Amarillo and rarely after I started working at the Amarillo paper in August 1966. Every once in a while in the mid- to late '60s, acts would come to town just to perform for black or Hispanic audiences. Kerr thought it was hilarious to assign me to "cover" some of these performances because he well knew that I was a skinny white kid, weighing in at about 115 pounds, who would be attending a show where 99 percent of the audience was black.

One night, for example, he told me to head over to a concert featuring a black artist, and I protested. "You know there'll be no story to write," I told Kerr. "This is a concert, not a news event." "You never know with these people," he said, grinning. "They may riot or try to burn the place down. Look what's going on around the country!" Yeah, right, I shrugged, and took my notebook and sat way up in the balcony hoping no one would notice my whiteness. People left me alone.

And I got to see what may have been the only Amarillo performance ever by the legendary James Brown. There was no story; I was happy about that, too.

So, in keeping with Kerr's campaign, he had H. M. sent me on a similar assignment that Sunday afternoon. I walked into work, and M. met me at the desk before I could even sit down. "Take a company car and get over to this address on North East Eighth," he said. Alarms went off in my head. I knew good and well that part of Amarillo was the very center of The Heights. "It's not a concert," he said. "It's an NAACP meeting." I started shaking my head. I knew about the NAACP from watching TV news. They did not have a great reputation. "Something might happen," he said. "Yeah," I said, "they might see a little white boy all by himself and decide to have some fun." "We gotta cover it," he said, and off I went. At least the meeting was in mid-afternoon, in broad daylight. My stomach was churning even before I pulled up into the dirt-and-gravel parking lot outside a big quonset hut. A lot of cars were driving up around me and a lot of black folks were heading into the building. Quite a few of them were kids, too, and I figured that was a good sign: The adults might not kill a white kid if the act was going to be witnessed by their own children. I went in like I fit right in (a ploy my mother taught me: when you don't fit in act for all the world like you do) and took a seat up close to the front and at the end of a row so I could make a quick exit if I needed to.

There were three speakers that day. They took the stage together and talked in turn. I have notes from those speeches somewhere. These three young men, one from Detroit, one from Watts and one from New York, told the audience about the riots and fires they had experienced in those cities and elsewhere. They talked about "whitey" and "honkeys" and about what should happen to whitey and honkeys. In angry tones, they shouted for the Amarillo blacks to burn down their town as a sign of rage against the white-dominated culture here and everywhere else in America. I suppose my hair was sticking straight up on my neck and head. I was taking notes as fast and accurately as I could. I was both scared shitless and galvanized by the fact that I would write the best, most important story of my life —possibly never to be eclipsed if I lived to be 100—for the Monday editions. Amarillo whites would be hysterical. I might be up for a Pulitzer. The situation was almost too good for me to be true.

After the meeting was over I milled around among some of the Amarillo residents to get their reactions. Most of the people I talked to were having absolutely nothing to do with these three radical missionaries of hate. One older man told me he was not about to burn down his part of town to make a point about white oppression. It made no sense to him.

When I had covered all the bases, I drove back to the newspaper as fast as I could and exploded to H. M. with the outlines of the story I had in my notebook ready for writing and putting on Page One! The more I talked, the bigger his eyes became. He went pale. "You just go sit down," he said, "I gotta call the boss." The boss was Don Boyette. Before long, he came purposefully into the newsroom and off into his own office, which had a glass wall opening onto the newsroom so you could see what he was up to. M. took me over, and I told Don the story, and he told me to type up all my notes, not for a story but for him to read through. Then he got on the phone. Over the course of the next hour or so, I typed up the notes, and I watched as the following people entered Don's small office: the morning

65

paper editor, Wes Izzard; the editor of the afternoon paper, Tommy Thompson; the publisher named Whittenburg; the sheriff; the police chief, Wiley Alexander; and the mayor. This high-level scrutiny of my story did not inspire my confidence. In fact, I had a bad feeling about it.

Some time that evening after all the editors and publishers and law-enforcement officials had left, Don came over with my notes and tossed them onto my desk. "No story," he said. And then he walked away. I turned to M: "This is the greatest story I'll ever cover and write, and you guys are spiking it!" He didn't say a word about that, just told me to start taking obit calls at the city desk. I did mightily resent this decision. I had no choice but to go along with it, but it made me mad as hell. I just ate my disappointment and disgust though, because I was only a cub and, thus, expendable. If I wanted to live to write another day, I would not need to fall on this particular sword. I did. Years later when I was the editor in chief of a newspaper I soon understood completely where Don and the white boys in charge of Amarillo were coming from. If we'd published my story on Page One, we would have had dead black people all over the place that summer in Amarillo, Texas.

Community leaders' pressure killed that story for the sake of the community. But, at any time since that summer did I feel forced into killing a story because of advertiser or community concerns? Not really. In fact, the opposite was the case in at least two instances. That is, in spite of what might be community or advertiser pressure, the publisher stepped in and protected my ass from those outside forces. I published in spite of economic threats.

Feb. 21: The publisher of the *Times Record News* in Wichita Falls in 1998 was either Bill Gulledge or Lynn Dickerson. That position was in transition, and I don't recall who was in charge, probably because it just didn't matter. Both of them left me alone to run the news operation. They trusted me. And why not? I'd run the newsroom as professionally as anyone could, and I'd been a good ambassador in the community for the newspaper. If you can't trust your editor as a publisher, you need to get rid of him or her because no one else will, either.

One Sunday morning in 1998, Dr. Robert Jeffress, the pastor of First Baptist Church of Wichita Falls, the second biggest Baptist congregation in Texas, got up in the pulpit, held up two children's books, condemned them as promoting homosexuality and said he had taken them from the public library and would not return them. The books were "Heather Has Two Mommies" and "Daddy's Room-mate." Jeffress railed against homosexuality as a mortal sin, and said the books helped lead people down that road straight to Hell. By the time I got to work on Monday morning, I had received several phone calls from people telling me about the sermon (of course I didn't hear it in person; I'm not a Baptist), and pointing out that I could hear it myself at the church's website. So, I listened to it. Yes, there was a front-page story here, and I got a reporter to start work on it. But, there was also an editorial to be written—about a church censoring what a community might choose to read. Before I started on the editorial I walked over to the publisher's office and told him or her what was going on and what I planned to do on the editorial pages. I don't remember any particular adverse reaction.

The story of the incident went on Page One on Tuesday morning and the editorial appeared in the appropriate place on the editorial page. The editorial caused a significant amount of consternation, and I'm sure the publisher got phone calls, although he or she never told me that. By the weekend, the uproar had only increased in volume, and that next Sunday, Dr. Jeffress took to the pulpit to attack the *Times Record News* for having the audacity to say he had no right to censor what the public might be able to find at the library. He put my contact information up on the screen of his televised sermon/show, and encouraged people to tell me I was wrong. My editorial page editor at the time was Eddie Barker, a seasoned journalist who I could trust to be accurate, meticulous and thorough. At some point after that second sermon, I left town to go to California to spend a few days with Julia, who was finishing up her PhD. in art history at Berkeley. I kept in constant contact with Eddie, who was completely inundated by letters to the editor about the homosexual books. From afar, I coordinated extra space in the papers for these letters, and I think followed up with an editorial or two that I wrote from out West. For us to take on First Baptist Church in a town that was heavily Baptist in a state that was heavily Baptist was no small matter. The potential financial damage probably kept the publisher up at night. But I never caught wind of any angst from that department.

Many years later in 2004 or 2005, another opportunity presented itself when the publisher could have yielded to pressure from the community to make me change an editorial stand. Darrell Coleman was publisher. Darrell had grown up in Burkburnett and attended Midwestern State University. He had many friends in both places when he returned to Wichita Falls as publisher after working for many years in Corpus Christi. Because of those relationships I always felt Darrell might be particularly susceptible to community nudges to get me to take particular stands on specific issues or to change coverage priorities. But he never showed himself to be anything other than a solid, professional publisher who recognized that if a newspaper loses its value as a conscience to the community it is no longer a real newspaper with any value to the community at all.

His ability to stand against the community was severely tested when the board of regents at Midwestern State University had what I immediately criticized editorially as an illegal closed meeting. I talked him into suing the board to make them redo the meeting and take action in public. After a hearing on the matter, the district judge ruled in our favor. The newspaper had won; Darrell's bottom line had lost $60,000 to fight the fight. He never griped about it and never held me hostage over it.

I was in an editorial leadership position in newspapers for many of my 45 years as a journalist, and I'm sure there were countless times when my bosses had to look to the higher gods of journalism to protect the newspaper's role as a conscience for the community.

Unfortunately, I spent the last four years of my career working for a woman who had absolutely no respect for her newspaper or for me, and no trust whatsoever in my ability to have the news covered and presented. It was a major, life-altering mistake for me to take a job as managing editor of the *Temple Daily Telegram* in Temple, Texas, in September 2007. I had retired from the *Times Record News* in June of that year, having accepted a buyout offer that was most generous for an industry in ugly transition.

Feb. 22: The new director of immigration appointed by Trump has issued two orders that essentially declare war on immigrants who are undocumented. We will spill billions to round them up and send them home. He wants to federalize anyone in law enforcement at every level, thus sanctifying them as bonafide agents of the state authorized to jackboot the country to lily whiteness. This will end very badly. Especially for people in agriculture, this may see the end of American dominance at the dinner table. I don't think out-of-work coal miners are going to move to California to pick grapes. White boys aren't going to do those jobs. Just like they aren't going to cook for your supper in a New York City café or bus your tables at Furr's or Luby's. Who's going to do the dishes? Better: Who in Texas is going to build the roads, houses, buildings? Maintain the parks and pools? These Trump people are so fucking crazy I can't even talk about it.

After I officially retired from the *Times Record News* in June of 2007, I found myself a low-rent little office downtown, just one room in a two-room suite. I bought a used laptop and set myself up with a place to go when I wanted to. At first, I had a little work to do editing major projects by a couple of my star reporters. They brought the stories to me because they felt I could help them polish things up. And I helped out with trying to keep afloat a group I had a major role in starting up to try to diversify the leadership pool in Wichita Falls.

Feb. 23: Of the many things I'm proud of after spending 24 years in Wichita Falls, I look back at the creation of a particular group with both a sense of satisfaction and frustration. The comprehensive results from the 2000 U.S. Census count of Wichita Falls' area didn't start showing up until 2002 or 2003. You didn't have to be a statistician to see that the city's trajectory was Hispanic. The white population was old and aging. The Hispanic population was young and was rising. But, when you looked at the people who ran the city— on city commissions and boards and agencies, all the way from the City Council to the board of the food bank—they were all white and older. Almost every single one of them. If Wichita Falls was going to grow and thrive in the next two or three decades, some of that leadership burden and responsibility needed to be shared by members of the Hispanic community. This revelation struck me at about the same time that it hit C.B., who was managing director of the Wichita Falls Area Community Foundation, an entity created to accumulate wealth from local resources and use that wealth in grants and loans to improve the community. We were like-minded and put together a plan to try to increase Hispanic involvement in leadership. We figured that, first of all, Hispanics with potential needed to understand they were wanted and that they could make a difference. Second, they needed to be exposed to leadership training and to limited involvement so that they could be successful. Third, they needed a way to network, to build a system of some kind that would help pass around what they knew and had learned. And fourth and least important the entire Hispanic community needed strong support to integrate into the larger community while not losing its unique flavor and identity.

Before going deeper into this, let me diverge and come at it from a different angle, an angle that's less institutional sounding.

I'm not sure when Lynda and I joined the Catholic church, but it was probably in the late '80s. Monsignor Charles King was the pastor at Sacred Heart Catholic church in downtown Wichita Falls, and he was a friend of Lynda's dad, C.D. Knight. We went through RCIA at that church under Charlie's wings, and then both got involved as time went by. Lynda got heavily involved in putting on the RCIA program, and I served as clerk of the parish council. When Charlie left, he was replaced by J.V., a man who had converted to Catholicism late in life from Methodism and then became a priest. He was a man who was in a lot of physical pain, and he was irritable, selfish and overbearing at his very best. He and Lynda eventually clashed at a fundamental level, and we decided to leave that church.

We had two choices if we were to continue as Catholics in Wichita Falls: We could go to Our Lady Queen of Peace, which was on the southwest side of town, or to Our Lady of Guadalupe, located in the center of the barrio. I refused to go to OLQP because it was too yuppie, rich and Protestant-like. I didn't much care for the people who went there. I didn't know anyone at OLG other than the priest, Father M. I knew him in a social way. I figured that over time we could nudge our way into OLG and in the long run be more comfortable there, so we started attending the service that was primarily in English with some Spanish elements. The people were very nice, if chilly, at first. But within a few months I had joined the small choir and was playing guitar with this group every Sunday while Lynda sat in the congregation. It did not take me long to fall in love with the people and the place and attendance became easy and familiar. We were always going to be strangers, but we were *their* strangers.

So, I knew people in the Hispanic community, and I knew what hard workers they were and what they could offer to the community at large if given the opportunity. I brought that background with me in discussions with C.B. and others about how to approach the Hispanic leadership challenge. We set out to meet, first of all, with the pastor of every Hispanic church in town, and had a young lady help us as an interpreter, Iliana Jaramillo. Ultimately, we pulled together a group of Hispanics and Anglos from a variety of backgrounds and called ourselves the Zavala Hispanic Cultural Initiative. Our goals were simple: Prepare Hispanics for leadership roles and get them involved. Iliana was the first president of the group, and our first efforts were to raise funds to send Hispanic members to Leadership Wichita Falls, a program that previously had involved basically whites alone. When I left Wichita Falls, this group was still intact, but I have since lost track of them. It's been 10 years. I hope they have done well for their sake, the sake of their friends and neighbors and the sake of Wichita Falls itself.

Today, I know Lynda misses the camaraderie of the church in the barrio, and so do I. I'm sure things would have changed, but that was truly a church home for us.

As I look at what Trump is doing with this group of people it both angers and saddens me. He has no compassion, no understanding that these are human beings not inanimate objects that he is threatening. His followers are so filled with hate of "the other" that they can't see the human misery they support.

I left more than a job and a career when I took that buyout in the early summer of 2007. I left an entire superstructure of psychological support. Of course, I didn't realize that at the time.

69

Feb. 24: Yesterday afternoon I sent an email to Julia and Becca explaining that the camp at Standing Rock had been dismantled, and that I had come down with bronchitis.

I got a nice reply from both girls. Maybe next time, and there will be a next time, you can bet on that.

The New York Times sent me an interesting email as a subscriber. In it, the publisher wrote:

"There has never been a more important time to share our story and what we stand for as an organization. Today, The New York Times launches its first major brand campaign in decades. This is the right moment to assert the value of quality journalism. The campaign is based on a fact — that the truth matters, now more than ever. The truth, as our journalists can attest, is also incredibly hard to get to. We remain undeterred in our efforts to reveal and report the facts with integrity and courage."

The New Yorker's emailed edition yesterday included a fine article about the 13 questions that Trump's nominee for the Supreme Court should be asked. He says he is an "originalist," which apparently means that he wants the Constitution's language to mean what it meant in 1778, when many of those signers of the Declaration of Independence and the Articles of Confederation still had slaves. For example, there is no right to privacy in the Constitution at all anywhere. The court over time has found one, however, in other rights statements. As I mentioned elsewhere, the Constitution does not provide for judicial review. That was asserted by the Court itself in "Marbury vs. Madison," and it has been the "law of the land" ever since. The evolution of our principles of due process has taken us to places never anticipated by the builders of the Bill of Rights. What do we do with all of that? Throw it out? The question, of course, is whether even a single Senator involved in confirmation hearings will have the guts to do anything other than preen and suck up when the time comes.

I have been waiting for Democrats to begin to act like they have spines of their own, and now I see in *The Times* today that there is a big argument among these few people about whether to combat Trump at every turn or try to appease him. For Christ's sake, People, let's recall the sterling history of the appeasers, starting with Americans like Henry Ford and Charles Lindbergh. Democrats must arm themselves with truth and reason and righteous anger and go forth to do armed battle with the people who want to have this country only for themselves and their golfing buddies. We must stay in the streets and we must stay in their face. Resistance is the only path or we will suffocate as the completely aberrant becomes normalized over time. Too often familiarity does NOT breed contempt but only withdrawal and ennui.

In August of 2007, I was very ready to find work, doing something. There just weren't many options.

About mid-month I got a letter in the mail from Sue Mayborn, publisher and editor of *The Temple Daily Telegram* in Temple, Texas, asking if I might be interested in applying for the job of managing editor. I did not give the offer a whole lot of thought, because I felt it was probably my last, best chance to stay in journalism. Lynda and Mom, who lived with us at that point, were willing to move if that's what I wanted to do. I don't think they knew how little effort I put into doing my due diligence on Mrs. Mayborn and the Telegram. I didn't even call the former managing editor to see why he had stayed only six months before leaving, a red flag of the first order and the first of many. After an interview with Mrs. Mayborn at the Telegram, I accepted her offer of $62,000 a year to be managing editor. I'll soon tell you what a terrible decision I had made.

We decided to rent out our house on Wenonah in Wichita Falls to our lawyer and to find a house while I lived in an old apartment not far from the Telegram in Temple. My first few days on the job at the Telegram should have warned me completely away. It wasn't too late to back off and back out. But, I didn't. I started work around Sept. 1, and the first Monday or Tuesday I was there I noticed on the side of the building a huge banner, stretching from roof to sod declaring that the Telegram was in its 100th year of operations. That afternoon, as I did every afternoon, I went to Mrs. Mayborn's office for our one-hour situation meeting.

Feb. 25: Trump went before an audience at a conservative gathering yesterday and blasted the news media again and then took shots at the FBI. Later in the day, his press secretary banned certain media members from briefings, including The New York Times, the Los Angeles Times, CNN and others. This, of course, will only inspire those newspapers and TV stations to dig deeper and broader. Trump will rue the day. His team has forgotten that he is king for only four years. If he has life after that he will play hell getting along with a completely alienated news media.

I started reading a new book about the life of Enrico Fermi, the Italian genius behind many of the scientific discoveries that led to the development of the atomic bomb. He came to be a scientist in the Rome of Mussolini and benefitted from il Duce's rise to power and acquisition of state wealth. It is good to be reminded once more about what the ascendancy of a madman looks like because it helps us to name the signposts as we come to them in the Trump presidency.

From the get-go I had no support from Mrs. Mayborn at the Telegram. The only feedback I got was negative. Nothing was met with enthusiasm. I finally concluded that she hated men, for the most part, and she enjoyed making my life miserable. That was because she herself was miserable. She had no understanding of journalism and made up for it by criticizing everything having to do with it. She had no courage, no gumption when it came to news coverage, and everyone in town knew they could come over to the Telegram, spit on my shoes and there would be no consequences. Worse, she might spit on them herself. This made it very hard to get the news. The police department in particular put up roadblock after roadblock as we tried to cover crime in Temple. The police chief would not publish the daily incident reports required by Texas law, and since Mrs. Mayborn wouldn't fight over anything and they knew she wouldn't they got by with it. The county judge, a lawyer, twisted and contorted the open meetings law so that no one reading an agenda could tell what would be discussed when. He knew the publisher would do nothing about it, so even after I talked to him about complying

71

with the law he only laughed. It was the same all over town. Nowhere was there respect for the *Telegram* and in many places only contempt. And to the extent I was the *Telegram*, that lack of respect and contempt tore at my perception of myself as a professional journalist.

When I was living alone in the apartment at the outset of my Temple experience, I worked long hours and then came home and drank wine until I could go to sleep. I began to believe that the only way I could get to sleep on any given night was to drink myself into that state. I was never really hung over the next day, so the consequences of drinking so much were nonexistent. Over the course of my adult life, I went through periods where I drank too much—never in the daytime or during work hours. But there were many nights when I was at the *Times Record News* when I'd fall asleep in my easy chair after having too many glasses of wine. I'm sure friends and family members have stories of me falling asleep in a chair after an evening of drinking at a local bar or restaurant.

In Wichita Falls, as editor of the paper, I had trouble sleeping, and I often drank to get to a nod-off point. The sleep problem became so acute that I finally went to a neurologist, and he tried me on several pills designed to get me to sleep. Most of them I took with wine, so I never really knew whether they would work by themselves. As time went by in Temple, I became so miserable and drank so much that I really had trouble going to sleep even with medication. I eventually wound up with a doctor at Scott & White who was pretty alarmed at what I was taking and what I was drinking—and what I was dealing with at work.

Feb. 26: I was reading this morning about a woman who got so angry at Trump back before the election that she put together an online boycott site called Grab Your Wallet. She began targeting stores that sold products that made a profit for Trump and his family, like Ivanka. She has apparently been pretty successful. I was a little surprised that *The Times* did not run a list of the Top 10 places where Trump-related goods are still offered so we could start boycotting them right away. I certainly would.

I hope that *The Times* and the *Washington Post* and other papers are looking at the small stuff as they track Trump troubles with the Constitution and law. For example, if and when the Secret Service and other services rent property in Trump Tower so they can be close to the president, to whom do they write the very substantial check? If it goes to Trump doesn't that amount to a conflict of interest? When a foreign government writes a check to cover the overnight stay of a representative at the Trump hotel down the street from the White House, to whom is the check made out? Isn't that a violation of the Constitution's emoluments clause? How many of those violations does it take to amount to a high crime or misdemeanor? If it were Hillary, maybe one?

The blatant hypocrisy of the spineless congressional leadership makes me want to throw up. They are utterly contemptible.

Everywhere I turned in Temple, I met either benign indifference or outright contempt on the part of government and public officials and even just the run-of-the-mill citizenry. Mrs. Mayborn must have been oblivious to this. She had no friends other than Edla, her secretary. She lived by herself out in the country. She did not go to church. One day Lynda and I ran into her in the middle of Lowe's.

She was pushing an empty cart around. I guess she had no place else to be and no one to be with. By that point I was not sad for her. I wanted out in the worst way. I think Mrs. Mayborn thought she could buy the respect that she could never earn. She put in hundreds of thousands of dollars for projects and buildings at the University of Mary Hardin-Baylor in Belton, a fourth-rate little Baptist school no one out of Bell County has ever heard of. She spent money on Baylor in Waco and at the University of North Texas in Denton. Her name and that of her late husband will go on those structures and those programs and when people ask who these folks were no one will know because their existence as journalists was so ignominious if not ignoble.

My sanity in Temple was saved by Baylor.

Feb. 27: I haven't explained very well about the way a community's power-seekers react when they see that they are not truly held accountable. It's important to address because we are seeing the kind of power shift in Washington right now that will inevitably mean trouble for the media's lesser gods when they try to deal with the powerful at their lower rungs.

After the tower attacks in 2001, the government reaction was predictable: close everything down, build up the security infrastructure and then see how far you could open everything up again without becoming a terrorist state. In fact, as I have written before about "Back Home," the tendency on the part of law enforcement and others in governmental power because of the War on Drugs was to crack down and ask questions later. The cops became militarized, the borders became less porous and people became generally more suspicious as the War on Drugs was waged.

Over time, we became more tolerant of having our rights infringed upon. So, when the cops, dressed in uniforms our first-line military troopers could only dream of owning, charged into a home with guns blazing, all in the name of curtailing drug sales and drug use, good people just looked the other way. When innocent people had their cars and boats and bank accounts confiscated without due process because they were merely accused of drug crimes, good people couldn't be bothered because this kind of thing was just necessary if the rest of us were going to be safe and secure. At our airports, we put up with the most intrusive, bullish, boorish behavior on the part of "officials" because it made us feel safe against "the other" that might be lining up to bring in TNT and blow up our buildings. A lot of media professionals were simply co-opted: We'll let you come along for the invasion of this house and you will get great video. Just don't ask too many questions. The overall effect of this top-to-bottom crackdown on citizen discernment of proper governmental boundaries was the shutting away of information, the closing of doors.

It became harder to get governmental entities to simply abide by things like the Texas Open Information Act. The more national political figures characterized the news media as a problem to be controlled, the more local political figures adopted the very same attitudes. Thus, in Temple, if you went to city hall and asked to see a copy of the minutes from the last City Council meeting the lady behind the counter would require you to turn over a Freedom of Information letter even though this kind of document was absolutely public record. You could appeal this nonsense to the city manager and he would stonewall you. We met this at every turn, especially at the police department, where the bald, tattooed goons were clearly controlling things.

Feb. 28: This is all more relevant now. The president calls the press the "enemies of the people." This is an echo from the 1930s in Germany or from early Soviet times under Stalin. The mere characterization will do damage as the attitude ripples out across America. But as Trump ups the attack and actually takes action, others will feel equally emboldened. The contempt will metastasize across the nation. Journalists everywhere will just have a harder time as information is cut off and as officials justify doing business behind closed doors because they are right and the watchdogs are wrong. Once elected people at all levels of power will come to feel they alone are the keepers of the American soul and pocketbook. They will refuse to realize there are a lot of other stakeholders in democracy.

Yesterday the president presented the outlines of his budget for the next year: Lots more for defense and national security and steep cuts in social services and the Environmental Protection Agency. I suppose education will be cut, too, but that's not in the newspaper today. House Speaker Paul Ryan doesn't like the proposals because he personally would like to cut the shit out of Social Security and Medicare and Medicaid. He's not against defense increases, even if they are completely irrational and unjustified. He is against Social Security, Medicare and Medicaid. This fight is like two jackals fighting over the carcass of something dead. We will not watch the president's speech to Congress tonight. The man makes me want to throw up.

In the spring of 2011, I was probably at my lowest point at the *Telegram*. I couldn't sleep even with strong medication and a lot of alcohol. Small things would disturb me at night, like a dog barking way down the street. Sometimes I would actually get out of bed and walk down to the dog's house and start screaming at the people in the house until they shut the dog up. Some people kind of behind us had a dog that barked at night once in a while, and I shouted at them one night that I would shoot the animal if they didn't shut it up.

The only thing that kept me from going completely crazy was a teaching assignment at Baylor in Waco, about a 30-minute drive away on Interstate 35. In 2008 or 2009, I contacted Sarah Stone, a journalism professor at Baylor, about teaching a night class. I had known Sarah when I was at *The Canyon News* in the 1970s. She was at the Amarillo newspaper. When I left the journalism department at West Texas State in the winter of 1982, she took over in my spot as acting department chairman. We had kept up with each other over the years through attendance at the Texas Associated Press Managing Editors conventions. She would be there showing the flag for Baylor, and I'd be there representing the *Times Record News* or the *Telegram*.

So, I called her up, and she had me over for lunch and I got a class to teach—editing. The class was for sophomores majoring in journalism. Each class had between 15 and 25 students, a good mix of men and women. The classes started about 6 o'clock in the evening, so I could leave the Telegram about 5 and get to the campus in time to get set up. I had nice covered parking right next to the journalism building. (For years, I worked on an editorial department manual that told new reporters and copy editors all of our policies and all of our style and performance preferences and rules. Everything had an example. And by the time I left the newspaper, just about every contingency was covered, including how to handle the threat of lawsuits. I gave a copy of this manual to every new newsroom employee at the TRN. After I left Wichita Falls I'm told that it became a prized possession. In fact, Deanna Watson, who was my replacement as editor, wrote a column three or four years ago about finding her copy and remembering how important it was to her. I was much flattered.)

I taught the editing class at Baylor for four semesters, I believe. In the background there was an ongoing conversation in the department about whether editing classes should be required of all journalism students. This discussion was, of course, due to the decline in the economic fortunes of print newspapers and the rise of online news services. Newspapers were hiring fewer copy editors and seeking more people who could post newspaper content at websites, a completely different skill set.

March 1: I had seen this coming. All around the country the talk in newsrooms was of how to put news up on a branded website that would draw eyeballs on a regular, daily basis and that would also generate money to replace the revenue lost when people went elsewhere to see what was going on. The publishers' idea was that our news products were valuable enough to be sought out in any format —print or online. And they were valuable enough to charge for in the traditional ways: a charge for access and a charge to be part of the news mix. Thus, if you read you paid and if you bought an ad you paid. This was the old newspaper in-print model. If this model was put into play it meant that you could repurpose your news and features from the print product to the online product and go on down the road. That would provide one level of support from readers or viewers. Or you could offer more online than you offered in print. That might get another level of funding. But, that was probably not going to happen in reality even if it were the model that everyone in the board rooms talked about.

In reality, for smaller newspapers the never-ending pressures to reap quarter-over-quarter and year-over-year profits were always going to force cost-cutting because in most cities there was not the kind of high single-digit growth required by publicly traded companies to elevate their bottom lines.

At the *Times Record News*, for example, we just kept cutting positions until we were down to the bare minimum in 2007. Wichita Falls and region were not growing enough to produce the ad revenue and circulation revenue to meet the company's ever-upward push for profits. We also kept losing readers. Many of them migrated to online sources for information, and many just decided they didn't need a daily newspaper. The deeper we cut, the less valuable was our news product, and the less able we were to catch errors. Our editing staff, like every-thing else, grew smaller and smaller and the work load on each individual grew heavier and heavier. In the Scripps corporation we were hardly unusual. I am going to use some rough numbers to explain what was happening.

March 2: When I got home from the church HalfTime Lenten service last night, Lynda told me that the national news was reporting this stunning idea: Oprah

Winfrey might run for president. That's a very interesting development. I had not thought about that, but in the real world today, where a Donald Trump can be president, it's not at all weird to think that a black woman celebrity might make the race and actually win. I certainly think the country is ready for a woman to be president, just not for it to be Hillary Clinton. And we've had a black man in the office, so it's not far-fetched at all for her to consider the race very seriously. At this point I could certainly support her, and I know Lynda could in a New York minute. Oprah is a very smart woman, she is a person of conscience, she has a great reputation and her name is probably among the best-known names in America. Lynda said that Oprah told the news people that she is only considering it because you obviously don't have to have governmental experience to get and do the job. Donald Trump has set a very low bar, maybe the lowest in history, and Oprah would leap over it with no problem at all. *The New York Times* had nothing on the subject this morning. I'm sure this is just a trial balloon, and if so I predict the reaction will be positive.

In about October of 2006, the stock of E.W. Scripps was selling for something like $65 a share. I remember that because I got stock options from the company at that price exercisable five or 10 years down the road. In February, the stock was half that amount. The market had finally figured out what we insiders had known for years: the newspaper industry as a whole was not going to be able to compete effectively with online news and commercial sources. There was no working model to look at. Scripps newspaper folks in Cincinnati went into a panic. Very soon after, the Scripps people convened a meeting in Dallas of all the Texas newspaper editors and publishers. The big boss, S.S., was joined by J.T., who had most recently been destroyed as a journalist by losing a long and very expensive battle for a major American city's newspaper market to one Dean Singleton. T. was editor of the Scripps paper. He reportedly lost more than $20 million over 10 years trying to beat out Singleton. Singleton absorbed the Scripps paper, and T. moved to Cincinnati where, I suppose, he could advise the rest of us on how to lose money and a newspaper and still survive.

At this meeting in Dallas, S. and T. told us in so many words the newspaper division was going down in flames and we needed to do something about it. Their advice: hire part-timers to cut staff costs and put on free-lancers or stringers. This was completely nuts. The *Times Record News* hadn't been able to hire a competent stringer in two decades. There was no one in our 18-county area capable of turning in a news tip, much less a news story. When I pointed out that this was the Wal-Mart way of doing business, nobody laughed.

This was not the first time Scripps' smart boys had come to Texas to try to set us straight on how to build circulations and make ever more money. Back in 2005 or 2006, the Cincinnati news guys got fed up trying to advise us long-distance on how to attract minority readers and minority newsroom employees. They just couldn't understand why you couldn't get black and Hispanic college graduates to come to work in a place that was going to pay them far less than they'd make as Texas teachers and that offered them no hope of finding a mate of the same color. They didn't get the fact that there weren't many literate black folks remaining to take the newspaper after the drug roundups of the '90s and that Hispanics were so disengaged from civic life in white Texas that they didn't need

76

a newspaper to tell them what was going on in their communities and families. The boys sent out a fix-it crew to Texas and New Mexico that consisted of the following members: a fat white guy from Washington state; a fat Hispanic guy from Puerto Rico and New York; and a skinny Hispanic guy from Cuba. In Wichita Falls, I invited a hundred or so folks from my church and from around town to come to meet the fix-it crew to give them feedback on how to make the newspaper more important to them, so important they would subscribe, etc. About 100 did show up on the night of the dog-and-pony show. It would be kind to say that the crowd did not warm up to the boys from Washington, Puerto Rico and Cuba. The group was polite, but utterly dismayed by the idea that they somehow owed it to us to support the paper. Wrong people with the wrong message at the wrong time. I was embarrassed but got over it. I found out later that the show didn't go over nearly as well in other Texas cities and in Albuquerque.

March 3: Nothing in *The Times* about Oprah. Maybe just a rumor? But, an interesting story about a company called SnapChat. It seems that this company's product is a cell phone app that allows you to take a photo and jazz it up and then send it. When the photo is opened by the receiver, it can be viewed and then it disappears forever. That's it. Now the company is valuing itself in advance of an IPO. The value is somewhere north of what several other apps that deliver real value are worth. The company actually produces something that has no long-term value at all, and the short-term value is debatable. This all reminds me of the so-called tech bubble back around 2000. All these Silicon Valley companies were floating IPOs for billions of dollars, but they didn't produce anything that you could buy and resell or hang on your wall or take out with the trash. The values were bullshit, and the people who paid those prices got took, to say the least.

Now comes Jeff Sessions, our attorney general, who admits he talked to Russians before the November election on behalf of one Donald Trump. But, gosh darn it, he forgot to tell Congress about that when asked a direct question during hearings leading up to his confirmation in the Senate. Not a problem, say Republicans, the whores that they are.

New South Wales had its hottest summer ever. Temperatures reached 113 degrees repeatedly. They traced it all to global warming. Austin had the warmest winter on record. Global warming? Our favorite weather guy, Jim Spencer of KXAN, says so. In The *Times* today, the Trumpists are finagling to get out of the Paris accords that are designed to reduce global warming.

In February 2007 after our disastrous meeting in Dallas to hear the Scripps boys' program for newspaper survival in Texas and New Mexico, the boys went back to Cincinnati to hatch other ideas. In March, this plan was handed down: Anyone in the company who was 55 years of age within a certain time window was offered a buyout. That buyout consisted of one full year of pay at current levels, plus one year of health insurance AND you got to keep all your stock options. This was the sweetest deal offered by any newspaper company at that time, and all of these businesses were offering buyouts to senior employees. Of course, I was eligible. So, I talked long and hard with Darrell Coleman, the TRN publisher. Ultimately, Darrell advised me to take the deal. He said I would not like working for the newspaper as it was going to be changing in the months and years ahead. More cuts would be coming and more changes that made us less a newspaper and more a money machine.

Lynda and Mother and I talked it over. I decided to take the deal at the end of May 2007. I loved the paper as an institution, and I loved my job, even though it was getting harder and harder to be enthusiastic about it. I had great respect for the people I worked with. But I also knew I would be miserable if I had to make more cuts and act like that was not a bad thing. I would not have been happy when Scripps sold the newspapers to Gannett, a company for which I had almost no respect.

I'm not at all sure I made the right decision even then. As I have mentioned I got a little office downtown and helped oversee the Zavala Hispanic Cultural Initiative. I also continued to interview Charlye O. Farris for the book I wanted to write about her. (Charlye O. was the first black female lawyer in Texas and lived in Wichita Falls.) And I edited two excellent stories by Lara Richards, my ace reporter, before they were published. Both had been in the developmental stage when I was editor, so my assistance was just an extension of that. Both stories were published and both won awards at the state level. I was most proud of Lara. Then I got the offer from Sue Mayborn to be managing editor of the *Temple Daily Telegram*.

March 4: E.W. Scripps gave me my year's pay in a lump sum when I left the company in June 2007, so I had quite a nice bit of money to invest.

The *Times* has an editorial today about Trump declining to fill hundreds of jobs in the federal government. The editorial notes his disinterest in the esoteric workings of Washington and cites that as the reason why he won't make these appointments. I think the reason is more obvious and more devious: He won't fill them because he wants the federal government to fail, not succeed. He and Steve Bannon want to leave things in a shambles because they hate regulations. They hate being told what to do even at the margins. And so do their big-money supporters like the Koch Brothers. Nothing would suit them more than having complete control over how they treated their workers and how they used the economy to their own advantage. Don't take my word for it: Consider what Republicans have done and will do to the Internal Revenue Service and the postal service. The Republican hatred for the postal service goes back decades; I don't even know the root cause. But the animosity runs so deep that the GOP does everything possible to make the post office fail: no staffing, higher rates, and in Wimberley even a lack of air-conditioning, bullet holes in the front windows that never get fixed and long lines for everything. The IRS is the same story for a different reason. If you gut the IRS you have a much-reduced chance of being audited. Fewer investigators mean more crazy accounting tricks can be deployed to avoid paying any taxes at all to run the government.

March 5: I put in four hours yesterday at the high school at the STEAM fair, promoting the library's ventures into the "maker" movement. I was in charge of our small drone collection.

Finally someone is writing about America's crazy obsession with "terrorists" who have become outsized bogeymen in the national imagination. Jon Finer and Robert Malley have an op-ed piece in *The Times* today with the subtitle: "America's politics have been distorted by our obsession with 'jihadism.'" No shit. The TV news reported last night that the Transportation Safety Administration has adopted new rules on personal searches at airport check-in terminals. A guy can feel you up all he wants in the name of finding some hidden weapon that is highly unlikely to exist at all. The Finer-Malley piece has some interesting figures:

"Since Sept.11, an average of fewer than nine Americans per year have been killed in terror attacks on American soil, compared, for example, with an average of about 12,000 a year who are shot to death."

The authors don't cite any figures about how many men and women armed with bombs, guns and/or knives have been stopped by TSA as they tried to enter the country to do mayhem. But the number is undoubtedly quite small.

One thing that seems to be lost on the people like Trump who want to beef up TSA security checkpoints and build a wall across the southern border is that people intent on blowing us up have thousands of miles of completely unprotected coastlines from Maine to Florida and from Baja California to Alaska to land a boat or two or a hundred.

Our irrational obsession with terrorism serves a political purpose, of course, because it keeps us off balance and at a constant state of war that requires an ever-increasing infusion of cash. ". . . our focus on terrorism has helped spawn a counterterrorism industrial complex, made up of new government agencies, private firms and an army of well-funded experts, who keep the issue atop the national agenda," the two authors write.

Yes, and as I have mentioned above, this obsession has had the trickle-down effect of militarizing our local cops and encouraging public officials at even the local level to close down public access and to heighten their arrogant hold on pitiful powers.

The authors continue: "The emphasis on terrorism diverts limited time and resources from other issues. It can lead to overreliance on military action. It can stifle conversation, since decisions justified by threats to the homeland are insulated from criticism. And as the counterterrorism rationales from internal arguments find their way into speeches and official statements, it ratchets up public anxiety."

What the authors don't say at that point is that a nervous and fretful public thus becomes willing to empty its purse to buy security even if the security is not necessary.

Their solution? Well, they don't have one.

March 6: We have obtained some pot, from around here, for Lynda to use. She has resorted to daily use for her back pain. Her source in New Mexico can't send any more because of a postal crackdown. If we can find a good source here then that would be great. Otherwise, I might have to consider heading to Colorado to buy stuff for her. Marijuana does ease her back and leg pain, and having it on hand is a must, one way or another.

As I was reading through the editorials in *The Times* yesterday, it struck me that in talking about my utter dismay working for Sue Mayborn in Temple I completely failed to mention what was probably the biggest burr under my saddle. Going into the job, Mrs. Mayborn made it clear that she did not want me to write a column or to write editorials. She was editor of the paper, so that was clearly her prerogative. I had no problem with that. But she did want to run an editorial page every day with syndicated columnists, letters to the editor, a cartoon and an editorial posted in the traditional upper left columns on the page. Before I really knew much about the production of that page, I put J. in charge of it. He didn't have much else to do; I needed his institutional knowledge, and Mrs. Mayborn liked him. Before too long I learned that the editorials were not written by J. or by Mrs. Mayborn or by anyone on the Temple newspaper staff. Instead, J. would go out to one of the syndicated services we subscribed to and download an editorial from one of the newspapers they represented and plug that editorial into a hole on our pages and *pretend like the editorial had been written by one of us.* No credit was given to the syndicate or the newspaper from which we took the editorial.

This was absolutely wrong, plagiarism of the worst kind. For a while I just figured nobody read the darn things and if they did they'd never know we hadn't written them. One day, though, I got a call from a local AM radio commentator, an asshole of the first order, asking me why we would print an editorial from the Detroit newspaper and not give them credit for it. I had no answer for him. This ran so absolutely counter to my nature as a journalist that I had trouble sleeping over it, and that just was one more thing piled on top of many others that made me miserable.

March 7: When your newspaper does not publish local editorials, it doesn't take long for people in power to figure that out. It's just one less institution to hold them accountable. Local editorials help bring things into the public eye. If you're an elected or appointed official and you're caught doing something wrong you can hope to keep the public from knowing about it, and if the local paper does not write editorials you're more likely to get by with whatever it is you're doing that's not right. The very possibility that you might be the target of an editorial works a little to keep you more honest than you might otherwise be. Without a local editorial capability, an editor can gum things to death but has no teeth. There is no threat there other than mere exposure. Robert Jeffress didn't take out after the *Times Record News* because we wrote a story about him stealing two books from the public library. He got his dander up because we had an editorial or two about the theft and what it meant. So, for more reasons that just deception I was not happy about the Mayborn no-editorial policy. I had virtually no pride in what I was doing in Temple. I was a perpetrator of a fraud and everyone in town who wanted to know that knew it. I hated being Sue Mayborn's "boy."

In the spring of 2011, I was beyond frustrated. I went to the doctor again to see about help in getting to sleep and sleeping, and we had a long talk about the pills I was taking, the amount I was drinking and the very real possibility that I was killing myself without just coming right out and doing it. He strongly suggested I retire. Otherwise, he said, "you will be dead before long." I went home and talked to Lynda and we agreed it was time to move on. Around the end of March I turned in my letter of retirement, setting the date right after the end of the Baylor semester.

Mrs. Mayborn certainly did not try to talk me out of it. I think she was probably surprised that I lasted as long as I did.

When I walked away from Temple I felt defeated. I had let myself down. I had ended my career on what I considered a low note. I was at the top of my game mentally, but I had been kept like a eunuch. I was disappointed in myself and my performance. But I was also relieved and happy to be gone from the *Telegram* and from Temple, a hateful little place if there ever was one.

I had always had pride in my work and in the places where I worked, with certain glaring exceptions.

March 8: Things are just getting wackier and wackier in Washington. Over the weekend, the "president" tweeted at an early morning hour that President Obama had tapped Donald Trump's telephones in Trump Tower before the election. He offered no proof. And all week long, his assistants have reiterated the verity of the accusation—with no proof whatsoever. Just must be true because He said it is. That's pretty incredible. As The Times points out, never before in history has a sitting president made such an accusation against his immediate predecessor.

Oh, but Wikileaks might know. Yesterday, they released thousands of documents revealing CIA secrets. Those secrets include the biggies about the CIA's abilities to crack into every electronic product on the planet. Think you're safe from the eavesdropping of your Mr. Coffee in the kitchen? Ha. Think again. Mr. Coffee is an informant! I jest, but only a little. There may be hell to pay over these revelations, or there may not. I'm not sure Trump knows enough about it to be outraged.

Then comes the leadership of the House with a plan to overturn Obama-Care, the Affordable Care Act, with something you could call the Be Kind to Millionaires Act. The bill would repeal the ACA and replace it with a measure that would throw poor people to the dogs and hand the keys to new Mercedes Benzes to the rich. The richest country in the history of the world will once again let the impoverished either die or go to the ER, not out of benign neglect, but out of deliberate, practiced meanness of spirit and heart.

And today we learn that Caterpillar, the megasuperstar of big equipment, has been cheating on its taxes big-time. I'm sure people who think that Caterpillar has those good ole aw-shucks values of the rural Midwest are shocked and saddened by the news. I know better. I've known a lot about how Caterpillar operates for many, many years. Back when I was regularly covering county government in Canyon, the county seat of Randall County, I learned to watch very carefully how county commissioners bought stuff. The most expensive gear a county could buy was the big road-building equipment that back then could cost in the $60,000 to $100,000 range. And somehow, Caterpillar always got the contract even with the highest bid. Why? For one thing, Caterpillar did make good equipment. But, they also went to a lot of trouble to sell their products to county commissioners. Every year, for example, Caterpillar would fly commissioners up to their factory town, where these guys would be wined and dined and treated like royalty. Nobody else in the business did this. They also helped write the specifications used to seek bids for heavy equipment. The specs almost always were written so that only Caterpillar gear could meet them. So, when bids were opened, other competing bidders would have to say they couldn't meet all the specs, and the commissioners would accept the higher bid by Caterpillar, because the law allowed them to take the lowest bid but also the best bid, regardless of price. Did Caterpillar buy off these commissioners? I think so, although I couldn't ever prove it. Doing shady deals was part of the corporate culture.

Also today we learn that Omaha, Neb., city officials are busy tearing up asphalt streets and returning them to dirt and gravel because they cannot afford to maintain them in an improved manner. It's estimated that the country has $1 trillion worth of infrastructure projects that need attention. The "president" promised to make this a priority during his campaign. We haven't heard anything about it since then, though. What's happened in Omaha has happened all over the country: elected public officials have for years refused to do their jobs in the hopes that someone on down the line would have the guts to raise taxes to the level required to do the dirty work of road repair and water and sewer line overhaul. The worst example of this I have ever seen was in the Temple Independent School District.

March 9: My last year in Temple, the new superintendent of schools was in a high lather over the ever-deteriorating state of most all of the public schools. Almost all of them needed major repairs. Some barely had running water. She put together a committee to look at a bond vote to fix the schools. And here's the awful truth her team, which I was a member of, turned up: In fact, there had not been a bond issue to repair old schools and/or build new ones since the late 1960s! That was about 40 years. Each school board since then had pretended like there was no problem with their physical plants, and when confronted with information that showed something different, they denied it and kicked the maintenance can down the road.

So, in 2010-11, every school had major problems, and the district needed some new schools to handle slow growth. I once asked the guy who was in charge of the Temple industry and business development program whether when trying to recruit someone to come to town he didn't just bypass all the public schools as fast as he could. He just smiled. Temple is the worst example of delayed or deferred maintenance, but I bet every town and county in America has its own hidden story of infrastructure gone bad and covered up.

In many areas crooked developers have strapped cities and counties with millions of dollars of problems related to lousy road construction, just as one example. Sometimes these guys are in cahoots with city or county officials who look the other way when construction is under way. I have seen numerous examples of that, especially around Canyon back in the '70s. One developer in particular comes to mind—Arch Hunsley. Arch bought several sections of land just north of Canyon and laid out Hunsley Hills in two or three big-acreage plats. Under the rules in place at the time, he had to build his own roads and lay his own pipelines. Arch started building a road, which to him meant getting a grader to skim off the top couple of inches of buffalo grass and soil, then following that with a machine that laid a very thin layer of hot mix asphalt. Bingo! You had a road. Yeah. Well. You had a road that would be good for a couple of years before it started completely falling apart. By that time, Arch would have houses built and the roads and related properties deeded over to the county for taxpayers to maintain. Thanks to a couple of savvy county commissioners he didn't get by with it. Arch was furious, but he was forced to build roads in a proper way so they could be well-maintained for years.

There's enough new-home development going on in the north part of Hays County to keep a road construction crew busy for decades. I haven't been around to look at what they're using in the way of material, but I sure hope, for the sake of the taxpayers who follow Lynda and me, that the county is making them toe the line.

I must interject at this point, while thinking again about my time in Temple, that besides the gig at Baylor, one other thing made my life a little less miserable. To get into that story I have to go back to my final four years in Wichita Falls. In about 2003, I got talked into being a mentor for a fourth-grader in one of the elementary schools. The school district sponsored an ongoing program that matched men with boys in fourth grade. The idea was that I as mentor would go have lunch with the boy chosen as my mentee once a week and simply talk to him or have him read to me after lunch. It was thought this might help get a kid who was on the verge of getting off onto the wrong track get back onto the right track. The youngster I was paired with was Franklin H. I came to learn that Franklin came from a family of drug-users.

March 10: I met with Franklin every week, and I felt that I never made much progress with him. His lousy attitude never changed. At the end of this sixth-grade year, I talked to him a long time about how he might shuck his reputation at Ben Franklin Elementary and start over completely new at the junior high. He understood what I was talking about, but his seventh-grade year was a disaster. I'm sure his reputation followed him, but he did himself no favors. I heard later that he had dropped out and been arrested for a series of home burglaries. Wow! What a favorable impact I had on that kid!

About a year into my tour in Temple, the school board hired a new superintendent from the Salado district. She was a young woman, very excited to be moving to a bigger district. One of the first things she did was have a day-long discussion involving community leaders and educators about how to face the challenges of the Temple schools. And they were legion. I have forgotten exactly how it came up, but we started talking about interventions for children in their elementary years, and I brought up the mentoring program in Wichita Falls. Everyone liked this idea, and all of a sudden I was volunteering to head up this new initiative. I worked with the superintendent and the district PR person and we put together the program, partly from pieces given to us by WFISD. I agreed to chair the founding board, and we set about recruiting board members and mentors. That first year we had more than 100 kids with mentors, and the program just grew every year. It was amazing. The program virtually sold itself. That's how eager people were in Temple to improve their children's educations. It was a huge untapped resource. I left Temple in 2011, of course, but the school people in Temple nominated me for an award as a Hero for Children, which I received, an honor bestowed on 15 people once a year by the State Board of Education.

The New York Times has a smorgasbord of stomach-churning news this morning. The health-care bill that aims to make the rich richer and the poor sicker and poorer. The shutdown of the news pipeline out of the State Department. The Wikileaks idea of helping FaceBook and Google fix their CIA leaks problem. The EPA chief's insistence that science has nothing to say about climate change. Two items stood out from that nefarious crowd: One about Baylor's descent into a brothel operated for the pleasure of its football players. The man most responsible for this reprehensible deflowering of a fine educational institution is none other than one Kenneth Starr, the guy who made millions trying to dig up dirt on Bill Clinton and went home finding nothing but his own treasure trove, a sanctimonious bastard if there ever was one. Ken Starr focused on what was important: win at any cost and ignore any collateral damage.

The other story that really hit home had this headline: "Profitable Companies That Paid No Taxes: Here's How They Did It." On Wednesday afternoon, Lynda and I took all of our tax forms to the library to have our returns prepared by a volunteer working through the AARP. After all the numbers were added up and subtracted, we have to come up with $1,100 in additional income tax to send to the federal government. That's $1,100 we really don't have but must pay under threat. If we were AT&T, we would actually be getting a subsidy from the U.S. taxpayer of $381 billion over an eight-year period. We would not be paying taxes at all if we were Wells Fargo, Verizon, IBM, General Electric, Boeing, Exxon Mobil. And the list goes on and on. But it does not include all those thousands of companies that don't pay any U.S. taxes, like Apple, because they are headquartered in Ireland or the Cayman Islands. This is un-fucking-believable. Where's the outrage over this kind of bullshit? The little guy who voted for Trump is obviously too fucking stupid to see who's really getting away with murder in this country thanks to Republican tax policies.

March 11: On the same note, *The Times* reports today that the Republicans' replacement for the Affordable Care Act sends all the money to people earning $200,000 and over and takes that money from the people who make under that amount. The losers? The Trump supporters! These fuckers deserve to lose.

I think I must have a funny attitude about work. With certain exceptions I've never felt put upon because I worked or had to work or wanted to work, and I never felt ashamed of any job I did. I've always felt that every kind of work is valuable and should be appreciated and also compensated appropriately. The word "menial" doesn't fit into my vocabulary when I talk about labor. Everyone who works deserves respect and support. I'm sure I had these attitudes before I got to high school. (I had certainly done plenty of work before then.) But, I had a teacher for metal shop class at Amarillo High named Archie Pool who put everything I thought about work into words. Mr. Pool only taught metal shop on the side; his real lessons were about how to work and how to fit into the world of work. His counsel was to respect everyone who put a shovel in the ground or a nail in a board or a word on a page. Put in a full day's work for a full day's pay. Don't just show up; put your heart into what you were paid to do. Work smart, work fast and work fair.

I recently re-read *Zen and the Art of Motorcycle Maintenance*, a book I first read when I was in graduate school at West Texas. The author is concerned with refocusing his life on quality, and he writes about how to discover quality and foster quality and develop habits of a quality kind. I think Archie Pool could have written that book. Our class was not just about how to weld, but how to approach the act of welding as a kind of art form. But he taught us boys way more than how to use a cutting torch and a lathe. Archie Pool was my favorite teacher of all time. He was a short man with a balding scalp. He wore glasses. He spoke with a firm command of the language of the shop and a firm understanding of boys of a certain age. Remarkably, I believe he had no sons of his own and perhaps no daughters, at least not in the DNA sense. Rather, he had lots and lots of boys he helped turn into useful and honest and hard-working men. I am proud to say I had him as a teacher.

Because I never shied away from working, and because I liked what I could do for whatever little dab of money I could get my hands on I started working at a very early age. The first job I remember was selling greeting cards from door to door in my extended neighborhood north of 10th Street and between Parker and Austin streets in Amarillo. I can't recall exactly how the deal worked, but as a young salesman I had several boxes of sample cards, and would take those to the front doors of my neighbors and sell them boxes of the cards that would be delivered at a later date by mail. I don't remember how many boxes of cards I sold, but I remember a lot of kind rejections. In those days, the early 1950s, a lot of women stayed home during the day; they didn't work outside the home. So, there were plenty of prospects. I can't even imagine a kid today coming up to the door to try to sell me greeting cards. But, door-to-door soliciting was kind of a gateway drug to the wider world of work. So, at some point I moved from selling greeting cards that way to selling the newspaper called "Grit." "Grit" was a weekly or a monthly tabloid publication that had family-oriented content. I don't really remember much about it, and I have no idea how many subscriptions I sold, but it was probably not very many. One or two summers I tried to cut lawns to make some money, but I was never very successful at that because we never had a good lawn mower with a motor that was dependable enough to truck around the neighborhood.

In those pre-junior high days, I really didn't need much money even though my "allowance" from Mom and Dad was only 50 cents a week. What I spent a lot of my earnings on were plastic model airplanes and model cars, paint and glue. I think I remember paying $1.50 for a very good model car or airplane kit, and 79 cents for models of lesser quality. I bought a lot of them from Skelton's Drug Store, which was located on 10th Street, before it burned down. For a little while I got involved in building little airplanes that had gas-powered engines that we flew over at the Maverick's Club on Lincoln Street in east Amarillo. Those took quite a bit more cash.

From early on, I was a car nut.

March 12: I'm getting very excited about going to Santa Fe with my three girls to celebrate my 70th birthday. I emailed D'Arcy a list of possible restaurants yesterday. Becca should be here this next Thursday, just in time for Laura's birthday. Then we load up and fly out on Friday.

March 13: I don't have an agenda for this weekend in Santa Fe, but I think that Julia is working on that. I might like to go to church Sunday at the big cathedral. It's a beautiful old church, and the music is usually above average because some of the professional singers in Santa Fe also sing in the choir or chorus. I don't have to go to church; it would just be nice. I think we can do some walking while there, because the condo is very near the plaza and the church and some of the restaurants. We can't walk up to Canyon Road, which is one area I'd like to visit. In my dreams, I have enough money to buy a huge, I mean really big, oil depicting the Southwest. One time when we were in Santa Fe all those many years ago I found the very painting I would have loved to hang in my house. It was gigantic, and it was somewhere around $50,000, so it was completely out of the question. It was a wonderfully unrealistic landscape of the Southwest desert around Santa Fe done in bright colors. We actually saw the artist while we were at that particular gallery, but did not try to meet him because we would never have been able to buy anything he produced.

March 14: The Congressional Budget Office issued its report yesterday on the financial impact of the Republican program to replace the Affordable Care Act. The cost will be borne by the poor, and the benefits will flow to the rich. About 24 million Americans won't have health care at all by 2026, and next year as many as 14 million could lose health care. This is the "just as good as Obamacare" plan promised by Donald Trump and his hitmen in the House and Senate. So, have the idiots in White Trash Nation taken notice? I guess they will when they have to go to the local emergency room and sit around waiting for ours to see a PA. What a country we are that allows so many people to suffer while the wealthy just cruise on down the road in their limos, and we all act like that's normal and to be expected from the greatest democracy in the world, the richest nation in history. I'm ashamed of my country.

The most important job I had as a kid was my paper route. But, I did work before that, and even spent a summer working for free. There was a Mobil gas station beside McGee Furniture in Wolflin Village where Alvin McGee, Mom's second husband, had all his vehicles serviced. Going into the summer between my sixth-grade and seventh-grade years, she talked to the guy who owned the station, and he agreed to let me work there and to train me that summer during the evening hours, from about 4 o'clock to about 9 o'clock. I was always a car enthusiast, and this was my dream job as a 12-year-old.

All during my elementary school years, I did a lot of just hanging out at the Phillips 66 station at the corner of 10th Street and Travis. John, the man who ran that station, was a World War II veteran who chain-smoked Camels of the unfiltered variety so that when he was smoking he was also doing those shallow spits required because you have tobacco bits on the tip of your tongue. John let me hang out when he pumped gas and wiped windshields and checked oil. I got to know important things like where the zerts were for a grease job, and which side of the car had the gas filler cap on which model and where the oil stick was on which engine. He also just talked about stuff, but I don't recall exactly what. On his right hand, John had a stub for a pointer finger. The rest of it had been shot off in the war. So, he held the cigarette funny when he had it in his right hand.

Sometimes I had the money to buy a Coke for a nickel from the red machine right outside the gas station doorway, and sometimes I had the money to buy both a Coke and a package of Planters Peanuts. John gave me the lesson on how to drink the soda down a bit out of the neck of the bottle and then carefully pour the peanuts in there, creating a concoction that was delightfully crunchy and sweet.

Once in a while I'd walk home from Lee Bivins Elementary School, and I'd get home and the place would be locked up and I would need to go to the bathroom real bad. I'd just walk very fast to the gas station and go to the bathroom there. John didn't care. So, I kind of knew my way around a service station environment when I went to work for the Mobil over on Georgia Street. What I didn't know was what happened on summer nights on that stretch of Georgia, and if I was excited about cars before, I was hyper-excited by the culture the car created when it got into the hands of teen-age boys and girls.

March 15: The health-care bill the Republicans are trying to shove through the Congress is so loaded with benefits for the wealthy in this country, you'd think the GOP would blush. You would be wrong. This bill is a gift and a large one. No longer do the Republicans even pretend that gifting the rich will benefit the nation as a whole or the poor in specific by the now-disproven trickle-down mechanism. They make no excuses and give no explanations. "We're going to make the rich richer and the poor poorer, and Fuck You if you don't like it," is their attitude. It's remarkably cynical and arrogant. At least Ronald Reagan pretended to believe that his tax cuts for the wealthy would make them spend more so the money would end up in the pockets of some of the poor, and he held to that lie even after his own budget people said it wouldn't work. I will shoot off an email to "my" congressman today and tell him not to vote for this piece of shit masquerading as public policy. Little good that will do.

It appears that all of us are meeting at the Albuquerque airport Friday afternoon. D'Arcy is getting there early to rent a car, and then we'll drive to Santa Fe. The forecasts call for great weather. All the bad stuff seems to be hitting the East Coast.

At Rotary yesterday, we had a program that made me want to stand up and scream. A married couple made the presentation. Both were in their 70s, I would estimate. Each of them had experienced death and then sudden rebirth, not once, but three times. The man focused on the last time he died, and his story was a wonder of strange details both revealed and oddly omitted. Upon his death he went through the stars and galaxies and landed in heaven and there encountered, first, Jesus, and then God the Almighty himself, who kindly asked the man to come and sit upon the lap of His Holiness while the Lord of All spent some time going over all of our correspondent's earthly transgressions, starting when the man was just a lad looking to buy some candy who stole Coke bottles from a neighbor's garage to do so.

March 16: After this long conversation, the Lord God Almighty let the man go, and our correspondent whizzed back to take up his earthen form and life. As this fellow told us about all of this, the woman was pantomiming the various emotions the man must have felt. She did so unaffectedly, but with such practiced vigor you had to wonder why they didn't take this show on the road—oh, maybe they did. After he had finished, she told us a bit about her experiences of death and beyond, and from what I recall I will say that two of them (she was six weeks old the first time she died!) involved the traditional bright white light and feeling of enveloping warmth and peace. They brought along a third man who was supposed to tell us his story, but we ran out of time. At the outset he was introduced as a fellow whose life-death story had been related in a front-page story some time back in the *American Statesman*. I did not read the story. But I sure wish responsible newspapers would stop playing up these fantastic stories that truly stretch the bounds of imagination and, of course, scientific fact. Extraordinary claims require extraordinary proofs, and that should be the standard applied to these kinds of "experiences."

The first Trump budget has been passed around Washington, and it is a stunner. It increases military spending by 10 percent right off. The generals must be dancing in the streets. I just wonder what in the world they can spend all that cash on. At the same time everything else gets cut.

Also in today's *Times*, this: The Great Barrier Reef is dying at an alarming rate, a victim of climate change, a reality denied by Trump and associates.

Also, this: Trump met with car makers to say he hopes to eliminate rules that require their trucks and cars to run cleaner, another initiative to make the world largely uninhabitable.

Also, this: A comparison between Trump and Old Hickory Andrew Jackson, calling them both populists. I don't think so.

March 17: Becca and I had an uneventful drive to the airport this morning, and we got settled in pretty quickly at our assigned boarding area for our Southwest flight to Albuquerque.

D'Arcy had picked up a car and met Julia, who arrived 30 minutes before Becca and me, and us at the terminal and we had a nice drive north to Santa Fe. The sky was clear and blue, and the temperature was around 70; it was perfect. We talked of many things, but Julia's description of a "small-food fair" that she went to in Baltimore stood out just for the oddity of it all.

In Santa Fe, D'Arcy was just mesmerized by the adobe homes and buildings. She couldn't believe an entire city would be made of such stuff and make it appear you had just stepped into the 18th century. We were all delighted by the fact that the fruit trees and the forsythia were in full bloom, the splotches of pink and white and yellow appearing here and there around houses and in medians. We easily found our AirBnb apartment at Fort Marcy compound, just down from where Lynda and I had a timeshare for so many years ending in about 2005. The apartment, a two-bedroom, had a large kitchen, two baths and a nice view toward the opera house and beyond. It looked to the northwest, I think.

At dinner, Julia told us about how hard it had been to get through the process to become a full professor, an event just culminated in February. She was especially hurt by a colleague at the University of Chicago who deliberately and viciously took aim at her in a letter in reference to her bid for promotion. The woman's name she refused to say, and this intrigued Becca and me so much that when we had returned to the apartment, we began googling around to find someone who fit Julia's very limited description. Finally, about midnight, Julia told us the woman was at the University of Chicago. Becca and I vowed to figure out something or another that would serve as payback.

March 19: On our trip together, a first-in-a-lifetime experience for the four of us, we talked little of politics. We all know what we think about what's going on. D'Arcy said, though, that she is thinking of running for office, something she would be good at.

It was a magical weekend with my girls. They were wonderfully sweet and kind to me. I was not a very good father to them, and they have refused to repay me with what I deserved. They have treated me with grace and forgiveness. I am forever grateful.

March 21: I did not keep up with the news over the long weekend. It appears that the Trump team will be investigated for colluding with the Russians in the November elections. We shall see.

One item in *The Times* caught my eye today—about hotel construction in Dallas, Houston and Austin. These cities apparently lead the country in this particular economic category. The writer tells one reason why: "Local and state governments, known to favor spending on business interests over social programs, compete to offer sales tax breaks, real estate tax abatements and other incentives to draw in developers. They also 'invest in roads and other infrastructure, which helps attract manufacturing, fill office space, and that drives demand for hotel rooms,' (one developer, a) Mr. Jacobs, said."

Very, very true. They bend over backwards for developers, but do less and less over time for, say, school kids and poor people. How proud they must be, them and their politician friends who keep cutting budgets for infrastructure improvements that would make life easier for anyone else in Texas other than developers. At one time, Texas had highways that were the envy of the nation. No more. We never had public schools that anyone would envy, and we have managed to maintain that reputation.

March 22: A new book is out that attempts to explain why Americans seem so willfully stupid. It's because they are willfully stupid and like themselves that way. To quote the reviewer in today's *Times*:

" 'Americans have reached a point where ignorance, especially of anything related to public policy, is an actual virtue,' the scholar Tom Nichols writes in his timely new book, *The Death of Expertise*. 'To reject the advice of experts is to assert autonomy, a way for Americans to insulate their increasingly fragile egos from ever being told they're wrong about anything. It is a new Declaration of Independence: No longer do we hold *these* truths to be self-evident, we hold *all* truths to be self-evident, even the ones that aren't true. All things are knowable and every opinion on any subject is as good as any other.' "

That seems a bit facile and over-general, but perhaps it isn't. I probably will not read the book because I know how it ends—with jackboots and barbed wire in this nation's future.

Another article in The *Times* caught my attention today: At the Anne Frank

House, school kids are not really up on who Anne Frank was and what happened to give her historical value. They are vaguely aware of Nazism. More reason to believe jackboots and barbed wire are in our future.

And then there's Judge Gorsuch, the man who would be a Supreme Court justice. His confirmation hearing before the Senate Judiciary Committee was conducted yesterday, almost all day. I listened to part of it on NPR as I drove to and from work. Regardless of what he said or didn't say, he will be the next Justice because that's what the Senate majority wants. Perhaps he will be restrained from pursuing his most base urges by the aura of integrity that accompanies the position. That is certainly to be hoped. I will say, though, that he came across on radio as a somewhat petulant patrician miffed at being asked tawdry little questions by United States Senators. Some of his responses made him sound like an aristocrat not being paid the proper homage by the riff-raff. I was particularly irritated by his continual use of the two constructions used by speakers who are trying to make the point very clear that they are right, period, as in: "The matter of judicial review addressed in Marbury vs. Madison is settled law, all right?" or "I did the hard work at Oxford to earn my doctorate in the law, Okay?"

At least it appears he will be neither as stupid nor as mean-spirited as Justice Clarence Thomas.

March 23: No way to read *The New York Times* today, very frustrating. I did start in on the latest New Yorker, which I sometimes see first online. Right there on Page 3 is a most interesting, almost startling letter from one George K. Yin, a professor of taxation and law at the University of Virginia School of Law, a little backwater college out yonder where the hicks live, don't ya know. Dr. Yin writes this:

"… A 1924 law, the result of conflict-of-interest concerns about the Treasury Secretary Andrew Mellon and executive-branch officials involved in the Teapot Dome scandal, *gives Congress the authority to examine Trump's (tax) returns and reveal them to the public without the President's consent.* Members of Congress cannot blame the absence of information solely on the President's intransigence. Indeed, they must explain why they favor the same secrecy that the President does."

One wonders, then, when members of Congress, including those few Democrats, will pick up on this and begin to push to see what is in the president's tax returns.

Lynda hollered at me that the AP is reporting that Trump's former campaign manager got $10 million from the Russians to make sure the election went their way. Who will pick up on this? The fact is that Trump has broken so many laws and crossed so many ethical lines it must be hard to know where to start to bring him to heel. But that *must* happen. The man is a danger to democracy in so many ways.

March 24: Paul Krugman writes this morning about the topic mentioned at the end of yesterday's comments in a tangential way. He warns about the news media's habit of presenting false symmetry: So-and-so said this; me-and-moe said this in response. Using false symmetry is a variant of covering things in a horse-race fashion. All through last year's election and even today, major media fail to report on the substance of conflicts and merely report that a conflict is occurring, with A saying X and B saying Y as if the points of view were equivalent. If one person is telling the truth and the other person is lying those statements are hardly equivalent. Last night, for example, NBC's Lester Holt had a long—deservedly so—story about the failure of the House to bring a new health-care law to a vote as planned.

The crux of the piece was the maneuvering by Paul Ryan and the president and the recalcitrance of House fascists, who would not agree to the bill as it would have been presented for a vote. The real story was about what the fight was about, not that there was a fight. The health-care bill is truly awful. It will eliminate health care altogether for millions of Americans. It will end the meager help that goes to the disabled through Medicaid. It will up premiums for everyone. It will lower taxes for the rich. The fascists want even more health care to be cut. They want more people to suffer. They want bigger bonuses for the rich. They want a bill that is so horrible that even the president doesn't want to go there. But apparently now he will. And his base supporters will get their very first kick in the head from a guy who doesn't give a shit about them and never will.

March 25: So far I have escaped the sinister Executioner of Irony. I have gone into the Santa Fe trip and come out on the other side without any kind of physical or mental problem. Now I have to make it through to the other side of May 8, my actual 70th birthday, to escape altogether.

The health-care bill is dead, and Trump is apparently walking away from the steaming carcass. The meanest of mean men in the House killed the worst of the worst bills in history *because it just wasn't mean enough*.

Now we will see what they do to find another route to give the richest people on the planet even more wealth while also, in the most satisfying way possible, screwing the poorest. Tax reform is next up. NPR reported yesterday that the last time a major tax reform bill passed it was 1986. Trump and Ryan may get their way on this issue, but many knowledgeable people are betting against them. The rich may have to settle for dismantling public education, warfare with North Korea, war on blacks and browns and Muslims and an astonishingly rapid rise in the pregnancy rate for 14-year-olds.

Lynda and I watched the movie "Genius" last night. It is the story of the relationship that developed between the great New York books editor Maxwell Perkins and the writer Thomas Wolf. Wolf came across as some kind of kamikaze storyteller and wordsmith brought onto the flight deck of publishing in a touch-and-go maneuver that barely slowed him down. It was a good movie; now I would like to see sequels about Perkins and Hemingway and Fitzgerald. To me, Wolf was the least interesting writer in Perkins' stable. Hemingway is my favorite author of all time. I discovered him through his short stories in high school and was gripped by his spare style and careful use of words.

The grip was not tight enough, though, to turn me into a writer myself. That took a life-changing couple of events, both of which occurred during my senior

91

year. In high school, I was a poor student. I did not flunk anything, although I came close to doing so in algebra, only to be saved by my math teacher who also happened to be my English teacher. I had Mr. Clyde Dale Martin for English my junior year and also had him for algebra. When he quickly learned that I could not do math but could do English, he told me that he would allow me to do English work in math class and give me a C grade at the end of the term—if I would never tell anyone who taught me math in high school. I promised, a promise I am breaking right now because I'm certain he will never read this and perhaps no one will.

My intention going into my senior year was to take a minimal load of "serious" classes, ones that would require homework and intense study. I planned to take subjects like speech and metals shop. At the same time I loved English and signed up for the optional fourth year of that. I also loved Latin and signed up for a fourth year of that.

On registration day, I did, in fact, get the schedule I wanted, which in those days was called a "blow-off" schedule, and I was swaggering around on the third floor of Amarillo High School bragging about it to whomever might listen. I was about to leave when a friend from elementary and junior high school ran up to me with a harried and worried look on her face. "Carroll Wilson," she said, breathlessly, "you have to be on the student newspaper this year!" Her name was Suzanne Thompson, she was the daughter of the editor of the afternoon paper in Amarillo, and she was to be editor of the student newspaper. Other than having been a newspaper carrier, I knew nothing much about newspapers. My dad read two a day, one in the morning and one in the evening, and some Saturday mornings when I was younger we would walk to town and go to the Bivins Memorial Library, where he would read the Dallas and Fort Worth papers. I might have looked at one now and then, but I was certainly not a regular reader. "No, Suzanne," I said, "I don't have to be on the newspaper staff this year." I showed her my yellow schedule form, already filled out and signed. "This is my blow-off year, and I'm not doing anything that takes a lot of time or a lot of work." I can't recall what she said next, but somehow she got me headed in the direction of the journalism classroom. "Just come down and meet our new teacher," Suzanne said. At the doorway, I peered into the empty classroom and standing there by the chalkboard was a woman with long dark hair who appeared to be just a little older than I was, and she was, well, quite a looker. She peered at me with one of those over-the-shoulder glances that seemed quite intriguing. Right then and there, I decided I could add journalism to my schedule.

March 26: The utter collapse of the Republican plan for health care for Americans has put into bold relief the utter corruption and treachery of the House leadership and the majority of its members. At the last minute to garner more votes, the Speaker allowed everything into the bill except the erection of gas chambers for paupers and Muslims. Now the dust is settling, and while everyone is breathing a deep breath many smart people are also reflecting on where we are and what happens next.

The latest issue of *The New Yorker* has a background piece that appeared before the health-care vote about one Robert Mercer and his family of neofascists.

The Mercers have accrued mammoth wealth and they have chosen to spend a little of it (a huge amount to normal people like, say, the Rockefellers or the Vanderbilts) to keep most Americans poor as dirt, sick, uneducated and always, always voting for their next surrogate. In this case, he is Donald Trump, selected by the Mercers some time back because of his colorful demagoguery and his stupidity writ large. Not only could the American people be manipulated, so could this dope from Manhattan. I won't go into all of it, but it is absolutely must-reading for anyone who wants to understand how our media and our institutions are being manipulated by the rich and powerful so they can keep on being rich and powerful. The author of the piece quotes David Magerman, who wrote an essay on the Mercers: "Everyone has a right to express their views. But when the government becomes more like a corporation, with the richest 0.001% buying shares and demanding board seats, then we cease to be a representative democracy. Instead, we become an oligarchy."

And that is also the point of Ganesh Sitaraman, whose new book on this very subject is the cover story on *The New York Times Book Review* this morning. The book is "The Crisis of the Middle-Class Constitution: Why Economic Inequality Threatens Our Republic." Alas, Sitaraman seems not to know about the Mercers because in his review of the book, Angus Deaton writes, somewhat sophomorically, it turns out: "Yet it is clear that we in the United States face the looming threat of a takeover of government by those who would use it to enrich themselves together with a continuing disenfranchisement of large segments of the population." YES, Angus, go read *The New Yorker*! It's already done!

This is also, tangentially, the subject of an essay in *The Times* Review section by Masha Gessen. When it comes to fraud, Mr. Trump is a king among princes. And he is winning at being a fraud and at fraudulent behavior because the rest of us actually cannot fathom that people like the Mercers are in charge of the whole freaking shabang—at this point. At this point. Ah, at this point only. So far.

Today, those in charge act with the worst of intentions insofar as what they do relates to the American people and not, say, to the Russians or the multi-nationals like Exxon Mobil, citizens of the Republic until that is not economically convenient. History shows us that when those in charge have even the best, the very best, of intentions, they are perfectly capable of doing horrible, ungodly things that may well doom the planet or despoil it so badly that even the richest will have no place to hide. I am thinking here of the men and women who joined together during World War II to build the atom bomb that ended the war in August of 1945. I am thinking of these people because I have been reading a biography of Enrico Fermi, one of the founding fathers of the bomb, written by Gino Segre and Bettina Hoerlin and published just recently by Henry Holt & Co.

Almost immediately after the bombing of Hiroshima and Nagasaki with two different kinds of atomic weapons, some of the scientists on the team pushed to go ahead and build a Super, a hydrogen bomb that would be much more terrible and destructive than the atomic bombs. While some pushed, like Edward Teller, others pushed back and pursued other lines of research. These others knew perfectly well that what they had created was the most destructive force in the history of the planet. That genie was out of the bottle; it might be used for good, which is how the country's nuclear power industry got its start, a product of scientific guilt. Or it might be used for even more destruction, a product of scientific hubris of the kind never even dreamt of by the Greeks.

I have written many editorials and many letters suggesting that nuclear power is not the way for us to proceed to provide electricity for ourselves or anyone else, all based on the notion that these materials are too dangerous for mere humans to handle over time. In the 1970s I was warning against nuclear power plants because we had nowhere to put the waste materials, which would be and are dangerous for thousands of years. Today, nearly 50 years later, we have waste sitting around in barrels at power plants because there is still no good place to store it. I am sure if the Mercers wanted us to find a way to do something else, we would do so and in short order.

The bluebonnets are out in wild profusion this weekend. They are everywhere, and they are beautiful. I also saw my very first grasshopper of the season yesterday, not a good sign at all.

It was 65 when I walked this morning. It was 82 as a high yesterday. It will be hotter today.

March 27: I finished reading "The Pope of Physics" yesterday, and came away with the nagging feeling that scientists like Enrico Fermi ought to have exercised stronger moral or ethical character when it came to development of the H-bomb and nuclear power. Fermi was agnostic on the development of nuclear weapons. He looked upon the entire enterprise as a grand experiment in physics neces-sitated by war. The depiction of him here is of a man unworried by the outcomes that might develop from his discoveries. Is this really good enough? Shouldn't there be a moral or ethical component in the doing of science? Many among those who developed the atomic bomb felt there was, and some even refused to go down the road toward the H-bomb. They felt it was morally reprehensible to plan for the very annihilation of the human race. At least Fermi and his friends were not doing science to profit from it, which is the way science is done today. In the pursuit of the dollar, today's scientists are willing to do anything, including lie about and distort their results.

March 28: I haven't even looked at the newspaper yet. I forgot. I went out for my walk and came back and Chi-Chi was still in bed with Lynda, and I guess that threw me off for the entire day!

The reason I wasn't interested in high school, to get back to that subject, was one thing, really—cars. I loved cars. I have mentioned spending a lot of money and time when I was in elementary school building and "customizing" model cars that I made from plastic kits. Any money I might make from my various sales and slave labor projects (like the one where I was paid to move five yards of dirt [which is one helluva lof of dirt, by the way] from one place in a guy's front yard to a garden area in his back yard) would go into car models and stuff to improve them. It blossomed the summer after my sixth-grade year when I worked for free several hours each night at the Mobil station east of McGee Furniture on Georgia Street in Amarillo where I was in a pre-teen-age boy's heaven.

Through the years I have made some serious mistakes on cars: the 1954 Austin Healey I had in high school! The Model A Ford I tore down and couldn't find

94

enough money to fix. The 1978 Corvette I couldn't afford to keep up. The 1968 Porsche 911 that was completely worn out. I eventually got it all out of my system—the drag-racing, the customizing, the expensive paint jobs—and settled for a dependable Nissan. What a major letdown!

March 29: For example, all that summer of my 12th year I wasted my days so I could revel in my nights over in Wolflin Village, and just about every nickel I made from my paper route went into a bank account dedicated to buying me a car. The route's purpose had moved away from providing income for a model car or two. I had the larger picture in mind. What before had been the daily drudgery of toting 50 papers from house to house every afternoon and getting up at 5 on Sundays for the same circuit now became the way to fulfill a dream.

In some ways I was like Don Quixote. The dream seemed impossible. I collected $1.50 at the end of every month from each of my 48 to 50 customers. The newspaper got $1 of that amount, and I got to keep the 50 cents. So, on paper, I could make $25 in profit every month. But, I also had to buy rubber bands and collection books and other miscellaneous items from the *Globe-News*, every dime of which came out of my pocket. And then there were the deadbeats, people who would not pay at the end of the month and would want me to come back later or who would put me off and never pay me. There were probably very few months when I actually made $25. But, it was tax-free money!

March 30: I took an arts/crafts class on Tuesday on how to use a gelli plate or something like that. It was somewhat useful information. After the class I had to rush to HEB to get a sandwich to eat before starting work at 1 o'clock at the library. As I was opening the sandwich package in our tiny staff break area, I was joined by Emily R., our youth services librarian. Emily was eating something and then pulled out a big black binder filled with papers and flipped over toward the back. She said she was finishing up a class on copy editing at Texas State University. I almost swallowed my tongue. "You know I taught copy editing at Baylor and at the University of Texas," I said. "Umhum," she said. I didn't know she was taking copy editing. She never had mentioned it. I was floored because I guess it just never occurred to her that she could ask me questions or pick my brain about copy editing. It was like I had been invisible.

I'm thinking this must be a generational thing. Bryan and Erin would never dream of asking Lynda or me a question about how to raise little Greyson. In fact, when they were having trouble getting him to go to sleep, they paid some woman in some foreign state to tell them what to do, when all they had to do was ask us. That's just beyond belief. I guess it no longer takes a village to raise a child; it takes a cell phone.

March 31: The whole story about Russian intervention in our elections just gets weirder and weirder. Now it appears that the Trump people are feeding disinformation to the Congress to try to get them to focus on the so-called wiretapping of Trump by Obama to deflect attention from their own Russian connections. The House committee that was supposed to hold impartial hearings on Trump-Russia has lost all of its credibility and that whole process is collapsing, which was probably Bannon's intended result to begin with. Over in the Senate, we shall just see how much they slobber over Trump to keep him from being tainted by treason. If the American people are not fatally cynical by now about who runs things in Washington, this whole sorry chapter will turn them toward a desire for monarchy.

I have been doing some thinking about why I was so car crazy when I was a kid. It's not good enough to say, well, all little American boys were car crazy. I think it had something to do with wanting something flashy and fast, something that would get you away from indoors and let you go out and play a long way from home and a long way from school and a long way from any kind of responsibilities. Cars were a bond for brothers. They consumed our allowances and our monthly checks and our passions. And they could be just flat fun.

I did adhere to a strict savings plan for my paper route money. Every month between $20 and $25 went into the kitty (Did I have a bank account? I don't recall.). I never got cash for Christmas or birthday gifts, so the route income was all there was to count for my goal.

April 1: Lynda and I were watching cable TV the other night when we saw a commercial that was so … so … so … so astonishingly graceless and crude that we couldn't believe what we had seen. The spot goes on for about 45 seconds and is animated, so it is very colorful. One character is a white unicorn. Another character is, as I recall, either a stylized man or a cow that stood on its back legs. The plot was this: The unicorn sat on a toilet and pooped colorful poop into an ice cream cone and then the cow/man ate it. To coin a phrase, I am not shitting you. Actually, the unicorn had a hard time pooping in the toilet until an unseen hand, undoubtedly a cousin of the appendage provided by Adam Smith to guide our entire economy, scooted a "Squatty Potty" right up so the unicorn could rest its back legs on the potty and therefore align its colon with the toilet just so, making the poop flow smoothly and without painful kinks in the plumbing right into the cow/man's ice cream cone. Yes, the commercial was for the "Squatty Potty," a product we had actually seen pitched on "Shark Tank" some time ago. I can't remember whether the inventor of the potty got any financial aid from a Shark, but I hope they did not sign off on a gross television spot clearly aimed at pre-teen boys. How many of them give a shit, to coin another phrase, about pooping rainbow-colored ice cream?

The Congress spent more than a year and untold millions of dollars to penalize Hillary Clinton for not paying enough attention to the isolated State Department field office in Benghazi. They were laser focused on holding her accountable for a situation that, in terms of world history, meant next to nothing. Today, the same Congress ho-hums at the virtually proven fact that the Trump campaign colluded with Russia to fix last November's elections so Trump would win. This is high treason of the first order, but Congress couldn't care less. We truly live in a time when almost no one in Washington cares about the future of this country so long as they make their money and go home to their horses and yachts.

Saving money from my paper route was not an easy thing to do. I still loved building model cars and airplanes, although I quickly ran out of space for those projects.

I pestered my parents long and hard enough that when I was about 13 they relented. They let me buy the real thing.

April 2: Yevgeny Yevtushenko's death was reported in The *Times* today. He was a Russian poet well-known in this country as well as his own. The death notice speaks of an uncertainty about his political loyalties. His poetry was universally liked. Yevtushenko is one of those people I was separated from by only 2 degrees. In 1966 or 1967 when I was a young reporter at the *Amarillo Daily News* and *Globe-Times*, I sat right across the desks from Buck Ramsey, the former cowboy who'd been thrown from his horse while chasing a calf on the Bivins Ranch north of Amarillo. His specialty was feature writing, and he wrote them beautifully, carefully, artfully. I wanted to write like Buck. Buck had some kind of long but flimsy connection with Stanley Marsh III, the eccentric Amarillo millionaire. One weekend Stanley scheduled a party for one Yevgeny Yevtushenko at his home out north of Amarillo called Toad Hall, or maybe at his house over on Harrison or Hughes or Lipscomb. I had never heard of Yevtushenko. Heck, I'd never heard of Russian poetry. Buck knew about both, and he really wanted to be invited out to Stanley's house to meet the great poet and to do a story. For some reason, he did not get the invitation. It may have been because Yevtushenko was avoiding the press. I don't know. The lack of an invitation did not stop Buck. He told the night city editor he was going to cover Yevtushenko at Stanley's house and would have a story good for Page One by deadline. I was working the day shift on regional stories at the time, so I was not there when Buck got back that evening. I did, though, read the story in the next day's paper, and Buck had done a great descriptive piece about the party and the man. No interviews. Just something right out of the New Journalism playbook. Our paper never did that kind of reporting even though it was all the rage across the country with Tom Wolfe and Hunter S. Thompson leading the way. I hoped this report would lead to more of this kind of writing assignment, but it did not. Buck told me later that he had to "sneak in" to the party and managed to do so unnoticed. Hmmm. A guy in a wheelchair sneaking into a party at Stanley Marsh's house?

Donald Trump's daughter and her husband have filed their financial holdings forms as required now that they are federal employees. What they filed showed that they have conflicts of interest as wide and deep as the Grand Canyon. Everything they will touch as presidential advisers will turn to absolute gold. They have hit the Mother Lode, and nobody in Congress will keep them from plundering it for every fucking ounce they can get away with.

Mom and Dad did let me use my paper route money for A Real Car. Daddy worked with his friend, later to be one of my mentors, Archie Pool, to find something suitable. When I outlined what I wanted and wanted to do with a car, at that tender age, I must have left out one very important stipulation: It needed to run. When Archie pulled the car up into our driveway I was ecstatic. It was a 1948 Plymouth sedan with dark blue paint that had faded to a dull gray with hints of blue pigment. We all pushed it up under the carport, and I got in and sat behind the wheel. The gray interior was still intact, but smelled like mold and long-forgotten gym socks. With some help from Archie Pool I popped the very substantial hood to get a glance at the engine. To my utter horror there was nothing there. Not only had I failed to stipulate that I wanted a car that ran; I had forgotten to mention that it ought to have an engine. Dad and Archie must have had a good laugh about that later, but at the time they treated it like it was something just a little shy of a limo maybe needing some hand-rubbing and a squirt of air in the tires. I had absolutely no idea where to start. Here I was with my very own car, and I was just clueless.

April 3: I dropped by the Shamrock station on Ranch Road 12 last week to get a bean and pork quesadilla for lunch, and a sign on the door said the lunch counter was closed. Later it dawned on me: They were very likely closed because the people working in the kitchen were undocumented Mexicans. And, too, many of their customers were undocumented Mexicans. The day laborers have disappeared from their usual waiting places in blue plastic chairs in front of St. Mary Catholic Church. Some church folks from around town had a meeting not long ago about what to do for these workers and their families. I don't know what the upshot was, but another meeting is set later in the month. Lynda says that ICE is picking people up just randomly around Texas, here and there. It's like a terror campaign. You never know when you will be next on the list. How many businesses will lose money, how many will close down in places like Texas before the Republicans see what a failed immigration policy looks like? See, nobody is going to cook tacos at the Shamrock station now that the Mexican ladies are gone. Nobody is going to do day labor now that the Mexican men are gone. They took jobs from not a single American citizen. Since jobs are now open here I wonder how many out-of-work coal miners can find their way to Texas. Those poor dumb bastards couldn't find the exit door with both hands. Talk about people wanting a handout.

There seems to be a dispute over who said, "First they came for the Communists, and I wasn't a Communist... ." You know the rest of the saying. The *Times* Book Review had a letter about the subject yesterday. I don't care who coined the term; it is nothing if not relevant now. First, they came for the Mexicans.

I read a lot of books outside of class assignments in junior high school, and almost all of them were related to cars and car culture. None of the books I read were about a kid with a car that had no engine and how he pieced it all together from stuff found at the junkyard and had the thing running so well it won its class at the dragstrip. Dad was not only not a mechanic, he had no interest in helping me figure all this out. At some point in some kind of rash, irrational act of terrible logic I checked a book out of the library to study how an automatic transmission worked. My car didn't have a transmission of any kind! I washed my car and cleaned up the interior and hosed out the engine compartment and I walked around and around it a lot, and nothing came to me about how to start. I cannot remember what happened to that car, but the experience did not do what Dad and Mom hoped. It did not dampen my interest in cars, not one whit. I was still saving my paper route money and still dreaming.

April 4: Almost every other page in today's *Times* has a story about one Trump infraction or another. It's astonishing how many ways he and his family have found to screw the taxpayer, make gobs more money and ruin the economy. On one page we learn that he's only the fourth president with active lawsuits pending during his presidency, and he has 75 to deal with. The number will only grow over time because the man can't help but work the wrong side of the street. On another we find out that while his White House staffers are supposed to open up about how many businesses they own or invest in that could benefit from their service, they have not done so, and apparently no one will hold them accountable. This man and his band of armed robbers and cat burglars may get away scot-free because the House and Senate refuse to do what they ought to do on behalf of the American people.

Then there's Bill O'Reilly, a Fox News lover boy who partners up with real writers to turn out a book a week on the theme "the real story behind the death of so-and-so," and also a serial molester of women. On Sunday, The *Times* reported that O'Reilly has paid out $13 million to settle claims he harassed women. Today, the newspaper says that Mercedes Benz and Hyundai are pulling their ads from Fox because of O'Reilly's outrageous behavior. The man, of course, is completely unrepentant. He couldn't care less as long as the money keeps rolling in from somewhere. These big Fox celebrities and others like them, such as Rush Limbaugh, think they are completely exempt from the rules and standards that apply to mere mortals. Who watches or listens to these twits?

I'm not sure what kind of car Mom and Dad had when they got married. My guess is that they didn't have a car for a while. They got married in Greenville while Dad was in the Army stationed as base historian at the airfield there. Mother worked at a retail shop as a bookkeeper in Greenville until the war ended, and they would see each other only when Dad had leave. He didn't need a car because he lived on the base. And a car might have been forbidden for a buck sergeant. Somehow they moved to Amarillo after the war; Dad's job as a teacher at Amarillo High School had been held open during the war so he could return to it when the conflict ended. The two of them lived in the Badger Apartments off Elmwood Park, from which both could walk to work. Later, or maybe earlier, they lived in an apartment somewhere else in town. They built the house at 914 Bowie Street, and it was completed before I was born in May 1947. This house was beyond walking distance for Dad, but Mom could walk to work at Northwest Texas Hospital, where she was in bookkeeping. So, Dad took the bus. At some point before I started elementary school (I did not have an opportunity to go to kindergarten) at Lee Bivins Mom took a job at Heath Furniture just a couple of blocks from Amarillo High School on Polk Street. So, both of them worked very close to one another. I remember that for some period of time we all took the bus to the high school, where we ate breakfast with other faculty members. I don't recall how I got back home.

And then we had a car, a 1950 or so Oldsmobile. It was a dark blue. The backseat was so expansive and buried beneath a huge slanting roof I felt lost back there when we would drive anywhere. I couldn't see out the back windows anyway. Later on Dad traded that car for a faded maroon Nash Rambler, an ugly little car if there ever was one. It resembled a giant mutant beetle on wheels. Still later, he traded for a 1957 Oldsmobile 88, which was the car he had for all but my senior year of high school. It was gun-metal gray, a beautiful car really and a fast one with an automatic shift. By the time I was in high school, Mother had been furnished a company car by McGee Furniture, where she was office manager and bookkeeper. That car was a plain vanilla white Chevrolet sedan, may be a '59 or 60 model. On the dirt roads west of Amarillo Mother taught me how to drive in that car. Or rather she helped me hone my skills as a driver in that car.

April 5: My first driving experience was actually not in Amarillo. It was not on a paved road, either. The summer I got my old engineless Plymouth John and I spent a week or so with my Uncle Basil and Aunt Marge in Mangum, Okla. Basil and Marge had no children, and they loved having us over there every summer until we got too old to want to go stay with them in their tiny town. They had a nice house in Mangum, and then several miles outside of town they owned a big plot of ground where they had a garden and a few head of cattle, including one bull we called "Toro," and a big cattle tank where we'd spend most of our time fishing for crappie and catfish. Basil had a dull green 1950 Ford pickup that we'd use to get out to the farm, and one day that magical summer he asked me if I wanted to drive. I was ecstatic. First he showed me where all the controls were, and there weren't that many—steering wheel, gear shift stick in the floor, turn signals, accelerator, brake pedal, clutch pedal. Pushing the clutch pedal to the mat floor almost required me to stand up to lean into it with all the weight I could muster, but not quite. The transmission had a granny low gear that he advised me not to use unless, God forbid, I got stuck in the mud. So, you actually started off in second gear and then double-clutched at every shift interval. It took practice, time I gladly put in out there on his driveway before we actually got on our way to the farm. Then, with him hugging the passenger side door and John sitting in the middle of the bench-type seat, trying to stay out of my way while I shifted gears, we got under way, as I backed out of the driveway and then put her into second gear and eased out on the clutch with Uncle Basil giving me a constant stream of directions. "Ease up now. ... Now put her in gear. ... Easy. ... Now double clutch. ... A little more gas. ... Whoa now. ... A little less gas." I'm sure I had a hard-on as big as Denver. Out on the dirt road toward the farm we sailed along in the highest gear, the old engine humming and me dodging the ruts and feeling the hot wind in my face through the open windows and just smiling.

After the engineless car was hauled away from our house, I set about trying to find a real car. Dad seemed to give in to the idea that having a car was not some fantasy that I would outgrow or get over. The best way to find a car was by poring over the classified ads in the daily newspaper, and I became a religious reader of the tiny print at the back of the paper. I cannot remember how it was that I decided I needed a very old car. It might have been that Mother and Daddy decided that I couldn't do much damage to myself or others with an old car. It would not go very fast, wouldn't be something I could race, if it ran at all. It would satisfy my hunger for a car, and it probably wouldn't cost very much to buy or maintain.

April 6: We had a regular Lenten season church service last evening, and the Gospel reading was from that part of John in which Jesus proclaims that he is the way, the truth and the light and that the truth will make you free. Sandy, the rector, went way deep into the theology behind that statement and ended up saying that if you follow Jesus you will forgive others and you will likely end up on the cross,

100

but that is what Christ requires or that is what is required to be Christ-like in the truest sense. I really wanted to discuss this with her because I think it is in this view that modern men and women become estranged. It's not that they won't sacrifice for something. It is that they won't sacrifice for the promise of eternal life. It's not enough somehow. In the post-Holocaust world we live in (Assad of Syria gassed his own people yesterday!) Christianity as taught in this manner threatens to become irrelevant. That's the reason, I think, that all the churches of Europe stand empty except for tourists. Frankly, any kind of religion seems to ring hollow when faced with the kind of evil that's so pervasive and that can do such damage in such a short period of time.

April 7: Last evening President Trump sent cruise missiles piling into something at a Syrian air base from which were launched the planes that use deadly gas to attack civilians the day before. I am of several minds about this. In a way, if we were going to be engaged in this large-scale conflict in a non-petroleum producing state as a surrogate for the Saudis, we should have engaged much earlier—during President Obama's administration. Why sit around and wait for bad things to happen when you can force Assad's hand? Well, for one thing, there's Russia. I guess, though, that since Trump and Vlad Putin are bosom buddies nowadays Russia will look the other way while we have a go at Assad. That seems to be the case this morning; things may change as the day goes on. The only dog we have in this fight is the Big Oil dog, and our new Secretary of State Tillerson knows all about that. He'll do nothing that will upset the oil production cart, which shows you how pitifully irrelevant Assad and Syria are, and ISIS, for that matter. If we are going to bomb every awful despot in the world, we will have to increase our bomber fleet, and we could start with Moscow.

Speaking of which, two interesting items that are separated into different sections of today's New York Times should stand together. They are twins. One is in the A section having to do with Putin's government banning a picture of Vlad as a clown. That's right. Now, Putin is on a par with Muhammad: If you desecrate his holy image, someone with big guns or bombs strapped to their tummies are going to come after you. The other story is buried back in the business section. There we learn that the government, that is, the Trump administration, is going to court to make Twitter tell them who is behind a Twitter account that is making fun of Donald Trump and his administration. And whoever that is isn't even using photoshopped images!

I was thinking more this morning during my power walk about Christianity today, and the conversation I had with Sandy the other evening, and the more I think about it the more I think Christianity has no real place in the modern nation-state. Here's what Christians are concerned about—enough to vote their beliefs and try to sway legislators to do the same thing: a woman's right to do with her body as she wishes; homosexuals; and who uses public bathrooms. That's it. I am recalling the lessons I learned from Ladon Sheats—No. 1 of which was that Christianity is deeply personal and lived out within the individual and how he or she relates to other people and social institutions. Ladon dropped out and refused to play politics because he recognized that his faith would never mean anything in the broader cash-and-carry arena. With that in mind, I'm not going to engage

Sandy any further on this, and, in fact, after I'm no longer on the Vestry I will probably just leave St. Stephen's and pursue religious studies and religious initiatives on my own.

April 8: When I was growing up on Bowie Street in Amarillo in the '50s and '60s, I enjoyed living in a neighborhood that extended well beyond the block I lived on, basically 30 houses on two sides of one street between Line Avenue on the north and 10th Street on the south. Amarillo itself was not a large place. In 1950, its population was only about 74,000, although the city grew from 74,000 to double that number in just the 10 years between 1950 and 1960 because the Strategic Air Command took over Amarillo Air Force Base. The total elementary school population in 1952 was about 9,000. By far most of those kids were white.

Our house at 914 was in the middle of the city block more or less. All around us were people more or less just like us. We weren't lower middle class or upper middle class or even middle class. We were nearer lower than middle. But I think of everyone as having been hard-working, honest, just plain good people.

Trump is getting credit from all sorts of people for sending cruise missiles into the Syrian base that launched the gas attacks on Assad's people last week. I'm not sure it was a bad idea. Rachel Maddow pointed out on her show last night, though, that the Trump action was completely inconsistent with what Trump has tweeted for years about the U.S. staying out of Syria, period. This actually was a great diversionary tactic. It pisses off Russia—maybe, wink, wink—so that calls into question his links with Vlad to steal the election last November. It shows he's a strong man unlike Obama, who, by the way, bombed the shit out of Syria numerous times in the normal course of doing business. And it does show North Korea and others that we might retaliate if they piss us off. The latter might not be a bad thing, either.

Adam Gopnick has a wonderfully written essay in *The New Yorker* blog that makes the very strong and horribly correct case that just three months into the new regime and we are already saying to ourselves, "Well, at least he's not Hitler." All that bullshit he and his family do, the corruption, the lies, all that is becoming normalized. We are becoming inured to living in a country where the leaders are running off with all the toilet paper and the bathroom fixtures, and we're essentially saying, "Well, hey, they did leave the shower head!"

April 9: Storm clouds are coming up, but we are ignoring that and heading to Bryan's and Erin's east of Buda to have some ribs (!) and to see the baby. And the goats and the chickens and the burros. It's an hour there and an hour back, but Lynda will love it.

Back in the early 2000s, when my friend John Binnion, a WWII veteran, was still alive, he invited me over to Crowell to be keynote speaker at the chamber of commerce banquet. Crowell is about 30 minutes west of Vernon and there are really only two ways to get there by car. Both ways take more than an hour, and I chose the route that would take me by the old reunion grounds at Margaret where the girls spent many a fun Labor Day weekend with Susan's extended family. I was feeling nostalgic, I guess.

Anyway, through John and the girls I had kept up with the

downward spiral of Crowell and Foard County. Both had their heyday in the 1930s, actually, when there were still a lot of farms and a lot of farm hands. Most big farmers had a farm hand and family on about every quarter section, and that adds up to a lot of mouths to feed and shoes to buy. At one time Crowell, the county seat and only real town in Foard County, had a thriving downtown with shoe stores, drugstores, a grocery store and various other outlets besides the *de riguer* farm implement and feed store. The schools had plenty of kids. But, over time, farms got bigger and they became mechanized, and farm hands just went away. They were no longer needed. Stores closed. People started leaving for places like Vernon and Wichita Falls, where there were better jobs. Kids would get out of high school and find absolutely nothing they could do to make a living in Crowell. So, they left. At the time John and his wife lived in Crowell—because she needed to look after a father who was in his 90s and watch over the wheat farm for him—Crowell was down to a few hundred people, most of them old like John. There were just two churches, one for Baptists and one for everyone else. And a preacher came to that church just once a month or so.

The whole situation kept John in a state of apoplexy. He'd taught at the University of Cincinnati and been a dean at Texas Tech, and here he was spending his later years in a two-bit town where you couldn't buy a decent cup of coffee or a one-penny nail. But, that's another story.

After I accepted the invitation to go over to Crowell to be the chamber banquet speaker, I tossed around a lot of ideas in my head. I wanted to make a good speech—for John if nobody else. I didn't want to embarrass him or me. What do you say to the good people of a town that's dying and they know it and they can't be bull-shitted about it? Well, if you're Donald Trump you just go ahead and bullshit them. You tell them that steel is coming back! Coal is coming back! America's coming back! It's all gonna be jelly beans and apple pie! Louis Hyman, director of the Institute for Workplace Studies at the ILR School at Cornell University, has a piece about this very thing in today's Sunday Review section of *The New York Times*. It's called, "The Myth of Main Street," and in it Hyman points out that what Trump is promising, even if delivered upon, would not fix small-town America. Small-town America depended on retail, strong retail, locally strong retail, and Wal-Mart killed that off in the bigger places, and the creeping decay seeped out into the hinterlands from there. Hyman kind of sidesteps the problems that presents in terms of erosion of tax base income and others. Instead, without saying so, he grasps the reality that there are a lot of people who would live in small towns if they could do so and make a living at it not related to things that are not coming back, like retail. In fact, here in 2017 he hits on the very idea I hit on 17 or so years ago: Wire rural America so that everyone who wants to live in a small town has the internet capacity to do so and compete head-to-head with people in the big cities.

It just so happened that I put my speech to Crowell together on the anniversary of the passage of legislation that created the Marshall Plan after World War II. With American dollars, the Plan rebuilt Germany and Japan in blinding speed. Why not, I asked my audience, create a new Marshall

Plan to rebuild rural America? Why can't federal money go to programs that wire up rural communities so their residents can stay put and still have access to the treasures and treasury that the internet provides? Today, that's Hyman's idea, but he doesn't cite the Marshall Plan as precedent. My speech was well-received in Crowell. I printed the whole speech a little later on a Sunday editorial page. I got exactly zero comments from my fellow Wichitans and beyond.

Hillary Clinton is interviewed for today's *Times*. It's a short piece based on a short interview. She says she won't run again. Who could blame her. She also blames the Russian email hacking and the perfidy of that dildo director of the FBI Comey for her loss. This man is a danger to America. Watch out for him. He is worse than Machiavelli. He will stab anyone in the back.

A long piece somewhere else talks about Steve Bannon's outlook, which is based on a dystopian piece of nonfiction that came out in the late '90s. The authors say nations go through four stages that are cyclically repeated, and that we are entering a stage of decline and danger. We'll need to be herded and handled like cattle to keep us from roaming too far from the barn. Bannon apparently sees himself as some sort of visionary cowboy savior of America while ironically shredding what he claims to love. Kind of like burning down the village to save it, *a la* Vietnam.

April 10: Over the weekend, several commentators sobered up long enough to take a long, hard look at the Trump cruise missile attack on a Syrian airbase and to call it for what it was: grandstanding. What will Trump do now? What happens if Assad bombs more children with chemicals? What if some dictator in another part of the world does the same thing? Trump is practicing the presidency as if it were a running videotape of discreet sound bites, each one to be taken separately and apart from others in the stream. We do this here, and we do that there, and we say this now, and we say that then, and none of it is intended to connect in any way that you might expect from the world's most powerful leader, who is, in fact, an inarticulate fool. Krugman in today's *Times* points out once more the false equivalency problems so many idiots in the news media have. They think everything, no matter how inequivalent, has to be balanced. I fought this as an editor many times. It's a hard thing to teach kids who are just coming to journalism out of college, which is what we mainly hired, but you would think that seasoned professionals would know better. They don't.

The Ringling Brothers and Barnum & Bailey Circus is folding up its tent at the end of May, and there is a valedictory of sorts in *The* Times today. If I'm supposed to feel sad or bad about this show going away, well, I don't. The people over at Cirque du Soleil have figured out how to put on a circus for today, and they deserve the audience. Animal cruelty can have no part in entertainment.

April 11: I got up this morning to go for my walk, and it was sprinkling. I went ahead around the corner and it started raining so I turned around and came back and have been sitting here drying off with a warm dog in my lap. We are due to have some heavy rainfall today, and it is very dark outside. We'll see.

Two Wells Fargo bankers have been forced to repay $75 million to the bank for bad behavior, requiring employees to fabricate accounts and make up fees so their books would look better. It's the bank that's taking this action, not the government or anyone else. Notably, I will remind you that after the 2008 housing debacle caused by Wall Street not a single banker was charged with a crime and not a single one went to jail. In fact, many of them were fatly rewarded for their incompetence. The market value of Tesla is now greater than that of General Motors, which is a stunning reminder to us all that people on Wall Street don't know shit about a lot of stuff. Elon Musk, who owns Tesla, is a mighty dreamer, but he is betting on the wrong technology. He's wanting batteries to be the fuel of the future, and they will be only if the government subsidizes his products to make them competitive with automobiles that burn other kinds of fuel. He has a nice little niche product for people who can live with the limitations of his cars. But, to think he adds value to the economy on a par with GM is hysterical.

In our neighborhood and many others in Amarillo, we kids were growing up in the shadows of World War II and knew little about Korea. We hated the Nazis.

Green Hill was an attractive place for all the kids of the neighborhood to play on for several reasons. For one thing, it was far enough away from the residential areas that we could scream our lungs out and not bother a single soul. For another it was grassy and flat, the perfect place to play football. It was so big that several games could be going on at the same time. On the north side of the hill where it met the railroad tracks, there was an underpass that took the train underneath a cross street. The underpass had steeply sloping concrete walls that were wonderful to slide down when covered with ice and snow. If you followed the tracks to parallel Line Avenue toward the west the tracks stayed below ground elevation for several hundred yards, and the water erosion on the walls of this manmade arroyo carved caves into the soil that were great hiding places. We played a lot of football on Green Hill all year long. And up until I was in sixth grade or so, we played a lot of "Army." In this replayed version of World War II, boys from several streets on the Bowie end of Green Hill would meet boys from streets farther away to the west in mock battles that we created out of thin air.

There was an Army surplus store on Georgia Street a couple of miles from where we lived, and for very little money you could outfit yourself with real Army packs, ammo belts, webbing, holsters and helmet liners. If you had a lot of money you could buy a de-militarized weapon of some kind. I had a shotgun that had never been used in any war and that was missing the parts vital to its use as a weapon.

On a Saturday morning, we'd get into our gear and head over to Green Hill to stalk and kill or to be stalked and to be killed by the kids from the west end, who were Nazis to us while we were Nazis to them. Those caves along the tracks were a regular target, but we roamed all over the neighborhood in our regalia reliving the action we'd only heard about second and third hand and see in war movies. When the snow fell and drifted on wintry weekends we'd head for Green Hill to build forts of snow and engage in prolonged battles with snowballs. I remember one fight that pitted John and me against Dwight and Donnie, two brothers who lived right behind us on Crockett Street, and John nailed Dwight right in the center of the forehead with a snowball that had a rock inside. Dwight bled all over the snow and then ran home wailing and holding his head like he'd been shot. When there was a good snow in that part of Amarillo, you'd find all the big metal trash-can lids from the neighboring alleys being deployed on the concrete slopes at the railroad tracks.

I don't think the girls in our neighborhood ever went over to Green Hill.

In general, the area north of Line Avenue, which formed the dead end for all the Texas hero-named streets, was industrial or commercial. Just north of the cave-like erosion features on the railroad tracks was the Navy Reserve Center. Out front were two big deck guns off some World War II warship. Sometimes we'd clamber up on those big steel weapons in our full Army regalia and pretend we were shooting down Jap Zeroes. But in our hearts we were infantry, not Navy, and we didn't play over there very many times. (In fact, I was completely enthralled by the idea of being an infantryman, and I couldn't tell you why. Daddy had been in the Army Air Corps and was base historian at Majors Field in Greenville for most of the Second World War. So, he had no war stories at all. My Uncle Raymond Gray of Greenville had been in the Army Expeditionary Forces in Russia during World War I, but he had never told me any stories even if he had any. My Uncle Gene Brady of Houston had been in the Navy. I don't remember seeing a lot of movies about World War II, and certainly did not see any at the theaters downtown. Maybe it's just that every little boy is fascinated by guns and the idea of using them. Whatever the attraction, from an early age I wanted to be a soldier. Until, of course, it came time to be one.)

April 12: Several makers of over-the-counter drugs are now marketing electrical devices that fit on the back to alleviate back pain. They are all battery operated and have a remote control. I bought one from HEB yesterday for Lynda. It's made by Aleve, and we hooked it up last evening. The protocol is to run the device for 30 minutes at a time, and it runs through a pre-programmed stimulation cycle. We ran through two of the cycles before going to bed, and Lynda said they did nothing for her. That's too bad. We will continue to try that device out, and seek out others. Meanwhile, we have an appointment with her back surgeon later in April to talk about the implantation of a device that would block pain signals in her back. We have both read and heard about pluses and minuses of the procedure. At this point it is worth trying.

I'm not the only person on the planet who thinks it is crazy that Tesla has such a high valuation, higher than GM. I read a blog piece posted by Fortune magazine yesterday by a guy who says that the investors who are driving up the Tesla price and value are heading for the same kind of bubble burst that happened when all the dot.coms went under 15 years ago because they were making things that either didn't exist or didn't make money or were sheer fantasies to begin with. Tesla kind of falls in that latter category.

We watched the second piece in the PBS series about the Great War last night, and it was disturbing, to say the least. The setting was mostly in America after the Congress declared war on Germany in 1917. Woodrow Wilson was so adamant about being right about getting this country into the war he could not stand any—any—comments to the contrary, and so he led Congress to the passage of some of the most outrageously unconstitutional laws ever written for a U.S. legislative body to consider. After one law, even church pastors were jailed for questioning the morality of the war. People were rewarded for telling on their neighbors. Civil liberties just went completely out the window. At the same time, black men were cajoled into joining up to fight and then put in charge of shovel brigades in France because white people were afraid they might learn to shoot straight and bring that particular skill set back to the United States to try to secure for themselves the rights they were prepared to die to defend for the French. Lawd. Lawd.

What otherwise civilized, informed people will put up with when they are fed a huge load of bullshit is just about beyond belief. We have been led to believe that the Germans had some defect culturally or genetically that allowed Hitler to lead them into the hell of World War II, but this movie shows in detail how good old Middle Americans can be hornswoggled into believing their lifelong neighbors deserve to be led off to concentration camps in their own country and without so much as a nod to due process. Unbelievable. So, YES, it can happen again, given the right set of circumstances. As we look around America today we see things being set up to lead us down that terrible path again. There are all too many people in Congress and in the White House who are prepared to sacrifice our freedoms for their dollars at any point in time. For them the Constitution means nothing.

Another reason to carry a revolver? Perhaps. But, seriously, one main reason I have weapons in my house is because I know history. The first people the Trumpists will come after are the professors, other intellectuals, the journalists and the librarians.

Speaking of Trump, now he is accusing Russia of being in bed with the Syrians when it comes to chemical warfare. Well, goshalmighty! Of course this is fakery, a public effort on the part of Trump to pretend that he is somehow alienated from the Russians just at the moment when a few people with a spine in Congress are trying to decide how the Russians funneled money and influence to Trump during the election last year. Nice try at floating a decoy, Donald. But, it won't work.

April 13: John's still looking into 5-shot revolvers for me. I can't pay high dollar like he can. He told me not too long ago, by the way, that he has 53 guns of one sort or another. That would include handguns, shotguns and rifles. The last time he came over he brought me a home-defense shotgun for my own use and several .22-caliber rifles he'd been tinkering with to test out different kinds of sights. He also brought over a lever-action rifle that he said was Joanne's. It was like the rifle used by The Rifleman in the TV show of the same name in the 1950s.

How did the parents and times that produced a liberal like me also produce a right-winger like John?

The last segment of The Great War TV series was on last night, and it was just as disturbing as the others because of what it revealed about Woodrow Wilson and this country's attitudes toward black men who had actually served overseas and fought for the French. Wilson, it turns out, was a reprehensible tyrant intent on stifling any and all opposition to the war, even to the point of stirring up racists and other assorted thugs to punish those who couldn't serve in the armed forces. The sedition laws were designed to have neighbor report on neighbor, turning entire groups of people against one another. It appears to me that Wilson was a megalomaniac just as bad as any others we've seen.

Again, the lessons are there for us to learn, and we ignore them to our peril. How much would it take for the propaganda machine that Trump runs to turn neighbor against neighbor right now? The cops are already at war with black men, and federal thugs are already rounding up brown people to send them trucking back to Mexico or worse. If push comes to shove what will Congress put up with and put forward? And what will the Supreme Court let stand? The way both of these organizations are staffed right now I'd say the odds are good they would suspend due process and civil rights in a heartbeat.

April 14: Yesterday I signed up for a constitutional law class taught by a professor at Yale named Amar. The course is 14 weeks in length, and involves reading a textbook about the Constitution written by the Yale law professor named Amar. No problem. I'll borrow the book through interlibrary loan. For my master's degree in political science I took several classes in constitutional law, most of them taught by Dave Matthis, who did not have a doctorate but who had a great legal mind and was a professor of political science at WT. I enjoyed Dave's classes, and I learned a great deal, but, mygosh, it's been about 45 years since I was in that particular graduate program. It couldn't hurt to review it. The first couple of lessons were interesting. Dr. Amar is passionate about his subject; he clearly loves the Constitution.

The class is offered through an online university affiliate called Coursera. I have taken many online courses packaged for Coursera students, including one about basic physics taught by a full professor at the University of Virginia; one about the music of the Beatles taught by a professor at a New York university; one about Big History taught by a team of professors at a university in Australia; and one about the political legacy of John F. Kennedy by a professor at Virginia; and one about philanthropy by John Peter Singer, professor of philosophy at Princeton. I completed all these classes, and I loved them. They help me keep sharp. I could never have imagined I would be taking classes with some of the big names in these subjects. Of course, the classes are not personalized in the usual face-to-face sense, but if you take advantage of chat rooms you can have one-on-ones with graduate assistants.

As an aside, the years I was studying constitutional law at WT also happened to be years of constitutional crises, the years of Watergate and debates over the limits to presidential power and presidential privilege. It was an electric time to be taking those classes because of the direct relevance of so many events.

One summer of high school I was driving my 1930 Model A Ford sedan, and my neighbor Joe Wirtz offered me a job on a crew that was shingling businesses and houses that had been damaged by a big hailstorm. And when in my senior year I was driving my 1954 Austin Healey, he really did help me build a complete walnut dashboard for the car and install it.

Joe was always dubious about my assertions that my goal in life was to be a mechanic and drag racer. One day I was over at his house, sitting around in the living room, and he was expressing his doubts about what I wanted to do. He asked me: Would you rather take apart a clock and put it back together or read a good book? I lied and told him I'd rather work on the clock. But, actually I would have liked doing both. I didn't see that one had precedence over the other. Joe didn't see it that way, though, not that it made much difference. He lived in his world and helped me in mine, and then I moved on and never really saw Joe after I left Bowie Street and then later started working at the Amarillo paper. He probably congratulated himself on being a good judge of character, though.

April 15: Lynda got up this morning and the first question she asked was, "Are we at war yet?" I had read *The New York Times* by the time she had risen, but, of course, they went to bed with their Texas editions probably around 8 o'clock last night, so there'd be nothing about overnight activities in there. Even now, about 9 a.m., I haven't bothered to look. If we are, we are. We seem to be on a train headed for oblivion regardless of what the people try to do to detour the track. We're living out Steve Bannon's wet dream: the end of civic life as we know it.

See, Trump has sent what he calls "an armada" sailing toward North Korea with the idea of showing their super-sensitive and uber-dangerous child leader who is boss around here. We're Marshall Dillon in the Trumpian mindset, and we are gonna scower the countryside for miles around to make sure all them dogies are safe and the coyotes and scofflaws are kept away. Several U.S. administrations have been just fine with calling North Korea's prevailing leader a kook and an outlaw and letting it go at that. I understand that the new boy-king is bent on developing a nuclear warhead on a missile that can reach Washington State, but I also know we have anti-missile systems in place, and we should have some kind of way to stop North Korea short of sending an armada to his doorstep to call him out and bloody his nose. Because this present Trump scenario will not end in a street fight that we can win. Instead, the boy king will turn his troops and his guns on Seoul, which is just a stone's throw from the 38th parallel, and millions of civilians could be lost in a few terrible days of attack. And then what will Trump have accomplished? His goal is clearly not to solve this problem. It is to make himself the center of world attention and bolster his own self-image as Much Man. This is the work of a megalomaniac and world-class sycophants who sup from his gilded cup. He may sit in Pyongyang but his twin lives in the White House and is far more reckless because of the very real resources at his disposal.

April 16: It's Easter Sunday, and I was up at 6 to get ready to go to church. I handled the audio-visual equipment at both the 8 a.m. and 10:30 a.m. services. Mom would have liked the entirety of it, from the little kids in their finest coming in before the 8 o'clock started to place flowers on the cross at the top of the altar, to the sermon, which was from Mary's perspective, a unique way of looking at the resurrection—from a woman's point of view (our rector and the author of the sermon is a woman).

I'm reading a book called *The Return: Fathers, Sons and the Land in Between* by Hisham Matar. It's this year's Pulitzer Prize winning work of nonfiction.

The book is set in the early 2000s in Libya and Egypt and then New York City and London. In it, Hisham Matar looks for his father, who has been taken captive and possibly killed by Qaddafy. It has taken me some time to get into the rhythm of the book. I am not finished yet. I read what must be a key passage yesterday and marked it for inclusion here:

"To be a man is to be part of (a) chain of gratitude and remembering, of blame and forgetting, of surrender and rebellion, until a son's gaze is made so wounded and keen that, on looking back, he sees nothing but shadows. With every passing day the father journeys further into his night, deeper into the fog, leaving behind remnants of himself and the monumental yet obvious fact, at once frustrating and merciful—for how else is the son to continue living if he must not also forget—that no matter how hard we try we can never entirely know our fathers."

How true that is. I knew of my father, but did not really know him and, sadly, for much of the time did not want to know him. Nor, though, did he know me.

Since it is Easter we will have Laura and Scott and Lyndsay and Bryan and Erin and Sarah and Greyson over for dinner this evening. Lynda really hurt her back yesterday trying to get stuff ready for this event. She went to bed crying, and there was not a single thing I could do to ease her pain.

April 17: Our Easter dinner was uneventful. Bryan and Erin "hid" some plastic eggs in our backyard for Greyson to "find."

The New York Times had a spread over the weekend about the steep decline in the last few years of retail in America. The story was prompted by an acceleration of the trend in the last year or so. Time magazine likewise had a story this last week. Then, this morning Paul Krugman expands on the situation. I quote, in part:

"Consider what has happened to department stores. Even as Mr. Trump was boasting about saving a few hundred jobs in manufacturing here and there, Macy's announced <u>plans</u> to close 68 stores and lay off 10,000 workers. <u>Sears</u>, another iconic institution, has expressed "substantial doubt" about its ability to stay in business.

"Overall, <u>department stores employ</u> a third fewer people now than they did in 2001. That's half a million traditional jobs gone — about eighteen times as many jobs as were lost in coal mining over the same period.

"And retailing isn't the only service industry that has been hit hard by changing technology. Another prime example is newspaper publishing, where employment has declined by 270,000, almost two-thirds of the work force, since 2000."

Lynda and I don't buy much anymore, and what we do buy we order through Amazon and have delivered by UPS or the postal service. I shop that way for two reasons: I can find almost anything I can imagine at Amazon, and I can compare prices for similar products. I can also see reviews by people who have made the same kind of purchase in the past. When I am looking for something at Amazon, I always look at reviews, and I would say that I have changed my mind about a product about half the time because of bad reviews. Why would I go to a retailer where I have to find parking, walk to the store, browse around to find what I want since none of them have floor assistants and then stand in line to check out, all without having any reviews to benefit my search? Yes, I have to wait a day or two to get what I ordered, but I consider that a small inconvenience.

About the only exception I will make is grocery shopping. I like going to HEB. I want to select my own meat and fish, and my own apples and other produce. We have to hope that specialty retail stores continue to be a draw for visitors to Wimberley. Our tax base in Wimberley is completely grounded on retail sales. There is no property tax levied. Likewise, at the library all of our tax income is from retail sales. (And sales have been so strong that the library board has money to burn—except when it comes to employee benefits.)

Krugman's column today was questioning why Trump continues to pretend like the most important sector of the national economy is coal miners when so many other sectors are hurting right now and will be hurting in the future. There are about 65,000 coal miners in the entire freaking country. Let's give all of them $100,000 a year and move on down the road and help people who really need help with things like accessible medical care and meaningful pensions.

April 18: Today we learn that Trump will not, NOT, release his tax returns, and thanks to that there will be no tax reform from Congress. Why would you enact legislation that would turn out only to benefit the president? And not even know it? That's fine with me. I don't care whether there is tax reform talk or not. Nothing that the Congress will ever pass will change the fact that in our America the rich will ever get richer and the poor only poorer. Talk of tax reform is only pandering.

We did not awaken today to a war with North Korea. I think that's still a possibility if not a probability, given the naive ignorance of those who run things in the White House. The dystopian Mr. Bannon would just shrug and say, "I just knew this was going to happen, drat it all." He would say this with a soft snicker.

I have canceled my attendance at the Texas Library Association convention in San Antonio Wednesday through Saturday. Lynda just isn't physically well enough for me to leave her here by herself. And, she wanted to try to get in to see Dr. B., her neurosurgeon, on Wednesday, Thursday or Friday. She desperately wants to have an electronic device implanted in her back so she can eliminate her back pain once and for all. Dr. B. does this kind of surgery, and even though his previous two surgeries on her back have been unsuccessful in stopping the pain, he's her doctor and he knows her situation and he's probably the best guy to go with. I have talked to other of his patients who have had the same surgeries Lynda had, and they are now pain-free. So far nothing has worked.

Besides the surgeries and the failed injection of pain-killers directly into her back by an anesthesiologist we have tried a substance called CDB oil, which is a distillation of cannabis that's supposed to kill back pain. You squirt a few drops under your tongue two or three times a day. We spent $300 on a couple of bottles, and the stuff never worked. All Lynda got out of it was a persistent stomach ache. We will give the rest of the oil away to someone who thinks it will work for them.

A week or so ago I bought an Aleve device that you stick to the back, and it emits some kind of electrical current that is supposed to ease back pain. It's probably snake oil, too. However, after a couple of days, Lynda thought it was helping a little. One interesting side-effect is that she can pee normally again, rather than dribble in the pot. This has been a big deal to her. It makes me wonder if there is something wrong with her bladder that is presenting itself in back pain. I poked around some on the internet yesterday to see what I could find, and nothing pointed me in a clear direction. I probably won't even bring it up to Dr. B. when we see him on Thursday.

April 19: Night before last we watched a very disturbing documentary on PBS about how Monsanto and Dow Chemical and a few other chemical giants have cornered the market on plant seeds to the extent that they almost completely control the world's food supplies. PBS is a small corner of the media universe. I wish this story could get better play elsewhere, but it probably won't.

I have been aware of the growing depth and breadth of this problem for years. You can't have been a newspaperman in farm country without knowing how Monsanto, in particular, took over corn production in America. First, Monsanto developed a miracle weed killer called Roundup. You could spray Roundup on your weeds, and they would go away for a long time. Then, Monsanto set about making a better hybrid corn seed, one that would be immune to the effects of Roundup, so you could spray an entire field and the weed killer would leave corn alone. Then Monsanto patented this seed, and began selling it to farmers with the understanding that they could plant the seed and harvest the corn but could not use the corn to reseed the next crop. Every year they had to buy new corn seed from Monsanto. In effect, this is kin to share-cropping. You are working for The Man in a very real way.

Now, you find that business model in wheat and almost every other crop that's produced around the world. Farmers buy their seed from Monsanto or Dow, and then they cannot reseed with what they produce. The PBS special lamented the decline in diversity that results from this kind of monopoly. Instead of having several varieties of corn seed or rice seed to use to develop crops, only one is sought and sold and bred and kept. The lack of genetic diversity may sooner or later result in disaster because something will come along that can attack the favored variety and there'll be nothing to replace it, according to the show.

The whole situation is worse than that, though, because here the basic food is controlled by a for-profit outfit that in the long run doesn't give a shit whether you starve to death or not. This has not been on the radar of the media because 99 percent of reporters don't cover farm news or agriculture and 99 percent of them did not grow up on a farm or ranch. Neither did the editors. They have no idea how anything related to agriculture works, and it would not surprise me at all if many of them just believed that corn shows up on grocery produce aisles after having gone through a manufacturing cycle in Detroit.

April 20: I've been assigned a series of verses from three books of the Bible to write my next group of devotionals from. I can pick one book. One of them is Wisdom. I'm completely unfamiliar with Wisdom—in any shape or form. I was thinking about it this morning: Who have I known in my life who was truly wise? No one. I cannot think of a single person I would classify as wise. I've known a lot of smart people and a lot of wise guys, though. The more I thought about it, the more I came to this conclusion: It's impossible to showcase the virtues of wisdom when everyone reveres only the vices of ignorance. That statement has particular application to this moment in history, but I surely have known a lot of ignorant people as well. What would a wise person be like? I don't know. Archie Pool might come close: the metals shop philosopher. He was a kind man, a man who was blind to the faults of teen-age boys, encouraging and in touch with the attributes we would need to grow up to be something besides dolts and dumb butts. Would that make him wise? I don't know.

I may just avoid the Book of Wisdom in this exercise and look at the Gospel or the letters of Paul that are also possible to draw on for the devotionals.

April 21: I was up at 6 this morning so I can update this paper, read the newspaper and then head to San Marcos to stand in line to get my driver's license renewed. This is the year I have to get a new photo and an all-new license. That means I have to take the following documents to the license bureau, thanks to the Legislature: a passport, my license to carry a weapon, a Social Security card, a DD 214 to prove I'm a veteran and the receipt for my automobile registration in Hays County. This is all, of course, to try to keep minorities from getting an ID so they cannot vote.

Over the course of the last several months, at least two federal courts have found that the Republican Legislature gerrymandered congressional districts in Texas so as to exclude minority voters and also instituted unconstitutional requirements for people to vote, again an effort to exclude minorities. You did not have to be a federal judge to see all of this going on. The Republicans took over state government in Texas with a vengeance and they don't mind at all doing stupid stuff that will appeal to their racist funders and other assorted misanthropes and ne'er-do-wells.

Not only will I have to take a sheaf of papers to prove I exist so that I can get a license renewed; I will also have to stand in line for hours because this same Legislature won't spend the money to build adequate facilities for a growing state population. They always claim they don't have the money, but they do. They just don't want to spend it rationally. Why not build big prisons when you could, instead, have reasonable drug laws? Big new prisons put money in the pockets of private prison companies and contractors. Strict drug laws just hurt poor people and minorities.

The measure of the irrationality of Texas legislators over time is what they have done to the funding of higher education. I have written earlier about my own experience as an example. The part of the equation that has hurt the most is state aid to higher education across Texas. The burden for paying for college has increasingly fallen on families or individuals. Thus, kids graduate with mountains of debt that they will pay on for years before they are free from it. A rational Legislature would see that it helps out workers and their employers if they spend less time standing in line for state services. The costs are real but hidden.

April 22: Trump and his staff just seem to be making shit up as they go along, over and over again. They are serial shitters. This past week has not been remarkable in that regard. First, you have Spicer, the president's press aide, suggesting that the Nazis didn't gas anybody during World War II, certainly nothing as bad as what Assad has done in Syria. Then he had his long "ooops opportunity" when it was pointed out that the Nazis gassed millions of people in concentration camps during World War II. Then, the president went to Detroit to a tool factory to sign an executive order about jobs that from all reports seems to have the effect of straw in the wind. The factory was run by Snap-On Tools, which has a supply chain that stretches around the world. The point of the Trump order, at least in the telling of his tale, was to stop overseas sourcing and manufacturing. Trump knows so little about so much, it's just hard not to laugh. But, it's crying time in America. Adam Davidson, a writer for the *New Yorker* who covered the Trump show in Detroit, is one among many reporters and authors and experts who point out that the trouble with this country's economy is NOT foreign competition for jobs or even for buyers. He writes:

"There is a real problem in the American economy. For much of the twentieth century, there was a wind at the back of working people—a steady increase in jobs, wages, and opportunity for those with basic education and a willingness to put in a hard day's work. We have shifted from the era of good work for many to the age of the hustle, where those with luck, good connections, education, and ambition can do far better than their grandparents could have dreamt, while those without see their incomes stagnate or fall and face a future filled with doubt. A sober and serious look at the U.S. economy leads, inevitably, to the conclusion that we haven't cracked this problem yet. In place of serious consideration from the White House, we have absurdist, self-contradicting theatrics."

Talk of the Germans' attempt at genocide during the World War wafted in the air last week in conversations at the library. On Wednesday morning, one of the volunteers was talking about a book she just read about the Israeli search for Adolf Eichmann, the Nazi concentration camp commandant. Eichmann was found in Argentina, I believe. Our conversation veered off into how incredible it was that the Nazis were allowed to get by with their slaughter of the different and the Jewish over the course of years. It's not like they operated underground. They herded people right out of their homes into the streets into long lines to board trains to go straight into the maws of hell, and nobody tried to make a run for it. Nobody pushed back. Those movies from those roundups leave me completely slack-jawed. And what about the people who lived right around the block from Dachau and Buchenwald and Treblinka? What the hell did they think was going on just over the other side of the barbed wire? Patty cake? Basket-weaving? Many years ago I went through the Holocaust Museum in Washington, D.C., and it was a horrifying experience just to be a witness so many years later. Absolutely beyond belief. Our talk then veered off into how and when you tell children about the Holocaust. They must know about it. All of it. But when? I don't know, but I will ask D'Arcy.

The visit to San Marcos DPS office to renew my driver's license began yesterday at 7:15 a.m. when I left the house for the trek over there. I got to the office about the time it opened at 8. There were already 20 or so people who had beat me through the front door. I took a number, filled out my form and prepared to wait until, oh, 11 o'clock. Instead, I was pleasantly surprised to be in and out with my paperwork completed by 9 a.m. Thanks to someone, the state has added people to the process, and there are now five stations where you can get assistance instead of two or three.

April 23: Because of some soccer or hockey game going overtime last evening, we ended up watching ABC news at 5:30 instead of NBC. I'm not sure it would have made much difference in the lineup, but it might have. ABC put in its first five minutes or so a story about Trump and family making a trek— for the first time!— over to the Bethesda hospital where the president pinned a Purple Heart on a U.S. war veteran wounded in Iraq or Afghanistan. A Purple Heart. The man trekked across the street to put a Purple Heart on a wounded veteran? And that's news? Not hardly. That's news management of the first order, and the poor schmucks at ABC fell for it. When the president farts, that is not news, people! If he is shot in the head on his way to Bethesda to pin a medal on a soldier, that's news, for Christ's sake. National media just have to do a better job at judging what to air out of the White House and what not to air. Their time is valuable and ought not to be devoted to a photo op of the most venal sort. Then, much later in the newscast we learn that 30,000 people, at least, marched on Washington to protest Trump's anti-science initiatives. Good grief.

The New York Times today has a whole spread devoted to what Trump policies and appointments will do to the environment – not today, but the day after tomorrow, almost literally. It's entirely possible that this legacy won't play out for our grandchildren, but for us! Our air will get worse. Our rivers will be more polluted. Our shores will shrink. Will that make Americans any more anxious about where we are headed on this Trump train to Hades? Probably not.

I sent an email to D'Arcy the other day asking her about when the girls will learn (did learn) about the Holocaust. I'm worried that as these events surrounding World War II fade into the distant past we will lose sight of the horror of it all and the lessons to be learned. D'Arcy wrote me back saying that the girls learn a little about the death camps and Nazism in fifth and sixth grades, and then in junior high they read "The Diary of Anne Frank" and another book on the Jewish genocide. I'm glad to hear that. They must understand what happened and why and what the world did in response.

April 24: Chi-Chi has fleas. Lynda bathed her on Saturday and she was OK for a while. I vacuumed the carpet, and we washed her blankets. I got almost no sleep Saturday night. Then she started really scratching herself yesterday. She got another bath. I vacuumed the carpet again, and we put the blankets in a hot dryer. Last night she woke me up three or four times scratching, and I finally got up at 5:45. I just gave up trying to get any sleep. I got her out of bed after Lynda yelled at me about 7 o'clock, and she is still itching like crazy. We will have to do something today.

Donald Trump is supposed to announce his tax reform plan by

Wednesday. Since nary a soul in his administration has a clue what he plans to do, it will be more than entertaining to see what he proposes. Let me guess: Big tax breaks for the rich so they will invest more and create jobs! The very same failed plan that Republicans cling to even in Kansas where this very package was made the law of the plains to the utter dismay of all those Kansans who are out of work and who shuttered their businesses because the Big Rich just took the money from their tax breaks and put it into the bank in the Caymans.

April 25: Today we learn via *The Times* that Trump plans to give big rich folks a tax rate of 15 percent, down from 35 percent. We don't know how his tax program will treat everyone else, but we do know that if that kind of tax cut is enacted for the wealthy, government will need to be cut by trillions of dollars. And we know what will NOT be cut: the military and anything that helps big investors. On Sunday, the *Times* published a spread of photos with short bios on the influential people Trump has surrounded himself with in an advisory capacity: All old white men with two exceptions. All businessmen or investors. Yesterday NPR reported that the Department of State has posted on its website what amounts to an advertisement for Trump's Florida "White House," a golf club and motel. This is literally taking the emoluments clause out of the Constitution and pissing on it in the gutter of Pennsylvania Avenue.

Meanwhile, The Pew Research Center studied the finances of the so-called middle class and found that it is – surprise! – shrinking. To quote one expert, who summarized the findings:

"It's a clear trend that the middle class in the U.S. is shrinking and not keeping up financially with the upper-income group," he said. "There is an aura of redistribution of income from middle income to upper income."

Robert M. Persig, author of "Zen and the Art of Motorcycle Maintenance," died yesterday. He was in his 80s. I read the book when it first came out in 1974, and re-read it a number of times over the years, most recently this year when I ordered a copy in paperback online. I did some research over the weekend for the devotionals I was assigned to write for church. I decided to use as the basis for them some readings from the Book of Wisdom. This book is not in Protestant Bibles, but is in the Catholic Bible and the one we use in the Episcopal church. Several scholars I looked at in my review compared some of the philosophical roots of Wisdom in the thinking of the Stoics, who would have been rough contemporaries of the Jewish author of Wisdom. The Stoics were rationalists, realists, and they believed in the power of reason. There are still websites out there devoted to Stoicism. Persig's book looked at the role of reason and also the role of unreason in describing modern life. The motorcycle's maintenance was a kind of stand-in for how to think about life and a rational way to approach it. On the other hand the pleasure offered by the bike's performance and the delight of riding the bike on the open road filled in the experience of living in that particular realm. What I have taken away from the book is the joy of living a life that is in the pursuit of something integrated, not wholly the result of the reasoning mind and not wholly the result of the passionate mind, an amalgamation of those elements. The result

116

can be a Quality life, a life truly lived.

I waited until sunset last night and then put on shorts and lousy shoes and went out and sprayed the front and back yards and porches with a flea killer I found at Ace Hardware. Bryan said it is the best to use for that purpose.

April 26: We took Chi-Chi to the vet yesterday and got a pill that supposedly killed all the fleas on her body. The cleaning lady came and went through the house like a hurricane. She vacuumed the carpet in the living room three times with her high-powered sweeper. We have done everything we can to get rid of the damn fleas, and I'll be darned if Chi-Chi didn't spend half the night itching and scratching. Maybe that's because of residual bites that bother her. I hope so; I have no idea what else we could do to protect her. She is in my lap right now and is being calm. She may just be tired out from all the work of scratching herself.

Trial balloons were released yesterday by the Trumpistas on his tax plan. It's nothing more than trickle-down revisited. It's never worked and never will, but there you go. Put a super-rich man in charge and he knows nothing but how to be a rich man. Today, he released the whole plan. It's a little hard to see how the coal miners of West Virginia are gonna like the tax cuts for the wealthy program, but they're too stupid to find a job so what can you expect?

April 27: A disabled Army sergeant, probably badly hurt in Iraq, used to live around the corner and down from us here in Wimberley. He moved to Houston, or that's what his brother told me. He left behind a 1965 Mustang, which I had seen parked in his garage for quite some time. The brother must have gotten the "sell" order because the car now sits over in the parking area facing Winter's Mill Parkway in front of First Baptist Church. Today, it was back in the driveway at the house with a handwritten sticker on the window. I stopped on my walk to see what it said. The car is yellow and looks original. The sticker ways it's a 289, three-speed, all just as it was when it was in the showroom 52 years ago. The price actually took my breath away: $45,000 "or best offer."

Donald Trump rolled out a one-page tax reduction plan yesterday so he could say he had made his proposal within the first 100 days of his presidency, a silly thing to do. It had no details whatsoever. No mention at all of where the budget would be cut or the deficit grown to pay for the cuts, most of which benefit the wealthy and, in particular, real estate developers like, well, Donald J. Trump and his son-in-law Jared Kushner. By the way, it seems that Jared's family's enterprises have benefited over the years from huge cash infusions from an Israeli guy who has been suspected of or accused of criminal activities in several countries. Birds of a feather …

April 28: The Trumpistas released their "tax plan" yesterday, and it is a complete joke. One page. No details. There are tax cuts for everyone on his one-page proposal. But, the biggest cuts are for their buddies in the 1 percent. Worse news: The Republicans who feign heart attacks when someone wants to increase their precious budget deficit are acting like they take the Trump plan seriously by saying that they no longer care about deficits! The entire group in Washington needs to be sent home, then tarred and feathered. These people don't care about the country; they care about themselves.

The contrast between the Washington of today and the Philadelphia of 1787-89, when our founding fathers were discussing the details of a Constitution to propose for adoption by the people of the 13 states, has never been more stark. Back then, every word carried the weight of a new nation, every comma was placed with care, every concept debated. The men who framed the Constitution knew well what terrible lies men could tell, what terrible deeds they could do, all to enrich themselves and their families. So, they tried to build in as many checks and balances as they could. They even conceived of someone like Trump being in the White House, but I'm not sure they figured on a Congress that would not hold him at all accountable on anything. The judiciary may be our only hope, and thank goodness there are still some federal judges out there who will put duty above party affiliation. This new man Gorsuch: We shall see what he is made of. I think on all of this as I continue taking an online course offered by Yale on the American Constitution. I took Constitutional Law when I was in graduate school, as I have mentioned. But, this refresher looks more at the document itself and not the law developed in challenges to it. I got the book for the class through inter-library loan and have started reading it. It's well done.

Story of the day in the *Times* is buried back inside in one outside column. It's the story out of Spain about how researchers are learning about a caterpillar that can eat and digest plastic. A Spanish scientist who is also a bee-keeper found these worms eating through her hives' beeswax. She rounded some up and put them in a plastic bag, and they ate their way out. Her fellow researchers ground some of the worms up and spread the resulting paste on plastic to see if the worms were just eating the plastic or whether they contained an enzyme that was digesting plastic. The latter seems to have been the case. That means at some point down the line the DNA will be extracted from the caterpillar and put into a bacterium and then mass produced to deal with our exploding mountains of plastic that take uber-eons to deteriorate and become benign.

Trump is not going to the White House correspondents dinner this weekend. None of his staff will be there, either. Now, these journalists should just cancel the whole sordid event. The *Times* doesn't support this display or egomania and for good reason: Readers wonder what these reporters will do for fame and fortune, and it may not always be in pursuit of the truth or what's best for people to know.

When I think back on influences that made me what I am, I start with family, of course, but also with Lee Bivins Elementary School.

At Lee Bivins, we children sat at a long lunch table with our teachers at the head. Before setting our trays down and taking a seat, we were obliged to sing "The Doxology" or "We Gather Together to Ask the Lord's Blessing." (At the start of every school day, we stood at our desks and said the Pledge of Allegiance and then recited from memory a Bible verse. The teacher would vary the sequence of who was called upon first, because the first kid was always going to recite the shortest verse in The Bible: "Jesus wept." There was very little separation of church and state at Lee Bivins. We even had a fish-only menu on Fridays out of respect for the Catholics among us, although I only knew one Catholic family, the Campbells, whose choice of faith was made manifest by the number of Campbell children, which was five.) Once we had taken our seats, we were obliged to sit there until we had eaten at least three bites of every item on our plates.

I suppose I would still be sitting there had it not been for paper napkins. When the teacher was not looking, I would scoop whatever happened to be the offensive portion of the day into the napkin, slip that into my jeans pocket and then toss it all into the bushes at the door leading out of the cafeteria to the playground after putting up my tray. This process of disposal became infinitely easier when the school got rid of glass bottles for our milk and brought in paper cartons. Then it was possible to drink all the milk and stuff brussels sprouts into the carton and just toss it into the garbage without anyone knowing anything different.

Week in and week out the food situation at school never improved. It was almost uniformly and always inedible.

When I was in sixth grade, along in the spring time, several of us decided that the cafeteria food was so bad we needed to make a statement. So, we got the word out that on a particular day all the kids should bring their lunches or go home at the appointed hour. If no one showed up in the cafeteria, teachers and Miss Boyles, the principal, would certainly notice, and maybe things would get better. The other ring leader in this plan was Kay Stinson, who had a big sister or two who may have egged us on. Perhaps we were influenced by what we were seeing on television, striking workers, sit-ins, calls for improvements in civic live. I don't know, but we got the idea of a strike somewhere. On the designated day, Mrs. Dalby, my first-period teacher, asked for a show of hands for those who would be eating in the cafeteria. When no hands went up, she shook her head and said, "Uh-oh. There's going to be trouble." Kay Stinson and I went to Taylor's Pharmacy for lunch, and when we got back I got called out into the hallway (not into her office!) by Miss Boyles, who told me how disappointed she was in me. She said I had been nominated for a Danforth Award, which meant something at the time, but she would not let my name go forward because of my leadership in the strike. The Danforth business meant nothing to me, and as long as my parents didn't know what I'd done I couldn't have cared less. Nothing improved in the cafeteria, though.

April 29: Page after page in *The Times* today is devoted to the first 100 days of the Trump administration. There is a bottom line: Nothing much has been done. His little tax plan ruse didn't work this week; everyone knew it was a joke. I think there is probably another more important scorecard that nobody seems to be keeping, and that is how much damage has he done in the first 100 days. I would say the damage is significant – from Ivanka's jewelry sales to his refusal to divest himself of investments that bring in millions from stuff he owns to his Russian election connection to his reckless talk about North Korea and Syria and Yemen to his choices for various Cabinet positions, most of whom are in charge of tearing up what years of bipartisan work have built, from education to environmental protections. Tally all of that up and you get a very large number indeed.

The story of the day is a 1A piece about the death of Florence French, a woman born in the Philippines of a Filipino mother and American father. She worked for the Japanese during World War II, sabotaging their fueling systems on the islands to direct gasoline and jet fuel to opposing forces, then snuck supplies into prisoner camps, and then was imprisoned for her work. She was liberated in

February 1945, came to America and joined the Coast Guard! She lived quietly and modestly and was only recently recognized for her actions during the war.

Time Magazine will go on without being purchased after months of speculation. Nobody wants to buy the outfit, and who can blame them?

A 1A story also tells us about how Mexican drug cartels keep killing journalists. The record is broken every month. I knew journalists along the border, including the ME of the El Paso paper, and I have wondered how they slept at night. I never did ask them.

If not the geographic center of my neighborhood at least the center of attention was Lee Bivins school, named for the very wealthy family upon whose ranch the entire housing subdivision had been built. The elder Bivinses lived just a couple of blocks south of the school in a huge Tudor-style home on several acres. The estate was two or three houses and out-buildings, and to the west of that property was St. Andrew's Episcopal Church, widely acknowledged to be the Bivins family's very own worship facility.

I started first grade at Lee Bivins in 1953 and finished there in 1959. The neighborhoods that fed Lee Bivins were stable, so the kids I started school with were the kids I finished with and then were the kids I graduated from Amarillo High School with. My first-grade teacher was Ida Lee Cope, a single woman whose age I could not possibly have guessed. She was a strict woman who believed, first of all, in the power of reading.

I may have known how to read when I started first grade. Mom used to say that I started reading early on her lap and Daddy's. I do remember them reading to me a lot. Dad was the best reader. I loved sitting in his lap while he read through the tales of Uncle Remus and adapted his voice to act out each of the characters. We had a lot of children's books in the house, and, of course, Dad read two newspapers every day, one thrown in the morning and one thrown in the afternoon. On Saturdays, we would go to the Mary E. Bivins Memorial Library on Polk Street in downtown Amarillo (there's that name again), and I would spend the morning in the children's section pulling out and reading books at random. On the hottest of mid-summer days the library, which had no air-conditioning, would be a comfortable place. The wooden floor was cool. The library seemed to embrace me and treated me kindly and without judgment or rebuke. I loved the place. So, I probably naturally slipped onto the right track at school, and I was rewarded by Miss Cope by being named a helper to sit with kids who couldn't read yet and encourage them.

I think at this point I probably need to digress to talk about something that affected my first-grade year and that might, in fact, have affected my entire life. At some point when I was 4 or just turning 5 I started waking up in the middle of the night sopping wet from sweat. Regardless of the temperature in my room, I woke up every night wet from head to toe. Before long, Mom and Dad took me to Dr. John Pickett, a relatively new pediatrician in Amarillo who had discovered that John had rickets when the boy was just a baby who cried through every waking hour, so he was well trusted. One evening Dr. Pickett came to our house and sat in the living room while he told my parents that I had primary tuberculosis. I was "hiding" at the time behind a big chair no one was sitting in, so I overheard the conversation without understanding anything other than that it was about me and it was serious because Mother was crying. The decision was made to put me into the Amarillo Preventorium for Children, located in the north part of Amarillo adjacent to the Heights and south of Thompson Park.

April 30: Chi-Chi had a bad night; storms blew through from the west at intervals all night long. When Chi-Chi doesn't sleep, I don't sleep, and I had to get up with the alarm at 6 o'clock anyway, which kept me up waiting for the alarm to go off because I can't actually hear the alarm itself but Lynda can and she kicks me when it goes off, which is just as good as the real thing, let me tell you.

Lynda had a bad evening last night. She took plenty of wine and pot and I think that did let her go to sleep.

May 1: Of course, I had no understanding of the conversation between my parents and Dr. Pickett on the evening he came over to talk about me and tuberculosis. I'm sure they were skeptical and asked for other opinions before taking the drastic step of putting me into a dedicated facility for children with the disease. I'm sure they wondered where in the world I might have contracted tubeculosis, which was still prevalent in the early 1950s. The germs were airborne, so I could have picked up on a sneeze at church or at a movie, although I don't think we went to movies much until I was older. Ultimately, they did take me to the Preventorium, and I held onto Daddy's legs and refused to let go when the nurses came for me in the foyer. It must have killed Mom and Dad to watch their little boy disappear behind doors and also to know they would not be able to hold him or talk to him for seven months. They suffered additionally from the approbation of my grandmother and Daddy's brothers and sisters, who never went along with the decision to put me into the Preventorium. Mother told me much later in life that she was singled out in particular for their anger over this and never felt part of the family after that, which was a very long time. Perhaps that's why she almost never went with us to Greenville for Christmas or for summer vacation.

I have very few memories of my time at the Preventorium. I was bed-ridden in a ward. The heads of the beds were up against a wall and the facing wall had windows that were slits set almost at the ceiling, so you could not see out, but you could know whether the sun was shining. The slits were wide and deep enough that when the rose bushes outside grew up the wind would blow them against the window screen making a scraping sound. For a while a boy was in the bed next to mine, an older boy, and at night he would tell me the scratches were of witches trying to get into our hospital. He successfully terrified me, and for some time after I got older I tried to remember his name so I could look him up and … what? Get some kind of revenge? I don't know …

For the entire time I was in the Preventorium, I had one day nurse. She was a short woman with braided hair that she pulled across the top of her head in an elaborate bun. I have since seen this hairdo on Scandinavian women, so I'm tempted to say she was from Norway or Sweden. She had no accent, however. I cannot recall her name. I could for a while, but then lost it along the way. Every morning she would bring me toast and eggs for breakfast, and then she would bring lunch. I could not move out of bed without her carrying me. At one point, I was put into the ward with the girls, which caused a ruckus among the boys and me a lot of embarrassment. I guess I thought at the time that there was some mix-up because my name was Carroll.

Eventually, I was allowed to go for lunch at the cafeteria, which was in a separate red-brick building, and I was excited to get dressed in normal clothes and to walk hand-in-hand with my nurse over to the building. But when I got to the doorway, I got a whiff of cooked cabbage, and it made me sick at my stomach, which was probably already unsettled by the anticipation of doing something new, and I threw up right in the doorway and had to go back to my bed and never got to go to the cafeteria again. One time I was allowed to play outside on the hill beside the red buildings, and the warmth of the sun on my face and the lilt of the breeze on my cheeks and the sweet song of the meadow lark lifted my spirits. Even today, I can hear a meadow lark and be taken immediately back to that hill and that day. One Sunday, Mom and Dad brought John out to see me at the Preventorium, and I was able to see him through the glass of the front door and to try to touch his hands with mine. For my birthday, Mother made cherry pies for the kids in the ward, and we were allowed to be together in a room that was long and skinny. I was released from the Preventorium after seven months, and that must have been in the summer before I started first grade in 1953.

May 2: Mother told me when she lived with Lynda and me and I asked her to review that time period that when I got out of the Preventorium she and I were shunned by the people at First Presbyterian Church. She would show up at things with me in tow and she would either be politely asked to leave or the crowd language of the people would signal their desire for us to be gone. Old friends of hers and Dad's also stayed away. I do remember walking down Bowie street way across 10th to visit a friend and having his mother meet me at the front door to tell me she would like for me to go away. In first grade, I had a lot of nosebleeds. I have no idea whether they were related, and I don't know how Miss Cope or the other students reacted. I just had them and they cleared up and we went on down the road.

When I think back on the Preventorium experience, I feel sorry for that little boy. Odd that I would see him not as part of me but as someone else. Maybe that's a way you deal with this kind of unusual situation, a long-enforced separation just at the time when you are so dependent on your parents and family. In 2010 or so I had a chance to go through some free psychological counseling because I was editing a book for a once-prominent psychiatrist in Temple. As part of that process I told him about the Preventorium, and asked him if he thought the experience might have affected me in some permanent way. He said, "Of course." But, then he didn't say how! Good lord. What might I have been like if I hadn't been in the hospital for seven months?

For a while several years ago I thought about doing a book about the Amarillo Preventorium, trying to supplement my meager recollections with some from other people who might have been there or had relatives who were there. I ran an ad in the Amarillo newspaper looking for folks, and nobody responded. I also made a special trip up to Amarillo to scout out the old buildings on the Preventorium campus. They had been torn down, and the only thing standing at that time were some city out-buildings. I gathered newspaper clippings from the

Amarillo paper, and they told something of the history of the place and the people who had founded it. I still have those. On that trip up there I talked with Dr. Pickett. He told me that he had discarded all of his patients' records just the summer before my visit with him, and he had no memory of my case out of all the thousands he had treated during his long tenure as a pediatrician. I thought maybe there would be some records about the Preventorium at the city or the public health unit or at the West Texas State history archives or the museum archives or, well, somewhere! But I couldn't find anything beyond the newspaper stories. I spent several days looking through records at the Texas State Archives and found some references to other preventoriums or sanitariums in Texas, but not one thing specifically about the Amarillo facility. A nurse with a PhD named Connolly has written pretty extensively about the "preventorium movement" in America, but she doesn't get to the state or local levels.

The most stunning thing I learned in all my research was this: **The preventorium existed not to help me get well, but to keep me away from people so they wouldn't get sick.**

We have made it through the 100th Day Celebrations of the Trump administration and the man has not been sanctified and crowned. Yet. His minions are busy undoing absolutely everything they can that was achieved by President Obama across the board. Yesterday, we learned that Scott Pruitt, the dumbass who is in charge of the EPA, has ordered his agency to take down from its websites anything having to do with climate change. This kind of revisionism smacks of Stalin and Hitler. He will rewrite science to fit his narrow industry-dictated view of things.

Yesterday, Trump "reached out" to the dictator of the Philippines to see if the guy might want to come to D.C. for a visit. This Duterte kills his own people with impunity. He never heard of due process. Yet, the president wants to be friends. He simply has no idea that there are nuances involved in governing for a reason.

May 3: All the librarians gathered yesterday morning to celebrate my 70th birthday at the library. They had bought a big blueberry pie from the Wimberley Pie Company, and Carolyn made some banana pudding. It was all very nice.

I finished reading a book about Christianity as practiced today by a guy in Oklahoma City named Meyers, and he is strongly, very strongly critical of this belly-button-gazing form of the faith. So many events today seem to require a real response, it seems irresponsible to sit back and do nothing, which is what we are doing. What should a church do to hold the faith against the likes of Donald Trump? What about the Republican Congress that cares not a whit about the poor and disenfranchised? The rich who are making off with our democracy so that their pockets will be further lined? An administration that cozies up with demagogues and despots around the world? A large portion of the electorate so ignorant that they cannot see that they are having their pockets picked and their futures mortgaged by oligarchs?

Lynda has talked with the wife of one of her cousins about back problems. S.L. has had tremendous back issues for years and years. She is apparently in nearly constant pain, and her husband stays in New Mexico to get away from her.

S. told Lynda it is OK to once in a while take a strong pain-killer, of which we have some remaining from our surgeries. I encourage Lynda to do the same thing when the pain gets so bad. She should not have to suffer like she has several days recently.

May 4: Last evening Lynda and I were watching a little television after supper, and the wind picked up noticeably. It was whistling down the chimney, which sets Chi-Chi on edge. I looked through the trees out the front door and the sky was a rosy, orangey, yellowy color with a slight tinge of dark gray. It was so much like what I have seen in the Panhandle when a dust storm is blowing through that I almost swallowed my tongue. I pointed it out to Lynda and she agreed that it was a frightening sight. I could almost feel my asthma creep up on me, and that is a kind of scary that feeds upon itself and can actually end up in an asthma attack.

The FBI director, James Comey, testified to Congress yesterday that he just had to tell them about Hillary's email right before the election last year because of devotion to duty. I say, bullshit. He certainly did not feel equally compelled to share what the FBI was doing about checking into Russia's hacking of the election on behalf of Donald Trump. The man is a danger to this country, perhaps not on a par with J. Edgar Hoover, but cut out of the very same cloth. What he has shone right out in public is what Hoover would only show in private: His willingness to use the power of his office and that of his men and women to undo any career or initiative, given the chance.

The New York Times reports this morning that first-quarter performance of its print division is off yet again. The print version of The Times is doomed; it is just a matter of a few years before it will be history. Meanwhile, the digital version is growing. In announcing the quarterly results, the newspaper's leadership employed the kind of nonsensical double-speak that tells me they either don't understand what they are saying or they are deliberately lying to keep their stock price up. These boys said that they are committed to a strong digital news product, but because the print paper is going downhill they will continue to make cuts in the newsroom. Right now, the digital product is simply a reconstitution of the paper product. What you see in print you see online. So, how will you improve the digital product if you cut the number of people who produce the print product that is the foundational instrument of your success regardless of platform?

I know from experience that it takes more, not fewer, people to produce an online and print newspaper, as well as different kinds of people. At some point I guess this will dawn on them, but it will dawn on subscribers sooner and by then it may be too late for management to, as usual, make a vain effort to recover.

In Sunday's book review section there was a short piece on a new book about George Washington. The book is called, "The Wonder of the Age," and it is by John Rhodehamel, published by Yale University Press. Here is the only quote about content: "Rhodehamel contends that a tension between ambition and reluctance to serve produced Washington's greatness. He eagerly sought out commands early in his career, but he hesitated to assume the presidency and could not wait to be free of it. In office, he used his tremendous prestige to consolidate American nationhood at an uncertain moment." The picture of Washington that emerges from the professor who is teaching the course on The

Constitution that I'm taking online from Yale is, of course, more substantial. Washington was so trustworthy, so smart, so knowledgeable, so courageous, a man of such moral character that when the founders thought of the presidency of these United States, they pictured George Washington and nobody else. How different are things today.

Turns out that Trump is so high on Duterte because his kids have a deal working in the Philippines for a new hotel, and he needs Duterte's support. Unbelievable.

Lee Bivins Elementary School was a two-story brick building of the old kind set on a full city block on 15th Street. You had a pretty good mix of kids, none of whom were black or Hispanic, and none of whom were poor, some of whom were wealthy and most of whom were just white-bread middle class. I knew one girl of Asian extraction, Mary Moc, who was in my first-grade class. Her father was a physician. I knew one Jewish kid, and I can't remember his name right now. Everyone else was Catholic or Protestant. The principal was a white-haired single woman named Ola Boyles. She didn't have much to do with me, because most of the time I was not in enough trouble to have to go to her office. Her secretary was Miss Crouch, who we called, of course, Miss Grouch. She did new-student interviews, and she asked me as I entered first grade whether I ever drank coffee or tea. When I answered that I did not, she seemed to doubt me. "Not even iced tea?" she asked. I had never had a glass of iced tea in my life, and hot tea was completely beyond my comprehension. I learned to read fairly quickly and was called upon by Miss Ida Lee Cope to help her with a group of slower readers. I must have been able to pull this off without making these kids feel bad because I don't recall feeling any hostility from them.

May 5: Miss Cope seemed like a very old, severe woman when I was in first grade. But, one thing is certain: She taught me how to read and how to love reading. If she did nothing else, that was enough. Later in life I met her at a funeral, and she seemed like an older lady then although she told me she was about to get married for the first time. She was still teaching first-graders. I had Mrs. Dalby for art and music. She was a big-boned woman with a hearty laugh. And she actually had a feeling for what kind of music the boys in her classes would enjoy singing. We learned The Air Force Anthem, for example (at'em boys, give 'em the gun!). When I was writing for Accent West magazine in the 1970s, I wrote a vaguely antiwar story about Amarillo, and I hit Mrs. Dalby pretty hard for teaching us those war-era songs. I feel bad about that now, because all she was trying to do was come up with something we would have a feeling for. She was actually pretty intuitive, because in elementary school we were definitely still thinking about killing the Nazis and the Commies.

For a long time I have traced my math-phobia to Mrs. Mathis, but it was probably something other than her efforts. Over the years I have really wanted to be able to do math, but I don't possess some undefinable something that lets me get it. I can understand broad concepts, big sweeps, but not the nitty-gritty of numbers. Oddly enough, I must have the gene for math because Mom was an accountant and a good one. Later in her life, she was so sharp at business books that she would go into failing companies and figure out how to fix them and then

125

do just that.

The House passed a revised version of the Affordable Care Act yesterday, finally giving Trump and Paul Ryan, the chickenshit speaker of the House, a victory they could brag about, which is sort of like getting up in front of the church every Sunday and announcing while thumping one's chest that one more time you didn't get up that morning and beat your wife. The bill if passed into law will – surprise – benefit the rich and hurt the poor. The Senate is unlikely to approve of it, though.

Just in case you need affirmation that I'm not off base when it comes to analyzing what's going on in America's print news media these days, let me present here a quote from Dan Rather, interviewed recently in *The New York Times Sunday Magazine*: "The crisis (in journalism) now centers on trying to make the transition from old media to new media – and then the second-most-important part of it is the changing dynamics of journalism as a business. What's happened is that nobody – well, with very few exceptions – has come up with a new business model that can sustain the most important kinds of journalism, like investigative reporting and first-class international coverage. To be a journalist is to be in a tradition, not a profession."

I wish I had the chance to ask Dan Rather who he means when he says that there are a few folks who know the business model that will produce good investigative reports, international reporting and money for the boss. I don't know who that is.

Trump recently called the dictator of Turkey to congratulate him on being able to consolidate his power after an obviously fixed election. This man Erdogan is nothing but another tin-horn tyrant in the mold of Mussolini, Tojo, Stalin, Peron, etc. The *Times* magazine published April 16 had an article about life in Turkey under Erdogan before the election, and it was a horrid place to be an intellectual or to question government. Thousands of people have been detained, jailed and tortured. Judges and prosecutors have lost their jobs. Policemen have been fired. Governors have been run off. Passports have been canceled so these marked men and women can only stay at home and worry about when the jackboots will knock down their doors and haul them off to prison. There is no freedom of speech or press. The script that Erdogan is reading from is the same one that animated his spiritual forebearers, the Hitlers of history. This is a man Trump admires and thinks enough of to contact upon the solidification of his iron-fisted rule.

May 6: The news today reports that the government announced that an unemployment rate for April that is at 4.4 percent. That's essentially full employment. Maybe even those pesky coal miners in West Virginia and Pennsylvania were able to find jobs! But, I do wonder about the veracity of the number. If the Trumpistas will have no shame when they take down climate data from the EPA website, why would they be any more likely to tell the truth about a key economic indicator? The answer is that they wouldn't. I suspect that we will find, after the dust settles, that we can trust no numbers and no information that comes out of the Trump executive branch. We have known for a long time that Congress just makes shit up, so that's two branches of government with zero credibility. We'll see how Gorsuch does on the Supreme Court that's already loaded with right-wingers.

I would have to say I got a darn good education at Lee Bivins Elementary. The teachers there set me up to be a good reader, a good writer and a good thinker. They didn't do too well in the mathematics department, but maybe that wasn't all their fault.

But, I really learned how to think from my dad. He read widely and he analyzed issues, and he had me reading widely, too, and asking questions. He never had a problem with answering them. And, probably most importantly, he made me do for myself. If I wanted money I had to make it. If I wanted to go to the movies, I had to make the money. Later, if I wanted to go to college, the financing was up to me.

So as a kid I was always looking for ways to make money.

May 7: We had a wonderful birthday celebration here at the house yesterday. John and Joanne came over from Kerrville, and John brought me a .17-caliber rifle that I can use for target practice. I'd been hoping to get one. It's what's called a varmint rifle, used to shoot squirrels and rabbits. I won't do that, but will have fun with it. Becca brought Trent, who was a very sweet and happy young man. I really got to see his personality shine through. Sarah came in from Austin, and Ian showed up. Scott drove over a little later from Canyon Lake. The Duncans came in from New Braunfels. They brought me the new book by Elizabeth Warren, who might make a run for the presidency in the future. The star of the show was Bryan, who brought six (6!) slabs of ribs and two briskets. Wow. The food was wonderful. Lynda had made some baked beans and Becca and I made potato salad. Lynda and I made banana pudding Saturday morning. All in all, a great birthday.

A long story in *The Times* today talks about how Apple may have hit its peak in the stock market because of lackluster growth in its sales. They are about 4 percent year over year, which Lord knows is not enough to keep the stock market happy. Still, it's the most valuable company on the planet. Oh, and it does not pay taxes in the United States. It parks its money off-shore and avoids paying taxes at all. But, the author notes, Apple might come back and pay some taxes if the U.S. lowers the corporate rate to 15 percent as proposed by Trump. I wonder why it would agree to pay 15 percent when it bears no penalty anywhere for not paying anything.

Another story reports that the sister to Ivanka Trump's husband is busy making deals around the world on the promise of getting her business colleagues in with the White House. This is now business as usual in Washington.

In its op-ed pages, the *Times* announces the hire of a fact-checker, that is, someone other than a copy editor. The fact-checker is a 24-year-old. She is very smart. She is all alone in trying to keep politicians and other congenital liars honest. Needless to say, she faces not just an uphill battle but one that is vertical. She may be joined by others sooner or later, but by then there won't be any facts to check because they will have been Trumpized.

May 8: It's my actual birthday, but most of the celebrating is over.

No doctor appointments this week!

The Republicans' health-care bill continues to draw well-deserved fire from across the political spectrum. In today's *Times*, both Charles Blow and Paul Krugman view it with alarm and disgust. Blow writes something I could have written: "Once again, the party that is vehemently 'pro-life' for 'persons' in the womb demonstrates a staggering lack of empathy for those very same lives when they are in the world. What is the moral logic here? It is beyond me." As Krugman notes, it is not about life or health; it is about making rich people richer. The Senate says it will start over, and let's hope that these 100 people show a smattering of conscience, although I certainly do not expect that from Texas' senators, Ted Cruz and John Cornyn, two plutocrats of the first order. They can't do the right thing because they've never been exposed to it and wouldn't know it if it bit them.

Ivanka Trump has a new book out about working women, a subject she knows as much about as she does about rebuilding a 1932 Ford. For certain, she is the daughter that Howard Roark would have had had Ayn Rand been more inventive.

May 9: More in the *Times* today about the Kushners' use of high-value immigration visas to attract Chinese money for their development projects in this country. This is no small thing; it speaks to how they look at the presidency and the government and the Constitution.

I found an interesting piece on the subject of populism in the *Washington Post* yesterday. I did some looking around to try to get a handle on a good definition for this term, which gets thrown around fairly loosely these days, at once describing Donald's Trump's political appeal and Marine Le Pen's and the subset of our population I have characterized as coal miners, the disaffected bubbas who can't find the energy or the will power to move out of a shithole of a state like West Virginia to find good jobs elsewhere. Several experts I ran across online suggest that populism is kind of a harum-scarum gut feeling that spreads through disaffected folks who want what they want and they want it now. It's not a movement with a center. Nor does it have a platform. It is probably more akin to anarchism than to anything else. Its root motivation is selfishness. I can certainly see all of that at work in the Trumpistas. Sherrod Brown, writing in the Post, tried to make it sound like populism was a soft pillow of a political brand that loves everyone and wishes everyone well, rooted as it is in the good old country values of trust and honor and blahblahblah. Of course, he is dead-ass wrong. I think he's mixed up his terms. Populism is a shithole of a public stand (look no farther than the Trump administration and its allies for evidence). He's talking about progressivism.

May 10: Yesterday Donald Trump fired James Comey from his position as director of the FBI. He gave as his reason the poor timing of Comey's announcements relating to Hillary Clinton's emails last October. What a laugh. At the time, Trump almost hailed Comey as a national hero for telling the world that he was reopening the FBI investigation into the email situation. Now, five months into his presidency, Trump wants to pretend that he's so outraged by what Comey did to Hillary that he deserves to be fired? Isn't it more likely that Trump is firing Comey because it gives him a chance to derail the FBI investigation into the Trump team's relationships with Russia, including the Russian hacking of America's presidential election in November? Well, heck yes.

Coming after the congressional testimony this week of a woman who was in the White House and told the president's people that they couldn't trust their new national security advisor because of his cozy financial ties to Russia, don't you think Trump started running scared? What huge elephant must be camped out in the living room over on Pennsylvania Avenue! This doesn't mean that an investigation will go forward. Trump now gets to select his own "boy" for FBI, and you better believe that "boy" will truly be a "boy" in every sense of the word. No Republican in Congress cares enough about the country to try to find out whether our president owes his election to Putin, so we may just go on merrily down the road toward the Tyranny of the Abjectly Stupid.

Meanwhile, to illustrate how thoroughly out of touch the administration is with normal people – as opposed to out-of-work coal miners whose brains now reside below their beltlines and their toothless mammies – the attorney general is thinking about going for the max again in all drug-related criminal cases. Obama backed off on the enforcement of idiotic laws that required the government to try to put a defendant accused of having even one joint into prison for life. He looked out at what's going on all across America, where drug laws are being ignored or being changed so that marijuana sales are now legal in a whole handful of states. He looked at the high cost of maintaining federal prisons that were full to overflowing with minor offenders. He looked at the cost to society of labeling every weed-smoker as an addict and a felon. And he decided that the battle wasn't worth fighting now, if ever. Jeff Sessions, our aw-shucks down-home dumbshit cracker of an attorney general, has been installed in an outhouse in the Deep South for the last 50 years, without a TV set or a telephone, peering out at the world through a crescent-shaped hole in the doorway to view an America stuck in the '50s. He truly sees things in black and white. And the less black the better, if you get my drift.

May 11: All the news media went berserk yesterday in the wake of the firing of the FBI director except, of course, Fox News, whose people suggested that it was time to "move on." I wonder if anyone in Washington has enough guts and enough interest in the future of this democracy to go forward with whatever it takes to bring down Trump and his Fascist friends before they completely dismantle this country, bleed off its wealth and sneak away to a nice island in the Caribbean. Right now, there are none of that kind in the Republican Party in the House or Senate. Not a single person of conscience will stand up to a bankrupt and corrupt leadership. What about that Panhandle cowboy Mac Thornberry? I'd like to know what he thinks, but it's very likely that after all this time in D.C. he is nothing but a guy who shoes horses or pulls ticks off cattle for the big boys.

Yesterday was the last day of the semester for me to go to Jacob's Well Elementary to have three second-graders read to me. Two of them have really improved. The little gal has not. She still doesn't seem to know how to attack words she doesn't know and sound them out. And she stumbles over many of the easy words that she has surely seen many times before. I'll come back in the fall to help out three or four more second-graders because it is so satisfying to see them improve and because I may actually be helping them in something that will serve them well for the rest of their lives.

Lynda started talking again yesterday about us moving into a smaller, more manageable place. I went to the web and found that the new apartments in Wimberley are taking reservations. They are advertising their two-bedroom units for $1,350 a month. I don't know what that includes – water? Cable? Electricity? I will try to call today and find out. Meanwhile, Cypress Creek Church, which is non-denominational, has announced plans to put an assisted living facility on property near the church, which is just off the Blanco River and Ranch Road 12.

May 12: Trump did an interview with NBC yesterday and was barely coherent if you try to compare him with other men in power who can do complete sentences and multi-syllable words. Nevertheless, he provided the information that he had met with the FBI director, James Comey, for dinner at the director's request and was told that he, Trump, was not under investigation. Then, during phone calls, the director reassured him of the same thing. Oh, and by the way, Trump did not fire Comey because of anything other than the fact that Comey was a show-boater and a phony and untrustworthy. This explanation does not square at all with what Trump's keepers have said since the firing. They said that the president fired the guy only upon the recommendation of the deputy attorney general, a guy named Rosenstein who was given his job by Trump just within the last few months. Now one hopes that Rosenstein will come before Congress and give us his version of this ever-changing set of lies.

Meanwhile, as Paul Krugman points out in an op-ed piece today in *The Times* today, the Republicans pretend nothing is amiss. They seemingly could not care less. This puts me in mind of one Mac Thornberry, longtime congressman from the 13th district of Texas who I mentioned earlier. Mac represents Amarillo and Wichita Falls in Congress. I wonder what he thinks. I did not agree with his politics when I was editor of the paper in Wichita Falls and I made no bones about that when he would come to meet with our editorial board. But, I thought he was trying to do a good job, and I thought of him as a man of conscience. I doubt my assessment nowadays because Mac is just as silent as everyone else in the Republican Party as the Trumpistas steal America and our democracy. I would write him a letter, but I know he wouldn't read it, and I don't need to expend the effort on something that will go from a clerk's hands into the trashcan. My own congressman, Roger Williams, is a worthless little man who has no guts whatsoever and is a mindless shill for whatever the Party wants.

I finished up my videos for the third week of the Yale online course on The Constitution and now have to write something to finish out the assignment and move on. I don't know what I am supposed to write about but need to get it done this morning.

May 13: Reports out yesterday and today indicate that Trump is looking to appoint John Cornyn as director of the FBI. Cornyn is a Texas U.S. senator. I'd say Cornyn is a good choice if you want a sycophant who is also a liar of the first order and a man who will do anything to forward his own interests. I have known Cornyn for his entire political career. Early on I was impressed with him. I thought him an honest and very smart man. He turned out to be very smart. In the Senate he has managed the incredibly acrobatic task of keeping his nose right up in Mitch McConnell's asshole.

Somebody pretty smart hacked hospitals and doctors' offices in 74 countries yesterday using a piece of software that the American spy agency discovered and then had hacked. Fortunately, I'm using Google's proprietary system, which I hope and think is pretty much very difficult to hack.

Timothy Egan, a writer for *The Times*, has an op-ed piece this morning asking where the patriots are in this entire Trump fiasco. The answer: They are nowhere. All of them have traded fame and fortune for otherwise human consciences.

A man named Henry Scott Wallace wrote an op-ed yesterday with the headline: "American Fascism, in 1944 and Today." H.S. Wallace is the grandson of Henry Wallace, who was vice president 75 years ago. That Henry Wallace wrote a piece for the *Times* 73 years ago called "The Danger of American Fascism." The grandson makes the case that there are some striking parallels between what his father called out back then and what it is easy to pinpoint in the political landscape today, namely the trend toward Fascism. Let me quote a couple of paragraphs:

"My grandfather warned about hucksters spouting populist themes but manipulating people and institutions to achieve the opposite. They pretend to be on the side of ordinary working people—'paying lip service to democracy and the common welfare,' he wrote. But at the same time, they 'distrust democracy because it stands for equal opportunity.'

"They invariably put 'money and power ahead of human beings,' he continued. 'They demand free enterprise, but are the spokesmen for monopoly and vested interest.' They also 'claim to be super-patriots, but they would destroy every liberty guaranteed by the Constitution.' "

May 14: It's Mother's Day, but we aren't really celebrating. Lynda told the kids to stay away. She doesn't feel well enough to have them around, and Greyson is a bubbly, busy little boy who never sits still and never shuts up. That drives her crazy. Bryan called Wednesday about what to bring, and he was upset when I told him not to come over. Lynda will be happier if it's just us two here. She doesn't have to posture or pretend, and she's not really comfortable about smoking dope when kids are around. Scott apparently beat Laura up over the pot situation. I fully understand that he is a teacher and cannot be linked to marijuana. But, this is in Wimberley, not New Braunfels, and nobody is watching a 75-year-old woman use a bong.

The *Times* had a very good column in its Review section this morning by Lee Siegel, a regular contributor, perhaps a staff member. I read his stuff quite often; he's a good straight-thinking liberal. The column is a contemplation about moving back to Norway with his family to live with other kinfolks. Siegel lists the reasons why he might consider such a move, and they jibe completely with my own reasons for wanting to abandon ship or, alternatively, to fight back as much as I can. To quote:

"Perhaps the most disturbing portent of a bleak American future is that for all the millions of words proving not just Mr. Trump's dishonesty and unfitness to serve but also the dishonesty and unfitness of most of the people he has put in positions of authority and influence, there is no clamorous outrage that is not easily dismissed as partisanship. Truth has lost its traction. Reality has become as fungible as a crosslisted stock. That is a development that goes deeper and will be more consequential than the advent of Donald Trump."

Siegel writes that he will not go to Norway, though. And he will not hope that it all just gets better or goes away. He will not be optimistic, either, or "positive thinking." He wants to fight. And so do I. I think that's the only way to get rid of the cancer of fascism that has overtaken our institutions.

May 15: For her Mother's Day, I fixed Lynda a big old filet mignon for dinner last night. She loves it, and we have had it at least three times in the last month. It is not an inexpensive meal: the meat alone cost me $22. Filet goes for $22 a pound at HEB. We did have some leftovers that I will have for lunch, which does stretch the dollar a little. Here is how I cooked it, just in case anyone is interested in preparing an absolutely excellent steak: Heat the oven to 415 degrees. In a good old iron skillet cover the bottom lightly with table salt and put it on the stove burner turned up high. Sear the steak for two minutes on each side, then put the skillet with the steaks right into the oven. If the steak is about an inch and a quarter to inch and a half thick, cook it for about 8 minutes. Take it out of the oven and let it sit for a couple of minutes. It should be close to medium rare. If you like your steaks more well done, then you don't deserve to eat something that costs $22 a pound.

I clipped the lead editorial out of *The Times* yesterday to save so that I will have it to refer to some years hence when the Republicans in Congress try to hold a Democrat president to some lofty standards. The editorial is a list of what Trump has done so far that defines his presidency and is a warning to Republicans that the bar has now been set at an historic low. The bottom line: lie, lie, lie. And never apologize for it.

While Laura and Scott were here yesterday we were talking about the New York plan to let high school students get into college free of tuition under certain fairly liberal conditions. Laura told me a little about the Tennessee program that is similar. Then this morning *The Times* had a story about the Tennessee program that's been in effect for several years. Under that state's plan, students can attend community college free of tuition. The number of students attending community colleges there has jumped 30 percent, I believe. And they are now graduating and heading off to universities without a huge amount of debt.

This is a great idea, and one that Texas almost had back when I was a student coming out of high school. Tuition and fees were so low at junior colleges that anyone could go who wanted to go.

Without Amarillo College I might not have gone to an institution of higher education at all because I didn't have the money and, when I was a freshman, I didn't have a car. There was a stigma attached to getting out of Amarillo High School and into Amarillo College. In the eyes of the rich kids who could afford to go to a big university elsewhere or the smart kids who got scholarships to do the same thing, AC was just an extension of high school. But I actually went to AC and took all the basics, the English, the history, the math, the science, and I am here to tell you it was no walk in the park. It was as good an education as any of my cohorts got and prepared me for the world just as well as their high-falutin', high-dollar courses prepared them.

May 16: We are off to Bastrop this morning for an 8:15 appointment with the pain doctor to see about having a device put into Lynda's back that will electronically eliminate the pain. We have heard that this is a good solution from Dr. B., her neurosurgeon. The first implant will be a test; B. will do the real one later, if the test proves to work. Bastrop is about one hour from here, so we will leave soon.

David Brooks had the comments of the day about Trump in today's *Times*: Our institutions depend on people who have enough engraved character traits to fulfill their assigned duties. But there is perpetually less to Trump than it appears. When we analyze a president's utterances we tend to assume that there is some substantive process behind the words, that it's part of some strategic intent.

But Trump's statements don't necessarily come from anywhere, lead anywhere or have a permanent reality beyond his wish to be liked at any given instant. We've got this perverse situation in which the vast analytic powers of the entire world are being spent trying to understand a guy whose thoughts are often just six fireflies beeping randomly in a jar.

May 17: Trump is imploding. In the last couple of days it has come out that he asked the FBI director James Comey to drop an investigation into the Russian connection between his former national security adviser and the Russians; he asked Comey to promise his loyalty to Trump and Comey refused; Comey recorded his meeting with Trump in a memo that he circulated to high FBI staffers; Trump told Russian diplomats secrets that he had been told by the Israelis.

There is talk of "obstruction of justice." No one is yet talking about "high crimes and misdemeanors," but that will surely follow after Comey and others are called before Congress for testimony.

Meanwhile, Republicans just act like nothing has happened. Were all this happening with Hillary Clinton in the White House, impeachment proceedings would already be under way. House and Senate Republicans have no morals, no scruples and no balls. They are a shiftless band of hyenas.

Writing in today's *Times*, Thomas Friedman had this to say, among other things: "The morally bankrupt crowd running today's G.O.P. are getting their way not because they have better arguments — polls show majorities disagreeing with them on Comey and climate — but because *they have power and are not afraid to use it, no matter what the polls say*. And they will use that power to cut taxes for wealthy people, strip health care from poor people and turn climate policy over to the fossil fuel industry until someone else checks that power by getting a majority in the House or the Senate."

I was thinking yesterday about how there seems to be no music associated with the anti-establishment movement these days. When I was learning to play and sing, thanks to my friend Malcolm Helm, the anti-Vietnam-War effort was in full swing and was propelled by music by the likes of Dylan and Peter, Paul and Mary.

May 18: The White House is in a well-earned and much-deserved crisis. The Justice Department has appointed a former FBI director named Robert Mueller III as special counsel to investigate the relationship between Trump and the Russians all the way back to before last year's elections. Mueller has a stellar reputation. If he does absolutely nothing else, he can do for Trump what that Nazi pawn Ken Starr did for Bill Clinton – tie his presidency in so many knots that nothing at all can get done. That would be salutary in and of itself.

There is some talk of impeachment in Washington, but not much more than that. After the Clinton impeachment the bar is pretty low for what it takes to get to a Senate vote on the removal of a president.

Trump heads off to the Middle East where he hopes to beat up the Saudis and kiss up to the Israelis. Both things will be hard to accomplish. The Saudis have successfully for many decades required that the United States act at the behest of the princes on every matter, even those involving loss of American lives in combat, in trade for oil. That won't change. And the Israelis are pissed because Trump told some visiting Russian spies last week some secrets that he could only have gotten from Israel! Good Lord!

It appears that while grocery stores are in trouble because of changing consumer habits retail stores are facing an even more uncertain future. The big-box stores appear to be going out of business very slowly. They are bleeding to death. I haven't been in a shopping mall or big-box store in years and won't go into one. I buy everything I need – with certain exceptions – online through Amazon. Long ago retailers treated me and other customers with contempt when they refused to have knowledgeable sales personnel in their stores. Sometimes I would go into a store and couldn't even find anyone to check me out at a cash register. Why would I want that experience when I can go to Amazon and find competing products with competing prices and, in most cases, user and buyer reviews to help me make an informed decision?

May 19: Trump takes off for the Middle East today, just a day after Kushner met with Saudis in Washington to arrange a huge arms purchase from American manufacturers. Obama had already approved billions of dollars in new weapons for the Saudis, and now Trump will try to go one better. This is very odd. The Saudis buy a ton of stuff to blow up from the U.S. and then never blow it up. They avoid conflict like Trump avoids the truth. I can understand buying a lot of new fighter jets because all those Saudi princes need to learn to fly something! But, what can you do with a bunch of track-mounted missiles? Kill rats in the desert? Trump will get stonewalled by the Saudis on everything over there and come away thinking he's King Kong because that's the Arab way of hospitality. Then he heads over to Israel where they will have to give him multiple blow jobs even though they hate his guts because they have to have those weapons to protect themselves from Arabs other than the Saudis.

Paul Krugman has a great piece in *The Times* today about the hollowed-out Republican Party, an institution of sewer scum and fecal bacteria. As I have written here previously, all the Republicans care about is making the rich richer and staying in power whatever the cost so they can continue to make the rich richer. Period.

David Brooks, writing on the same page in *The Times*, warns that nobody wants to work for Trump, which is kind of a problem because he has hundreds of openings to fill. Well, actually, the only people who want to work for Trump have their own petty and avaricious agendas, so you can kiss the hope for good public policy a fond adios.

May 20: *The New York Times* has an interesting story today about the success achieved by *The Washington Post* in the digital era. Apparently the *Post* has expanded its scope and reach online and is thriving with digital subscriptions and advertising. I certainly hope so. The *Times* and the *Post* must stay strong to provide a balance against Fox News and the other dedicated disseminators of fake news, better known as propaganda.

May 21: Nothing new on the Trump front today, although the column writers in The *Times* continue to take him to task, and deservedly so. Even the most conservative of columnists hate him because he has not even come close to doing what he promised on a number of issues, and even though as The *Times* reports today, the EPA is eliminating regulations for oil-and-gas drillers and operators all across the country, which was a Trump promise being carried out in spades. The *Times* on Saturday showed the damage caused by the melting of Antarctica, and it is extensive and expanding. One columnist correctly points out that it is unfair to 4-year-olds to compare Donald Trump to them. They are much better people at that young age than he is and perhaps ever has been.

In *The Times* magazine, Gary Rivlin has a revelatory column that argues for states to make the first two years of college free if students go to a community college for them. These two years would be treated like Grades 13 and 14, paid for by the states and communities just like high school is paid for by everyone right now. The idea does have merit. Students can get a good education in community colleges at a reasonable price, and they can move on in life without the monumental debt associated with a college education now. Society has a huge interest in educating kids beyond high school, and our failure to do so will come back to bite us. (Just like our policies restricting immigration will eventually make us a less-creative, less-interesting place to be – and more expensive.)

May 23: Trump is far away, and things have calmed down a little, although today is the day his henchmen are to release details of his budget request. His budget officer had a press conference yesterday to give out some details, and it's fair to say that Trump did what he said he would do: He asked for vast increases in help for the rich and for defense and vast cuts for the poor and the hurting. I haven't seen details about his budget for the EPA or Education, but he promised to cut the heck out of them, and I'm sure he will. *The New York Times'* first take on the request included this information:

Of 13 major initiatives in the budget, nine are drastic spending cuts, mostly aimed at low-income Americans. The biggest of those, by far, is an $866 billion reduction over 10 years in health-care spending, mostly from Medicaid. That would be achieved if the Senate approves the House bill to undo President Obama's Affordable Care Act. But many Senate Republicans oppose it; Senate Democrats are dead set against it and the vast majority of Americans don't want it, and for good reason. It would deprive an estimated 10 million low-income Americans, many of them nursing home residents, of Medicaid benefits; it would also defund Planned Parenthood, reducing or ending health services to 2.5 million people, mainly women.

The budget also calls for slashing food stamps ($192 billion over 10 years) and disability benefits ($72 billion over 10 years), including a big chunk from the Social Security disability insurance program. The rationale is that the cuts would force Americans back to work. But some 60 percent of food stamp recipients already work and an estimated 15 percent more work most of the time, availing themselves of food stamps only when they are between jobs or when their hours are reduced. The remainder are disabled and elderly. They will not go back to work if their food stamps are reduced. They will go hungry.

The budget does show the man for what he is, an insensitive asshole only concerned about his friends in the top 1 percent.

Lynda said she watched a video of Trump getting off the plane in Saudi Arabia or Israel yesterday with Melania trailing him down the ramp and across the tarmac. She said Trump reached back to grab Melania's hand and she fluttered it away like it had been pissed on. Does she dislike him as much as many of us do? How could she listen to what women have had to say about him and not feel icky?

May 24: The Trump budget is not only dead in the water; it has sunk to the bottom of the legislative pool. Not even the rankest of conservatives like it, although it does kill some of their most hated programs like National Public Radio, the National Endowment for the Arts and the National Endowment for the Humanities.

Frank Bruni opines today in The *Times* about a speech given by the mayor of New Orleans this week after that city took down four monuments to Civil War Confederacy leaders, including Robert E. Lee. It was less an opine than a rhapsody. Bruni called it one of the best speeches he's ever heard. I followed the link to the transcript, and I must say it was a very, very good speech, and it outlined very clearly and very forcefully why it is no longer just fine, thank you, to give places of honor in our cities to these men of the great lost cause. They weren't just on the wrong side of history; they were on the wrong side of morality.

The mayor's speech pointed out the noxious bullshit that passes for reason on the part of pro-monument people. They claim the statues simply honor an historic past. If we are to recall that history in monuments, the mayor asked, then where are the marble likenesses of slave ships and lynchings? He also notes that the monuments were constructed across the defeated South about 20 years after the end of the Civil War as part of a revival of Southern sentiment that swept through the region at that time. I have not read much about the time period between 1865 and 1900, but I know Southern states were slow to return to the United States, and I know that resentments ran deeply in the South, including Texas. The New Orleans mayor listed the number of lynchings during that period at 4,000. That's an incredible number when you think about it.

This whole business of trying to expand the library is shrouded in some kind of weird silence. Two board members came in to meet with Carolyn Monday morning, and she said nothing about the meeting. I did give her the name of the architect that designed the new Seguin library along with contact information and the name of Kevin's company in Pearland that does library projects.

May 25: Kristoff has a great opinion piece in today's *Times*. He has gone back to the transcripts of the 1999 impeachment hearings conducted to try to get Bill Clinton removed from office. There he found quotes of outrage and bluster from men who are still in the Senate or associated with it concerning what it might take to get a man kicked out of office. Wouldn't it be something if they held this president even to the same low standard that led to the impeachment of Clinton?

I have just about finished up Week 5 of the Yale online course on The Constitution. The most interesting details I learned so far have to do with how short-sighted the founding fathers were when it came to slavery and its impact on the country after adoption of The Constitution. They really did nothing to bring slavery to an end, and so Southern slave-owners ran the country right up until they get their asses whipped in the Civil War.

John sent me something last week via email lamenting the relocation of all the Confederate generals from various pedestals and parks in the Old South. I didn't email him back. It would just be another source of irritation. Amarillo has its own Southern soldier set up in Elmwood Park near downtown. I grew up wondering about this Confederate trooper. I remember there was an inscription on the statue; I don't remember what it says.

When you think about it, it is very odd that Amarillo would have such a commemorative piece of outdoor art. Amarillo didn't even exist until around 1900, well after the end of the Civil War and after the end of all the bullshit that surrounded Reconstruction. The statue was erected well after the revisionary period that Texas went through in the 1880s and 1890s when the Civil War was looked at through glasses that promoted astigmatism. It really has no link to Amarillo's history whatsoever and is just a gratuitous symbol of black intimidation.

May 26: The traffic getting out of Wimberley on Ranch Road 12 yesterday was horrendous because of a road-paving project. I finally made it to the Dietz shooting range in New Braunfels after 10:30 and got signed in with no trouble. At the range, the master, a guy named John, helped me sight in the .17 rifle that John gave me for my birthday. He showed me how to get the scope working right. I shot 50 rounds through the rifle and felt good about it. I'm pretty shaky, but if I watch my breathing and take careful aim I can hit a pretty tight circle of shots.

The president's budget, which cuts everything but defense, has been declared DOA by many in the House and Senate. And it should be. As if to give the finger to the entire process, the president sent over a budget that not only makes no fiscal sense but that literally does not add up. In fact, it counts some numbers twice either as an effort to put a bigger batch of lipstick on this pig or to fake out the Republicans who are slobbering to do anything they can to make their tax cuts for their rich buddies look good.

Then, the president went to NATO and pissed on the shoes of everyone in Europe. As the *Times* notes in an editorial today, the president treated the leaders of the world's great democracies with contempt, and this is a man who can't wait to nuzzle up to Putin, Duterte and the Saudis, world-class dictators and autocrats. The man cannot be clueless; he must just be a tyrant at heart, although not a world-class one. The president lectured the Europeans about not paying their fair share for NATO, leaving the U.S. to do the bulk of the financing. It was a little frustrating to find no table or other information in The *Times* about how much the Europeans do pay for NATO and how much they owe. I will have to Google that.

May 27: Trump's kin are making a killing off his golf courses. He manages to have "meetings" with "officials" at these courses, lugging along the press corps that duly reports on his whereabouts, thus giving him advertising on the national news that he could never buy. He has had his underlings take golf pros on tours of the White House as a way to pat them on the po-po. He and his henchmen have no ethical values at all.

May 28: Trump's son-in-law is also making a killing as an unscrupulous landlord in New York and New Jersey, as detailed in The *Times* Sunday magazine today. He has the compassion of Caligula. Will this come back to haunt him? Probably not. The rich in this country are almost beyond accountability.

And speaking of the rich, *The Times* has a rundown on executive CEO pay in today's paper that will make your hair stand on end. The best paid of them made about $100 million last year. Last year. Last year. For one year. These people, mainly men, are shameless as well. And their stockholders, who insist on quarter-over-quarter and year-over-year growth regardless of circumstances, are shameless, too. They reward profitability growth over all other values; treating employees right or having a good pay scale – these things are not even in the calculus. It is clearly time for labor unions and socialist workers to rise and assert worker power again. Of course, to do so we'd have to figure out some language the idiot out-of-work coal miners speak. They're too stupid to understand English. Latest case in point: The *Times* reported yesterday that the West Virginia governor told them that coal is not coming back, period. The future in West Virginia is NOT coal, but solar and wind and natural gas.

I see that the Wimberley school district is hiring janitors. Maybe the coal miners who are out of work in West Virginia might be smart enough to put 78676 in their GPS systems and find their way out here to take the kind of work they better get accustomed to after Trump kills welfare as they know it.

May 29: Back in this country, Trump is trying to figure out what to do with Jared Kushner, his rogue son-in-law, a pipsqueak with a mean streak. Jared has had communications with the Russians about who-knows-what, and made some deals, I have no doubt, because that is what he and his family do: They make deals. Trump is also going to have to live with the fact that he basically dissed the Europeans and made them feel abandoned by this country, a geopolitical mistake that's about as big as anyone has made since George W. Bush sent troops into Iraq and then Afghanistan. It may actually be more significant, because the

Russians read these things as extraordinary weakness on the part of a president they must already sneer at and make fun of. Imagine what Putin has told his inner circle about the fact that Trump couldn't find the energy to walk around in Europe with the heads of other countries and had to have a golf cart to haul him around.

Today, *The Times* reports on the very real damage the Trump budget would do to our nation's health. Here is an excerpt from the article:

"To help offset a 10 percent increase in military spending, much of the government would take serious hits, including agencies tasked with biosecurity.

"The Office of Public Health Preparedness and Response, which tracks outbreaks of disease, would be cut by $136 million, or 9.7 percent. The National Center for Emerging and Zoonotic Infectious Diseases — a branch of the Centers for Disease Control and Prevention that fights threats like anthrax and Ebola — would be cut by $65 million, or 11 percent.

"The C.D.C.'s Center for Global Health would lose $76 million, or 18 percent. Its Emergency Operations Center, which conducts real-time monitoring of outbreak responses, and its Select Agents Program, which sets regulations in lethal toxin labs and helps researchers stay ahead of bioterrorists, face unspecified cuts as well."

We had quite a storm blow through last night. Lots of bluster and not much rain. Lightning strikes seemed to hit all around Woodcreek, but nothing came close to us. Our rain gauge is not set up properly, so I don't know how much rain we actually received. It was cloudy and 70 degrees this morning when I got up to walk, and it felt so good I walked the three-mile loop from our house around and down and then up again and back to the house.

May 30: John sent me an email yesterday that included a video someone made by copying and pasting photos from various service members funerals and then overlaying a bagpipe version of "Amazing Grace" for audio. With the exception of the very first image, which was the photograph taken of the Marines raising the flag at Iwo Jima in World War II, the others were all shots taken at the final services for troops killed in either Iraq or Afghanistan. I emailed John back a message that said that we should doubly mourn those men and women who were sent by stupid presidents into stupid and endless wars. John wrote back a huffy note that I had ruined the spirit of the thing. The boy is just up to his ears in bullshit. And since when is "Amazing Grace" an appropriate hymn for troops killed in combat? Were they saved? Were they wretches? Sorry, but the selection of that particular song just seems totally inappropriate for the event. I think maybe nobody knows the words or understands the words or gets what "grace" is all about.

May 31: Now is the 50th anniversary of the Beatles' issuance of "Sgt. Pepper's Lonely Hearts Club Band" album, and *The New York Times* suggests that not only was it old hat when it came out but it is really, really old hat now. Rock, *The Times* says, is now on the fringes of American pop music. That must be true. Or at least that seems to accord with my own feeble observations. Rap and hip-hop are institutionalized nowadays. They are mainstream. Country, which is just another way of saying "pop", is out on the margins as well. It would be interesting to take an online course in modern American music just so I'd have a better perspective. I'd like to know who's making money and who isn't, and why. This is as much about taste as it is about the formers of taste. I don't remember much about my reaction to "Sgt. Pepper" when it came out in June of 1967. Susan and I got married at the end of that month in that year, so about June 1 we were absorbed in other matters. I never bought the entire album, which is what you had to do to get the full experience of the band's experiments.

Tom Friedman, writing in *The Times* today, likens the administration to an emirate in the Arab world. At the center is the emir, Trump, surrounded by his toadies, the crown princes and princesses. And to curry favor with our United American Emirate you have to do the same things you have to do to curry favor with the royal family in Saudi Arabia: You have to pay. It's a very apt description. Another news report in the newspaper says that Trump is having trouble finding people to come work for him in the White House. Little wonder. He's a tyrant and a back-stabber, which I guess are similar creatures. The story, like many others, doesn't mention the hundreds of top-level jobs that Trump has not yet filled across the executive branch of government.

June 1: Trump released the names of the lobbyists he's hired to oversee the agencies they lobbied for before he hired them. What? Yes. That's right. After going through all of last year's campaign promising to "drain the swamp" in Washington, he is surrounding himself with people who worked for industries to lobby government for special favors and putting them in charge of policies affecting those businesses. Suddenly it's not a swamp? Or maybe there are no scruples in the White House these days. *The Times* also reports today that Trump's kids are all over the planet hawking their wares to governments and big businesses that desperately want something from America's president.

Yesterday, I heard on the news that China is standing by while the United States craps on Mexico and plans to extend its hands in cooperation when our neighbors to the south need some help. Before the election they might have looked north, but no more.

Like all good newspaper publishers everywhere, the ones at *The Times* are lying through their teeth over another round of buyouts announced today. They will get rid of copy and line editors, mainly. This, the publishers assure us, will not do any harm to quality. Yeah, right. Then, why did they have them in the first place? Why are we seeing so many errors even in the Sunday magazine? Because they have killed copy editors. The *Times* story goes into the whys and wherefores, all of which involve declining revenues in advertising:

"But those gains (in digital revenue) were not substantial enough to offset a continuing, industrywide decline in print advertising, historically the main revenue source for newspaper companies. Print advertising at The Times *fell 18 percent in the most recent quarter, causing an overall decline in advertising revenue of 7 percent."*

I talked briefly to the rector last night after the Half-Time service. She told me that for the first time in her life she has been busy writing letters to her congressman and our U.S. senators and the president. She said, among other things, that she is embarrassed by the presidency. That's the least of our problems – that he embarrasses us. I think as she realizes that she is aging out of her job she will become bolder and less willing to sit back and let events of the world that challenge her faith just go by without comment. I hope that's the case because all across the world, mainstream Christianity is rudderless and clueless. There is not a single U.S. religious leader who can call out the president and have it stick because of his or her moral standing. All of them are in retreat.

June 2: An odd friend named G.G. Pulley helped me get a job my senior year in high school. George got me a job where he was working – Howard's Hickory Hut on 15th Street just off Washington. George was the cook, and the main thing he prepared was barbecue brisket, beans and potato salad. George used a wood pit and he'd put the meat on early in the morning so it would be ready by 11:30. After he put the meat on he was supposed to clean up the Hickory Hut and the business next door that was also owned by Howard. It was called The Gay '90s Club, and it was decked out in kind of kitschy period decor on the walls and on the floor.

In Amarillo in those days you could serve alcohol as a private club only if you also served food, and The Gay '90s got its food from the kitchen via a back hallway that linked the two businesses together. The idea was that bar customers would order barbecue from the menu and then we'd fill the order at the Hickory Hut and shuttle the plates on big trays back and forth. That was the idea; nobody ever ordered barbecue from The Gay '90s Club. Ever.

Nevertheless, we had to stay open at Howard's until the bar closed down, which meant we had a lot of time to do absolutely nothing but talk. In fact, 90 percent of the time we had nothing to do but talk because nobody came into Howard's, either. The whole point of the restaurant was to act as a front so the owner could make his money off the alcohol. He didn't care if he ever sold a plate of beans at either joint.

I was hired to help George clean up the club and the restaurant and to bus tables at the barbecue place. I would meet G.G. at the club around dawn every day, and we would, first, take out all the broken tables and chairs busted up during the festivities of the previous evening. We would wash all the glasses, toss all the empty bottles, wipe down all the tables and the bar and clean the carpets. While we did that we listened to the jukebox because G.G. had figured out how to get it to play without us having to feed it quarters.

There was a big walk-in refrigerator between the Hickory Hut and the club, and some evenings the waitresses from the club, all of whom were long-legged and bosomy in their dark red Gay '90s outfits, would drop off a mixed drink like a gin and tonic on an ice-cold shelf in the fridge for G.G. and me to share. One night we all got caught by Howard himself, and we were fired right then and there. I was actually not disappointed because I was so bored all day long.

Trump, as promised, has announced he will pull the United States out of the Paris Climate Accords. We will thus join the ranks of other thriving and robust nations who have likewise distanced themselves from the treaty, namely Nicaragua and Syria. Quite naturally, the move has been criticized by just about everyone except that coal miner in West Virginia who is still stuck in his outdoor shitter and doesn't realize yet that it is actually 2017.

This ignoble exercise in illegitimate power will benefit mainly the Chinese, who are stepping in all over the place to take over where America once was preeminent. Need a little cash to help jumpstart your new power station? The Chinese will furnish the money, no strings attached. Yet. Need a few new missiles to ward off an enemy? The Chinese have just what you want! Like some bad guy in a Dickens novel out of the 19th century, China will be just around every corner with a satchel full of knockoff watches or a fistful of ready cash. And the world will beat a path to its door.

The question now is whether everyone will just stand there slack-jawed and weepy eyed and let this fraud continue apace. If I can find a good way to say, NO, in a very loud voice I will pursue it. Today, I'll fire off a note to Roger Williams, my esteemed Republican congressman, to protest, for the absolute zero effect it will have on him.

Yesterday, I finished up my class on the American Constitution, an online noncredit course offered by Yale. It was very, very interesting. I took a lot of constitutional law in graduate school, but those courses were all about how the Constitution was changed by court cases and had nothing much to do with the original version and the amendments. I want to go back and read the Dred Scott decision for just one reason: It shows just how far from reality, truth and justice the Supreme Court can tread.

Lynda got word yesterday from the pain doctor that she can go in next Wednesday for the trial implant of a device that is supposed to electronically reduce her back pain. We are very excited about this. The trial will go on for seven days, and if the device works as advertised she will have a permanent implant after that trial period ends.

June 3: I awoke at 2 o'clock this morning because of pain in my lower back. It was not excruciating, but enough to make me wake up. First, I thought if I just used the bathroom I'd be OK to go back to sleep. That didn't work, so I took a couple of Advil and pretty soon I fell back asleep and stayed in bed until about 6:45, when Chi-Chi decided it was time to get up and get moving. I'm not at all sure what to do about the lower back. I know definitely what I will not do: have surgery.

The *Times* reports that the owners of small businesses across America are just atwitter about Trump, "the new sheriff" in town. WhooHoo, cowboys! Wait until he wades into that High Noon shoot-out with the Russians and the Chinese carrying his pea shooter. The man has now given up any remnant of moral authority he had, and that's about all that carries America into the hot sun of international engagement as a credible leader these days. That and dollars. If we go ahead and do what Trump wants to do and cut off the flow of dollars in and out of the country, then even that will be unavailable and we'll be shot down like the tin-horn little goat-ropers we're becoming.

The Roto-Rooter guy had to come out because our drains weren't doing their job, and he said we needed to have our septic tank pumped out. The Hill

Country Wastewater people came out yesterday and confirmed that. So, now it will cost us around $600 to deal with the problem. Maybe that will fix the plumbing drainage issue. I don't know.

I have signed up to take an advertising class through Coursera. It should be about the history of advertising and what can be effective, what isn't. I looked through a lot of the Coursera catalog to find a course to take online. I toyed with the idea of taking a five-course concentration in creative writing. But, I'm not too keen on doing a bunch of stuff that's peer reviewed by people who may or may not know what they're reading and then having to pretend to be happy about that. I really don't appreciate being critiqued anymore. The class doesn't start for a couple of weeks, so I get a break.

The Pew Trusts research people in Florida issued a new report yesterday about the status of daily newspapers in this country. They have tracked statistical data since about 1940 for total circulation of all U.S. dailies, for example. That chart shows that weekly circulation for all papers stood about about 40 million in 1940. The high point was in 1985, when circulation was at about 63 milllion. In 2015 that number was about 35 million. While the number of households in America has boomed since before World War II, the weekly circulation of dailies has actually dropped below the number in 1940. The peak period overall was in the late '60s and the '70s and early to mid-1980s. Those just happened to be the years when I was a journalist, so I was there during the boom times.

I knew that without having to refer to any circulation charts. For most of the years I was a reporter and editor I was treated with respect. I could generally call the police chief and the city manager and the mayor and my congressman and get them to answer their phones. I had the power to get things done and I did.

With the advent of the internet and the rise of outlets like Fox News my standing in the community faded, and by the time I was ME in Temple, it had all but evaporated for a variety of reasons not entirely unrelated to the silly woman I worked for.

Another interesting chart shows revenue by category since 1960 in billions of dollars, unadjusted for inflation. In general, revenues from advertising and circulation peaked in about the year 2000, then dipped, then went back up to the peak level in about 2005. The growth in revenue was steadily upward from 1960 to 2005. A third chart shows that the number of newsroom employees in U.S. newspapers has fallen from about 62,000 in 2004 to about 38,000 in 2015. That decline began much earlier, though, because publishers put constant pressure on newspapers to show double-digit profit growth quarter over quarter and year over year every single year. That profitability model could not falter or even waver. It was mandatory. And that kind of goal was impossible to reach in cities like Wichita Falls where household growth or population growth was stagnant.

You cannot grow newspaper ad and circulation revenues by 6 percent year over year if the population of your town is not growing by that amount or greater and certainly not if it is flat or declining. Making this argument with HQ in San Antonio or in Cincinnati would only get you fired. So, as editor I shouldered on. When I took over the newsroom in Wichita Falls, I had 54 or 55 employees putting out two newspapers every day for five days a week and one paper on Saturday and another on Sunday. That was in 1995. When I left there 12 years later, I had about 35 people or fewer working on one newspaper. If it was hard to grow circulation when you had a growing community base, it was much harder to grow circulation as you cut staff and coverage, giving people a product of ever declining quality and expecting them not to notice and to pay the same or more over time.

June 4: Thunderstorms moved in last evening and they have stayed around. We don't have a rain gauge anymore so I have no idea how much rain we have received. Chi-Chi hates the thunder and lightning and spent almost all evening in my lap. Then this morning as the storms increased in intensity she was right back up there. The thunder that rolls across the Hill Country is much different sounding than the thunder I remember shimmering across the flat plains of the Panhandle. There, there was nothing for the sound to bounce off of. Here, the noise echoes from hill to hill and sticks around for a long time.

The *Times* reports that Marissa Mayer, who runs Yahoo, makes about $900,000 a week. That's right: a week. And she does that by operating a company that is in steep decline. Advertisers want nothing to do with Yahoo. So, how does she make that kind of money? Stock options based on the earlier Yahoo purchase of shares in a Chinese search engine and one in Japan. She made some good deals for the Yahoo board, so they keep rewarding her. Meanwhile, she loses market share for her company and her employees leave for better jobs. As with so many other stock-based companies, the CEO and all those around her get absolutely no credit for keeping good people and keeping their morale high, for giving people a decent wage, for giving them health care benefits.

A front-page story details how the Koch Brothers used their money to hijack the Republican Party and turn its members against the idea of climate change. The KBrothers own all kinds of petroleum-related businesses. By the way, Citizens United, thanks to the Supreme Court, only helped the KBrothers become the de facto shadow government that runs America.

A coworker at the library handed me a photocopy of an article appearing in the June 2 edition of Commenweal by Blase J. Cupich. The title: "Signs of the Times: Witnessing to a Consistent Ethic of Solidarity." Cupich, who is archbishop of the Archdiocese of Chicago, cites the usual litany of threats to the people of the world, like nuclear war and greed, and, of course, abortion, and entreats his readers to hold together as a religious faith to fight these blights in unity one with another. He quotes one Cardinal Joseph Bernardin of Chicago as suggesting that Catholics are uniquely positioned to do this:

"Cardinal Bernardin was convinced that the church should not shy away from her unique contribution, even if it meant standing apart from the prisms of political decision-making used by other groups, even if the integrity of our social teaching was met with hostility because it could not be made to fit into the partisan political framework that governs American public life."

Nor should any so-called Christian faith shy away from calling out those who would lead us in directions away from solidarity and community with those who are afflicted by the wealthy and powerful in every realm, not just the political.

144

But, here is where Cupich and Bernardin get it wrong, in my estimation: "We should maintain and clearly articulate our religious convictions but also maintain our civil courtesy. We should be vigorous in stating our case and attentive in hearing another's case; we should test everyone's logic but not question his or her motives." This is utter bullshit. At some point, you have to quit being Mr. Niceguy in the face of tyranny and those who would literally starve you to death and instead speak Truth to Power in the most forceful way possible. It is not enough to have a conversation over tea and crumpets in some big bishopry in Chicago. It may not be enough to call out the perpetrators of unseen violence from the pulpit or with a sign in one's hand in the crowd at a parade. In too many churches today, the signs of solidarity all point to those at the top being at one with those in power and those who will be powerful.

June 5: A couple of years ago I was over at Scott's and Laura's in Canyon Lake and I was browsing through the history text Scott was using for his high school course in world history. One of the chapters was about evolution, and I asked Scott what kind of reaction he got in New Braunfels, America, when he broached that subject. Actually, he told me, he did not broach that subject at all. He just let the kids read the chapter if they wanted to, but he did not cover it in class. I was not surprised. All it takes is a parent or two calling the principal to make a teacher's life more miserable than it already is.

So, neither was I surprised when I read in The *Times* today about a student at Wellston, Ohio, high school who challenged her teacher on climate change and just refused to back off when confronted with any factual or true information. This 17-year-old acted like a brat and a bully in the classroom and basically got by with it because of the subject matter, as if the academic world in little Wellston were so fragile it could not stand up for a teacher telling a snotty student what is right and what is wrong and making it stick. This subject was climate change. What do Wellston teachers tell students about evolution? My guess is that Wellston students will grow up to be as stupid as their parents. They'll inbreed there in Ohio and then not be able to find jobs that are simple enough for them to do and then they'll complain because they can't find work and have to live in shitholes that they actually don't mind inhabiting at all because they're accustomed to what stupid smells and tastes like.

Then at another end of the stupid spectrum there is the board and chairman at Mylan, the company that makes and sells the Epi-Pen, a device that delivers a dose of a medicine that stops an asthma attack in its tracks. A year ago, Mylan was all over national TV as an egregious example of capitalism gone wrong because the company was charging about $600 for a product that cost about $5 to make and market. Mylan gave "price gouging" a whole new definition. Now, a year later, the Epi-Pen still costs $600, and the whole brouhaha has blown over. A *Times* reporter looked into this ignoble experiment in public shaming.

Isn't there a competing product? Why not?

June 7: Today we go to Austin so a doctor can implant a test device in Lynda's back, along the spine, to see if it won't eliminate her pain. She will wear the device for just a week, and then they will remove it. If it works, she'll have another more sophisticated version implanted permanently. We have high hopes that this will work. Her pain is getting worse by the week.

I started my online class in Advertising and Society, offered by Duke University, yesterday morning. It was pretty good, actually, probably the class with the highest production values of any I have taken. The physics class I took a couple of years ago, offered by a professor at the University of Virginia, was the best. The prof had a lot of props and had a lot of activities. He was very engaged in the whole thing. In the advertising class, we will look at television spots and ads on the internet, and probably to a lesser extent, ads in newspapers and magazines. I think this will be a good course (even though I taught advertising at WT back in the early 1980s).

Earlier this week, Trump announced that he wants to privatize the air-traffic-control system. As usual, he defaulted to hyperbole to describe the present system, which, by the way, gets millions of air passengers to and from international destinations day in and day out without accidents. It's an antique! It's horrible! It's spent millions of dollars with nothing to show for it! It's scrap and bubble gum!

I have no idea what kind of shape the system is in, and it is possible that a private company could take on the whole enterprise and make it much better, but I wonder how the finances would be worked out. A private company will need to make an ever-increasing profit, and the more the better. So, let's say the company invests in new gear and higher pay. Right now, everyone who pays taxes in America has a financial stake in the air control system, so the costs are spread over a huge pool. The private company won't have that kind of reach to tap into unless, of course, it can count on subsidies from the taxpayers to take up the slack. So, the taxpayers will still be players, but they probably won't have the kind of oversight over operations that they have now because that function will be proprietary.

There are numerous examples of problems all across the country. But, Texas toll road 130 is one that's close by. The southern portion of the toll road is a partnership between two companies, one in San Antonio and one in Spain. They built the road and they operate it and they get the tolls. But, the tolls haven't been enough, and in 2016 the toll road authority filed for bankruptcy. I don't know what's happened since that, but it's a good bet that in the backs of the minds of the owners is the idea that the state will sooner or later kick in some cash to save their butts.

And then there's just the simple fact that The People do benefit from having some shared operations, such as water service and sewer service and police and fire protection, just to name some that are obvious. The companies have a narrower concern — maximizing financial returns.

The fight in Wimberley right now over wastewater is a good local example. Aqua Texas, a for-profit, privately held company, wants to take over the city's wastewater system, but in exchange the company wants a way to provide the city's water and also wants the city to agree to let Aqua provide utilities to everyone in the city's extraterritorial jurisdiction. That effectively means the city will not be able to control growth outside the city limits, and Aqua will promote growth because that's the way it makes more money – by increasing demand for its services and products. The question for the City Council is whether the citizens don't have an interest in controlling their destiny when it comes to growth and the extension of services.

Thanks to Malcolm Helm, my grade-school buddy, I noodled around with guitar-playing and -learning during high school, and the summer after I graduated I joined up with a kid named Bobby Hertner and another kid named Gary Edwards, and we formed a band called Public Works with the idea that we'd learn some popular songs and then play some gigs and make a little money, but mainly have fun. In our own way we came to terms with a few songs by The Doors and the Rolling Stones and some other groups, and then we played our debut for a talent contest in Elmwood Park where the crowd was nice enough not to boo us off the stage. We never got a single job, so Bobby and I played together on a couple of stages, notably the Agora in Canyon, and then the entire project just fell apart for lack of interest.

After Susan and I were married in June 1967, my time was so full of college classwork and full-time work that I just put the guitar aside. Then in 1970 before I went into the Army I sold the guitar to Buck Ramsey. When I got out of the Army in July 1972, I had several hundred dollars paid to me because I hadn't taken any leave in the previous year or so, and I took some of that money and talked to Art Nizzi, who owned a music store in Amarillo, about a new guitar.

It took a while for me to redevelop the callouses on my fingers and to recall the chords to some songs, but I kept at it on an irregular basis until D'Arcy got big enough to enjoy singing and hand-clapping. When we got involved at First Presbyterian Church, largely because we wanted D'Arcy to have some exposure to religious stuff, I did some playing for older kids, and then when Julia and Becca came along we made some memories on nights when we'd gather around the coffee table and sing folks songs. Susan and I were divorced in 1980, and I just put the guitar away in a closet. Playing it reminded me of the girls, and those memories were hard for me to deal with. It was better to tuck them away.

June 8: We drove up to Seton Northwest hospital just after noon yesterday and Lynda had a device implanted on an experimental basis in her back. Two electrodes were threaded on each side of her spinal cord. The idea is that electrical signals that carry pain from the lower back and leg to the brain will be interrupted enough to make her, if not pain-free, then relatively so. She will wear the device itself on a belt for about seven days, and then we will go to the doctor's office in Austin and have it taken off. Two weeks later, if the experiment is successful, a permanent version will be implanted. I am very hopeful this will work. Lynda has been very patient for a long, long time, and she is not by nature a patient woman.

The FBI director Trump fired, James Comey, released his written testimony yesterday, just before he is scheduled to appear today before a congressional committee to testify about how Trump tried to get him to stop investigating the administration's ties to Russia. In the written statement, it is crystal clear that Trump did obstruct justice or try to do that. He will no doubt get by with it, because the Republicans don't care about such niceties. Trump could take a dump in the chair of the Speaker of the House while everyone was watching on national TV and every Republican in Washington would applaud the productivity of his bowels.

Major news about the past of the human race, rather than its very bleak future, came out of Morocco. Archaeologists have found that homo sapiens go back 300,000 years, about 200,000 years farther back in time than has been thought possible. Several skeletons have been discovered there, at a place called Jebel Irhoud, and they are co-located with objects that can be dated with accuracy. Here is a little about them from *The New York Times*:

"The people at Jebel Irhoud shared a general resemblance to one another — and to living humans. Their brows were heavy, their chins small, their faces flat and wide. But all in all, they were not so different from people today.

'The face is that of somebody you could come across in the Metro,' (one expert) said."

I was playing around in the Google News file yesterday and found a fascinating story about how Kansas is faring these days under a very conservative governor named Sam Brownback who has proudly led that state into bankruptcy thanks to his close adherence to trickle-down economic theory. His state has been held up as a model laboratory for what trickle-down, which is a centerpiece of Trump's tax and economic plan, can do. Here is what The *Times* reported today:

"But this week, Mr. Brownback's deeply conservative state turned on him and his austere approach. Fed up with gaping budget shortfalls, inadequate education funding and insufficient revenue, the Republican-controlled Legislature capped months of turmoil by overriding the governor's veto of a bill that would undo some of his tax cuts and raise $1.2 billion over two years.

"The move amounted to a shocking rejection of the tax-cutting experiment Mr. Brownback had held up as the centerpiece of his conservative governing. But economic growth and revenues lagged, and even his allies began to publicly criticize the tax cuts."

And so it goes in LaLa Land, where up is down and left is right and right is wrong. No doubt the true believers (who aren't really, but who must pretend to adhere to some rational school of thought beyond mere greed for the sake of tradition) will find something Kansas did wrong in the implementation.

As I was approaching my 50th birthday in 1997, it occurred to me that I could enjoy playing the guitar without having an audience of kids or other family members. But it also occurred to me that other than a handful of chords that I had learned in high school I was stuck. Plunking three-chord songs was no challenge, and I wanted to be challenged, so I told Lynda that for my birthday present I wanted guitar lessons.

My intention was to try to learn to read music. I stopped by a couple of music shops, and their instructors were all busy, and then I went over on Jacksboro Highway in Wichita Falls to Sam Gibbs Music, the largest and nicest music store in town. The boys there hooked me up with Leon Gibbs, who was nearing 80 years of age. Leon had a Saturday morning time slot, and we started out with the very basics on how to read music.

June 9: The testimony of James Comey, the FBI director fired by Trump, proved to be just as scintillating as anticipated. He called Trump the liar that he is, among other things. David Brooks, writing on the op-ed page of The *Times*, predicted that this investigation will be around a long, long time, and that is certainly something I would hope for. Every single day, Trump needs to be pricked by this probe, just like the Clintons were when the Republicans ran the Whitewater investigation for seven freaking years, turning up essentially nothing. Comey has emerged as a hero for not being pushed around by Trump, the Bully in Chief. And rightfully so. During his testimony yesterday he time and again underscored the fact that Trump may be in league with a Russian plutocracy that desperately wants to run the world and wants to rid the world of American influence. Someone pointed out yesterday that Trump has spent an inordinate amount of time trying to cover his ass and not a single word has been said about Russian interference with America's elections and American democracy.

The *Times* finally got around to the story that has been hanging out there waiting to be plucked from the ethosphere for months: The lack of foreign workers to take over menial jobs Americans won't take on a bet. I'm not sure what got the editors' attention, but the story begins in Mackinac Island. There, nobody can find enough workers to clean rooms, wait tables, walk horses. And the reporter learns that the same thing is happening up in Maine and in other places where summer is an important part of the economic scheme.

Did these people not see the movie "A Day Without a Mexican?" Well, they don't need to find a copy because they will be living it from now on thanks to the Republicans' and Trump's new policies about immigration. Hotels on Mackinac Island may have to close entire wings. Horses may have to stay in their stalls. I guess they will have to start having meals that are available at buffets. I wonder when The *Times* will figure out that this clamp-down on workers from other countries is going to hurt industries all across the country not just on a single island of wealth and privilege.

I looked forward to my Saturday lessons with Leon Gibbs. He was a soft-spoken man who obviously knew his stuff, and he was an eager teacher with a vast reserve pool of humor and goodwill. Over time, we began spending a little part of every lesson with me asking him questions about his background and then probing a little deeper and a little deeper still. It actually did not take long before I figured out that the man and his career were worth book-length treatment, so I talked to him about that. He agreed, and, better, he had some notebooks that he'd kept over the years in which he'd written out bits and pieces about his life.

One day I drove over to Midwestern State University and talked to James Hoggard of MSU Press about the university publishing a book I'd write about Leon. Jim went for it immediately, and so Leon and I began setting aside times on Saturday specifically to work on the book, primarily with me doing the interviewing with a digital tape recorder and him doing the talking. We also continued with the guitar lessons, and before long I had written a few songs that Leon polished up and made sound right.

After a year or so of interviewing and doing other research I wrote the book and got it to Jim and he published it. It came out in 2003, and then the work began! We had one launch party at Sam Gibbs Music, and my three daughters came, which tickled me to death. That same weekend, we had a big launch party at the Knights of Columbus Hall, and we sold hundreds of books. Then, we took books to Archer City, Petrolia, Waurika, Walters and a few other small towns and played and sold some more. I never kept a good count on how many books we sold, but it was in the range of 1,000. Neither of us made a single dime off the book. All the money went to Jim to pay for the printing. Julia told me that was just the way things work in academic publishing. Books don't pay for themselves and authors make zero on them. We did make a little money on a related project, though.

June 10: Trump had a press conference yesterday and called Comey a liar and said he would testify under oath about Comey's claims. We'll see. I think that Trump lies and then believes them, so having him testify would be useless.

An interesting development from the Senate hearings: Apparently John McCain has dementia of some sort. His questioning made no sense. McCain is in his 80s. He's a very, very stubborn man. I understand he is also a very, very mean man. He will not leave the Senate on his own two feet. It would be wonderful if a Democrat could take his seat, but that won't happen. If he leaves he will leave so that the Republican governor can appoint himself and then be set up for election.

A major storm blew in last evening about 9 o'clock. Lots of thunder and lightning. We still don't have a rain gauge. Chi-Chi took refuge under Lynda's chair.

As the date for publication of the book about Leon Gibbs came closer, Leon and I decided it would be fun to do a record with him playing some of his songs and some of my songs and some old-timey hits. I checked into pricing at a Dallas company that produced CDs in nice packages. Each CD package would cost us about $1.50. We could sell them for $15. Not bad.

Sam Gibbs had on staff two salesmen who were gifted musicians. One of them had been a session musician for shows and recording studios in Branson, Mo. So, we recruited these two guys to play keyboards and bass and do the recording a couple of evenings after Sam Gibbs shut down. We recorded about 15 songs, only a couple of which Leon actually wrote because he didn't have the copyright on any of his hundreds of songs. He'd never bothered with the paperwork. When the book came out, we had the book and the CD to sell, and we made back our CD production costs and a little more. The songs I wrote for it were not very good, but they were songs, and I did write them, so I was proud in that sense.

June 11: Today is Lynda's birthday, and we have nothing planned. We have told the kids that we will not be celebrating here and we will not travel to celebrate there. The back device is still a work in progress, and we are hopeful as the experiment progresses.

This morning about 7:15 I was walking on my usual fast-walk/slow-walk route toward Woodcreek Drive and ran into Joanie, a woman of about 62 who lives in the cul-de-sac one street to the south of us. She has a big house on a big lot on the corner and lives by herself. She moved here just a year ago from Massachusetts so she could live near her only child, a daughter, and the daughter's husband. They live in Austin. Joanie wanted to be here for the birth of her first grandchild, and that happened about six months ago.

Now Joanie has her house on the market, and she told me this morning she is moving back to Massachusetts —"home," as she put it. She said she does not want to grow old here, and she was dismissive of her relationship with her daughter and her granddaughter, saying that the child will grow up and be busy and so on.

I completely understand where Joanie is coming from. My children and stepchildren have never even come close to depending on me in any way, shape or form to help raise their kids. They have never asked for advice. They have never asked for money. In the case of Bryan and Erin, they have been resentful when Lynda and I tried so much as to visit them in the hospital on the day Greyson was born. The resentment hardened when I told them there was something physically wrong with him that made him cry all the time, so to show us they spent a few hundred dollars for an "expert" in California to tell him over the phone how to get Greyson to go to sleep at night. The same advice could have been had for free from 30 miles away, but the dynamics of child-rearing with my kids' generation is different. They don't need us, and that's just a fact, something Joanie has recognized at a good time because home prices are at historic highs in Woodcreek, and she will get her money back. We are baffled by the kids' resistance to the idea of us helping or being asked for advice.

The front page of *The Times* today is dominated by a story about how the religious Left is trying to coalesce into a force to oppose the Trumpian enterprise that America has become. They will need to do far more than their forebears did when those few good men walked at the front of marches arm-in-arm with Martin Luther King Jr. For one thing, modern American churches are losing membership in startling numbers. St. Stephen's is an example. We are seeing steep declines. People just aren't going to church anymore. There's not much there for them. If they don't need family, they certainly don't need the extended family that church, in part, represents.

Or, if they do have a need, they can have it fulfilled at a megachurch where nothing makes them uncomfortable or challenges their way of thinking about things. An expansive theology that requires people to be forgiving and understanding and welcoming and not judgmental seems like a quaint idea in an America run by the Party of Doom and Domination.

June 12: Lynda did not feel better all day yesterday, and last evening she said she hurt as badly as she has ever hurt. So, it was a terrible birthday for her. We called the woman who is in charge of Lynda's case/device situation, and she had Lynda do a minor adjustment. We will have to see how that worked through the night and then this morning, when the woman is supposed to call again.

Time magazine had a cover story this past week on the millions upon millions of dollars the Trump family is raking in from the hotel they run just down the street from the White House in Washington. Foreign governments hoping to make points with the Trumps are spending thousands of dollars for food, booze and rooms, and events that were originally scheduled elsewhere in Washington are now being planned for this hotel. Back in January, the Trump family said that any money that came to them through the hotel from foreign governments would be donated to charity, but a couple of weeks ago the managers of the hotel said they couldn't separate out the money so that would be impossible.

It increasingly appears that it will be up to the courts to hold Trump accountable. This kind of thing is clearly unconstitutional. But the Republicans who control Congress will not do one single thing about it. Meanwhile Democrats and those in opposition to the Trumpistas need to run good people to take over Republican positions in coming elections.

During the time that I was taking lessons and working with Leon Gibbs, Lynda and I were members of Sacred Heart Catholic Church in Wichita Falls, a matter I will discuss in more detail elsewhere in this document. For now, it's enough for you to know that we left that church and made the conscious decision to join Our Lady of Guadalupe Catholic Church. That church had three Masses on Sundays, and one of them – at 9 o'clock – was in English with some parts of it in Spanish. The 9 o'clock Mass had a small musical group consisting of two guitars, a bass, a piano and a flute, four men, three women and a teen-age girl who was the flautist. I was vaguely acquainted with the bass player and his wife, the pianist, and I asked them if I might try out for the group. They were kind enough to invite me to their home for a practice, and I ended up playing with this band every Sunday for several years. I really loved these people and playing with them. They broadened my musical horizons and helped me become a better musician and a better person.

June 13: The attorneys general of the District of Columbia and the State of Maryland have sued Trump saying he is violating the Emoluments Clause of the U.S. Constitution by accepting stuff of value from foreigners. The courts have never dealt with the Emoluments Clause, but if it means anything it means Trump cannot continue to rake in the cash from his Washington hotel and his various properties around the world. Even if the lawsuit never makes it to the Supreme Court, and it might not, we may get to see a lot of the president's previously secret tax records among other things and those could give us some insight into whom exactly he is most beholding to.

A new study reported on in today's *Times* found that brisk walking can be good for the discs in one's spine. I do a fast walk four days a week, so perhaps I'm doing something other than just helping out my heart and lungs.

The Norwegians are completing work on a huge underground storage facility where they will store their spent nuclear fuel rods and other nuclear wastes, all extremely dangerous for thousands of years. The rock caverns they have created will be filled with the waste and then filled on a go-along basis to further isolate the containers.

Absolutely nobody wants high-level nuclear waste generated in this country, and that has been the situation since after World War II when nuclear scientists and the government began to pretend that atomic fission would be the salvation of mankind instead of its destroyer.

I made this issue of the storage of nuclear material a matter of study for years starting in the early 1970s when I was pursuing a graduate degree in political science at West Texas State. At the same time, I was editor of The Canyon News, and I found out one day that a team of drillers were in town to punch some test holes in the ground near Canyon.

Over a very few days I discovered that the drillers were working for a geologic research lab at the University of Texas at Austin on a contract with the federal government. The focus of their study was on huge salt formations buried under Randall County, having been created eons ago when a deep saltwater sea existed below the Caprock and lapped at the rock surfaces underpinning it. The salt formations were believed to be deep, stable and impervious. In the newspaper I wrote stories about what was going on and why, and that was the impetus for my research into nuclear waste disposal.

I soon came to believe that there was no good place on the planet to store nuclear materials for the long term. The products are hyper-dangerous for thousands of years, and there's not a site that will be stable for that time period. As I continued to dig around and also to apply Christian thought to the whole atomic milieu, I decided that the pursuit of bigger and better nuclear weapons and the development of nuclear power plants, actually unnecessary with a little creative thought given to how to produce power from the sun, the wind and the oceans, was immoral. In particular, the continued development of nuclear arms, which threatened the future of the human race and every other living thing on earth, was a moral outrage.

Coincidentally, the Reagan administration announced at about the same time that planners were looking at the area north and west of Canyon for placement of an MX-Missile system that would be placed on railroad tracks so the individual missiles could be rotated around as in a shell game so Soviet satellites couldn't keep an eye on them with accuracy. The MX-Missiles had nuclear warheads on them. So, here was another regional threat to life on the planet with its basis in atomic fission, the material and process that destroyed Hiroshima and Nagasaki to end World War II.

June 14: The device that is supposed to alleviate the pain in Lynda's back is not working, still. We are to go to Dr. Ramirez' office here in Wimberley this afternoon to meet with Jessica, the representative of the company that makes the device, to try to figure out why it isn't working. The temporary implant is to be removed Friday morning, so we have exactly two days remaining on this experiment. I have no idea what we will do if this does not take care of some of the pain. Neither does Lynda. What would the options be? I guess they would be drugs of some sort. My friend Phil Duncan was on a moderate dose of morphine for pain administered a little at a time throughout every single day until he got off that with something better and newer and less deadly.

Poor old stupid Jeff Sessions wouldn't tell the Senate anything about his dealings with the Russians. He completely hunkered down and came up with every excuse in the book when asked questions. The man comes across as a simpering fool, kept on a chain around his neck in some dark basement in the

Justice Department by the Master Mr. Trump.

One of the more interesting stories today in The *Times* had to do with the opening of a play in New York City, a part of its outdoor cultural offerings during the summer months. The play is "Julius Caesar" by Shakespeare, and it is a modernized version with a Caesar who is very Trumplike and who is, as scripted by The Bard, very dead about midway through the action. Corporate sponsors of the production have now pulled out because of the depiction. The *Times* story is about how this has become something of a trend – companies killing their ads when they don't agree with the political tone of a work of art.

Well, welcome to the Trump era.

In the mid-'70s, two or three forces came to bear on my slowly congealing thoughts about America's commitment to nuclear power and nuclear arms. One was religious. Susan and I tried to discern what the Gospel writers were telling us that might be plugged into the issues we faced in those times. We felt that it was pretty clear that any plan adopted by a government or other group of people that had as one of its possible outcomes the destruction of all life on the planet was wrong-headed and needed to be scrapped in favor of an alternative with less drastic results. That just seemed to flow from the teachings of Jesus and Paul, among others. We became aware of that flow because of the influence of Baldwin Stribling, the pastor of First Presbyterian Church in Canyon, a man who was something of a scholar on the writings of Paul and their application to modern times.

A second influence on what I was thinking and doing came from the books I read and the professors I studied under when I was working toward a master's in political science at WTSU. Without exception these men and women were liberals, and they made no bones about that. When I studied under Vaughn Nelson, the head of the physics department, I found that he, too, was a liberal, and because of his understanding of the science behind nuclear energy he was very much opposed to what was going on across the world to force dependence on nuclear fuel for power production and for weapon development. They all helped me understand what it meant to be socially conscious and socially responsible, traditional viewpoints we were well-prepared to embrace because of what we had come to believe about social justice and human rights.

Several of my professors and their spouses were members at First Presbyterian, and we socialized with them. So, we spent evenings talking about current events and how they might be dealt with from a Christian perspective. Some of that social conscience I developed through interaction with Buck Ramsey, the cowboy poet and feature writer who had such an impact on me when I was a young reporter at the *Globe-News*.

June 15: Lynda and I met with a representative of the company that makes the electronic device that they have implanted in her back on a trial basis to try to relieve her leg pain. The device hasn't worked as we'd hoped, so he met with us here in Wimberley to look at the device and to change out programs to try to make it more effective. He is a bright young man, and he asked good questions about Lynda's pain, and his first observation was that her pain pattern was very unusual and not at all like anything he had experienced. Most people who have back pain have pain 24 hours a day, he said. Lynda's pain starts about 4 o'clock every day. Some days it starts earlier, but 4 is about average. So, the pain is intermittent. I personally have thought that the pain could be caused by the way she sits at her computer and in the car and everywhere else. She has very poor sitting posture, and I think she's done something to the nerves that is not associated with the usual back pain problems.

I told the man that my fear is that from the get-go we have had it wrong. "I worry that we decided the problem was a rabbit and we have chased that rabbit all over West Texas and we have never been able to catch it, and all the while the problem has been the roadrunner, and he's standing out in the highway giving us the finger." That's what I told him. The laminectomy didn't work. The fusion surgery didn't work. The electronic device doesn't work. The injections in the spine didn't work. Maybe we need to chase the roadrunner not the rabbit. So, the guy adjusted the program, and sent us home promising to call us at 6:30. He never called. Lynda woke up this morning crying because she had pain right off the bat after waking up, and that's highly unusual. Her great fear, of course, is that nothing can be done for her, that there is no relief in sight.

I wish I could reprint here the entire op-ed piece today about cultural appropriation that appeared in The *Times*. I have a hard time believing that otherwise smart people in this country are having a very hard-edged argument about whether a white guy can put together a piece of art that uses techniques or subjects borrowed from American Indian or Black culture—uh, sort of like (or exactly like) what Elvis did. I'm not even sure where the idea comes from that it is a bad thing to borrow from different cultures. Will we remove all the Remingtons? Will we stop white urban women from making North Carolina-style barbecue? What about stopping white directors from making movies about Black history? The list is so inexhaustible that just thinking about it tires me out. What passes for intellectual integrity these days is as laughable as what passes for knowledge about foreign policy.

Speaking of which, it is now a possibility that Trump will go to Florida and announce he is clamping down again on Cuba, undoing what President Obama did and releasing that tiny island nation from the grips of iron ignorance and vengeance. Trump may want to cozy up to his Cuban buds in Miami, rich guys who golf with him, and thus give them the screws to tighten on Cuba again. What a disaster that would be. Not speaking of stupid.

And then there are the dumb bastards who ruined the Flint, Mich., water supply because a) they didn't want to spend money to do things right, and b) didn't give a shit about the poor people who live there. Finally, someone is holding them accountable, and they are being charged with crimes.

This is the kind of government that Trump is establishing as the gold standard in Washington – bean-counters who have no clue about the people they are governing and who don't care.

June 16: We go to Austin to the anesthesiologist to have the pain device removed from Lynda's back and to talk about options. He may not have any ideas, but I hope he does. I don't want to come home with nothing at all for Lynda to look forward to.

I sat down yesterday and made myself write the six devotionals I was assigned for distribution to subscribing members of the church. I felt pretty good about one of them, a take I did on the Last Supper. I hope it is read as satire and not taken literally. I get absolutely no feedback on these devotionals from anyone. The woman who receives them and massages them before sending them out via email doesn't even send me an email telling me she has received them. Nine months or so ago, I got an email from her complaining about one I had written that said something unfavorable about preparing for war or maltreatment of soldiers or something, and she came back to me to change what I said. I did, but it kind of hacked me off. I don't think everything that is done at church has to be provocative, but people do need to know they are at a Christian church and not a meeting of the Rotary Club.

The jury for the Bill Cosby sex-assault trial is deadlocked, and there may be a mistrial. Lynda says that the key witness, the woman assaulted, made a poor showing by changing up her story over the years and during the trial. I don't know about that because I haven't paid attention. I did find it odd that Cosby would be charged with just one offense when something on the order of 60 women have accused him of drugging them and assaulting them. Why did the prosecutor agree to going forward with one accuser rather than several? If this is the state's strongest case, and it ends in mistrial, then the other women are shit out of luck getting any justice, assuming their accusations are true.

I was thinking on my walk this morning about how lucky I am to have this job at the age of 70. I think every day I can work and can do what I've always done is a gift. It's a gift on top of a gift on top of a gift, actually. Every day after I got home from the Preventorium when I was five or six years old has been a gift. Every day after June 30, 1972, has been another gift. That's the day I got out of the Army. And now every day past May 8 of this year is a gift because I've hit 70 and I'm still doing quite well.

Trump is to be in Florida again today, this time to say he is cutting Cuba off again. This will hurt everyone but Trump's fat Cuban ex-pat buddies who run casinos and related projects in Miami. Trump will say that opening Cuba up for American involvement after 50 years of enforced isolation is not working. What's never worked is what America tried to do there for five decades. Now, The *Times* reports that when the U.S. leaves Cuba this time, the Russians will be back with a vengeance. If the Russians can't get there fast enough the Chinese will. After all, Cuba is only 20 miles from the United States. What a great place to have a naval base so as to put pressure on this country to do whatever it is China or Russia wants.

June 17: We met with Dr. H. at his office in Austin and he removed the leads from Lynda's back. We asked what the next step might be, and he said he would talk with Dr. B., the neurosurgeon, about where we go next. Lynda and I both doubt we will ever hear from H. or B. again. We both think it's possible that we got a wrong diagnosis right out of the gate, and the case needs to be reviewed by someone else, so if we don't hear from these two guys again that's probably for the best anyway.

Amazon has bought Whole Foods for $13.4 billion. That's kind of a surprise to me, although I figured some big shakeup was coming to Whole Foods because of its stock situation. The *Times* plays the story as a prelude to a clash of Titans: Amazon and Wal-Mart, both of which want to own the American consumer experience. I'm not entirely sure what Amazon gets out of the deal other than 450 real, actual stores and some inroads with the producers and distributors of organic foods. From the perspective of a consumer, I'm curious but not worried. At least here in Wimberley, we have our HEB, and I don't see that changing anytime soon.

Today I am supposed to put together a recording studio so that Rotary members can record stories for kids overseas. This should be interesting since I really don't know anything about all of this.

For awhile I have toyed with the idea of writing a book with a subtitle of, "How the Texas Panhandle Produced a Single Lone Liberal." But the more I have thought about that the less able I have been to figure how I came to be what I came to be. Part of the answer is that, while I was not encouraged to study and do well in public school, I was given the tools to ask good questions and to examine things. I had a good ear for bullshit. I attribute that, in part, to Dad, who developed and taught a course at Palo Duro High School called "Critical Thinking." His skeptical take on the world of politics had to have rubbed off on me in a big way, and I remember that if I read nothing else around the house when I was in junior high and high school, I read "The National Review," a magazine edited by William F. Buckley Jr. I admired Buckley for his erudition and for the fun he poked at most sacred cows. He was a genteel iconoclast whose targets most often were liberals. It was the way he thought about things that I enjoyed, not necessarily what he thought about things. He threw in a little Latin here and there in his magazine, and that appealed to me.

My favorite magazine growing up, though, was "Mad" magazine, which in those days provided a zany and irreverent sendup of absolutely everything. When student leaders came along who talked about not trusting anyone over 30, they were preaching to this one-man choir. I didn't trust anybody of any age, which probably made me a perfect candidate to be a reporter and editor, although it took a while for me to realize that. The world around me in Amarillo was all white-bread and unthreatening until I got on at the Amarillo paper and started covering the police beat, thus seeing the results of some pretty bad stuff I never knew existed.

June 18: The internet was down from 10:30 until after we went to bed yesterday. So, all the things I wanted to get done did not get done, including setting up the radio studio. Everything needed to set that up was available only online. So, I spent a lot of the day reading Jack London's works, loaned to me by a Rotarian. I remember reading a few of the London stories when I was a kid, but I never read anything by him in high school or college. I'm now kind of surprised by that because he was a good writer, if a little over the top sometimes. In some things that he did in his writing I saw foreshadowings of Hemingway, who most assuredly read London works at some point. For example, London uses a stylized English, incorporating "thees" and "thous" and "thys" when his Indian-speaking characters use their own languages. It's a very effective way of letting the reader know right away that what's being said is not English. Hemingway uses the same literary device in "For Whom the Bell Tolls," some of which needs a way for readers to "understand" Spanish without actually having to read Spanish.

June 19: Up at 5:30 so I could shower and get to church by 7 o'clock to get set up and rehearse for the 8 a.m. service. After that, I had to get everything ready for the 10:30 and then do the projections for that service.

In the wake of the Amazon buy of Whole Foods, there is a lot speculation, of course, about what this will mean for retailing in general and the grocery business specifically. The *Times* speculates that Amazon will bring skills in robot placement and use to play in the checkout line and behind the scenes in product shelving and maintenance. Thus will a trend be accelerated. And thus will millions of jobs go away. To quote from The *Times* article today:

"Companies won't invest in technology unless it's less expensive than employing people, and most retail workers make near minimum wage. But in a case study of grocery stores, McKinsey found that the savings from automation were three times the cost, and 68 percent of the savings were from reduced labor costs."

Most likely, the elimination of jobs won't take place as quickly as some think, because even in the grocery checkout line sometimes things require human intervention. At HEB, for example, the checkout clerk is also the last point-of-sale opportunity: They ask if you need ice or stamps. On several occasions, I have actually needed ice and have forgotten about it until the clerk asked the question.

Playing at Our Lady of Guadalupe Catholic Church in the choir required me to practice, which I probably would have avoided. I kept at it. The songs we played during mass were not your traditional Christian hymns. Instead, they were from a two song-book collection of more modern hymns and chants with music designed just for guitars. For a few years, the choir on Sunday mornings was joined by Miranda Rodriguez, the daughter of two other members. Miranda played flute, so she added a bright dimension to our music.

Besides being a talented musician, Miranda was a smart and personable young woman. I hired her to write obituaries for the newspaper, and she did a stellar job before she went off to college.

Meanwhile at the newspaper, forces were at work that led me in another musical direction. One of my better reporters, Lee Weaver, was undertaking a series of stories that put him into immersive situations he would experience and endure and then write about in the first person. For one of his stories, Lee signed up to become a rock star at a local music shop that offered crash courses in rock stardom. Want to be a singer? They'd team you up with someone who could make you a better singer and show you tricks of the trade in the recording studio, but it would happen fast, like over a six-week period and it would come at a cost. At the end of that six weeks, you would join with others in similar boot-camp-type programs as guitarists or drummers and put on a mini-concert to show off what you all had learned.

Lee wanted to be a singer. As his training period progressed, his idea of what would make for a fun story morphed and broadened to include me on guitar and Lee's sports trainer, who was a very nice-looking young woman who knew

158

how to play drums, on drums. Then we had an idea:

We would pull together talent from within the newspaper and have a group that would play for nonprofits at no charge. It would get the newspaper name out there as hip and groovy and fun instead of boring and old-fashioned and stiff. We recruited the foreman of the night press crew to be lead guitar player because he was, in fact, a very good lead guitar player. We talked a business writer into being the drummer because he could actually play drums. And we ended up with someone not affiliated with the paper at all on bass because in the whole newspaper there wasn't one. We called ourselves Media Circus, and we played various gigs around town for about a year. Overall, we took in exactly $20 apiece and that was from a show we did for the city's concert in the park series. Our best, most enthusiastic audience was the folks who attended the Association for Retarded Citizens (ARC) banquet. We had our worst show at the Electra goat cookoff and festival, where we had a kid who was interviewing to be a reporter sitting in on bass, trying to play songs he'd never heard of. We never got asked back. You gotta be pretty bad to be dissed by a goat cookoff.

June 21: I made a huge fruit salad yesterday for a Rotary installation banquet last evening at the library. I used watermelon, cantaloupe, grapes and honeydew melon, and it was all wonderful. Every melon was just at the peak of flavor. Frankly, I have avoided buying cantaloupe and honeydew melons at the grocery store for many years because they just never taste like anything other than cardboard. I've always liked ripe cantaloupe, with an emphasis on the "ripe."

My Uncle Basil and Aunt Marjorie had some ranchland outside of Mangum in southwestern Oklahoma, and John and I would go over there in the summertime to spend a week or so with them. Basil was a great fisherman and stocked the cattle tank on his property with several kinds of fish so that when John and I came over we could go fishing with him. Our brand of fishing was to use cane poles with grasshopper tails for bait. Whatever we caught, Marjorie would fry up for us for dinner. I'm sure those were very hot days in the blistering Oklahoma sun, but I don't remember them that way. I loved being with Basil just above the mud line beside the little lake, watching for turtles and snakes, seeing the neon-colored dragonflies skim over the lake just above its quiet surface, anxious not to miss seeing the bobber wobble, doubly anxious about what to do if the catch was too big to bring in on my own.

Up on flat land above the cattle tank, Basil had planted cantaloupe. He might have had other fruits and vegetables. At least once on one of our visits, he took salt and pepper shakers along for the trip, and right there in the field, he cut open ripe cantaloupe for us to spice up and enjoy on the spot. It was kind of a guilty pleasure to get all sticky from the sweet orange pulp and juice. John didn't like cantaloupe. I loved it. I guess when I shop for cantaloupe I make the mistake of seeking to revive that experience.

On some summer days when I was working Saturday evenings at the *Times Record News*, our farm editor Joe Brown might drop into the newsroom after visiting the cantaloupe festival at Walters or Waurika, Oklahoma, bearing with him several specimens given by a grateful farm community. We'd spread out some newspapers and slice them open. Boy, they were good. And they were probably the last memorable cantaloupes I had.

Trump tweets that China has failed to rein in North Korea. Whether that reflects reality is problematic.

The Senate is meeting in secret to develop a health-care bill. It must be so singularly rotten that even Mitch McConnell, the manager of the stench that arises from that house of government from time to time, won't let it out into the fresh air.

We're off to Dr. Ramirez today for Lynda to see what's next. Then, we have an appointment Friday in San Marcos to see her back surgeon with the same purpose in mind.

June 22: Dr. Ramirez was attentive and compassionate and a great listener as we told him about what's happened since last we saw him about Lynda's back. But, ultimately he had no ideas and no solutions. We will go see Dr. B. tomorrow afternoon and see what he has to say about the direction we take.

Headlines in newspapers and on TV are reporting that shopping malls are doomed. A quarter of them are closing within a few years. Thus:

In 1966-67 or so, downtown Amarillo went into a steep nose dive from which it has never recovered. When I was a kid, downtown was the singular shopping destination for the entire Texas Panhandle area. There were a few national chains represented along the length of Polk Street, like Woolworth and Kress and Levine's, but most of the stores were home-owned. There was Blackburn Bros. and White & Kirk, where you could buy clothes and shoes, small hobby stores, independent shoe stores, music stores, shops where you could browse for records, bookstores and even a newsstand, where you could buy newspapers from all over the United States and magazines from all over the world and cold soda pop out of a squat red top-opening vending machine that stood by the doorway.

As boys John and I would walk with Daddy on Saturday mornings from our house on 10th Street all the way to Polk Street. On our way, we passed the Westerner, Central Grocery, Skelton's Drug Store, several apartment complexes, the Porsche dealership, a big tire store and many others. At 10th and Polk, we would just walk right into the Mary E. Bivins Public Library, a huge mansion that had at one time been Mary E. Bivins' home, when that was all ranchland.

On a typical Saturday sojourn with John and Dad, we would walk to the library and spend an hour or so there while Dad read the Fort Worth and Dallas papers. Then we would walk on the west side of Polk past the outdoors shop and into the newsstand with its scuffed and worn wooden floor and its exotic aroma of printer's ink and cigar smoke. Then, we'd walk on past Blackburn Bros., which had a big integrated awning that stretched halfway across the sidewalk. We'd ask Dad for a nickel or a dime to put into the hat of the one-legged beggar who sat there in the shade with one pants leg folded neatly up over his stump, the man a discarded remnant of World War II reduced to exchanging yellow No. 2 pencils for chump change. On up the street we'd go to Hi-Lo Records, where Dad would pore through the new albums and search in the racks for old ones that he could buy to listen to on the fine home hi-fi set Mother had built in to one wall of the dining room. We weren't yet sophisticated enough to buy 45s. We didn't listen to the radio. In fact, we didn't have radios, and I never heard the ones in our cars.

If we went to The Silver Grill, we would turn that direction, have a big lunch and then walk back home on 10th Street. Most of the time, we made that one sweep down Polk Street and then headed home. When John and I were a little older and deemed mature enough to make the Saturday walk by ourselves, we would hike up 10th to downtown with differing agendas. At some point, we joined the YMCA. I'm not sure why because neither of us knew how to swim and we were not compelled to learn. That was about all you could do at the Y besides play pool and maybe a pickup game of basketball, which neither of us were good at. Nevertheless, we might head, first, to Fedway to ride the escalator, and then to the Y to hang out a little and then we would spend 25 cents for a hamburger at a stand right across from the Y.

June 23: I went to see "Wonder Woman" with Laura and Scott, Lyndsay and Ian last evening at the Alamo Drafthouse in New Braunfels. The movie was great fun if not a great film. Unlike many in this genre, it actually had a solid plot and some pretty good characterization. The woman who plays Wonder Woman is quite beautiful. I hear she is Israeli.

Yesterday Trump took his show on the road again, this time to Iowa, where his people turned out by the hundreds in rapt adoration. Then, as he does, he lied to them. *The New York Times* reports on exactly 12 lies he told them in his speech. Did he tell any truths? Probably not. The man doesn't "do" the truth.

The Senate has released some details on its health-care bill, which, of course, would take from the poor and give to the rich. Even some Republicans don't like it, but they don't like it because it's not mean enough. Among them is the slimy salamander Senator from Texas, one Ted Cruz. So if Mitch McConnell can't guarantee that X number of poor people will actually die because of the bill, these senators will withhold their support and the bill will itself succumb.

The 25 cents John and I each spent on a burger at the little joint across from the YMCA was probably the best quarter I ever spent on anything ever. It was a great hamburger. After we got the burger, we would walk straight east to Woolworth's where we would buy some bridge mix candy. They'd put it in a little white paper sack, and we would stick that in the pockets of our jeans and then go to the Paramount or State for the matinee. There, we'd pay another quarter for admission, and it was possible to sit through two movies in one afternoon before we had to walk back home.

Long before I was in junior high school, a guy named Wolflin developed Wolflin Village east and west of Georgia Street starting at about the 2200 block. McGee Furniture was on the west side of Georgia, and that's where that gas station was that I worked at when I was in 7th or 8th grade. Blackburn Bros. opened a store there even before McGee Furniture was built. East of Georgia was the older part of Wolflin Village, and it contained a pharmacy, dress shops, shoe stores, a big candy store and Colbert's, a huge department store that had The Top O' the Village restaurant right adjacent to it. Nizzi Music Shop was in Wolflin Village.

I'm sure that Wolflin Village bled off some retail business from downtown for quite some time. Even when I was in elementary school and junior high, we

161

were walking over to Wolflin Village. In junior high, several of us would walk on nice days to the pharmacy to have lunch and then walk back to Stephen F. Austin Junior High School. By the time I was in high school, Sunset Center had also been open for quite some time on 10th Street at about Western Street. Sunset Center had a Penney's and a Montgomery Ward and a store called Woolco. More retail traffic must have moved in that direction, too. So, at the point in time when all of us kids were converging on Polk Street to rev our engines up and down, there was not much left of retail there. It was the Drag, but no longer the main drag, in reality.

Instead we tended to gather in herds around our respective turf centers. For Tascosa High students, that center was Stanley's Drive In on Georgia in Wolflin Village, just behind McGee Furniture. For Amarillo High students, the center was at The Ranger on the Canyon expressway.

June 24: Our visit to Dr. B. yesterday yielded no new information. He promised to go back and look at all of her X-rays and other documents to see if he missed something important that might be causing her continuing back pain. He also said he would talk to the pain specialist about the possible implant of a drug-delivery device in Lynda's back. It would send a small amount of a narcotic into her spinal chord. We should hear from him early this next week. I think Lynda is losing hope. I don't know where we go if the narcotic drip doesn't work. She wants to investigate that possibility more in depth, and she talked to her cousin Susie in Wichita Falls, who has a bionic back, about the proposal. Susie endorsed it, I suppose. But, Lynda is doing more research as we speak.

The *Times* today had a long article on the art show in Kassel, Germany, that Julia and Mel are attending. I knew nothing about it. The item makes it appear to be very political this year, which is right up their alley. Many of the works of art are films.

The Senate version of the health-care bill is, just like the House proposal, a finger to everyone in America who isn't a millionaire. Only millionaires will benefit from its passage. If you make over $1 million you will see your taxes cut by at least $54,000 a year. If you make under that, you won't have health care or you will pay thousands of dollars for it. And we pretend that we live in a democracy.

A decision was made in 1966 or 1967 to close Amarillo Air Force Base. This was a monumental blow to the city of Amarillo, even as early as '67. That announcement put the stake in the heart of downtown. Nothing could revive it from that point on. The chamber of commerce or the downtown merchants group tried to have big merry Christmas celebrations there, when they would block off the streets and erect big lights. There was no magic in that, either.

Susan and I got married in June 1967 and moved into a duplex at the very southernmost end of Polk Street near the railroad tracks. We paid $45 a month. A year later, we could have bought a nice house in the eastern part of Amarillo for $7,000. That's about what my parents paid to build the house at 914 Bowie Street in 1947. Susan and I drove all over east Amarillo, and there was block after block of houses up for foreclosure and for sale. We looked at a three-bedroom, two-bath brick house in south Amarillo that would have cost us $13,500. We were not smart enough to cut a deal for something like this, and so we just rented and rented. Eventually, Amarillo began growing again in a southerly direction, and that's where new shopping malls were installed. Western Plaza on Western Street came online at some point, and that was the big mall when I lived in that area. Now, malls are in demise.

I personally haven't been to a mall for the purpose of shopping since right after we moved to Wimberley in 2011. For the last six years, both Lynda and I have done the vast majority of shopping online, primarily using Amazon. Why? Three reasons: 1) you can find what you want from your chair in your home office; 2) you can read reviews of the product, sometimes from literally hundreds of people; 3) what you buy is delivered right to your front door. Price is sometimes an issue, but not often. Having said that, we don't buy much these days; we are past the acquisition phase of our lives. We spend a lot of money on groceries, and sooner or later (probably after we are no longer around) we might be able to order food and household goods via Amazon for same-day delivery, but we're not there yet as an economy, so I still go to the grocery store just like my dad did – two or three times or more a week.

Lynda buys all of her books through Amazon. She uses a Kindle Paperwhite. I would guess she buys one book a day, and the average price is probably under $10. But, that's her only real entertainment, something she truly enjoys. I don't use a Kindle, so I don't buy books through Amazon. How many people are like us? Probably not many, but enough are changing their buying habits to directly impact the future of shopping malls.

June 25: I was up at 6:30 today to have some coffee and shower before picking up Tom Dawson for a drive to Buda. We played the 10:30 service at St. Elizabeth church there. A very nice crowd was in attendance, and they were most appreciative. We had seven or eight people in the choir behind us, so we did make a lot of noise. Oh, and a drummer!

Then I was off to Kyle to get Lynda a printing cartridge, then the grocery store, and now back at home. I did read some of The *Times* today, but didn't get far before I had to get ready to go. I got an email from The *Times* that included a definitive list of Trump's lies, and, boy, is it a long one. The man can't talk without lying. I've never seen anything like it. And his Fox News buddies let him just yammer on and on as if the man made good sense.

The problem here is that there is no great front-runner to go against Trump in four years. Bernie is way too old. Elizabeth Warren: I don't know about her age. Others? I don't know them. Someone has to get up and get moving! Maybe they just haven't told enough big, fat whoppers to get media attention required to get name recognition!

A storm may be coming, so Chi-Chi is in my lap, fretting over it all.

Lynda is doing a lot of research on the web about the pain pump. She latches onto the worst cases, of course, because they are so alarming. I wonder about how many people have had good experiences and why we can't see more of those. I just haven't looked yet.

June 26: A page one story in today's *Times* outlines the rippling effect of the massive downturn in brick-and-mortar retail, particularly in shopping malls. The story originates in Michigan or New Jersey somewhere and features the people working for a dress shop in a mall. The shop is closing, as are so many others in similar situations. From The *Times*:

"Small cities in the Midwest and Northeast are particularly vulnerable. When major industries left town, retail accounted for a growing share of the job market in places like Johnstown, Decatur, Ill., and Saginaw, Mich. Now, the work force is getting hit a second time, and there is little to fall back on."

At the same time, people in advertising are also fretting over how to reach the eyeballs of all those folks who no longer shop at the mall but shop instead online. The advertising industry had a big convention in France over the weekend. From The *Times*:

"Given that the limit is no longer the number of channels on the television dial but the daily human capacity to consume media, the rush is on to get even better at divining what you want before you even know you want it — and to make sure it's available in ample supply."

Part of the solution will be commercial spots online that are under 10 seconds apiece. This makes sense because the traditional 30-second spots are just not being watched. I can't wait to skip a commercial when I'm watching a YouTube video. So after 5 seconds or so, I click out of the spot and get right to the content. If the message were 5 seconds, I'd probably stick with it.

And in another place The *Times* has a related story, this one about how art dealerships are closing, and only the big galleries are surviving. From The *Times*:

" 'People are not coming to galleries,' (their source) said. 'It's been a simultaneous perfect storm of the convenience and plethora of the art fairs and the Instagram mentality of seeing something and immediately having a yes or no response to something — it's not the world we signed up for.' "

In the news today, there is a lament that the Secretary of State hasn't a clue and can't seem to figure out what Trump wants him to do. Rex Tillerson says one thing, Trump tweets another. And the problem is literally all over the map. In Qatar, for example, Tillerson says everyone should sit down and be calm and work things out. Trump says Qatar pays for terrorists and the Saudis ought to shut them down (notwithstanding the fact that we have a huge and vital military operation in Qatar).

The advent of indoor shopping malls didn't kill downtown Amarillo. But the closing of Amarillo Air Force Base did – that along with the persistence of parking meters and the lack of free parking space.

I didn't do much buying when I was a kid because I never had much money, and the money I did have went into my car projects, for the most part. (My senior year, I did splurge on clothes, though, and I did a lot of buying at Brent's Menswear store in Wolflin Village, around the corner from McGee Furniture. Brent's carried Ralph Lauren and Polo and Gant shirts, and I fell in love with the colors and fabrics offered by Gant – especially the madras items. The shirts at that time were $6.95, and I don't recall paying more than $9 ever for a shirt. I had 60 of them. I'd wear them a couple of times, then take them to a laundry lady who would wash and iron them and put them on hangers for me. Wasn't this a rich-kid-wannabe kind of thing to do? Maybe, although I knew I would never be rich. I wasn't born into money, my parents weren't going to have much money, and my own trajectory in high school was toward jobs that didn't pay well. While I had a few dollars, I spent them on shirts that made me look like a million dollars even if I would never have that kind of money myself.)

I might go to one of the malls in Amarillo to look around, but I rarely bought anything at a mall. When I married and we lived in Canyon, we never went to any mall. We were so poor we never bought anything anyway other than groceries. When I was in the Army in Indianapolis we never found the mall. After Lynda and I moved to Wichita Falls, I discovered pretty quickly that the only stores worth doing business with were at the mall. There was a Sears and a Dillard's. If I needed appliances, I went to Sears. If I needed clothes, I went to Dillard's. Sometimes I would shop at J.C. Penney. But, here's the thing about why I eventually just quit trying to buy anything at all at Sears and Penney's: They quit trying to help me. In fact, sometimes I couldn't even find anyone in Sears who would go to a cash register with me so I could give them money in exchange for a product. That happened to me more than once at Penney's. So, I quit going in those stores. I was not alone. Both of these once-huge retailers are on the ropes. Sears may be out of business. I don't know. I don't keep up with either of them.

June 27: The Supreme Court issued rulings yesterday. The big headlines were reserved for the one that delays Trump's Muslim travel ban while allowing implementation of small parts of it. But, to me, the big ruling was a case that got inside-page coverage from The *Times*. In that ruling, the court said it is constitutional for a church-affiliated school to receive money from a government agency to use for paving for a playground. Sonya Sotomayor dissented, rightly arguing that giving any money to a church crosses the line. She is a hard-liner (pardon the pun) on the issue of church-state relations, and she knows her Constitutional history. The founders would not have said it is all right to fund anything that promoted religion. But, we live in the kind of days for the court that this country has endured before (consider the ruling in Dred Scott).

We had some rain last night, but I have no idea how much. The truth is that it doesn't much matter when it comes to watering ground cover because water just flows right past grass and through the rocks under this thin soil and heads downstream.

For a number of years Lynda and I had a time-share condominium in Santa Fe, N.M. We'd go over there in late October or early November and stay a week or two. Early on we made the decision to try to save up some money to buy some artwork that we both liked to go in our home. Shopping for art in Santa Fe is like being a kid at FAO Schwartz. The city has hundreds of art galleries, something for every taste. We gravitated toward works that had some connection with the Southwest, and we loved pieces by R.C. Gorman of Taos in particular. But, desert landscapes spoke to us as well. Over time we did buy some nice art in Santa Fe and Taos and in some other New Mexico places.

But, we found art we really loved in Prague, when we spent two weeks there with Sarah. The street artists were leaving Prague because it was becoming too expensive, Sarah told us, and that created a sense of urgency to find and buy what we could while we could. We figured we would only be there once in our lives. We bought quite a number of pieces, and then had a booger of a time trying to get them home by carrying them onto the plane. We royally pissed off one airline waitress, who finally found a place for our canvases, but not without being rude and mean about it.

We now have those works hanging in our living and dining rooms. Other works we have acquired are in other places around the house. We have space for one more big piece, right above our bed. But, that size of an original work would be very expensive, and we don't have that kind of money anymore. I toyed with the idea of really looking for something when the girls took me to Santa Fe for my 70th birthday this year, but we did not make it up Canyon Road to the shops that had the really wonderful Southwest artists' stuff on display.

I made $50 on the Buda church gig Sunday, and I had to go buy Lynda a new ink cartridge for her printer at Target in Kyle Sunday afternoon. So, there I was in Target with $50 to burn, and I didn't even look for anything to buy.

June 28: Bryan came to the house yesterday afternoon to start picking grapes off the huge vine in our front yard. These are mustang grapes, and they don't produce every year. In fact, I think this is only the second or third year we have had them. There are still some green grapes in the clusters, but enough are nice and deep purple that they are worth picking. He got a big bucket full and will come back this weekend to gather in some more. The deer eat the grapes off the lower branches, and they also like the leaves. I've seen bucks stand up on their hind legs to get at the grapes higher up on the vines.

Bryan plans to make mustang grape wine. There are several videos about how to do this on YouTube. I've watched a couple of them. The process is pretty basic. Bryan and Erin came over two years ago when we had a pretty good crop, and they picked what must have been 50 or 60 pounds of grapes. Bryan bought some equipment in Austin, and then manufactured some vinegar. I guess it's still not ready for prime time because he hasn't brought us any of it yet. I am not sure what he will do differently this time, but he's going to a lot of trouble if all he comes up with is vinegar.

The *Times* has a nice piece about a printer/photographer named Richard Benson, who died recently. Accompanying his obit were a couple of photos he was credited with shooting and printing. One of them was called "Texas Panhandle 2006," and it was a picture of an ancient wood outbuilding that was leaning toward the left. I'm not sure that anyone who is not familiar with the Texas Panhandle would get the joke. Everything leans away from the wind in the Panhandle – trees, buildings, weeds, fence posts. I haven't seen that particular building, but I could probably find a similar one pretty easily by driving in any direction out of Amarillo.

The Senate version of the health care bill is dead. And it should be. The Congressional Budget Office reported that it would eliminate funding for 22 million Americans to get health care. That wasn't enough pain to suit Ted Cruz, the Nazi

Senator from Texas. Cruz wanted more people to be hurt.

Tom Friedman has a column that everyone should read in The *Times* today. It is about how Trump killed the Pacific trade alliance in his first week in office only to let the Chinese take over that part of the world, figuratively speaking, not literally – yet. Trump thought China was part of the deal; of course, the deal was hammered out by Obama to try to keep China in check. And China was the target of the deal, not the center of participation. This kind of bull-in-the-china-closet reaction by Trump will hurt us all over the world. The fucking out-of-work coal miners in West Virginia won't care, of course, so long as they have their opium pipes.

I need to make a decision about working more hours just to focus on the library expansion project. I don't want to work eight more hours; I don't think there's enough to be done to warrant that amount of time. But, I could work four more hours and get a lot done.

June 29: The news that will keep on biting us in the ass was on Page 1 of The *Times* today. It's about code stolen from the National Security Agency (NSA) that's being used to hold major computer networks and big companies for ransom. You don't pay them, they don't tell you how to unlock your computer. In other words, the NSA's top-secret juju has been swiped and is being used against everyone. This is not simply troubling; it's outrageously insane. If this were the Obama White House, Republicans would already be holding hearings on why and how the NSA was so sloppy and stupid, probably in cahoots with Hillary to give the country to the Aleutians or the ancient people of the Andes, for God's sake, in exchange for having her visage on a voodoo doll. But, Trump gets off scott-free on this one, too.

One of The *Times* columnists writes today about the back-to-the-future aspect of the grocery business, what with Amazon buying Whole Foods. He speculates that part of the reason is so that Amazon can deliver groceries to your front door like or better than Blue Apron. Wow, he says, what a concept. Indeed.

Like the columnist I grew up in a time when ice in block form was actually delivered by truck to people on Bowie Street. I remember them chopping the ice with an ice pick. As a very small child, I remember the milk man – from Goldsmith Dairy – coming right up to our kitchen door and into the house, while we were eating cereal, and putting glass milk bottles into our refrigerator. We would have left the empties out by the back door for him the night before. I remember one of the milkmen because he had a 1950-ish Chevy that was two-tone brown. He told me about it, I believe in the context of wanting to better himself so he could hotrod the car. So here we are 70 years later, and there is talk of home delivery. Not by a milkman-kind-of-guy, but by drone. I do believe this will happen and in my lifetime. Drones are just too cheap, almost in the expendable category, and gasoline and drivers are just too expensive. And drones can carry heavy bombs; why not watermelons?

June 30: Fifty years ago today Susan Bryan and I were married at First Presbyterian Church of Amarillo. John was my best man, and Susan's sister Misty was her maid of honor. We spent our honeymoon in Cimarron, N.M., before I got sick and we had to head back to Amarillo. I was working at the *Amarillo Globe*

News as a night cops reporter. Susan wasn't working at the time, but she very quickly got a job as a unit clerk at St. Anthony's Hospital. We lived in a duplex on South Polk Street. On the other side of the duplex Cindy and Gary Burgess moved in. We paid $45 a month. We were about 100 yards from the railroad tracks. Our next-door neighbor was a Hells Angel.

Inside the business section of The *Times* today we find a story about reporters and copy editors staging a protest at the newspaper. Their complaints had to do with the elimination of a central copy desk, the firing of about 70 copy editors and the firing of an undisclosed number of reporters. The *Times* management announced these changes a few days ago, and they are clearly and admittedly a response to the decline in print advertising that's plagued all of newspaperdom since the advent of the internet. Frankly, I'm surprised The *Times* has held on this long.

Fifteen years ago or more, the people who owned the *Times Record News* in Wichita Falls started cutting back because of internet pressure. I lost a complete edition of the newspaper—the afternoon version— along with a reporting staff and copy-editing staff, and over time the goal became not to produce a reasonably informative and vital newspaper but the creation of greater and greater wealth for the investors.

In a town like Wichita Falls, which wasn't really growing in population or retail trade, the idea of having 6 or 7 percent quarter-over-quarter and year-over-year profit growth was ludicrous. But that was the expectation, and we lost at least one publisher in the late '90s because he couldn't and wouldn't promise the kinds of margins that management expected. I think that the year he was fired, he had put together a budget that called for 3 percent growth year-over-year. Keep in mind our margins were in the range of 20 percent, an amount unheard of in American business.

The *Times*' managers, like mine in the '90s, say that eliminating the copy desk, culling the staff of oversight editors not responsible for copy, and cutting reporting staff will merely streamline the news production process, resulting in a better newspaper. This is pure, unadulterated bullshit. You do not cut supervisory and copy editors and get a better newspaper.

Right after I was named the editor of the *Times Record News*, I found myself on an airplane seated next to the new editor of The *Washington Times*. I asked him what his goal as editor of this big, major newspaper was, and, by extension, what my goal should be. He did not hesitate in his response: "Get it first and get it right." I tried to remember that over the years and also to instill those values in my staff. Doing both became increasingly harder as I lost copy editors, supervisory editors and reporters.

Over the course of my first 40 years, newsrooms across America embraced computer editing and typesetting. We were streamlined in the name of efficiency and because the advent of computers in so many areas of production revealed the need for fewer people to do those specific jobs. For example, when I started at the *Times Record News* in 1983, we probably had 50 people working in the backshop forward of the press room. When I left, we had three or four.

July 1: When I retired from journalism in 2007, we had 33 or 34 people in the newsroom at the *Times Record News*. That included six or seven in the sports department, three photographers and three people who worked as imagers, meaning they toned photos for the press and, by rights, should have been backshop employees. Another was my secretary who doubled as the newspaper librarian. We had two full-timers on the features desk, one farm editor, a city beat reporter, a county beat reporter, a schools reporter, an editorial page editor, a business beat reporter, a features designer, two cops reporters, a Sunday general assignments reporter, a couple of obituary clerks and a complement of copy editors. The copy desk had to be fully staffed, and the other positions were negotiable. But, this I thought was the minimum number we needed to put out a daily newspaper and one on Sunday.

Remember here how the work flow happened when I started out at the Amarillo paper. In my newsroom of 2007, the story went from a reporter to a city editor to a copy editor. And the copy editor had by then become a glorified typesetter and stereographer, someone who actually built newspaper pages in a design program, laying in the stories, the photos and the headlines and then sending the finished page to the press. So, not a lot of intense editing actually happened at the copy desk level.

July 2: I forgot to include in these paragraphs something about my adventure into very high-dollar steak preparation. Thursday I went to HEB and bought two big rib-eye steaks, each weighing about 9 ounces. These steaks were special because they had been dry aged for 21 days, according to the signs at the butcher counter. I paid $38 for these two steaks or about $26 per pound. I routinely pay about $23 a pound for filet mignon, but these were the most expensive two slabs of beef I have ever bought.

When one spends $19 on a steak, one wants the steak to be cooked to perfection. So, I was very careful on the timing, and my steak came out a little overdone. Lynda's was perfect. She declared it the best steak she had ever eaten, which made me happy and made the expense worthwhile. But, I could probably get by with something a little less pricey. One time dining at that level is plenty for me.

I remember when I first moved into a house with two other guys in Amarillo while I was going to AC and also working at the *Globe-News*. We went to the grocery store to buy our first bags of stuff to cook up, and the hamburger meat we bought was 33 cents a pound. Thirty-three cents a pound! Of course, most of it was water or grease. So, you'd start cooking with a raw hamburger patty the size of a dinner plate in your skillet, and by the time it had cooked down it was the size of a dime.

Lynda had another pretty good evening, in terms of pain, thanks to those small candies that B. brought back from Washington state. One-half of one seems to do the trick. She is happy as a clam, and has asked him to see if he can find some more. We all hope that this simple remedy will do the trick.

Gorsuch, who has been a Supreme Court justice for less than six months, gets his early due in an editorial in The *New York Times* today. He is even more conservative than Clarence Thomas, who has the distinction of being too stupid to understand the Constitution. For example, the *Times* points out that Gorsuch and Thomas were not completely on board with the court's recent ill-argued decision to let states put taxpayer money into playgrounds built by church schools. But Gorsuch took the matter beyond what the court said when it declared that the ruling at hand would have an effective reach only at the playground level and said that states should never be stopped from supporting religious education. What is this man thinking? Would he be OK with having the taxpayers of Texas pay for the construction of a building for a Muslim school? And so we learn right up-front that Justice Gorsuch is not really conservative as a matter of belief or propensity; he is a conservative because that's where the money comes from.

As the copy desk at the *Times Record News* (and all across America in newspapers that size and larger) shrunk and the demands that editors be designers and page-builders intensified, the pressure built on city editors and other line editors to do a much better job of copy editing. They were already doing that while also juggling the task of supervising story development, keeping track of payroll information and time off/vacation time and holding reporters' hands. I went through a lot of city editors because the job was just overwhelming for the most of them.

The overall result of the mounting pressures on newspapers to make unholy profits was to cut what the editorial departments could cover and offer, to increase the number of errors and to make these places not much fun to work at, to end a sentence badly with a preposition. I wish I had a dollar for every time a source or subscriber called me up or collared me somewhere to ask, "Don't you guys have proofreaders anymore?" They didn't want to hear the answer: "Hell no. We haven't had proofreaders at the *Times Record News* EVER! And we never will." When I left the newspaper in 2007, we were still trying to figure out how to get our stories and photographs onto our internet pages without adding personnel.

July 3: Tomorrow I'm up and off to be in the 4th of July parade with the Dark Sky Committee. I think we have a Jeep and a banner and our T-shirts, and we're going to hand out some candies. Lots of candies. Or, at least I hope we have lots of candies. It's hard to get people who have not ridden or participated in big parades to understand how much candy it takes to make people on the parade route happy.

Trump is doing such asinine things it's almost impossible to keep a running total. Fortunately, last week the NYT published a full page of lies he has told. Someone responded when I told them of the collection: "Just one page?" But it goes beyond lies. This is a sick, sick adolescent we have here. The Republicans love him to death because he's their little boy. Charles Blow, a columnist for The *Times*, hates him. From Blow today: *"The presidency has been hijacked."*

No shit.

And so has the Supreme Court. And Congress. The Koch Brothers must have arms broken from patting themselves on the back so many times and so hard. Likewise, the Walton family. At some point, though, people will tire of Wal-Mart, won't they? Probably not.

July 4: On this 4th, one wonders what Thomas Jefferson would think of Donald Trump.

July 5: The 4th parade yesterday was the biggest and best ever. I walked alongside our Jeep that had speakers that blared out "Deep in the Heart of Texas" as we crawled along Ranch Road 12. I handed out dark sky information cards, and I was pleasantly surprised by how many took them and thanked me for them. Many said they were supportive of the idea. I'm sure there are kids growing up all over the world who have never actually seen a night sky with all those wondrous stars and planets. I joined the dark sky group that's just getting started here, and it includes Louis Parks, a member of the CARD group that reviews proposed construction projects around Wimberley. He said I am being considered for membership. It is a group I'd like to be a member of because it has an impact already and I think I can help out.

This week, Trump's challenge is how to deal with a North Korea that keeps testing our patience by launching intercontinental ballistic missiles capable of reaching Alaska. Will he negotiate with Kim? Trump bills himself as the great negotiator. We shall see since he is also a great bully and a great sulker and whiner.

July 6: This morning we go to Kyle for me to see Dr. E. about this bowel situation. He is not a friendly person, but maybe he will listen and fix the problem without much trouble. It's a real perplexing thing to me; I have never had this before.

Trump will meet with China's president and Putin in Europe this week. He will spin the results his way, but I have a bad feeling that he will be badly used by these two sneaks. And if he is badly used, our country will be badly used, too. He hasn't a clue what to do about North Korea. But neither does anyone else. A writer in The *Times* today suggested that we will have to depend on deterrence, ala 1969, and give up trying to stop the North from deploying nuclear weapons. He is probably right. We have to stifle the urge to "do something, anything" about what the North is doing.

Hobby Lobby, whose conservative owners close shop on Sundays to worship the Lord and who pay their employees minimum wage with not enough hours to qualify for health care, are in trouble for smuggling antique cuneiform tablets out of the Middle East for their collection of Bible stuff in Oklahoma. "We just like Bible stuff," they told investigators. Why? Because their little god of The Way Things Ought to Be in Hobby Lobby Land is in there, right there on those pages where he belongs, not out in the world where he might frown on corporate greed.

I have signed up in Coursera for a class on how to tell stories across many platforms. I hesitated about this because it may tax my brain. My brain needs taxing. So, I will go for it. I am finishing up the class in Advertising and Society. It's been just so-so. The ads have been interesting, but I didn't really learn much I didn't already know.

July 7: Trump is in Germany making disparaging comments about Obama and others in American government, something only a moron would do. The man is loyal only to himself. You just don't go overseas and crap on your own people in public. Everyone learns that in kindergarten; stand by your people. If the coal

171

miners of West Virginia don't know anything else they know to stick with their clan. Hell, that's why they stay in those freaking hills and won't try to seek jobs where there might actually be jobs. He is meeting with Putin today, and the thing is that Putin is a liar and a cheat and anything at all he says or promises cannot be trusted. This is a great show for Putin, a silly thing for Trump to be making into a big deal.

Be careful what you wish for: Americans may want to feel safer, and cops may want to make them safer, but let's look to China for a cautionary tale about the route not to take. Actually, it was all laid out in the book "1984." We made the mistake of reading it as fiction rather than prophecy. The Wall Street Journal, in its June 27 edition, has a story on 1A about how the Chinese are using face recognition technology to track jay-walkers, among others. They put cameras everywhere, like American cops want to do, and then run your facial features into a database and then match every time they see you. If you are caught jay-walking, your picture goes up on a big screen with lettering telling people you are a criminal.

I'm reading a book now called "Shop Class as Soulcraft," by Matthew B. Crawford. A reference to it caught my eye somewhere so I got it through interlibrary loan. Crawford's thesis echoes that of Robert Pirsig, author of "Zen and the Art of Motorcycle Maintenance." Crawford's prose is denser, almost deliberately so. And I think if I were him I'd be a little embarrassed to steal the idea from someone who wrote a book on the value of doing stuff by hand with an eye toward achieving some kind of rough analog of perfection back before 1970. I guess the notion of doing good work with your own two hands has staying power and is worth reframing now and then.

The idea appeals to me as I reflect back on Archie Pool and my high-school shop classes. But, Crawford goes a step further and places shop class in a larger field that essentially pits workers versus managers with managers the tools of corporations that mainly want to suck the life out of the workers and then discard them as soon as possible and with as little financial obligation as possible. That's certainly been my experience for the most part with certain powerful exceptions. I ended up my working career with two pensions, one for $350 per month and one for $850 per month, and I am grateful for both, as meager as they are. I'm especially so now that most corporations don't offer any kind of pensions at all to their retiring workers.

July 8: I have some vine-ripe organic tomatoes I'm going to make some gazpacho out of today or they will go bad before I can get around to it. That would be a real shame, because good tomatoes are really hard to find even at the farmers markets, where so many vegetables seem to have been imported from the Valley or California and labeled as if they were locally produced.

Trump met with Putin yesterday and it is reported that he asked Putin about hacking American elections, and Putin denied it and so they moved on. Today, all the other nations in the conference in Hamburg are supposed to issue a statement that highlights how the United States has abandoned international leadership in the world community, and how the rest of them will move on with someone else at the wheel. The *Times* reported yesterday that all over the world, trade deals are being worked out without U.S. involvement so that new partnerships are emerging that do not require our billfolds or our participation. This will not be a good thing in the long run for this country.

Reports today indicate the U.S. is at full employment or very close to it. Anyone who wants a job can get one, and companies are having a hard time filling positions. I see signs in several windows here. So, in reality, the issue facing the government is not how to create more jobs but how to create more people. And we aren't going to do that because we're going to close our borders and make it hard if not impossible for new workers to get to these shores. Already, smart kids from China and India, who once might have come to study in America, are going to Canada or elsewhere.

July 9: *The New Yorker* for July 10-17 has a devastating piece as its main longform journalism offering about Texas and its politics. The writer, Lawrence Wright, who lives in Austin, is just dead-on accurate in his description of what goes on in the Capitol. What's at work there is a fraud and a parody launched by sycophants and psychos who are beholding to the most heinously stupid people on the planet, many of whom live right here in Texas. I cringed at every paragraph because Wright so honestly portrays how absolutely idiotic the officials are who run the state, from Abbott on down. I have talked intermittently with Lynda about moving completely out of Texas and going to New Mexico. In fact after last year's election I did some online research into places to live over there and found some attractive-looking little towns near Albuquerque with low costs-of-living. She won't hear of it.

If something happened to Lynda I would very seriously consider moving because the people in this state are just too dumb for me to associate with, and I'm not being vain about that or egotistical. I'm just saying that it's hard to stomach being around people who are so intellectually careless or unimaginative.

In the same issue of *The New Yorker*, Sheelah Kolhatkar writes in the Financial Page about the bad-boy of new companies, Uber. I know that in this piece Kolhatkar is not trying to cover the waterfront when it comes to describing corporate misbehavior, but he doesn't even get close to doing that: "There are many examples of corporate behavior that violates rules but bolsters profits, from emissions cheating at Volkswagen to the creation of false bank accounts at Wells Fargo and alleged sexual harassment at the highest levels at Fox News ..." Really, those are the best examples? Not even close. In today's *The New York Times* there's a review of a new book about how nobody—nobody!—was prosecuted by the federal government for the misdeeds and lies and other outrageously illegal acts perpetrated on the American public by the big banks when they caused the meltdown of our economy in 2008. If you wonder why, the book answers the question: the lawyers involved at the banks and at the Justice Department were either buddies or they were linked together by things like the schools their kids attended or the churches they went to or mutual friends. It was a classic example of the Good Old Boys taking care of one another. If a Justice lawyer got too close to prosecution he would remind himself that after his stint in government service he would need a good job, which would be provided by the very people he was supposed to consider prosecuting.

And then there is this in the latest New Yorker from David Remnick: "Trump began his national ascendancy by hoisting the racist banner of birtherism. Since then, as candidate and as President, he has found countless ways to pollute the national atmosphere. If someone suggests a lie that is useful to him, he will happily pass it along or endorse it. This habit is not without purpose or cumulative effect. Even if Trump fails in his most ambitious policy initiatives, whether it is liberating the wealthy from their tax obligations or liberating the poor from their health care, he has already begun to foster a public sphere in which, as Hannah Arendt put it in her treatise on totalitarian states, millions come to believe that 'everything was possible and that nothing was true.' "

Finally for today, Robert H. Frank, an economics professor at the Johnson Graduate School of Management at Cornell University, has a great essay in The *Times* about how a single-payer system would save everyone money on medical care. In layman's terms he makes the case, which is basically this: if the government pays for health care, you have just one set of administrators, you have a big pool of people most of whom are not sick and you have negotiating power that one company or even a group can never hope to achieve. Lynda and I are hearty supporters of a single-payer system because it just makes sense for the reasons Frank discusses, but also because it leaves no one behind. Consider this, which Frank includes: "In 2012, for example, the average cost of coronary bypass surgery was more than $73,000 in the United States but less than $23,000 in France." Why? France has a single-payer system.

July 10: Trump tweeted yesterday that the United States should join up with Russia to protect all of our cybersecurity. He is so flabbergastingly naive that I think people around the world were just too stunned to say anything. You know, he skipped all the secret security briefings before and after his election, so he probably still thinks of Putin and Russia as people over there who speak a funny language and drink too much vodka. Both of those things may be true, but Russia is far from a friend or even a potential friend. Surely someone in Washington will try to talk some sense into Trump. At least we can take heart in the fact that he cannot sign a treaty without Senate approval. Oh, what am I thinking: this Senate is full of sycophants and pantywaists and drunkards. He might round all of them up for a night of Russian spirits and women who look like Melania and have them eating right out of his hand. Or maybe he's already done that.

The *Times* reports today that Bloomberg, the people who publish business news, believes that the American public will be buying huge numbers of electric-powered cars by 2030, enough to dwarf production and sales of internal-combustion-powered vehicles. To quote:

"The reason? Batteries. Since 2010, the average cost of lithium-ion battery packs has plunged by two-thirds, to around $300 per kilowatt-hour. The Bloomberg report sees that falling to $73 by 2030, without any significant technological breakthroughs, as companies like Tesla increase battery production in massive factories, optimize the design of battery packs and improve chemistries."

The *Times* is somewhat skeptical and quotes people who think Bloomberg is a little too optimistic. Consumers buy cars and pickups for more than their propulsion systems. They buy them for long and short trips and they buy them because they like to go fast and sound mean. Not everyone who drives these days is a little old futsy woman with flowers in her hat. Or a balding boomer worried about gas mileage. It is entirely possible that battery technology will move beyond where we are right now. At least that would be something I would hope to see. The traditional lithium-ion battery is dated technology, but it seems to be the only technology out there. Isn't there some other chemical way to make a cheap and effective battery? I don't know enough about it to say.

July 11: The *Times* is having fun reporting little secrets kept by the Trump family about meetings with Russians during last year's campaign. A little bit leaks out every day, the more to keep Trump in the news in a way he'd prefer not to be in the news. *The New Yorker* is also taking apart every move the administration makes so as to show who is actually running things, and that would be the very rich for their very own ends.

David Brooks reviews a book in The *Times* today that tells why the American wealthy classes get to keep being that way without some kind of intervention. Rather, not why, which is explained in gradations of greed, but the how. They have their own way of doing things, and if you don't know that language or those ways, you will not break into their hierarchy. It's always been just that simple. That's one reason those at court in tsarist Russia spoke French. In another disturbing news report in The *Times*, we learn that Trump is thinking about out-sourcing the war in Afghanistan to the guy who ran Blackwater, Erik Prince, and his associates. As when George W. Bush was president, that would mean contractors would make gazillions of dollars providing shoddy services and watching American boys get killed on their behalf.

It has been argued, and is probably transparently true, that the single most compelling reason for American involvement in the Iraqi war was to enrich companies owned by or run by friends of Vice President Dick Cheney, once the head of Schlumberger.

Our visit to Dr. Ramirez yesterday yielded a little of help for Lynda. The doctor prescribed an antidepressant, which she will try for three or four weeks, and then he will try her on Lyrica. Our plan right now is for me to fly to Colorado within the next week to buy her some edible pot and send it home via mail. I'll get there, spend the night with a friend, and then transact as much business as I can before I have to return home. I might have to spend two nights. I will need to concoct a couple of cover stories to explain why I need to buy so much of the product, and then why I need to mail it all back. I think I'll go to a minimum of three shops and three post offices. There is some risk of detection involved but it is tiny. The reward far, far outweighs the risk because Lynda does get some pain relief from edibles.

I returned "Shop Class as Soulcraft" to the library yesterday without finishing it. The author was just a pretentious asshole who had a single message: find something you can do really well and do it." I just couldn't wade through the self-referential bullshit of the Shop Class author, although he did get me to thinking about why shop classes were ever invented – as ways for big businesses involved in manufacturing to inculcate certain values in worker bees they could hire out of high school and put onto the assembly line. Archie Pool certainly did talk up those values of hard work, thrift, patience, and so on, but it is a stretch for me to believe Mr. Pool was a tool of the big boys. I saw him more as an advocate for us, trying to build us up in terms of our character and to strengthen our ethical fiber.

July 12: Thanks to The *Times* we know that Trump Junior met with a top Russian lawyer last year in the hope of getting dirt on Hillary to help Trump win. He might not have gotten what he wanted, but he did in fact meet with her. What constitutes Treason, one wonders? The media is talking about "collusion." Who will bring up the "T" word because that's what we are talking about here? And what about a conspiracy to violate the Constitution's emoluments clause by trying to accept a huge gift from a foreign power?

In two other stories today, The *Times* reveals what the Trumpistas are up to in Washington as they try to dismantle the government. In all executive branch agencies, Trump has set up teams to look at regulations and how to undo them to the benefit of business and industries under their regulatory umbrella. Many of the people appointed to the teams are also or were also lobbyists or lawyers representing those very industries and businesses that would benefit from changes in the rules. This is not just an incredible breach of trust from a man who promised to "drain the swamp" when he got to DC. It is also wholesale, state-sponsored and state-sanctioned conflict of interest. The other story may deal with a situation that will have the harshest long-term effects. It's a story about how this country is pulling back on helping other nations that desperately need help and instead pouring our wealth into our military.

Will he leave behind a world and a nation that is better for his having served? Maybe "served" is the wrong word. Maybe the right word is "exploited." Or "abused." Or "destroyed."

I watch all of this in despair and outrage. I am too old to do very much about all of it. I might run for office, but by the time I could get to the level to do something I'd be too old to get any votes. And I'm not at all sure I'd be electable to dog-catcher. I have left a trail of very liberal newspaper columns and editorials behind, dating back to my days as editor of The *Canyon News*, and, I guess, especially then. I also would not lie about being a socialist just to get a vote, and I certainly would not curry favor with those who want to do terrible things to the planet or other people. But, most of all: I don't have any money for such things.

I have tickets to go to Denver in two weeks to buy Lynda a year's supply of edibles. I'll stay with P. there, going in on a Tuesday and coming back on a Thursday. I think I need to buy about 400 pieces of candy and have them shipped home in discreet, unassuming packages. It is absolutely crazy that Lynda could get a prescription for a powerful opioid today over the phone, but I can't buy a little weed to relieve her pain. This is truly "reefer madness."

July 13: I have been reading *The Taste of War: World War II and the Battle for Food* by Lizzie Collingham. It is remarkably well researched and detailed and unveils the role of hunger and the lack of food products in the drive of the Nazis and the Japanese as they grew to yearn for war and then for an end to it. In the first chapters, as Collingham recounted how the Nazis adopted a policy of food for

Germans first and starvation for everyone else, I thought she was sounding like a revisionist who would blame the Holocaust on Germans' need for food rather than on antisemitism. However, in Chapter 9 she lays it all out: "It had always been the intention of Hitler and a section of the National Socialist leadership to eradicate the Jews from Europe. The food crisis of 1941-42 provided an ostensibly rational reason as to why the crime of murder should be committed. The Jews could not be allowed to continue eating the precious food which the German workers deserved; they must die in order to free up desperately needed food supplies. Thus food worries gave added impetus to the Holocaust." In other chapters, Collingham tells how Hitler and Goering and others in the Nazi leadership dictated that everyone else but Germans would be systematically starved to death so that not a single German would be hungry. I had not read anywhere about the way the Germans starved out the people in western Russia, but that's exactly what happened. This is a terrific book for anyone interested in learning about World War II at a greater depth.

The big, big news in the *Times* today is not about the Trumpistas! Instead, it is about something else altogether:

"A Food and Drug Administration panel opened a new era in medicine on Wednesday, unanimously recommending that the agency approve the first-ever treatment that genetically alters a patient's own cells to fight cancer, transforming them into what scientists call 'a living drug' that powerfully bolsters the immune system to shut down the disease."

Perhaps I will live to see the day when drugs are tailored to individual bodies as this one is. There is just one drawback with this approach at this point: The cost for this new treatment is estimated at about $300,000. That is for one patient.

July 14: We had a frustrating day yesterday. Lynda took a new antidepressant Wednesday evening, one prescribed by the doctor when we visited him together on Monday. It knocked her for a loop, and she slept most of the morning. She felt groggy and out of sorts, with chills at times. She called the doctor, and he told her to stop taking the medicine. So perhaps he will adjust the dosage later, and she can try again.

The Republicans unveiled their latest version of a health-care bill yesterday, and it was not exactly DOA but nearly so. Early reports are that it leaves more than 22 million people on Medicaid without health insurance, doesn't cover pre-existing conditions and doesn't give deep tax cuts to the rich like the previous Republican version did. The Senate might pass it, though, so the senators can enjoy their August holiday without worrying about it anymore. That leaves a conference committee to work it all out, and that may be impossible. But, at least the Republicans can say they actually did do something, even as bad as it is, the appearance of being effective accruing more value than actually being effective. This is the way it is these days in the Land of Hocus Pocus and Tom Foolery that is Donald Trump's Washington.

On the business page of today's *Times*, this headline: "Tough Times for

Disciples of Ayn Rand." And they are legion, believe it or not. The Randites are finding out that Objectivism takes you only so far, and that is generally to the bathroom mirror where one can gaze upon one's glowing countenance for only so long before it becomes a little nauseating even for narcissists. For generations, Ayn Rand has appealed mainly and almost exclusively to adolescent boys. Which makes it a perfect set of books for Trumpistas and the technocrats of Silicon Valley.

I read Ayn Rand's works when I was in high school – early high school – and they made me want to pump iron, except I was never a very good pump-iron-type kid. Then I discovered Herman Hesse, and that was more my style.

I scanned through to the end of the book about hunger and food shortages in World War II and then returned it to the library. I probably finished the first 10 chapters, but the rest was just too much, and it was too poorly organized. At least I gained a hugely valuable perspective on just what role the search for food played in the war.

July 15: A lot of articles these days concern growing old. Even in the debate over Medicaid, the subtext is what to do about old people, many of whom use up a lot of resources while giving nothing back to society in return. I see this not just as a problem having to do with economics, but a moral problem as well.

The fact of the matter is that the retirement age of 65 is too young. Most people live far longer than that, and at 65 they are just as good as they were at 45 and probably better because of the experiences they have had in the other 20 years. It would probably be more realistic to set the official retirement age at 70 or 72. There'd be some whining about that, but the data show that a whole lot of people are not actually retiring at 65 anyway. They don't want to quit working. I certainly didn't. That doesn't deal, though, with the problem of providing health care for people as they near death, like in the last year or two before they die. We need to have serious policy discussions about this with serious people, so that isn't going to happen because those kinds of people aren't setting public policy these days. We probably need to put a brake on government spending for extraordinary health-care fixes once a person enters a period of serious decline. Why would it be reasonable for anyone to pay for a knee replacement for someone who is 90 years of age, regardless of their physical abilities? There has to be some cost-benefit discussion.

It's my understanding that in certain Native American cultures, the old and infirm were encouraged to go off and deal with death on their own terms – for the good of the tribe. The aged didn't want to be a burden. (Maybe I'm putting too much weight here on "Little Big Man.") I feel that is a responsible way to look at this situation, and my own plan is to voluntarily leave and wrestle with the final outcome on my own terms and in my own time. I'll be damned if I'm going to sit around and act like I'm entitled to something as the end closes in. I'm entitled to what I work for and nothing more.

July 17: I have started in on a new class offered by Coursera called "Transmedia Storytelling." It has a very impressive list of contributors and is already very interesting just as I work on the first week of assignments. I am going to have to come up with a good story that contains a lot of visual elements that will let me use video to create part of the story line. I have some ideas, but they are not fleshed out. I hope that by crowdsourcing the ideas I can come up with something that is actually good enough to get me through the class with some knowledge of how these things work.

I have been elected to the CARD steering committee. CARD stands for Citizens Alliance for Responsible Development. Of all the groups that exist in the valley it is the one with the most credibility when it comes to growth in Wimberley and environs. CARD members sat down with HEB, for example, to work out details of their store design before they opened in Wimberley – even before they got approval from the City Council. And CARD was instrumental in keeping public the details of the plan that Tractor Supply put forward to have a big store on the outskirts of town, just south of the river. It was a bad plan, the council understood that thanks to CARD, and the TSC proposal went nowhere. My first meeting as a member is tomorrow night.

I think maybe a story that ran inside in the Business section of the *Times* on Sunday actually belonged on 1A. The story is about the big pharmaceutical companies and how they spend their money. The subhead: "Companies budget more for share buybacks and dividends, a new academic study shows."

So, who benefits? Not customers or sick people. The beneficiaries are the share-holders and the managers who own stock or options. The goal is to drive up the stock price regardless of anything else. This is what I was, in part, talking to Sarah's best friend about Saturday at Greyson's birthday party. Until this stockholder-first mentality is overcome with some rational sense that customers have a place at the table, too, then nothing will change. And I just don't see this happening in my lifetime.

July 18: The health-care proposal is dead in the Senate. Two more senators said they won't support the measure, killing it for now and possibly forever. It's not clear to me why they won't support it; at first blush, it looks like it just doesn't give enough tax breaks to the rich to make these senators happy. That would certainly make sense. No Republican in elected office wants to raise taxes on the wealthy or expand medical care for the poor.

Over on the business page, The *Times* notes that the median home sales price in San Francisco is now $500,000. That's double the median across the country. In Austin, I believe the median is more than $300,000, however. From the story: "Housing prices in Los Angeles, San Francisco, San Jose and San Diego have jumped as much as 75 percent over the past five years.

I'm not surprised about this. I've been watching these prices for a number of years. In fact, at one point in his career John got a job offer in the oil business based in San Diego and couldn't take the job because he could not have afforded the housing out there. Not long after that, I talked with an editor at the San Diego paper who I ran into at a national conference of some sort and I asked him about housing prices. He said he had a hard time hiring staff members because of the cost of housing. The *Times* report suggests that this kind of pricing crisis will over time really hurt California. Perhaps. But if that's where the good-paying jobs are then that's where the people will go and they will figure out what they have to do to live out there.

The *Times* editorializes about the number of companies that are going into the electric car business, citing Tesla, of course, and Volvo. I still think that the Achilles tendon of this business is the battery. Tesla has a big factory in Nevada to make lithium ion batteries for cars and homes, and the increased availability may drive costs down somewhat, but batteries are still expensive, not particularly long-lasting and some may just catch fire and blow up. A major breakthrough in battery type would no doubt push Americans into cars with electric power, but we aren't there yet.

July 19: Since the Senate cannot come up with a good health-care bill, Trump is simply going to destroy the Affordable Care solution bit by bit until Americans are begging him and Mitch McConnell to give them anything. It is a nasty use of brute force to do great damage so that one can get what one wants and is a reminder of the childlike tantrums that Trump is capable of throwing. Imagine the spoiled-child-on-the-playground scenario playing out without the child asserting that he will take his ball and go home if things don't go his way. Instead, the child, after having been told he cannot do as he pleases, finds a hatchet and chops the ball into tiny pieces and then huffs off to his mansion to find another ball he can play with all by himself. Or, he finds a hand grenade and blows up the entire playground!

I attended my first meeting as a member of the steering committee for the CARD group last evening. It is a collegial crowd of good people all intent on doing the right thing, something of an anomaly in this day and age. It appears we will be focusing in the near term on "low-impact" living, including low-impact development. This is an excellent road to go down because it can include so many initiatives.

July 20: Trump sat down for an interview with The *Times* yesterday, and the story about it today says he grumped about the special prosecutor looking at connections between him and his family and Russia. That's nothing new.

I sent Julia a clip from another *Times* article about an art show in Italy that has been closed amid allegations that many of the paintings were frauds. I imagine this happens quite often in high-end art because of the astounding prices people will pay.

I will spend hours this weekend doing research for my trip next Tuesday and Wednesday to Denver. I need to write down addresses of all the shops and also of all the post offices. I also need to do some research on kinds of pot that will relieve pain. Last night, Lynda got really high, and she also was pain-free when she came to bed. This obviously underscores the solution to her problem. This whole business about the trip has me sleeping fitfully every night. Last night, I lay awake worrying about how I might be in prison – that is, how I might live and survive. I worry about an arrest scenario that has the cops storming in our front door with guns at the ready and shooting Chi-Chi because she barks at them. I will be very glad when this whole episode is behind me.

July 21: As I mentioned on July 19, Trump is now setting about to kill the Affordable Care Act's benefits, thus also killing untold millions of Americans who depend on that law for health-care insurance. It is a spiteful act by a little man. I have rarely seen anyone more bereft of empathy. If there is any justice in the world there will be a special place in Hell for this man and his minions. The *Times* outlines the three things Trump has already done to kill the health-care program, plus four more he plans to undertake. His vow to "let it fail" is not at all what he intends. He means "let me kill it."

Today's *Times* gives blow-out coverage to the new movie called "Dunkirk" by Christopher Nolan. I have been to Dunkirk, and I would love to see the film, which the Times reports is simply brilliant.

July 22: I can't seem to sleep much beyond about 4 o'clock. I don't look at the clock, actually, but it is dead dark when I wake up and Chi-Chi is not restless yet. I lie there and think about everything in the world, worrying about this or that. This morning I was up a little after 6. I just couldn't stay in bed any longer, and Chi-Chi was ready to start moving. So, up and out, walking at a fast pace around the neighborhood. It had to be about 80 degrees with no breeze, but that's OK. It's still a whole lot cooler than 100-plus, which is what it will hit for the 19th straight day here this afternoon. We could easily have 60 or more days of 100-degree highs this summer, and that would put absolutely everyone in a terrible humor. I have been through summers like that, over and over again, in Wichita Falls, where 90 days of 100-plus days aren't unheard of. It's relentless, never-ending-seeming, and it just wears you out.

The *Times*' lead editorial asks a very good question this morning: When Trump met with Putin in Europe recently, how many times did they talk and what did they talk about? And why were there no other Americans present, including an interpreter that was hired by Trump? (Only a Russian interpreter was there.) Putin will do nothing for Trump unless he gets something really big in return. What will that be?

On an inside page of the *Times*, we learn that Ivanka and Jared are making upwards of $200 million a year on their various companies, including that hotel in Washington where *el presidente* continues to get the profits because he can't be held accountable under U.S. ethics laws. Is it naive to wonder what the Kushner kiddos would do to keep that stream of cash flowing?

July 23: There's just not enough space on the front page of the NYT to publish all the outrageous stuff the Trump people are doing to this country. In today's paper alone:

+ They and Trump are backing off on promises to fix the infrastructure. They have no plans to do so.

+ The Trump appointee to the CDC head job is from Georgia where she was in bed with Coca-Cola. This is the woman who is supposed to make a big deal out of things like obesity and diabetes, both of which are exacerbated by sugary drinks.

+ Trump announced that he has the absolute right to pardon anyone he wants, including his son and his daughter, etc., etc.

Over in the *New Yorker*, there is an interview with a former Carrier worker out of Indiana who just lost her job, the very job Trump and his vice president, a former Indiana governor, promised would not leave that state.

Meanwhile, in a brazen act of courage unheard of in the annals of Washington in the last 30 years, House and Senate appear ready to pass a bill that would penalize Russia for hacking our elections and for invading various neighboring countries. Will the president sign it? Hahahahaha. We shall see.

July 24: From the *Times* today comes the revelation that Scott Pruitt, the head of the EPA and its avowed executioner, just can't seem to stay put on the job in D.C. Travel documents made available to the newspaper show "Mr. Pruitt spent 43 out of 92 days from March through May in Oklahoma or traveling to or from the state." But, whaaaaa, Mr. Pruitt said, it was all on business. Right, Mr. Pruitt! There's so much environmental stuff going on in Oklahoma you, personally, have to be right there to oversee it all.

From Charles Blow, editorial columnist in The *Times*, writing about the appointment of a new White House communications director he calls The Mooch: "Nothing will change with the arrival of the Mooch Communications Office because nothing has changed about the kook in the Oval Office. (Some may find that descriptor harsh, but I find no appellation too coarse to express my outrage over Trump's character, behavior and agenda. If anything, no word feels grave enough to properly express it.)" I pull that quote and print it here because it expresses my own view of Trump and his co-conspirators.

I have put together a new postcard for Julia and Mel that has John McCain on it, and a pretty mean description of this picayune little man. Lynda saw it, and she asked me not to send it because it was in poor taste. It is time for liberals in this country to stop worrying about what is in good taste and what isn't. We're in a fight for our lives and for this democracy, and unkind words should be the least of the weapons in our arsenal.

NPR had a special report of some kind on the radio Saturday that I just caught brief snippets of concerning the 50th anniversary right now of the Summer of Love – 1967 in San Francisco. I'm a little surprised that this summer is passing by without more media about that summer, the music back then, the Flower Children, the love beads, the LSD and pot. It's quite remarkable, really, that mainstream television and even cable channels with specific focuses have just ignored this significant event in Baby Boomer history.

I was never a participant in any of the Summer of Love stuff, except for the fact that I got married in June 1967 at the ripe old age of 20 years. I was working full-time as a night cops reporter and a daytime regional reporter at the Amarillo newspaper in the summer of '67, and I was focused on learning to write and learning to report, just generally learning the ropes of journalism. I recall reading about the Hippies and LSD and all of those things going on out on the West Coast, but they were so remote from Amarillo and the Texas Panhandle as to be on another planet altogether. I actually probably paid more attention to the riots in Detroit and in other major cities, because the impulses that led to the burning down of urban areas could be felt, if one were in touch with them, right there in Amarillo, right below the surface. Hippies and flowers and The Dead were not even close to being part of the landscape in Amarillo in 1967, but racial tension was certainly part of the vibe. In fact, it was actually probably in 1966 and 1967 that I became conscious of the differences between the black population in

Amarillo, which was just as poor as dirt, and the white population, which was way, way larger and vastly more affluent even on the bottom rungs of the ladder.

July 25: I'm off just after lunch today to Denver. I need to find and buy the right stuff, and then load it into boxes and mail it back to a couple of addresses in Texas, and I have tonight and tomorrow to do that. Should be plenty of time. Should be no worries. Still, I'm nervous about the whole thing.

Kushner told Congress yesterday that he met with Russians four times last year, but he did not collude with them to throw the election to Trump. Yeah, right. I imagine they talked about how many potatoes it takes to make a bottle of vodka. A columnist in the *Times* suggests today that the Republicans are pretty quickly moving away from Trump in small ways that will be significant. Harrumph. Oh, and yesterday, Trump spoke at a Boy Scout jamboree and acted like an asshole. What a role model. "Boys, here's what you want to grow up to be like: a serial sexual assault perpetrator, a serial liar, a back-stabber, a braggart, a conniver, a traitor and a charlatan."

There were no hippies in Amarillo or at Amarillo College in the Summer of Love, at least I didn't know of any. And there were no love-ins. I never heard of LSD in or around Amarillo, and marijuana was as foreign to me as any exotic Indian or Middle Eastern spice. In fact, when I was in high school and college, I was never offered marijuana and never ran into it. Even as a cop reporter during the summer of 1967 in Amarillo, drugs were just not a problem or even on the radar. The problem I ran into over and over again was alcohol. On a Friday or Saturday night, I would typically be covering a bar fight that invariably involved two white guys who were vying for the attentions of the same girl. Pool cues were the weapons of choice. The Amarillo Police Department had no drug squad, no SWAT team, no drug-sniffing dogs.

July 26: On Tuesday, I drove over to Austin airport, and got there in time to check in at the Parking Spot and get a sub sandwich from Thundercloud Subs, an Austin institution. It was actually pretty good. I will have to remember them because there is a Thundercloud location in Dripping Springs by the HEB store. The United flight wasn't bad, although the seats were so close together that even I could not figure out how to move my legs. I have never been in a tighter seating arrangement on any kind of transportation. But I dozed for most of the flight.

P. touched base with T., who is the father of P.'s grandchild, A. He has never been married to P.'s daughter, C., who is A.'s mother. He is unemployed, but takes care of A., who is 20 and can't seem to hold down a job and doesn't attend college. T. had volunteered to take us around on Wednesday to various places to make our purchases. He had worked at two dispensaries, so he knew the folks there, and he had a medical prescription for pot, so he could get access to better quality, more potent stuff. We agreed to meet at 10 o'clock Wednesday at his house. Planning the outing with T. in the lead and P. as moral support made the whole enterprise less stressful. I was in bed by 10:30 Denver time.

July 27: I was up early, much earlier than P., although she rose in time for us to get to T.'s house by a little after 10.

Before we left P.'s house, D. took her aside and warned her not to go into any post office when we mailed the stuff back to Wimberley. This made her nervous and that made me a little nervous.

T. was one cool character, though, and I had complete confidence in him, oddly enough. The first shop we hit was a converted bungalow. We walked in the front door into what had been the living room, and there sat a young man behind a desk. Off to the side and behind him were two closed doors. One led to the room where medicinal pot was sold, and the other to the room where recreational pot was sold. T. showed the kid his prescription, and he was allowed into the medicine room. He soon emerged with a small brown paper bag, and motioned for me to follow him. Outside, he explained that he had stopped at this location only to buy a vial of hash oil in the medicine room because he could get it cheaply there. It was about $40, but the small glass container had more than 100 doses in it, a great bargain if there ever was one.

Next, we went to a regular store front building where T. had worked and knew all the staffers. We bought recreational materials there, and I bought T. some weed to thank him for his help. Then we were off to another place where T. had worked, and again we found some items we wanted. By that point, I had just given T. a wad of money so he could handle the transactions since he spoke the language and was familiar with the products, of which there was a dizzying array.

Our last stop was at a chain store, where the choices were just about unlimited. This store even had a whole counter filled with Willie Nelson branded items. We were allowed to buy only eight pieces of merchandise apiece, so T. did some quick figuring. We bought a sleep tincture recommended to us by P.'s doctor and some Green Hornets, which are T.'s favorite edibles.

After that, we had a brief discussion with P. about how to get the goods back to Wimberley, and T. was an expert on that subject as well. He recommended that we go to a nearby Office Depot to pick up a couple of Federal Express boxes, then fill the boxes off-site, then return and send them via the FedEx counter there because that particular location was mostly self-help. So, we did that, while P. waited, now really nervous, in the car.

After lunch, we headed for a parking lot and filled up one of the FedEx boxes with our purchases, then sealed it up and took it to Office Depot and paid $123 to have it sent overnight with an arrival time guaranteed by 10 a.m. in Wimberley. T. recommended that schedule because it gave FedEx no time to inspect the package. At that point, I had spent right at $800 on pot and on the FedEx service. That did not count air fare or rental car or the Parking Spot fee. All told the trip probably cost us more than $1,100. But, for that amount I bought more than 400 pieces of edibles and other supplies for Lynda, so it was well worth the trip.

July 28: I awoke yesterday at 6:30 Texas time, got up and had some coffee and read two newspapers and then left P.'s house for the airport. I got there a little after 8, so I had a long wait for my 10 o'clock flight.

The Frontier flight was better than the United because the seats were not so close together, but there were no snackies! I got home about 4, and the package from Denver had already arrived – some time around 10 a.m. I was vastly relieved to know that I had pulled this off and not gotten caught. Lynda tried out a couple of the gummy bears, and they had some effect but didn't kill the pain. I suspect that killing the pain will depend on the level of pain on a given day and not on the amount of THC in an edible.

On my walk this morning, I was thinking about how much easier and cheaper this whole acquisition process would be if I could make my own edibles for Lynda. A kid I know offered to show me how to make marijuana butter the other day, and I think I will take him up on it. This trip cost us, all in all, more than $1,000, including air fare, car rental, etc. I spent about $700 on the pot, the rest was for travel expenses. I spent $123 just to send the stuff back to Wimberley via Federal Express. It cost me that much to get the package here at 10 o'clock after I put it in the system in Denver at about 2 o'clock on Wednesday.

The Senate is acting like a bunch of junior-high boys. They are giddy in indecision and abject stupidity as they try to eliminate Obama's health-care law. This is no longer about government. It is no longer about health care. It is not about insurance. It is about testosterone poisoning.

And speaking of that, it appears that Trump's people will roll back every single advance made by people in the gay community. I suspect that before long it will be against the law to provide health care for gay couples and there will be an assault on gay marriage. You read it here first.

The Boy Scouts issued an apology yesterday for Trump's performance at the jamboree, during which he acted like a complete asshole and jerk. He spoke not of anything remotely related to scouting, but instead about his own trivial and small-minded vendettas. Everywhere he goes, the nastiness rubs off and lingers.

Krugman goes after the witless and mean-spirited John McCain in his column today. McCain deserves it. He's a mean little man whose goal is never much beyond caressing his own ego. McCain is the sanctimonious enabler of evil-doers.

July 29: So, McCain ended up being the deciding vote in the Senate that doomed the health-care plan. A hero? Not in my book. It will take a string of such votes to tell me he is anything more than a grand-stander and an opportunist of the first order.

Nadia Popovich has an article with huge graphic in The *Times* today with this headline, "Hotter Summers, Once Exceptional, Become the Norm." I don't need to say much more than that the graphic is all that any smart person needs to see to know we are in deep trouble in North America because the trend line is set and unchanging. Today, the forecast temperature in Austin is 106 to 108.

During the spring before I graduated from Amarillo High School, several of my friends and I spent some time talking about college. Before my senior year, I had not even considered going to college because I really wanted to do something with cars. My senior English teacher, Clyde Dale Martin, told me flat out when I started my last year of high school that I shouldn't bother about studying hard because, he said, "You're just not college material." (When I got my bachelor's degree I sent him an invitation to graduation, and when I got, first, a master's in political science and, second, a master's in English, I sent him invitations to those ceremonies, too.) But when I found that I could do journalism and be a reporter and writer, I fell in love with the whole of newspapering, and I knew I needed to go to college to get a decent job on a newspaper. Our discussions then began centering on where we might go, and some of my buddies already had scholarship offers and schools in mind. I was so clueless about all of that that I knew nothing about the SAT until the day before, and I got drunk that night and went in with a full-blown hangover. I had no idea how important those scores would be, and didn't care very much. I had no money to go to college, no prospects for a scholarship and no promise of help from my parents or anyone else.

Jeff Anderson and I decided we should go to Amarillo College for the summer of 1965 just to check it out. So, we signed up for two semesters of history and biology, which would allow us to get 12 hours out of the way right off. The cost was minimal: $78 for tuition and less than $22 for books. But, I didn't have that kind of money saved up, thanks to my car, so I decided to get rid of the car and use the money for college. I sold it for $500 to R.B. And he ruined it over the course of the summer.

July 30:

Q: So, you're saying that you took off two days from work last week and flew to Colorado and back to buy marijuana for your wife and to send it home via Federal Express?

A: Yes, that's right.

Q: Did you know that it is illegal to send pot back to Texas in that way?

A: Yes, of course.

Q: And you did it anyway?

A: I felt the opportunity to get medicine to provide pain relief for my wife was worth the risk of getting caught. Getting caught did occur to me, but I reasoned that I am really too old to be sent to prison for such a simple, very low-threat activity. And I could live with probation.

Q: You felt that it was unlikely you would get caught?

A: Unlikely, yes. But I did take a precaution or two. For one thing, I did not try to bring anything back with me through the airports. Instead, I loaded the packages I bought into a Fed Ex box obtained at a very busy Fed Ex facility inside an Office Depot. Basically, the whole mailing process was self-serve, so only a cashier was involved in the mailing at that point. We sent the parcel overnight with delivery to occur before 10 a.m. the next morning. The speed with which the package had to be handled, we felt, would make it unlikely that anyone would bother to look inside or sniff around.

Q: Why not let your kids take the risk and arrange for purchase and mail?

A: I'm responsible for my wife; they aren't. While the risk was very manageable for me, it was not for them.

In today's *Times*, Elon Musk's new Tesla is unveiled at its assembly plant in California. Musk plans to sell his new battery-operated car for $35,000, which puts it within reach of quite a few would-be buyers. The question is whether that $35,000 is a price subsidized by the U.S. government. If so, then what is the real cost of the car? Oops. Turns out his cars are heavily subsidized by the American taxpayer. From Investors Daily:

For every Tesla car sold (up to No. 200,000), federal taxpayers kick in $7,500 to lower the costs. State taxpayers in a multitude of states pony up still more. In Colorado, they contribute another $5,000 to the electric car kitty, in California, it's $2,500.

When the *Los Angeles Times* crunched the numbers two years ago, it found that Tesla buyers had received more than $284 million in federal tax incentives and more than $38 million in California rebates. And that was before Tesla's banner 2016 year.

The taxpayer help only starts there. Tesla also collects hundreds of millions from competing automakers by selling environmental credits in California and more than half a dozen other states to car companies that can't meet the states' "zero emissions" sales mandates.

Plus, Nevada ponied up $1.3 billion in incentives to convince Tesla to build its huge battery factory near Reno.

And this doesn't include the fact that electric car owners don't pay into the Highway Trust Fund — which is financed by the per-gallon tax on gasoline and pays for road construction and upkeep.

Whether Tesla can survive without all this taxpayer largesse isn't altogether clear.

Also from The *Times* today, word from a guru on American manners that it is perfectly OK these days to host your very own baby shower. Feeling that this is wrong is a leftover from some past era, the guru writes. Really? Not around here, buddy. It's pretty gauche for a woman to ask for presents herownself.

Time Magazine that arrived yesterday has a good story about the 2,000 people who showed up in rural Virginia last week to get health care. They camped out for treatment of everything from cancer to gum disease to bad eyesight. Time calls the lack of good health care in many areas of the country, "a slow-boiling catastrophe." The Senate would neither know about that nor care.

The *Times* magazine explores where new ideas are coming from for big-ticket movies. The conclusion: There aren't any new ideas. The new movies are coming from old intellectual properties, such as the DC comics and Marvel and Lego. Projects are increasingly spun off from known products. Where, I wonder, does someone with an original idea get a hearing? Not in Hollywood right now. I wonder, too, whether my instructors in my transmedia story-telling class are thinking about this and what they are thinking, as well.

July 31: The "cold front" we expected over the weekend was either a no-show or a joke. It was as hot and muggy as any other July day this morning when I went for a walk. We seem to face another 30 to 45 days of 100-plus temperatures. I'm not sure that even our drought-tolerant Texas plants will make it through unscathed. All the grass around here is dormant, and the leaves on green plants are wilted and sad.

Krugman in today's *Times* traces the present-day Republican decrepitude back many years, and says we should have seen this moment coming. We are at some kind of pivotal point. Will the American people continue to buy the lies and propaganda of the GOP? Only if the people are exceedingly stupid, and I'm not betting they are not. Charles Blow takes on Scaramucci, a profane Mafia-type called in by Trump to be the enforcer in the West Wing. The guy is a scabrous archetype of the bad-acting Sicilian who enters each room with his shotgun roaring.

The *Times* has a bit of good news. The story is about how public libraries around the country are stepping up to provide summer lunches for hungry kids who otherwise would go hungry. Hundreds of libraries are taking federal funds that Trump will probably kill when he learns of this generous program and giving children good food and a chance to read.

Aug. 1: Trump has put former Marine General Kelly in charge of the White House, and the very first thing he did was fire Scaramucci! After about 10 days on the job, which included one curse-laced rant to *The New Yorker*, The Mooch was tossed out on his butt. Just one more example of terrible judgment on the part of the man who would be king.

Congress appears to be in recess even if not physically so. Mitch McConnell must be drinking his breakfast, and his lunch and his dinner these days.

The *Times* reports today that ad agencies have finally awakened to the fact that Amazon is kicking the butt of every retailer in America, including Wal-Mart. Here's the thing: When you are looking at a product class on Amazon, you get all the products and related products in that class on your screen. And each of those products has a description, a series of questions that have been answered by consumers and reviews, along with a statistical rating. Do you get that when you go into Wal-Mart? Good grief, No. Why would a rational shopper shop anywhere but Amazon when you get all that information for free?

Aug. 2: For some inexplicable reason, members of the Senate have decided, albeit reluctantly, to act like adults. Or, at least, they are moving in that direction. Trump demands they stay in Washington this summer until the Affordable Care Act is repealed; they are acting like they want to move on to more damaging legislation, like altering the tax code so that the rich get fabulously wealthy and the poor come to resemble migrants in Syria.

The stories about Trump cronyism keep populating the front pages of the *Times* and other papers. Today it's about a guy who served in Trump's campaign who has opened a shop to help businesses, etc., get what they want out of the White House without calling himself a lobbyist. Another story reveals that the White House now has a group working on making sure minorities don't get any special treatment in college admissions. They want us back to "white-only" in the upper reaches of society—or just about anywhere, actually, because Bubba don't want no stinking competition when it comes to the drinking fountain or the latrine.

I spent some time yesterday trying to figure out why the Texas governor and Senate believe it is so important to make people use public toilets that correspond with their birth genders. If you try to follow the money on this issue, you have a hard time. I can't find anyone outside the governor's mansion and the halls of the Senate who want this bill, and yet it continues to be pushed and pushed in this summer's special session. Businessmen all across Texas, and Big Oil, Big Retail, Big Industry, Big Insurance—all these folks do not want this bill to pass. I think it will, anyway, and Texas will receive some measure of punishment that will not be nearly harsh enough.

Aug. 3: The story of the decade is at the top of the front page on The *Times* today. Here is the second paragraph:

Scientists for the first time have successfully edited genes in human embryos to repair a common and serious disease-causing mutation, producing apparently healthy embryos, according to a study published on Wednesday.

The research marks a major milestone and, while a long way from clinical use, it raises the prospect that gene editing may one day protect babies from a variety of hereditary conditions.

But the achievement is also an example of human genetic engineering, once feared and unthinkable, and is sure to renew ethical concerns that some might try to design babies with certain traits, like greater intelligence or athleticism.

Back in the 1970s when I was covering West Texas State for the *Canyon News*, a close friend and source for me was Dr. David Labrie, a full professor of biology and a member at First Presbyterian Church. David was a geneticist, and he and I had long discussions about the ethics and morality of pursuing deeper and deeper changes in human genetic material. This was long before we even knew there were such things as stem cells, which gives you an idea of the state of the scientific art.

The path from where we were in the field to where we could be with time was clear, and made clearer, of course, by science fiction in books and on the screen. The Boys from Brazil were Hitler knockoffs made possible by jiggering with human genetic material. So, the ethical and moral questions have been out there for quite some time, and I'm not aware of any Big Decisions about how to proceed from this point. Given the nature of our polity I would guess that there will be a well-funded Wall Street venture capital drive to customize babies, and no one will stop it because it will all be done in the name of Making America Great Again. My point is that we had plenty of time to take a mature, long look at the issues and build in some safeguards and have not done so. My second point: Just because you CAN do something doesn't mean you SHOULD.

Pope Francis may yet get me back into the Catholic church. Today's *Times* also has this story about the pope's folks taking on the White House in an article in a Vatican-approved journal.

The authors, writing in a Vatican-vetted journal, singled out Stephen K. Bannon, Mr. Trump's chief strategist, as a "supporter of an apocalyptic geopolitics" that has stymied action against climate change and exploited fears of migrants and Muslims with calls for "walls and purifying deportations." The article warns that conservative American Catholics have strayed dangerously into the deepening political polarization in the United States. The writers even declare that the worldview of American evangelical and hard-line Catholics, which is based on a literal interpretation of the Bible, is "not too far apart" from jihadists.

Clearly, the goals of fundamentalists of whatever stripe are world domination by whatever means appear the most promising. They are winning in the Texas Legislature by default, the "bathroom bill" being the most recent and most outstanding example of their malignant agenda.

189

Aug. 5: Last evening we watched the Meryl Streep movie about a woman who wanted to be an opera star but could not sing and did so anyway. It was a very funny movie but also moving, a cautionary tale about self-delusion. How often do we believe we are something when we are not seen that way by our family and friends at all? In a way it was sad.

The kid Martin Skreli, who arbitrarily raised the price on a drug for AIDS patients by 5,000 percent overnight a few years ago, was found guilty on charges of swindling investors in another business. The boy is completely unrepentant. He is a smart thug. But he is also a poster child for American free enterprise in this day and age, a whole world centered on greed and mean-spiritedness that is absolutely OK with a president of no moral character whatsoever. There are no penalties for avarice, as we learn every day and learned very well after the 2008 housing debacle when not a single banker was charged with a crime. Tangentially, we are learning that there is no moral force on the planet that can oppose American free enterprise and its spawn, Skreli and Trump.

Two stories in an edition of The Wall Street Journal published last week caught my attention and the attention of one of our library volunteers who brought the paper to me to read. The first story was about the steep and continuing decline of the grocery business across the country. Grocery owners have expanded beyond what they need to have to meet an ever-decreasing demand for what they have to offer. And that demand is down because young people are eating out more, and other folks are finding alternatives to the traditional supermarket. I would be perfectly happy getting my foodstuff through something like Blue Apron, but Lynda would not go along with that. The other story of interest begins this way: "Hopes for a U.S. nuclear renaissance dimmed Monday when the owner of a partially built power plant in South Carolina pulled the plug after its costs ballooned by billions of dollars." The story goes on to say that only two plants were under construction in this country at the time, and now both seem doomed and nuclear power along with them. We should abandon nuclear solutions once and for all time. They are too expensive to build and will ultimately cost us much more either in damage control or in loss of life and property when they "do a Chernobyl."

Aug. 7: Storms blew in this morning, and Chi-Chi had a hard time trying to rest up. She has to be right up under my chin in bed when the thunder and lightning are going off outside. Even then, she is restless. She is in my lap right now, trying to feel good about the bluster outside.

Krugman wants us to move on and talk about what Progressives can do when the Trump era is ended, and that could be pretty soon (or one hopes it will be soon). He writes about health care in his column in The Times today, and suggests that liberals should not plan to toss out the Affordable Care Act when it is their turn to rule again. Instead, he thinks it should be fixed and made better.

Aug. 8: Trump is so busy undoing trade agreements around the world the people most affected don't have time to intervene or get their problems aired out. The cattle industry is an example. Right off the bat in January, Trump walked away from an Asian multi-nation trade agreement that would have meant billions of dollars in sales to the beef industry. Now, Trump's people are looking at agreements elsewhere, i.e., NAFTA, that could cut back beef exports out of this country even more. Tough shit, cowboys. You voted for him, you got him. Another example has been the steel industry. With some agreements breached and others in limbo, foreign steel-makers are dumping their products in this country at bargain-basement prices. So, those steel-mill towns that thought they would be back in the money after a Trump election—and thus voted for the dumb bastard —are seeing their little dreams evaporate. Tough shit, steel-whiners.

On the front page of The *Times* today we learn that scientists and other experts in and out of government have prepared, as required by Congress, a once-every-four-years assessment of the climate, and they say things are worse than four years ago and getting worse by the day. The report has to pass through the hands of Scott Pruitt, the dumbshit Oklahoma oil lackey who runs the EPA these days, and he is a climate-change denier of the first order. So, he probably won't sign off on the report, thus making its "leak" imperative. Despite efforts by Jeff Sessions to silence people who know things Trump doesn't want us to find out, the leaks will continue out of Washington and environs. The truth will out – one hopes.

Another *Times* story today talks about the liars who have been our presidents. Many tell whoppers, but not as consistently and as irrationally as Trump:

"But President Trump, historians and consultants in both political parties agree, appears to have taken what the writer Hannah Arendt once <u>called</u> *'the conflict between truth and politics' to an entirely new level.*

"From his days peddling the false notion that former President Barack Obama was born in Kenya, to his inflated claims about how many people attended his inaugural, to his description just last week of receiving two phone calls — one from the president of Mexico and another from the head of the Boy Scouts — that <u>never happened, Mr. Trump is trafficking in hyperbole, distortion and fabrication on practically a daily basis.</u>*" (Emphasis added.)*

Aug. 9: Last night after supper, Lynda got a call from P. in Colorado. P. wondered how Lynda was doing on her edibles, and Lynda reported that she was not doing well at all. Later, she told me that the caramel edible she took about 5:30 was causing nausea. I think she is giving up on this potential solution, so I'm very frustrated by the whole thing. We have $800 worth of pot that is now not useful or potentially not useful, and we have no solution on the horizon. I wish I could get her to go see an acupuncturist. I hear there is a good one in Austin, and I hear that from some people who aren't dumb about such things. It is surely worth a try. Maybe I've gone too easy on Lynda by not insisting that we look at other alternatives. I hope we can find a way for her to take the edibles – with something at the outset that will contravene the nausea – so she can get some relief that way. I have suggested just recently that she consider taking an opioid on days when the pain is really bad. That would make opioid use only occasional and shouldn't seriously disrupt her digestive system, which has been the source of her main complaint about opioid use. Perhaps if she could knock back the pain to zero one day with an opioid, she could get ahead of the pain the next day with an edible.

Trump is rattling sabers with North Korea. Good luck with that. Has he really ever looked at a map to see where Seoul happens to be relative to the DMZ on the peninsula?

The *Times* has a story about some reports just issued about immigration and immigrants and the impact on the U.S. economy. The bottom line is that we really need immigrants to take the low-level, low-paying jobs that Americans won't take. Gosh. What a revelation! Wonder if the Trumpistas have seen them. Wonder if any of the Trump White House people have ever considered who is washing dishes and turning burgers out in the real world that these elites certainly do not inhabit.

Aug. 10: Trump is doing what Trump does best: Bellering about something he knows absolutely nothing about and looking like a tragic fool in doing so. This time it could get serious fast. He is tweaking the nose of the dictator of North Korea, who has threatened nuclear war. Trump is like a poorly grounded adolescent boy. His first reaction on everything is to raise his fists and thump his chest. He is almost a caricature of a president, a kind of Saturday Night Live parody. Unfortunately, his idiocy could pay off big-time in a small war centered on Guam or the Hawaiian Islands. It seems to me that if the boy king of NK threw off a few nuclear rounds on either of those places there is not much the United States would do about it. He has the "trump" card: If he wants he can just lob a few warheads over into Seoul. He could almost get a couple of strong warrior types and just hand-throw a nuke from the north to the south. We have to be the adults in this standoff, because we already have a child on the North side. We don't need two children in this particular sandbox.

Lynda took a small dose of hash oil on a nut last evening about 4:30, and it put her into a deep funk. It was a downer for her. She probably should have waited and it would have been a good sleeping aid. She was pretty lost all evening long, and waited until 10 to go to bed. She slept well, though. I don't think she moved a muscle all night long. It's 8:30 a.m. right now, and she is still sleeping. So far, we are 0 for 5 or 6 on the edibles. Nothing has worked as well as she wants.

Aug. 11: Big News Today: The *Times* reports that researchers at Harvard have successfully pursued the implantation of pig organs into humans and believe the first normal or routine set of procedures can take place within the next two years. The *Times* says that about 40,000 get organ transplants every year – human to human – but more than 110,000 are on waiting lists. (Of course, if you're someone like Steve Jobs, you get to move to the front of the line.)

Trump had a press conference yesterday at his golf course and bucked up his threat to nuke North Korea if they nuke Guam or anyone else first. If we are not careful, this will all creep into the realm of the inevitable and there'll be no stopping it. Remember World War I? How does the young and inexperienced leader of North Korea save face now? I don't see how. This all reminds me of the scene in "A Christmas Story" where the two kids face off in the schoolyard on a sub-freezing day in Cleveland and enter into a dare, double-dare, double-dog-dare blustering contest that ends up with one kid's tongue stuck to the flagpole.

Remember that?

Trump also now officially dislikes Mitch McConnell. Join the Club! I personally hate Mitch McConnell, but I'm not inspired by the same insipid things that move Trump to disparage this Kentucky coonhound of a loser. McConnell may now join the rest of us in saying, "Oh Yeah, Trump, well, who gives a shit what you think?"

Aug. 12: Lynda has now officially given up on the edibles. They are not killing the pain in her leg, but are causing her an upset stomach. She thinks having an upset stomach on top of the leg pain is not offset by the minor amount of relief she is getting. A friend told Lynda she can sell our remaining products, so maybe we can recoup some of the $1,200 or so we spent on this project.

Now Trump is talking about military action in Venezuela. Venezuela? Are we going to intervene all over the globe when a tin-horn dictator comes to power? What will we do? Who will we hand power to when we topple Maduro? How will we bring down the staggering rate of inflation? Where will we find cheap groceries to put into stores? Where will we get jobs to put the people to work? Jesus Christ, what an idiot Trump is.

The *Times* reports that Scott Pruitt at the EPA has installed a regime of secrecy so that nobody within or without the agency knows what he is up to as he dismantles this corner of government and turns Big Oil, Big Gas, Big Plastics, Big Chemical and Big Crime loose to despoil everything under the sun they can get their hands on.

Wonder when our congressman, one Roger Williams, will have a town-hall meeting this August holiday period. Never. That's when.

Aug. 13: You do not need to have a doctorate in psychology to know what Kim Jong-un, the dictator of North Korea, is up to. For years he has used the United States as the Enemy So Huge It Can Consume and Destroy Us – also known as the Big Bad Wolf—to keep his own people in tow and cowed as he consolidates his power in a tiny, otherwise inconsequential and notoriously shitty little country in a nowhere corner of the universe.

Now, our own Trump is learning from the little guy's playbook and turning it on his very own people, who seem to be a little too stupid to understand that Trump the Tiger is all about power and nothing about anything else at all. Jean H. Lee writes about this situation in today's *New York Times* on the Sunday Review page. She details how Jong-Un has been able to keep his people in check by threatening them with a U.S. takeover. What's going on in North Korea in terms of propaganda is pretty inventive stuff. Trump doesn't have to ramp up a huge multi-generational hype and terror machine because his right-wing journalist buddies do that for him, and his partners out there in coal mine country just nod and pop opioids and vote! Instead of dismissing the Trumpian hyperbole as ridiculous, the media, even in the mainstream, just go along as if the man is not insane. Who will finally stand up and say the Emperor is buck-ass Naked?

Chucked away inside the *Times* is an article I wish had been written about 15 years ago, back when I was gathering material for my News & Numbers classes and for inclusion in the ad hoc bible about how to do journalism that I put together for editors and reporters joining the *Times Record News* staff. The story is by Jeff Sommer and has this headline: "Why the Dow Isn't Really the Stock Market." In the next 24 inches or so, Sommer shows how the Dow Jones Industrial Average is skewed by the performance of a very small handful of stocks, such as Boeing and Apple. I have long thought the news media's manic concentration on the DJI average was misplaced but I didn't know why—until now. The Dow doesn't really describe anything that touches reality in terms of the broader economy or even the broader stock market. If you really want to know how the market is performing, Sommer suggests you look at the S&P 500, which aggregates the performance of more than just a mere handful of companies. This really does make sense, but it won't change how the major media report market activities. They will continue to report the DJI average as if it is a biblical truth. And so, the result will eventually be that people will act on bad information and the cows will come home at some point and we will have the pop of a bubble.

And finally today there is the story of Sears, which is in freefall. The *Times* gets into the weeds about corporate financial strategies, but let me tell you what happened on the ground when you shopped at Sears. When I was a young man, you could get your Sears catalog and order what you wanted, and it would be shipped to you. The catalog had almost everything under the sun. It was a vast array of stuff, an amazing shopping world.

Over time, though, Sears decided to move me away from the catalog and into the store, and at first that was OK because there were people on the floor at Sears who knew about appliances and tools and tires and clothes for kids. But, pretty soon, you couldn't find anyone on the Sears floor to help you find what you were looking for. In fact, you couldn't find anyone on the floor to check you out with the products you had tracked down for yourself and to take your money.

Sometime along in there, Sears started urging you to put everything on a credit card or on credit, and the interest rates were outrageous. I got the distinct impression that Sears no longer cared about selling Craftsman tools or Kenmore appliances; Sears just wanted to make money off its loans to consumers in the form of credit cards. So, I stopped going to Sears altogether. And I haven't been in a Sears in years and years. I quit going to Sears before I ever stopped going to shopping malls. Adios, Sears! Don't let the door slam you in the butt as you exit American retail.

Yesterday in West Virginia, white nationalists (i.e., Nazis) took torches into the streets of a small town, and there they met resistance from some folks who think diversity is not a sinful thing, and they bashed each other's brains in for a while. Trump, of course, did **not** call on white nationalists to stop acting like juvenile delinquents. Regardless, this kind of thing will continue to play out because his administration has aided and abetted it, and won't stop doing so.

Aug. 14: Trump will not condemn the white nationalists who trashed Charlottesville, West Va., Saturday and clashed with anti-Nazis there. He just walks away from the whole thing as if fascism is fine with him, and it seems to be. Meanwhile, the Nazi who put the thing together was pleased as punch with the melee he caused.

Aug. 15: Trump finally figured out that his family and friends were going to absolutely pester him to death, so much so that it might affect his golf game, about taking white nationalists to task for the Saturday riots and deaths in Charlottesville, and so he went on TV and smirked his way through a statement saying that these hoodlums and thugs were evil. The *Times* had this to say in an editorial:

His aides _reportedly_ urged him to express that straightforward sentiment on Saturday. Yet even as he now managed to get some of the right words out he could not bring himself to assign blame for Ms. Heyer's death, saying only that she "was tragically killed." Contrast that with _his eager invocations_ of Kathryn Steinle — "the beautiful Kate," as he _started calling her_ in tweets and speeches more than two years ago, after she "was gunned down in SF by an illegal immigrant."

The double standard goes to the heart of Mr. Trump's simplistic, racialized worldview, where the criminals are black or brown and the victims are white. In fact, white supremacists have been responsible for 49 homicides in the past 16 years, more than any other domestic extremist movement, _according to a joint intelligence bulletin_ produced by the F.B.I. and the Department of Homeland Security in May.

There is talk of a white supremacist rally in College Station in September. If that is actually going to happen, I'm driving over there to be part of the counter protest. Go back and read "In the Garden of the Beasts" and see what happened in 1930s Germany when common Germans declined to stand up to the Brown Shirts and Nazis. There are distinct parallels to events of our own time and many, many lessons to be learned from the weak response to the rise in racial hatred in Germany during that decade leading up to the invasion of Poland to set off World War II.

Aug. 16: We did not order nearly enough eclipse-viewing glasses from NASA for Monday's solar event at the library. We are getting 10 to 15 calls every day now with people asking if we have the glasses and if they can come by and pick them up. At first, last week, we said, Yes. Now, we have to say, No, because we only have about 300 left, and we expect to have about that many people at our party on Monday morning at the library. The teen librarian seems to think we ordered and received 1,000. That would mean that we have already given out 700, and I just don't think that is the case at all.

Trump utterly stunned everyone in the country yesterday when during a press conference he declared that those on the Left in Saturday's confrontation in Charlottesville were just as wrong and wrong-headed as those on the Right. That is, he depicted them as morally equivalent. That is, he said that Nazis and other assorted fascists, who were yelling their hatred for Jews and black people, were in the same moral ballpark as lefties who were telling the Nazis and fascists that they were full of shit. Wow. The man is such a nut case that even Fox commentators were forced to gasp and struggle for breath.

Over the long weekend, after Trump's initial refusal to condemn the Nazis, several CEOs of major corporations who had agreed to serve on Trump boards at the Washington level quit in disgust. Yesterday, the CEO of Wal-Mart walked away, too. You would think that the Trump Ship is sinking, but I doubt it. The Republicans, especially people like the Koch brothers, who are neo-Nazis at heart, will not let him fall.

The Guardian reported last week on a series of revelations made in pretrial proceedings in a lawsuit involving Monsanto Co., revelations about how Monsanto fixers made sure that research that might have shown Monsanto's lead product "Roundup" was harmful to human health was rigged to show the opposite. The lead on the story is a good summary:

Monsanto Co. started an agricultural revolution with its "Roundup Ready" seeds, genetically modified to resist the effects of its blockbuster herbicide called Roundup. That ability to kill weeds while leaving desirable crops intact helped the company turn Roundup's active ingredient, the chemical glyphosate, into one of the world's most-used crop chemicals. When that heavy use raised health concerns, Monsanto noted that the herbicide's safety had repeatedly been vetted by outsiders. But now there's new evidence that Monsanto's claims of rigorous scientific review are suspect.

Actually, the evidence reported on by the Guardian shows that the claims are far more than merely suspect. Monsanto's people were meticulous in making sure that not a single claim of human risk was associated with Roundup. They fixed the data. They fixed the documents. They just rigged the whole thing so Monsanto could keep making money. That's bad enough. But, the whole story about Monsanto, Roundup and American agriculture is just a very sick tale of corporate greed and stupidity on the part of producers. I heard on NPR one day recently that there is now a movement afoot to sustain an open-source seed revolution that will let farmers get back into the business of planting real crops with real seeds not purchased and owned from DNA through the finished grocery product by Monsanto. I wish them well. Monsanto will not let them go quietly into this territory.

Aug. 17: Chief executive officers of a whole lot of big American corporations started leaving two councils set up by the president. The defection started with a black CEO who said he didn't want to be part of the president's anything after Trump refused to condemn the fascists who killed a girl in a parade in Charlottesville last Saturday. So, Trump just dissolved the two councils, while accusing some of those CEOs of being bad actors in the economy!

Trump's Tuesday performance was of one piece with everything else he says and does and what he stands for. He appeals to the lowest common denominator and stays there in the gutter with his fellow incompetents and haters. He will never lift us up; he will always tear us down because that is just who he is. In his own words, SAD.

Every call we have received at the library since Monday morning has been an inquiry about getting the glasses for the eclipse. Yesterday, K., the teen librarian, got on the web and went to the sites of every single vendor of these glasses to try to order some more. She found some glasses at one location, and those folks wanted $25 each for flimsy, one-time-use paper glasses. There are sites on the internet selling the glasses for upwards of $1,000! In a hurry yesterday, I looked up how to build a simple viewing kit, which is two pieces of cardboard with a pinhole in one and a white piece of paper on the other to act as a viewing screen. I went over to HEB and got several really big sheets of cardboard, some duct tape and some heavy-duty foil. Then I made a prototype, and had my volunteers make some.

Diane Thuesen sent Lynda a Facebook post this a.m. that said, "Dear God. If you want us to impeach Donald Trump, send us a sign. Like, a blot on the sun. Anytime in the next week or so."

Aug. 18: Krugman today calls out Trump's enablers, the cynical Republican leaders who will add gasoline to the fires of corruption and insanity at the White House and do nothing about the devolution of the American presidency into something on the far side incompetent. We are truly almost there, and they do nothing. Why? As Krugman notes, a third of their voters are white and a substantial number of them are white supremacists. So we still – still – have a race problem in this country. I honestly don't know how you get beyond that. I mean, it's not like we haven't tried an unbelievable number of social experiments in this country to get us to tolerate one another. Now that the Trumpistas are in power, though, it's easier to empathize with the haters because I absolutely cannot stand to be around anyone who supports this creature. I don't want to walk on the same side of the street with them.

Aug. 19: Steve Bannon is out. Trump's chief of staff and Trump himself fired this Supreme Asshole yesterday. Bannon was the architect of Trump's strategy to get and keep votes among the neo-Nazis and Fascists. Trump will keep them now that Bannon is gone because Trump will continue to pander to them. He just leans that way by nature; he doesn't need a strategist to help him figure out how to be a racist.

We started watching "20/20" last evening. The program was about the Nazi groups and the groups that have formed to protest and counter then. One of those groups is Antifa (for Anti-Fascist). We changed channels when it became clear that the producers of the segment were guilty of the same kind of intellectual dishonesty that so describes Trump: they strived to show a false equivalency between the two sets of groups. What they failed to do, which is what eludes Trump, is to declare without doubt that pro-Nazi forces are anti-democracy and anti-American. These people are traitors. If you oppose them, are you in the same boat? Not even close.

And where is Netanyahu? MIA, that's where. Even The *Times* noted his absence in the imbroglio in today's editions. And where are our congressional leaders? MIA as well. There is no moral leadership in Washington.

Aug. 20: During the afternoon, I taught about 12 people how to make devices so they could enjoy looking at Monday's solar eclipse without hurting their eyes. We had boxes and duct tape and cardboard and aluminum foil, and everyone went home with something satisfactory for the experience.

Aug. 21: I'm worried about today's solar eclipse activities at the library. We have told people various stories about how to get the now-very-precious viewing glasses that we have remaining. We seem to have about 300 glasses out of 1,000 we got from NASA. That is not going to be enough, I fear. We have told people that these will be handed out on a first-come, first-served basis this morning. We have told people that if they come to the event they will be given a pair of glasses. And we have told people that when they come to get their glasses they will get a pair only if they promise to stick around for the solar eclipse party at the library AND to share with someone who didn't get a pair. I have no idea where people will park. I am clueless about who is buying ice and tea and who is setting up tents in the vacant field north of the library.

Lyndsay and I saw "Dunkirk" at the Alamo Drafthouse in Austin yesterday afternoon. A main criticism I had heard of the movie, not from "official" critics but from others, was that there was no real story line or plot to follow and no character development. I would disagree. The plot was nontraditional in form and trajectory, and in fact, there were several plot lines. Characters were developed almost in cameos, but those short appearances were enough to tell you about a lifetime of experiences embodied in each person. I thought the movie was thoroughly entertaining and also just a very powerful way to tell a true story.

Trump goes on TV tonight to tell Americans about Afghanistan. I will boycott it.

Krugman directs his ire in The *Times* today at the Republicans who have enabled and continue to support Trump. One line from his column: "The point is that progressives shouldn't celebrate too much over Trump's legislative failures. As long as he's in office, he retains a lot of power to betray the working people who supported him. And in case you haven't noticed, betraying those who trust him is a Trump specialty."

Aug. 22: When I got to work yesterday virtually nothing had been done, and no plan was in place, for our solar eclipse watch party.

I asked Carolyn to take a lead on getting ice and water and the "tents" set up in our field north of the library, and K. and I concentrated on getting the inside ready to go. At 10, we opened the doors and there were probably 75 people waiting to get in. I told them we would be distributing the special solar eclipse glasses at around 11:45 in the field, and we were asking people who got the glasses to share with others since we did not have an unlimited supply. Many of them started filtering into the multi-purpose room where I left all the viewer-making supplies from Saturday's session. And I started showing people how to make their viewers. We had three types going at one time, and everyone was very cooperative and happy. It was great fun.

About 11:45 everyone left the building with the exception of a few folks who wanted to watch the eclipse on our big-screen projector in the main room of the library. Even before then we were out of Moon Pies and Milky Ways. Out in the field, about 150 people had gathered under the shade of our tents or under the trees to watch, and at about 1:10 p.m. the eclipse reached the maximum, and everyone oohed and aahed and then they left. We had many, many compliments on the party and what we're doing. Maybe I was a little too uptight about the whole thing.

Trump had a televised speech last evening, and we skipped it. He's grandstanding, trying to dig his way out of the heap of manure he's positioned himself in. I won't be part of it. The *Times* reported that he spent time trashing Obama's strategy in Afghanistan and then turned around and, his campaign promises notwithstanding, adopted the Obama strategy. Clearly, instead of bringing troops home, he will increase the U.S. military commitment in this 14-year disaster.

Aug. 23: Trump was at it again last evening at one of his fan-only pep rallies in Phoenix. He spent most of his time attacking The *Times*, the *Washington Post* and CNN. Meanwhile, the *Times* reported this morning that the feud between Trump and Mitch McConnell the Spineless is percolating right along and threatens to overshadow everything else going on in Washington after the Senate returns in the fall. This will be the duel of the emasculated, the fight of the toothless, gumming each other with profane lies.

The *Times* also reports this morning that Wal-Mart and Google are teaming up on e-commerce to try to deal with Amazon. I love Google and don't like Wal-Mart one iota, so I'm afraid that they will not have my support.

I stepped outside to feed Miss Kitty this morning and it was just a little cooler than usual. We might even have a shower this afternoon, although I'm not counting on it. Nor am I counting the plus-100-degree days any more. We must be past 50 by now.

I marvel to this day at how Daddy managed to survive as a young man trying to write his way into a job by pecking at a portable typewriter in the attic of his folks' home on Fuller Street in Greenville, Texas. In the '20s and '30s, they had no air-conditioning, and the afternoon heat in Greenville was stifling, what with the temperature coupled with the East Texas humidity. I can't imagine what hell that must have been. John and I spent a couple of weeks every summer when we were growing up in Greenville, and we were never hotter, especially at night. In Amarillo, after the sun went down even in summertime, the planet cooled off and sleeping with an open window could actually be a chilly affair. The heat never followed the sun in Greenville, so it seemed just as hot at night as during the afternoon. I would lie there on the top of the sheets in the bed in the middle bedroom on the second floor of the house on Stonewall Street and just sweat and sweat and pray for sleep. Even the mornings weren't cool.

Aug. 24: Trump keeps attacking the news media, and he is setting the tone for a lot of people who never liked the media in the first place. Today, several articles deal with the subject, and they come pretty close to a chorale of whining. Can't stand the heat, boys and girls? Get out of the freaking kitchen. President gets tough; get tougher. The press is called upon at this time to gather together as the Hounds of Hell and chase this sonofabitch out of town.

In other Trump-related news, American Jews have suddenly awakened to the fact that a Nazi is in the White House. From The *Times*:

"All four Jewish groups — the Central Conference of American Rabbis, the Rabbinical Assembly, the Reconstructionist Rabbinical Association and the Religious Action Center of Reform Judaism — said they could not participate in interactions with Mr. Trump around the fall holidays.

"We have concluded that President Trump's statements during and after the tragic events in Charlottesville are so lacking in moral leadership and empathy for the victims of racial and religious hatred that we cannot organize such a call this year," the statement said.

And another story on Page One outlines what global warming is doing to the permafrost in Alaska. It is in essence going away, and the more permafrost evaporates the faster the temperature rises. From The *Times*: "In Alaska, nowhere is permafrost more vulnerable than here, 350 miles south of the Arctic Circle, in a vast, largely treeless landscape formed from sediment brought down by two of the state's biggest rivers, the Yukon and the Kuskokwim. Temperatures three feet down into the frozen ground are less than half a degree below freezing. This area could lose much of its permafrost by midcentury."

The lead story in the newspaper today has to do with Trump's alienation of Republicans, including one spineless creep named Mitch McConnell. Little Mitchie has been such a good boy, always there to lick the president's boots, and now that mean old president is pooping on Mitchie's party! Get a pair of balls, Mitch, and then tell us about how things are going in Washington!

Today I take Lynda back to see Dr. Ivy Ramirez, this time about her stomach upset. She can't seem to eat anything that doesn't make her feel bad. I asked her not to sell all that edible pot I got for her in Denver (which she wanted to get rid of because her stomach hurt and she figured that was the cause) until we had seen the doctor. She may have something entirely unrelated. I have no idea what it is, but having a routine stomach ache is not normal.

We are supposed to have rain today. HAHAHAHAHAHA!

Aug. 26: A Volkswagen engineer pleaded guilty yesterday to writing code that would let VW diesel engines pass emissions tests while polluting to high heaven. He got 40 months. I guess that is the best you can hope for.

Another *Times* article tells us about evening hours at the Trump International Hotel down the street from the White House, the place where Trump rakes in money from foreigners, in violation of the emoluments clause of the Constitution. It's a wonderland for lobbyists and conservatives, kind of reminding me of those plays and movies that show the glitterati of Nazi high society in the '30s Berlin. All is gay and shiny and bright! And why not, when you can screw everyone else in America and eat a $60 steak on their dime?

Sixty dollars for a steak! I can't even imagine that today, and never would have. I have worked hard my entire life, but that just sounds ridiculous.

Sixty dollars would have been about three months' profit from my paper route, the first steady job I had. I threw 51 papers on two city blocks on afternoons and Sunday mornings. The Sunday part of the job was no fun at all. Daddy usually woke me up at 5 o'clock, and I certainly would have preferred to stay in bed late on Sunday because it was fully half of the two-day weekend that I was off from school! I would get up, take a leak, dress, get my bag and head out on the route and try to finish by 6 o'clock. (I had a bike at some time during the three-year period I threw that route, but I never used it. I could walk the two blocks faster than I could ride them because I'd miss so many porches when trying to keep my balance.) In nice weather, I would finish the route and then I might walk a few blocks east to the Toddle House and have a piece of chocolate icebox pie and a big, cold, frothy glass of milk.

If there was going to be bad weather, it was going to fall on Sunday mornings, and I walked the route through some doozies. One storm left all the trees and lawns completely shrouded in ice. All along 10th Street the power lines were down, and I stepped over them carefully so as not to kill myself. I had to crunch through the ice-covered snow around fallen tree limbs and fences to get papers on porches. I was very cold and very wet. There were several Sundays like that. Fortunately, though, it never rained on Sunday mornings when I was throwing papers. We did not have plastic bags in those days, anyway, but we did porch the papers, which kept most of them out of the weather. When I couldn't trust a porch to protect the paper, I would put it between the screen door and the heavy front door of a house.

On those stormy or particularly cold Sunday mornings, Mrs. Helm, Malcolm's mother, would be waiting with her porchlight on and her front door open, and she would call for me to come in and have hot chocolate and warm up. Except for a lamp light in the living room and the dim light in the kitchen, her house would be dark, and Malcolm would be asleep upstairs. I would sit quietly and sip hot chocolate until I was warmed up. It was a wonderful gift from a very nice woman.

Aug. 28: Trump did give a pardon to the racist asshole former sheriff in Phoenix, who had been convicted of criminal contempt of court.

I am sad that I'm not a young man. I would be signing up for an army to combat Trumpistas and their collaborators.

Aug. 29: Several stories in various media are making the obvious link between climate change and Hurricane Harvey, which was driven by warm Gulf waters. One writer on the op-ed page of the *Times* this morning lays out the evidence in a scientific way that will most certainly be pooh-poohed by the idiots in charge.

Less discussed so far is how unbridled, balls-to-the-wall real estate development doomed Houston and the area around there. Houston has never had zoning, so you could wind up with your mansion next door to a pig farm and nothing could be done about it. It's all concrete and rooftops for as far as the eye can see out of downtown Houston, and that's all mighty fine and dandy if all you care about is making a buck off housing and retail and property taxes. If you want to see how not to build a city, go to Houston and wade around in the water. What you see will have you wondering why they didn't grow a few trees and parks and put in a little drainage here and there.

My paper route taught me some valuable lessons, from making myself gut up and get out there when it was below zero and ice was on the streets, and when I had to ask for money from a woman who I knew wasn't going to give it to me. I learned to stick to it, to do what you have to do. I learned not to be stupid with other people's property.

Aug. 31: Today's news is much about Houston and the aftermath of Hurricane Harvey, and rightly so. People in the media are beginning to make the strong link between overdevelopment, balls-to-the-wall development regardless of consequences, and the flooding, which is massive and unprecedented. Houston has proudly given big breaks to business and caused them little or no grief as they set about ruining the landscape in all directions. Houston is one ugly place and it is only going to get much uglier. Growth seems unstoppable.

And, who has been supporting all this growth without any need to declare responsibility: The prosperity Gospelites like Joel Osteen, who refused to open his megachurch until Tuesday, and Republicans, that's who. This column is by Anthea Butler:

"So while the storm churns through Texas and Louisiana, causing floods, death and misery, it is time to consider the damage the prosperity gospel has done to America. Mr. Trump and Mr. Osteen unwittingly revealed its ugly underbelly: the smugness, the self-aggrandizing posturing. It has co-opted many in the Republican Party, readily visible in their relentless desire to strip Americans of health care, disaster relief and infrastructure funding.

"Now Ted Cruz and Texas Republicans seek federal disaster aid, although they voted against the same in the aftermath of Hurricane Sandy. The Republicans in states affected by the disaster will find out soon enough what it feels like to come to Washington and relief organizations with their hat in their hands.

"The survivors of Hurricane Harvey do not need empty tweets and platitudes from people like Donald Trump and Joel Osteen. They have shown beyond a shadow of a doubt that, as we say in Texas, they are all hat and no cattle."

My church is gearing up to help people in the flood-impacted areas. Lynda and I will send some money through some avenue, although we don't have much we can spare. We will not be giving to the Red Cross, which has managed to tarnish its once-good name by failing to do the right thing in places like Haiti. The *Times* even editorialized against donations to the Red Cross earlier this week, noting that they have decided not to be held accountable for the gazillions of dollars they take in on a regular basis. One thing we can do is fill up one-gallon plastic bags with items people need right now. The church is distributing those bags, and we can fill them up. I think that's a pretty good idea, because there are thousands of people in shelters right now and more will be entering shelters. The storm is still wreaking damage across parts of Texas and Louisiana.

Sept. 1: The president of our Rotary Club sent out an email yesterday asking members to bring things like water and paper towels and baby wipes, toothpaste, soap, etc., to her business over on Ranch Road 12. She plans to drive to Rockport with whatever she can gather up and give the stuff to the Rotary Club there for distribution and use. The church also put out an email asking members to put together kits of stuff in one-gallon plastic bags so they can be handed out at the various shelters around the state. So, I went to HEB and bought $122 worth of stuff, including huge boxes of disposable diapers, and Lynda and I stuffed four one-gallon kits and I took the rest of it over for the Rotary collection.

I don't know what else we can do. I'm too old and out of shape to go down there and help muck out houses or cut down tree limbs. I can't carry anything heavier than a lunch tray, so I'd be more trouble than I'd be worth. I hate that because my impulse is to pitch in and help.

Sept. 2: People are returning to their homes in Houston and other cities in that part of Texas, and what they're finding is far worse than they could imagine. Everything is ruined by water. And following the water in this late part of summer will be mold and other awful stuff. I'm honestly not sure how people will go back and rebuild some of these areas because they will just be uninhabitable.

Unfortunately, there are no lessons to be learned by the Houston flood situation because while there are teachable moments and teachable situations, there are no students. The people who might be paying attention are the ones who abetted the problems of unregulated development in the first place and the people in charge now are dedicated completely to deregulation. If lessons were spoken, they would have their fingers in their ears and their mouths would be clucking to shut out the jabber.

Sept. 3: I guess that I have been pretty darn lucky all of my life when it comes to weather and related events because in many roles I actively sought out bad weather and often went into places already victimized by storms. That 1978 flood along the Tierra Blanca Creek in Canyon is a good example. Our house did not fill with water over on 11th Avenue, and by the next day when I was roaming around trying to get pictures and the full scope of the disaster, I never was in danger.

When I was a young regional reporter for the Amarillo newspaper, I went into several towns that had been hit by disaster right after disaster hit, and when I was with the television station in Amarillo and later was city editor in Wichita Falls, I would cheerfully and eagerly go out chasing tornadoes all over the Panhandle and southern Oklahoma.

Oddly enough, for all the times I went tornado hunting, I never actually saw one until one day when Lynda and I were on vacation, visiting daughter Laura, in Denver. At that time, she was living with D.O., who had a house with a second-floor view of downtown Denver. It was amazing. One day, I was up on the second-floor balcony, ostensibly to watch D.'s dog Rudy jump from the balcony into the swimming pool, and I saw the very dark and threatening storm clouds building over downtown and then watched as a tornado formed and twisted through downtown before withdrawing and moving on eastward and away from the mountains.

After that, the only other time I have seen a tornado was – back in Denver! And that was just a few weeks ago when I was standing around waiting to get a rental car at the Denver airport. Off toward the mountains, I saw the clouds brewing and out came a small tornado that dissipated before reaching the airport itself. I never heard any sirens or alarms, so maybe this was just par for the course

203

there.

I do remember being scared just once when out chasing storms north of Wichita Falls and across the Red River into Oklahoma. I was riding shotgun in an open Jeep driven by Lee Anderson, who was regional editor at the time. I was city editor of the afternoon paper, and my shift had ended at 3 o'clock. In that part of Texas, storms generally built in mid- to late afternoon (the storm that destroyed a quarter of the homes in Wichita Falls on April 10, 1979, hit at about 6 o'clock in the evening). We drove lickety-split under some very dangerous-looking clouds on our way to the other side of the river and back, and the hair on the back of my neck stood up several times as the wind shifted directions and the sky changed colors. Snowstorms, however, were an altogether different story, as were windstorms.

Sept. 4: Trump has been out of the news for the most part over the weekend. His generals made some sword-rattling comments about a bomb North Korea blew up in an underground test. In a Tweet, the commander in chief suggested the U.S. cut off all trade with countries that trade with North Korea. That would be, mainly, China and South Korea. Can you imagine not having trade with China or South Korea? Really? What is this guy smoking?

It's estimated it will take at least $180 billion in federal assistance to get Houston back on its feet. That's federal assistance, with an emphasis on the "federal," as in the people who Texas lawmakers love to hate. You know, those lawmakers who turned back federal dollars for Medicaid, leaving thousands of families to go without health care. If you drilled a hole in a place rotten with hypocrisy you'd put up your rig in Austin, Texas.

Sept. 5: On my walk this morning, I thought about really retiring. I have been working since I was a kid, and I'm kind of tired of having to deal with people in a work setting. I'll probably feel better later today.

A story on the front page of today's *Times* notes the bare-bones hypocrisy of Texas elected officials, who "hate" the federal government until it's time to take a huge handout, for Hurricane Harvey cleanup. We're talking $180 billion, in all probability. So, where's the tough talk, Governor Abbott and Senator Ted Cruz, you fucking jackal?

Sept. 6: Now comes Hurricane Irma. Today it is hitting Puerto Rico. By Sunday it is supposed to hit Florida as a Category 5 storm, the worst.

Yesterday, Trump's henchmen announced he will kill the program designed to let young people from other countries who were brought to America by their parents when they were children stay here and work without threat of deportation. In six months, they can be deported. The announcement said these kids are taking jobs from other Americans, blah, blah, blah, as if those fucking out-of-work coal miners who never graduated from high school could do what these many motivated college graduates with white-collar jobs are doing! Obama gave these kids hope by making them safe from deportation. After all, their being here was not their doing or their fault. This is just another way for Trump to appeal to his racist base.

The Agriculture Department is also setting about to undo anything and everything done by the Obama administration and past presidents, specifically targeting requirements that school lunches be healthy. Scott Perdue, the secretary of agriculture, told school lunch people yesterday that their jobs were going to get easier because they weren't going to be so constrained by concerns about the health of children. I mean that's what they heard him say.

I guess school lunches have come a long way. The last time I ate a lunch at school I was a mentor for a student at an elementary school in Temple. Once a week, I would go have lunch with him, and the fare was generally inedible. Even the pizza was bad.

Back at Lee Bivins Elementary School, the cafeteria ladies cooked as if they alone were in charge of fattening all of us up. They were like grandmas with a very limited palette. So, they would cook up stuff like cooked cabbage and brussels sprouts and spinach. We had Spam for lunch sometimes and other sorts of hot mystery meats. I remember being served a salmon patty one time that seemed to have fine hairs stuck all over it. I couldn't find the courage to eat it.

Sept. 7: The *Times* today has a big report, of course, on Hurricane Irma, which is heading directly for Florida, a fact that seems to have eluded Congress and the president. Yesterday, they reached an agreement that would send $8 billion in aid to Houston and that area to start the rebuilding process after Hurricane Harvey. So, after Hurricane Irma lays waste to Florida, are they going to go back and try to come up with a similar deal for that state? I would guess so. It just seems pretty stupid to do the Houston aid dance while Irma is in the wings. And, oh by the way, $8 billion will barely touch the amount needed in South Texas. The estimates are closer to $180 billion. If Irma is as bad as they say it is, that would be roughly what it would cost to do repairs out there, too.

To my way of thinking $360 billion is not chump change, and it will go in a lot of cases to people who want to rebuild right where they are right now, which is a definition of insane public policy if I ever heard one. If people build in coastal areas that are subject to flooding now and will be even more susceptible in the future, the government should be discouraging them, not encouraging them. It's irresponsible public policy to reward stupidity.

I'm actually surprised to learn via The *Times* that some Republicans are joining Democrats in suggesting to the Supreme Court that gerrymandering districts for political gain is wrong and ought to be outlawed. Perhaps there are some statesmen in D.C. after all.

Texas is likewise a perfect example of what happens when one party draws up the maps without any consideration given to the actual political makeup of the state. The House and Senate are completely dominated by, not just Republicans, but the most conservative of Republicans. No one else gets a voice. So, we have a legislature that spends days and days talking about which bathroom transgender people can use, as if anyone actually gives a damn about that other than Joel Osteen and his cult of cultural cadavers.

Sept. 8: Last evening in California, Julia introduced her new book called "Fray." She did a reading and had a party, and Bryan got to be there. I do wish I could have been there, as well. This is, of course, a very big deal for Julia, and I am most proud of her and her accomplishments. She is so smart and such a hard worker. I worry that she is too hard on herself and will burn out or otherwise flame out in some scary way.

Stunning news on two fronts today, both shining a huge searchlight on how vulnerable we are to hacking in this day and age. Both stories are on 1A in the *Times*. One highlights the hack of 200 million accounts held by Equifax, one of the Big Three credit reporting agencies in the United States. Millions of identities, to include Social Security numbers, were stolen, and you can bet they will be sold and resold for years to come, causing untold misery for many, many Americans. The Equifax CEO said he was sorry in a televised report last night. Thanks for that, asshole. This sonofabitch needs to be fired – now. But it is quite likely that his board will give him a bonus next year instead. That's the way it works these days in American corporate culture. You screw up bad, and the board throws money at you. Unbelievable. This hack means I will need to figure out how much of our information was compromised and what to do about it. That could take hours online. Will I be paid for my time fixing the problem that Equifax caused? Hell no.

The other hacking story is more interesting, actually. It is about how the Russians created at least 100,000 false identities during last year's elections to hijack Twitter and FaceBook and turn them into engines of support for Trump. No one will be held accountable here, either, and it is not clear that anyone will learn anything for the next time around.

Elsewhere in the news, Hurricane Irma is churning disaster toward Florida. And Krugman takes Jeff Sessions apart for his speech announcing that kids here under the DACA program would no longer be protected from deportation. Sessions tied the decision to the unfair taking of jobs by these kids from all those thousands of poor Americans who couldn't compete and win them fair and square. What happened to the conservative notion that folks should pull themselves up by their own bootstraps? Here is a group of kids who did just that, and they are punished for it? Somewhere when this nightmare is over we need to erect a huge statute of Hypocrisy across from the White House.

I started the Coursera class on terrorism and counter-terrorism yesterday. It promises to be very, very good, so I'm excited about that. It's offered by the University of Leiden in The Hague.

Sept. 9: The hurricane is bearing down on all of Florida this morning, but I have not looked at any news sites yet, so I'm not sure when it will hit with full force. The forecast is for Irma to be a Category 4 or 5 hurricane, with 5 being the most violent and deadly. Cissy and George are counting on the storm going more to the east, but yesterday it was predicted to take a little bit of a westward shift.

The big news for the last couple of days has been the hack of Equifax. I went to their website yesterday morning to try to figure out how to protect our data, and I got almost nowhere. I got a message that I could check back on the 13th to file for protection. I went ahead and looked at all three credit reports that are out there on us, and they seemed to be in good order. We shall see. Thieves would be wasting their time trying to get any money out of us. We don't have any.

Sept. 10: I haven't looked at TV or the internet this a.m. to see what Hurricane Irma has done to Florida. The storm was 300 miles wide when it was approaching the Keys, and it was supposed to be a Category 4 storm when it hit Fort Myers. Some weather expert pointed out on the news last night that this is the START of the hurricane season, and they quoted a hurricane expert as saying that the Atlantic is unusually warm this year and that will make hurricane development easier and hurricanes more powerful. I think they edited his sound bite before he got to the part about global warming, and then minimized the effect.

What we are seeing is a retreat on the part of news media from the Big Truths that are out there but disputed by Trumpistas, I suppose so that the media will be removed from the Trumpista Hate List. I surely do not see that happening, but I do see some of the weak-kneed TV people lurching away from controversy so they can keep their pitiful little jobs.

Sept. 11: Sandy's sermon yesterday was one of the best I have heard her deliver on a Sunday morning. (The truth is that I don't actually 'hear' many of them because of where I sit and the acoustics of the place. I heard yesterday's sermon because I had on a set of headphones.) It was about how the brain reacts when engaged in the act of forgiveness and how the brain reacts when engaged in activities such as revenge. Her message, of course, was that not only is forgiveness required by Jesus but it is good for the brain. I don't know about the physiology of that, but the whole thing got me thinking about acts of forgiveness that I've seen in person.

Undoubtedly, the greatest act of forgiveness I have ever seen occurred about 15 or 20 years ago and was performed by Pam, Lynda's cousin. All those many years ago, Pam had a son, Alex, who had just graduated from St. John's in Santa Fe. One very early morning he was riding his motorcycle, with his girlfriend as a passenger, in Albuquerque, and he was hit by a pickup driven by another young man who had been drinking. Alex was killed. Lynda went up to Denver immediately to comfort Pam and to stay for the funeral. The driver who survived was charged with manslaughter.

Within a few weeks after the funeral, Pam met with the district attorney who was handling prosecution of the case and asked that the charges be dropped with the understanding that the boy would do community service and stay out of trouble for X number of years. And that is what happened. Pam's reasoning was that the incident had already ruined one life and should not ruin another simply out of revenge. She wanted to be able to move on, and forgiveness helped her do that just as it helped the young man who was behind the wheel of the truck.

Sept. 12: The weather news reminds me of one summer I spent roofing houses for Joe Wirtz. I made more money than I had ever made doing anything. The way I figured it out later, I made more money per hour that summer than I made until I became managing editor of the newspaper in Wichita Falls!

While earning a lot of cash at that job, I also learned a number of valuable lessons. When you're roofing houses with other guys, you learn very quickly how important it is to work as part of the team, not as an individual. I probably weighed around 100 pounds that summer, so it took a lot for me to lift a bundle of composition shingles from the ground to the rooftop. I could get the bundle up about halfway on the ladder, and then someone had to come take it from me and put it where it needed to go. Popping chalk lines was a job for a team, and sometimes you just needed help when you were trying to cut shingles around roof structures.

The value of teamwork on a roofing job was driven home to me after that summer when I was hired by a neighbor to put a new roof on his house. The roof was steeper than any I had encountered out in South Amarillo, so the guy tied one end of a sturdy rope around the chimney and the other end around my waist, and I had to navigate the roof like a spider. That job would have been infinitely easier with a partner.

After I finished the summer of roofing, Mom talked to Zeke Powell, the guy who owned Uncle Zeke's Pancake House in Wolflin Village, about putting me on as a part-timer during the school year. Zeke put me to work as a busboy, and I worked breakfasts and lunches on Saturday and Sunday mornings and a few days after school. I think I worked 30 hours a week, and I made 75 cents an hour.

Sept. 13: The *Times* reports this morning that the housing market is still strong in Houston, citing the example of one family whose house was devastated but still got an offer to purchase. For a long time it's been one of the hottest housing markets in the country, and even the thousands of destroyed properties will only increase demand for a limited supply. One thing is certain: The disasters in Houston and in Florida will ensure that there are no tradesmen to do work anywhere else in the United States and, maybe, in Mexico. Puerto Rico and parts of the Caribbean are also demolished, and they will be rebuilt, too.

Apple introduced its new iPhone yesterday. From The *Times* report:

"With the $999 iPhone X, Apple moved to a new premium level of pricing. The smartphone will cost $300 more than the iPhone 8 and $200 more than the iPhone 8 Plus."

I'm not sure I understand the draw for this phone, but I'm no longer in the demographic that would care about it.

Sept. 14: The *Times* has buried a very interesting story in its business section about Kaspersky Labs, a company that I have scrupulously avoided since the dawn of my own personal computer age. I found out early on that Kaspersky's security software for computers was invented in and made in Russia by Russians. I thought that buying such a thing to make sure my computer was secure would be ridiculously risky. Why would I buy something from Russia that gave Russians a chance to break into my computer? Not everyone was as prescient as I was! And I'm not kidding. Today's *Times* story is about U.S. government officials ordering that Kaspersky Labs security software be removed from government com-April 30, 2019 computers because of the fear of HACKING.

The *Times* front page is all about the talk in Washington of big tax cuts for business. The fight is over how much businesses should pay in taxes, and there is not even an argument that they should pay more than they are paying now, which was the case even during the Reagan years. That tells you about the political environment. The 1 percent can't decide what it wants to have; it just knows it wants more and more.

Sept. 16: One of the librarians stopped by the front desk on his way out yesterday evening. Under his arm was the book on Vietnam that is a companion to the big-event-style series on the war that airs starting tomorrow night. Ken Burns, the well-respected documentarian who produced the Civil War series that I liked so much, is producer on this project, too, so it should be splendid. It has received glowing reviews from all the sources I'm familiar with. "You want this after I'm done with it?" the librarian asked. "No, thanks," I said. I won't look at the book and I won't see the series. The whole thing makes me sick at my stomach: the war, my part in it, my reaction to it, the 56,000 dead U.S. boys and girls, the untold thousands of dead Vietnamese and Cambodians and Thai. All of it. The whole damned thing. As you can tell, I have not done a lot of planning in putting this diary together. Nevertheless, I had originally thought I would include my Army experiences when I was writing about my place in the world of work. But, now that the documentary is at hand, I might as well go ahead and skip forward to that part of my life.

In my mind, the story begins during my senior year in high school – 1964-'65. I didn't watch much television news during high school, and read only bits and pieces (i.e., the comics pages) in the Amarillo newspaper, so I was not so informed by the developing war in Vietnam that it was pressing on my consciousness. I knew I would have to register for the draft when I turned 18, and I knew that joining the military was an option after high school graduation.

During the spring of 1965 the idea of the military became reality when Greg Vitarelli, angry over not winning a short-story-writing contest (that I won) and angry over losing a girlfriend, Janis Parks, dropped out of school and joined the Army. Almost before I heard he was gone, he was, in fact, gone, and then he was in Vietnam. Greg's sudden move was an isolated situation. And it provided no persuasive impetus for my own brief survey of options in the military.

Even though I was doing well as a student newspaper reporter, I still felt there was no real place for me in the broad and wide world I envisioned entering after high school. It had been laid into me that I was not college material, and I had pursued my lessons in high school as if that were the case. Going into graduation, I had a low-C overall grade-point average. I couldn't have cared less. I guess I felt so bad about my future that at one point I called up Jerry Raines, my wrestling coach and an old friend of Dad's, and talked to him about getting into the Marine Corps. He had served, and you could tell he was proud of that service. He was not encouraging. I don't know why.

I turned 18 in May 1965 and signed up for the draft and also graduated from high school and was confronted for the first time by the fact that if I did not get into college and stay in college I would be drafted and would be, in all likelihood, going to Vietnam. Several of my friends were in the same situation: We didn't have enough money to go off to a university, we had parents who were not going to pay our way, we were healthy enough to be drafted and we didn't want to go into military service at all. So, we all went to Amarillo College, starting that very May. I had sold my Austin-Healey for $500 to pay for college, and I used some of the money to buy a bicycle that I used to go back and forth to classes. (For part of that summer, Jeff Anderson and I worked at a moving-and-storage company. I will detail that particular job in a later entry.)

I was riding my bike to classes one day thinking about a Dan Rather report out of Vietnam, and it occurred to me that at that point, the war in Vietnam had been going on for two or three years. The longest war in American history had been the Civil War, and it lasted only four years. So, I thought, if I can stick with it in college another year or so, the odds are very good this war will be over and I can be free of having the draft hanging over my head. Boy, was I wrong!

Sept. 17: I didn't mention this earlier, but the Census Bureau issued some new economic data a week or so ago, and The *Times* spent quite a bit of space today writing about it. The story by Patricia Cohen notes that incomes are up and poverty is down, according to the Census data: "The disconnect between positive statistics and people's day-to-day lives is one of the great economic and social puzzles of recent years." Indeed. So, she sets about trying to solve the puzzle and does so mighty well, in my opinion. The American Dream is not back on track even with this blip. Middle America is not moving forward. Statistics she cites show that, "in 1973, the inflation-adjusted median income of men working full time was $54,030. In 2016, it was $51,640—roughly $2,400 lower."

That's 1973, she's writing about, but the disparity began building far earlier than that, back in the 1960s, when I was just getting started in the workforce. In fact, since I have started the part of this project that will deal with my world of work, it might be good to just go ahead and throw out some numbers that you might find of interest.

Every year before I retired (let's use 2011 as the official date because that's when I started getting Social Security) I received a nice letter in the mail from the Social Security Administration called "Your Social Security Statement." This document was fascinating to me because it showed my earnings by year. The first year for which I had taxable earnings, according to the report, was 1963, which would have been my first year at Uncle Zeke's. I had earnings that year of $497. Remember, I was making 75 cents an hour. That would be the equivalent of $6 an hour today, adjusting for inflation. (These inflation numbers come from the Bureau of Labor Statistics.) The next year, I made less: $174. And the year after that, 1965, I made $196. I went to work at the Amarillo newspaper in August of 1966, and for the remainder of that year I earned $893. That would be about $7,000 today. The next year I worked full time at the paper, and my earnings totaled $3,623, which would be worth $28,000 today. I am going to put a table below showing the year, the total earnings and then the amount that would buy in 2017 dollars.

Year	Earnings	Today's purchasing power
1970	$6,090	$39,555
1971	$5,700	$35,162
1972	$8,631	$49,946
1973	$9,275	$53,455

1974	$10,250	$54,003
1975	$10,450	$49,245
1976	$12,963	$57,242
1983	$22,388	$56,203
1995	$51,224	$83,675
2007	$97,500	$118,261

I selected those dates for the following reasons: I went into the Army full-time in 1970; there was massive inflation in the 1970s, and you can see my salary didn't keep pace; I went to work at the *Times Record News* in 1983; I was made editor of the newspaper in 1995; and I retired in 2007 from the *TRN*.

I never felt that I made a lot of money anywhere I went and I especially felt used by the publisher at the *Canyon News*.

Sept. 18: *The Times* reports this morning on the status of *Rolling Stone*, a magazine that has been around since 1967. It was an icon in the trade, but I never paid much attention to it because I couldn't keep track of all the rock groups and their various doings even in high school, much less in college and later when I was working 65 hours a week and going to school and trying to raise three girls. Still, you could count me among those who thought *Rolling Stone* would go on forever. It appears that is not the case. The founder, Jann Werner, is retiring and trying to sell the publication. It may continue in someone else's hands, but will it be the same?

Sept. 19: We go to the doctor this morning so Lynda can report in and get more of the medication that's helping her get a life back. There seems to be a question about whether insurance will pay for the medicine. If it doesn't I don't know what we'll do because she says the cost is about $1,000 a month.

Republicans in the Senate are trying to pass another bill that would undo Obamacare and leave millions of Americans without insurance or health care. The vote apparently hinges on a couple of iffy Republicans, one of whom has said he will bite the bullet and vote "yes" on the bill, no matter how awful it is. These people are worse than cretinous jackals. They are zombies that nothing will kill. My frustration and anger over their willingness to cause unmerited suffering and death has never been greater. I could spit bullets. But, what can I do? I'm now 70 years old, and I have no clout whatsoever.

The Times has a front-page story on how no hurricane of any force will keep people from wanting to live in Florida and Houston and invest in real estate. When you look at that and the Republican majorities in the House and Senate and the Republican in the White House, you can only conclude that the Republican decades-long effort to reduce public education to babysitting has worked and worked very well, indeed. People are too stupid for self-government!

At Amarillo College, there was no talk of the War in Vietnam, no student or faculty expressions of concern or outrage, no protests, no marches, nothing. It was as if the war existed on the other side of the world and involved aliens from other planets, which was true in part.

The nightly news with Walter Cronkite might show us what was going on in Vietnam, but who had time to watch the news? Those images on TV of the monks setting themselves on fire and burning up in the streets of Saigon: horrible, but not my problem.

It was only after I got a job at the *Globe-News* in August of 1966, a year after I graduated from high school and a year after my freshman year at AC that I took even a passing interest in Vietnam, and I did so mainly because of Buck Ramsey, who introduced me to the Angry White Liberal, and some assignments I pulled as a young reporter, among them covering a speech by a Green Beret at a conservative forum.

Still, the whole war was barely a blip on my radar. I held firmly to two comforting notions: One, that as long as I stayed in college and passed 12 hours per semester I could keep my student deferment from the draft, and two, that no war in American history had gone beyond four or five years, max.

My complacency was threatened during my first semester at West Texas State when I found that I could not pass the second year of college algebra, a subject required as part of my degree program. But, I had gotten myself into a terrible double-bind: I couldn't pass, but I also could not drop the course because I was taking only 12 hours at the time. I waited until late in the semester to go talk to the professor, who, of course, knew I was failing. In a very awkward and uncomfortable conversation at his office, he let me know in an oblique way that he had a son right then serving in Vietnam and that he would not wish that fate on anyone simply because of a failure to grasp algebraic functions. He gave me a C in the course, a gift of pure grace. It was not the last act of compassion I experienced as the war droned on.

That junior year in college at West Texas, 1967-68, much turmoil was brewing over the war and over race, and I was deeply involved in all of that because I was associate editor of the student newspaper, The Prairie. (The anger over race relations was palpable, mainly because about half the players on the WT football team were black and a higher proportion of basketball players were black. These guys were a very, very small minority on the WT campus, which was with those few exceptions redneck white.)

Sept. 20: Trump made a fool of himself at the United Nations yesterday, and the *Washington Post* blistered him for it. The *Times* was less visceral in its reaction. The leaders of the free and not-so-free world must have wondered what in the holy heck was happening in America. The Trumpian schtick is straight out of a seventh-grade locker room, where bullies learn the art of posturing before foggy mirrors.

Sept. 21: Carolyn sent me a link yesterday to a report that appeared in a higher education publication this week. Here is an excerpt, which should make your hair stand on end:

The Brookings Institution has released <u>survey results</u> showing that many college students lack understanding of or support for the legal principles of the First Amendment. Among the findings:
Students are more likely to believe that hate speech is not protected by the First Amendment than to believe it is protected (44 percent to 39 percent, with the

remaining saying that they don't know).
A slight majority (51 percent) of students believe that it is "acceptable" for students to repeatedly shout at a controversial speaker to prevent that person from being heard in a campus talk.
Nineteen percent of students (and 30 percent of male students) said it would be acceptable for a student group to use violence to prevent a controversial speaker from speaking.
A large majority of students (62 percent) said that when bringing a controversial speaker to campus, a student group is legally required to also have a speaker with an opposing view.

The Senate is pushing toward a vote on a health-care repeal bill that would put block grants for health care distribution into the hands of state legislatures across the nation. Holy Shit! What would it be like if Dan Patrick and Greg Abbott got their hands on a bunch of money intended for the health care of poor people? Well, "poor" would suddenly be anybody with an annual income of OVER $100,000. Ambulance service would be available only to residents of River Oaks in Houston and Highland Park in Dallas. You'd be able to get opioids of any kind if you could show a platinum Bank of America card. Right now, just about everyone, including insurers, are against the bill, but it may well be passed. If not, it will have been because all of these interest groups offered some kind of payoff under the table to keep it off the table.

As late as the fall of 1968, I guess I operated in a state of denial about me and the war. Being a reporter and editor and photographer afforded me the mental opportunity to shield myself from the stark facts about Vietnam, particularly the fact that it will still be raging on while I was approaching the official end of my IIS deferment period, which would be in May 1969, the moment I graduated from WTSU.

At some point in 1968, my brother John decided to join the Army. He said he wanted to be a helicopter pilot, but after he went through basic training at Fort Bliss, Texas, he was sent to advance training at Fort Knox as a tank crewman. (John's decision had nothing to do with patriotism, I must say. He had become engaged to a girl in Amarillo who was pushing him hard to get married right away, and he developed feet the temperature of an iceberg. He saw no other way out.) Right out of Fort Knox, John was sent to Korea for 13 months as an infantryman with the 2nd Infantry Division.

Over that winter of 1968 and 1969, many of my fellow seniors started getting draft notices calling them to come in right after graduation. It was clear that I might be getting that letter myself. I had a long conversation with Mother, exploring the idea that Dr. John Pickett, the man who diagnosed my tuberculosis in 1953 or 1954, could be approached about writing a letter to the draft board saying that I was physically unfit for service. She asked him; he would not.

Here I was then: physically fit with a brother in the Army, a dad who had served in World War II, an uncle who had been aboard ship in the Pacific during World War II, another uncle who had been in the infantry in World War I and two great-grandfathers who had fought for the South during the Civil War. I honestly did not see a way out. And then it came to me that if I was going to have to serve in the military during wartime, I needed to do it as an officer, not as a grunt.

213

Sept. 22: It just so happened that the lieutenant colonel who was in charge of the ROTC detachment at West Texas had a background in journalism, and I became acquainted with him in a class or two he took that I was also taking. I knew him, of course, as a news source, but being a fellow student changed our relationship a little.

Early in the spring semester of 1969, leading up to my graduation, I walked over to the ROTC building one day to talk to the colonel. At that point, I figured that ROTC was not an option for me because it was a two-year course of instruction and I was about to graduate. Not to worry, said the good colonel. He signed me up for a one-year course of instruction that would have me going to Fort Benning, Ga., for basic training in the summer of '69, then pursuing a doubled-up class load in '69-'70, then going to Fort Sill, Okla., for advanced training in the summer of '70, with immediate commissioning as a second lieutenant to follow that.

Susan was not happy about this. She was not happy about any of it, actually. At one point, she pushed for us to move to Canada, but she couldn't push hard enough. I couldn't figure out how to face my dad and my uncles and my brother if I went to Canada. Neither Mom nor Dad were elated by the idea of me going into the Army, but there wasn't much to be done about it. So, in May 1969 I got my degree in journalism from WTSU and in June of 1969 I went to Fort Benning, Ga.

Sept. 23: During those years of 1968 and 1969, I'm sure my dad found himself in a real bind about his boys. He had positioned himself in our minds and in the minds of his friends and colleagues as an arch-conservative, a hawk, almost a card-carrying conservative John Bircher. And now his sons were about to be used as instruments of his government's policy, good or bad, in Southeast Asia. Perhaps he saw it as his and our patriotic duty to go off to whatever war came along regardless of whether it was just or right. Perhaps he believed that U.S. interests in Vietnam merited having two sons in harm's way. Neither of us asked Dad what he thought. Nor did we seek his permission or his blessing about going into the Army. We didn't ask for his counsel or advice. We just went.

Before I took off for Fort Benning, I had a long sit-down with a major and a captain at ROTC headquarters about how things worked in the ROTC program and how to play the ROTC game. In part, it was their duty as instructors to tell me how the game was played, and in part, I think they just wanted to see if I could game the play.

Here's what I mean: All across the Army, in every course of education and training aimed at making officers out of civilians or out of enlisted troopers the basis for advancement was competition. The scoresheet for each competitive venue was called the Order of Merit List. Every top grade, every win in hand-to-hand, every bullseye on the rifle range moved you as a soldier up on the Order of Merit List. At the end of basic training, you got a cumulative grade, and that grade was weighted and went into the ranking mix on the OML. At the end of advanced training, same thing. Of course, you got grades for classroom study and for drill, etc. All of that went into the mix.

At the end of your course of instruction, you were then ranked against your peers on the Master Order of Merit List for your unit, and if you were at the top you got an award and a medal.

But, in ROTC and at West Point, you also got something else, something more precious than a medal or a pay raise or a vacation in the Caribbean. You got to choose the branch within the Army in which you would serve. There were four combat branches: infantry, armor, artillery and air defense artillery. And there were noncombat branches: medical corps, adjutant general's corps, finance corps. Once you were assigned a branch, you were there for your career. You would not be reassigned. I quickly figured out that if I ranked at the very top of the Order of Merit List I could pick a noncombat branch and not have my ass shot off in Vietnam!

I was not alone. Thousands of men at West Point and in ROTC and in officer candidate schools knew the game and played it to the end that the best of them did not go into leadership roles in combat units. The perverse outcome was that the troops in Vietnam were not led by the best and brightest but the dumbest and least qualified. (I have proof of this in the form of an article about a survey that was published in 1970.) You can bet that Ken Burns will not have this dirty little secret included in his TV series.

Sept. 24: Trump is spitting angry at Sen. John McCain, who is in a position to kill the so-called health-care bill the Senate just dug out of some sick swamp somewhere. McCain won't back it; so Trump is name-calling, as usual. That's his only real expertise. The measure of the strength of the stranglehold the big rich have on the Senate is in the completely blind support senators are giving to this plan to kill health care for all but the wealthiest. At least 50 of them are completely in thrall to the 1 percent.

Everything I read tells me that Trump is playing with fire when he taunts and taunts and taunts Kim Il Jung. Kim must protect his position at any cost, that latter being the operative phrase. He will do anything to continue to be king. And regardless of what Trump seems to think, the cards are with Kim, not with Trump. The ace in the hole for this dictator is a few old artillery guns that are aimed straight at Seoul, South Korea, where a few million innocent civilians live and work. Trump does not have that in his hand or the deck he is playing with.

At Fort Benning, we had eight weeks of basic training pumped into six weeks, so we were up earlier than ordinary draftees and asleep later. Our days were packed. I lived on the second story of a two-story clapboard World War II barracks building that had no heat or air-conditioning. Our Company A, 6th Battalion, 2nd Training Brigade senior drill sergeant was Sgt. First Class Maldonado. His assistant was Staff Sgt. Futch. And his assistant was a buck sergeant whose name I don't recall.

The physical training was very hard for us, but we got harder and leaner and meaner over a short period of time. We ran everywhere with steel pots on our heads, boots on our feet and M-14 rifles in our arms. That's right: We had M-14 rifles to train with. We went to the rifle range with M-14s and qualified on M-14s. We never saw an M-16. They were all in Vietnam. We qualified with old hand grenades; we found out they were old when one went off in a kid's hands on the

215

Friday before A Company was supposed to go to the grenade range.

We did get a couple of weekends to take leave, and several of us went into Columbus, Ga., and got a motel room and some beer on those outings. I was drunk and in a motel in Columbus on July 20, 1969, when Man First Walked on the Moon.

It was not lost on me that I was being trained to kill people – at long range with a rifle and at close range with a knife or my bare hands. Nor was it lost on me that I needed to learn to do these things really, really well because my life might well depend on these skills and others that I left Fort Benning without knowing. I did OK at Fort Benning, OK enough to get me up the ladder on the Order of Merit List.

Sept. 25: Trump really stirred things up, and perhaps they will blow up in his face. He called out NFL athletes who take a knee during The National Anthem to protest police brutality against blacks on Friday or Saturday, and yesterday just about everyone in the NFL, from the owners on down, took a knee and also raised a finger. However, I'd much rather see Trump trying to run the NFL from Washington than trying to run the country. Maybe he'll keep himself mired in these inconsequential issues and leave the rest of us alone.

It's hard to overstate the hypocrisy of elected Republicans from Austin to Washington. Greg Abbott, our brain-dead governor, hates, hates, hates Washington and everything it stands for, even to the point of refusing to take money earmarked for the needy in Texas. But, here comes Hurricane Harvey, and Abbott has his hand out like some poor street beggar. The insult is made worse by the fact that Texas has $10 billion in its Rainy Day Fund, and Abbott won't spend it on the hurricane cleanup. What the ever-lovin' hell does "Rainy Day" mean if that hurricane doesn't fit the definition? And, of course, the Republicans in Washington are pushing and pushing on that bill they say is about health care, only – ONLY – because they have promised for nearly eight years now to repeal the Affordable Care Act and because their Big Donors are pissed off at them.

At the close of training at Fort Benning, it occurred to all of us in A-6-2 that we had not learned anything about how to lead men into battle, which is what ROTC was all about. We were not just dismayed but frightened by the oversight. How was it that within just 12 months for some of us we were going to be expected to pit 50 of our own men against an unknown number of the enemy's and win?

I returned to Canyon disgruntled and fearful. Some years later as I reflected on that Fort Benning training, it occurred to me that the Army was not at that point trying to make me into a leader of men. They were trying to make me into a basic soldier, which is entirely different. They wanted to tear me down and build me up as something new, something they could work with in the formation of a leader who was tough, confident and smart. They did accomplish that goal. In August 1969, I signed up for and started taking a double load of classes in what was laughingly called Military Science.

Sept. 26: I got a letter from John via email this a.m. He writes about finding a box of stuff that included letters from Dad and other memorabilia. He wants to bring it over, and I did invite him.

Story of major interest in The *Times* today is about how six White House staff members, including, most notably, Jared Kushner, have used private email to do government business, something that approached the Deadly Sin category when the Republicans found out Hillary Clinton had done that. So, will we have months-long investigations by Congress into these lapses? Will entire nightly news reports be taken up with this? Of course not. Congress is nothing but a rightwing shill machine for the Big Rich, and being hypocrites doesn't bother a single one of them because it's not about being honest or having integrity, it's about getting rich, too!

Sept. 27: Today I start the year as a Reading Buddy at Jacob's Well Elementary. I'll be assigned two or three second-graders who are running a little behind on their reading skills and have them read to me for 20 minutes or so. These are kids whose parents don't read to them at home, which is something I just don't understand. Surely most parents today know how important it is that their kids be able to read and how important reading at home is to that end.

The anti-health-care bill is dead in the Senate. That was announced yesterday after another senator announced she would oppose it, making a total of three who wouldn't vote for something they had never read, that had never been vetted by anyone in the government and whose only fans were the leeches at the top of the income heap, like that stupid asshole who ran Equifax until he "retired" last week.

The House and Senate are about to hand the 1 percent a huge tax cut. Will it make them invest in new jobs and new businesses? Probably not. A story in today's *Times* tells us what happened back in 2005 or so when there was a tax holiday that allowed companies with dollars stockpiled, to be untouched by taxes, overseas to bring the money back home. Some of the money came back. But ...

"The jobs, however, didn't come."

What kinds of patriots are the folks at Apple, Starbucks, Facebook? What kind of corporate citizens refuse to pay their fair share and go to such lengths to keep their money? Something is rotten in a society that produces these billionaires and then allows them to get by with robbery without consequence.

Sept. 28: The Republicans rolled out their tax plan yesterday, and as usual they had no specific information about anything so there was no way to see what kind of impact it would have. The *Times* editorial board looked it over and summarized it this way: "It would do little or nothing to improve the lot of the working class, a group President Trump says he is fighting for. It would instead provide a windfall to hedge fund managers, corporate executives, real estate developers and other members of the 1 percent. And can it be just a happy coincidence that Mr. Trump and his family would benefit 'bigly' from this plan?"

As 1970 dawned, Susan and I had our first child, D'Arcy, and so the pressure was on me like never before to be the very best I could be so I wouldn't have to go to Vietnam and leave these two alone for a year or, if my worst fears were realized, far more.

In June of that year, I went to Fort Sill in Oklahoma for another eight weeks of training crammed into six weeks. We were at Camp Eagle, a rocky, hilly, desolate spot on the edge of the main fort, the home of Army Artillery. We lived in eight-man tents, and on the day of arrival I was put in charge of erecting my squad's tent. I had never erected a freaking pup tent, much less one big enough for eight. Somehow I found guys who knew how to put up a tent, and they helped the rest of us, and we all worked together to get all the tents up in our company area.

Sept. 29: Trump is coming under fire from all corners because of his lack of response to the dire situation in Puerto Rico after Hurricane Maria. That whole island is a huge, huge disaster, and the problem is only going to get worse due to lack of electricity and water. In the first days after the hurricane, Trump spent his energy blasting the NFL's owners for not firing guys who protested during the playing of the National Anthem during football games. I'm not sure how aid will get to and be distributed in Puerto Rico, but I'm sure that the president, who has the attention span of a 2-year-old, has already lost interest. His only interest is stroking his own ego.

Sept. 30: Trump's housing secretary resigned yesterday after failing to move anyone closer to a new health-care plan and after riding around the world in luxury jets at taxpayer expense. He is now the only Cabinet-level official hired by Trump to be caught doing what he thought Trump hired him to do: plunder the public till until no cash was left to do government business, thus effectively killing off the very entity Trump and his allies hate so much. An innovative plan! This guy Price just didn't have the right moves.

It was about 75 when I went out walking this morning, a bright and beautiful day after four days of rain. We ended with about 3 inches, which is about average for the entire month of September. I hope the rainy period has broken the hot spell so we can get some relief and head into fall.

At some point in the final weeks of training at Fort Sill, I learned from our captain that I was going to be No. 2 on the Order of Merit List at WTSU and that I would thus have my choice of Army branches in which to be commissioned. I had no interest whatsoever in getting into a combat branch, so I chose the Adjutant General's Corps, a small group of officers who handled the Army's personnel system, computer and paperwork systems. The AGC's unofficial motto had to do with the medallion we all wore on our lapels: "Twinkle, Twinkle Little Shield. Keep Me Off the Battlefield." If you were an airborne Ranger this shield was not necessarily a badge of honor or courage. But, it was a sign that you were smart enough not to get your ass shot off in a war that was absolutely pointless.

So, on a Saturday right after the end of training, I walked across the stage at Fort Sill and was sworn into the Army as a second lieutenant in the Adjutant General's Corps. Susan and D'Arcy were there, and Susan pinned the gold bar on my shoulders, and Dad pinned the gold bar on my cap. I'm sure that even before that point in the summer of 1970, the generals in Washington knew in their hearts that the best and brightest were not leading the troops in Vietnam; they were opting for something that would not have them dying for nothing.

In July or August of that year, I got two sets of orders from the Army that were to be in effect after I got out of officers' basic school at Fort Benjamin Harrison, Indiana. The first set assigned me to the AG office at Fort Gordon, Georgia, for one year. The second set assigned me to an AG office in Vietnam. Drat! I was still not off the hook. I might have a job that was relatively danger-free in Vietnam, but I'd still be in Vietnam, where there really was no good place to hide.

In October, Susan and D'Arcy headed to Houston for eight weeks while I went to Fort Harrison for officer basic training. I flew up there with my gear and stayed in a bachelor officers apartment that had been built during World War I. On my second or third night there, I attended a reception for incoming student officers hosted at the Officers Club. I wandered around and chatted over drinks with various other new officers and with the older guys who ran the school and the post. One of the senior bird colonels asked me a couple of questions about where I was from, where I went to school, what I had done before the service, and I told him I'd been a reporter on a daily newspaper and then a country weekly, that I had a degree in journalism, blah, blah, blah. He moved on; I moved on.

At mid-morning on the following Monday, the very first day of class, a fat major opened the back door of the classroom and hollered my name. I thought, Holy Shit! What have I done? Dad's only piece of advice for me when I was leaving for Army basic was this: Don't let them know who you are. Blend in. The instructor excused me, and I walked with the major over to his office.

Oct. 1: The major who pulled me out of class at The Adjutant General's School at Fort Harrison on that Monday morning in October 1970 was named Smith. He was a blusterer, a big shot, I could tell that much. And he was a talker. When we got to his office, he offered me a seat and then started asking the questions: Did I have a degree in journalism? Had I been a reporter? An editor? How long? Where?

I couldn't figure out where all this was going, and then he told me that the school had just started up a new magazine and had an editor at that moment who was going to be leaving the Army soon and so they needed an associate editor who could take over when he left. Would I be interested in the job? Oh, hell yeah, I told him. Well, he said, there's a catch. To get the job, you'll have to sign up for a third year on active duty. Whoa, I said. I don't know about that. Think about it, he said.

You better believe that is all I thought about. That evening after class let out, I headed over to the Officers Club with a couple of guys who had quarters in my building, and we went straight to the bar. There were a couple of other lieutenants there, so we sat around with a few drinks, and I told the group my story, about how they wanted me to stay at the school and be editor of this magazine, but to do that I'd have to sign up for a third year, and it was just pushing off the inevitable tour of duty to Vietnam. I might not go my second year, but there was no dodging that bullet for the third.

The only first lieutenant in the group, a guy named John, listened, then said, "Not So!" It so happened that John was commander of headquarters company for the school. As such, he was in charge of processing and initiating and altering orders for those who worked at the school. If I stayed, that would include me. I would nominally work for John as well as the bird colonel in charge of the magazine's operations. "Any officer assigned to the school is given permanent duty for three years, period," he said. "You won't go anywhere but right here."

The Gods of an otherwise random universe were smiling upon me again! "But," the lieutenant added, "you ought to try to get a little sweeter deal if you can. The Department of Defense Information School is right here at Fort Harrison, too. You oughta see if they'll let you take the information officers basic course before you go to work for the magazine." That night, I called Susan. She was initially very much opposed to the third year, but when I told her that I had the skinny from the very guy who cut orders at headquarters, she agreed to the deal. The next morning, I signed up for a third year with the agreement that I'd go to DINFOS at Fort Harrison right after officers basic, then I would join the magazine staff in January.

Oct. 2: Yesterday or Saturday, Rex Tillerson, the secretary of state, announced while in China that he was seeking face-to-face negotiations with North Korea and had made some progress. Later yesterday, Trump tweeted that Tillerson was on the wrong track and shouldn't be trying to get through to Pyonyang. This was not just a rebuke but a stunning one, a chastising done not behind closed doors but right out in public, big as life. You have to wonder if Tillerson is going to accept this kind of insult and just swim on through. I don't know why he would. He's got more money than God and he had almost more power when he was head of Exxon Mobil. If Tillerson does stay on, it will only show the world the man has no balls whatsoever. How do you face your colleagues and contemporaries in other nations if they know you have no balls and no support from the man in the White House?

Oct. 3: The death count is up to 59 and the number of wounded is up to 527 in the Las Vegas concert shooting incident that happened Saturday night. The guy who did all the shooting and then killed himself was a loner millionaire gambler who had more than 50 guns at his home and in his hotel room. Some of them must have been altered so they could shoot automatically, meaning that if you pulled the trigger once and held it you'd fire off an entire magazine of rounds one right after another in rapid succession. It's hard to buy those rifles if you're just John Q. Citizen. It's not hard to buy kits that will allow you to modify a semi-automatic weapon so that it fires on automatic. But you need to know what you're doing. And if you're going to fire the thing you need to live out in the country where nobody can hear you because automatic rifles do sound like what they are. And they're scary to the normal ear. The mystery here is motive. Even his brothers can't pinpoint a reason why this guy might go berserk. It turns out his father was a convicted bank robber who escaped and was considered armed and dangerous and crazy. Like father, like son? I don't know.

GM and Ford both announced major commitments to electric cars yesterday. They are adding new models and developing new product lines. They say they are kissing gasoline goodbye. Good luck with that. Enthusiasm for electric doesn't make the problems with that technology go away. Battery life and dependability and replacement costs have to be dealt with at some point, as does range. Until you can jump into your car with your rucksack and your dog and head across country without worrying about running out of battery power, this effort will be severely hampered.

So, when do those incentives go away? And what are they, anyway?

Oct. 4: The Supreme Court heard arguments yesterday on the practice of gerrymandering legislative districts so as to get and perpetuate a political majority that's bulletproof. In Texas, especially, state legislators have drawn lines that make it impossible for Democrats to ever get back into power in any sense of the word. The districts are drawn in such a way that Republicans don't have to do much heavy lifting to win. The result is not good for democracy or the future of this country, as some of the justices acknowledged when they heard testimony on the matter.

The *Times* had this terse sentence in an editorial this morning: "No one can honestly defend partisan gerrymandering, but no one is quite sure how to stop it."

My first encounter with gerrymandering was in 1966 or 1967 when I was covering the Amarillo school board's decisions in response to a Justice Department mandate that they desegregate Amarillo's schools, which meant closing some and consolidating others. For example, the board decided to close Booker T. Washington High School, the all-black high school in north Amarillo. New high-school boundaries had to be drawn up, and the school board drew a map that had boundary attendance lines between Palo Duro High School and Amarillo High School. The boundary was drawn meticulously so that at its edges, it went around every home occupied by a black family so that family would go to Palo Duro. Blacks were arbitrarily skewed into Palo Duro and out of AHS. I learned the word "gerrymandering" from Buck Ramsey, who I'm sure used it as an epithet.

Then, when I was covering the Randall County commissioners court in Canyon before I went into the Army, a rule or law was passed that required county commissioners in Texas to be representative of the districts they lived in. Every county had four commissioners. In Randall County, Canyon was the county seat and was just about in the center of the county. But Amarillo was situated very close to the Potter-Randall line, and in the early 1970s all growth in Amarillo headed southward, spilling out of Potter and into Randall. At the time, the county's four commissioner precincts were laid out so that the county was cut into similarly shaped and sized quarters. That worked OK as long as the county was rural. But when the quadrants that contained south Amarillo began to swell in population, those people were not happy to have the same representation on the court as the few hundred folks who lived in Ralph's Switch south of Canyon. One-man, one-vote laws required that each precinct have the same number of people, so the power soon shifted to South Amarillo.

Looking out at Texas and other states, it's easy to see that we are no longer a democracy, and that's by design. Unless the Supreme Court deals with gerrymandering, this lack of representation will only worsen until something else gives out of the political playbook.

Oct. 5: Nobody seems to be able to explain why Rex Tillerson sticks with Trump.

The man cannot have any pride. He's not stupid. So, he must be getting something out of the relationship. I'm guessing he has a silent benefactor or two or three who have promised that if he will stick in there they will pay him off handsomely when he leaves the government. What is their motive? I don't know.

And so far nobody can explain why a gunman went into a room on the 32nd floor of the Mandalay hotel in Las Vegas and shot hundreds of people, killing 59. His girlfriend came back from the Philippines yesterday and couldn't shed any light on the motive for this killing spree. Trumpistas have stifled the urge, for the moment, to blame the murders on Muslims and the Islamic State. It would be a world-class whopper if they could make that stick. After all, this guy Paddock was a 60-something white guy who gambled professionally for a living. Not many Muslim terrorists match that description.

Oct. 6: Still no motive for the guy who killed 58 and wounded 500 at the Las Vegas country music festival on Sunday. An old white guy with two dozen weapons, including automatics.

So, it turns out that there is this invention out there that allows you to turn a semi-automatic AR-15 into a full automatic. It's called a bump stock. That's what the guy in Vegas had on his rifles. I'm sure you probably couldn't find one anywhere today at any price. If anything about weaponry should be outlawed it is this device. Nobody but the military needs an automatic rifle.

Oct. 7: This week was the low-key 60th anniversary of the launching of Sputnik by the Soviets, the first man-made object to orbit the earth. I would have been 10 years of age at the time, but I really don't have any recollection of the event itself. I'm sure I was made aware of it, though, because Dad was so aware of things political. Of course, from that point on my childhood and growing-up years were shaped by Sputnik and America's reaction to it. It went from being a curiosity to being a mortal threat capable of delivering nuclear devastation right to our doors in Amarillo, Texas. Thus commenced the bomb-shelter craze, which Dad looked into at one point, and the regular classroom drill of ducking under one's desk and covering one's head, and the space race that transfixed us as we sent John Glenn and others into orbit. Oddly, the rise of the Soviet threat did not change our "enemy" on Saturday mornings when we would head to Green Hill to fight the kids from Austin Street. That enemy was still the Nazi. Sputnik changed how we were taught math and how we were exposed to science, even though we did not know that as students. Really, it changed everything for this boy and so many others.

I was thinking today of a conversation I had yesterday afternoon with a patron. He was C. R., pastor of a major Protestant Church of Wimberley. C. was checking out some books from Juniper, the retired Catholic priest, and something had C. going on and on about how he no longer watched the news, no longer listened to public radio, no longer read newspapers or magazines – all this a measure of his frustration and anxiety over Trump. I couldn't help but overhear what he was saying, and at one point, he kind of threw up his hands and said something like, "I feel so helpless. There's nothing I can do. I'm just one man in a small town. I can't make any difference." I jumped in. I said something like, "Of course you can make a difference. You're a preacher. That's your job! That's why you got the brass balls. It's up to you to tell people the truth!" Juniper, a librarian who retired as a Catholic priest, jumped in, too, and said something like, "When I was a parish priest and after I had pissed people off with a homily, I would tell them it was my job to make them uncomfortable with where they were." C. didn't seem to be persuaded. So, there you are: a mainstream Protestant preacher who is so fearful of his congregation or so unsure of his theology or something that he won't speak out against injustice and cruelty and sexism and the preparations for war. Oh my.

Oct. 8: In May of '72, a message came down to the school from Army HQ in Washington that was pretty startling and potentially life-altering. It represented the most important stroke of grace I had received having to do with serving in the military during the Vietnam War.

Oct. 9: So, I did read it through, and I honestly could not believe what I saw on the pages. By way of this message, the president through the secretary of the Army was offering an early discharge from the military to any first or second lieutenant then on active duty so long as the soldier left active duty between June 1, 1972, and January 1, 1973.

Oct. 10: I must have read through that message about early discharges two or three times before I headed downstairs to the office of the school adjutant, a red-headed major. I showed him the message and asked him if it was actually from the Department of Defense and meant what it said, and he said that it was, in fact, authentic in substance and in promise. That night I talked to Susan and I called Troy Martin, publisher in Canyon, about having a job for me if I got out of the Army that summer instead of a year from that summer. They both said I should take the early out, and so I filled out the paperwork the next day to get out of the Army on June 30, 1972, and that's what happened.

I had dodged the Big Bullet of my generation, thanks to the Order of Merit List and a few good people who were in the right place at the right time.

Now, here I am at age 70, and sometimes I wonder if I didn't get off too easy. That sounds crazy, but I had a great job in the Army in a great location. I didn't have to break a sweat to do my job and do it well. What if I'd gone to Vietnam? Could I have cut it? I don't regret that I didn't go, exactly; I just wonder.

Driving away from Fort Harrison on that last day, I was filled with relief and gratitude. I had a job waiting for me in Canyon, I could use the GI Bill if I wanted to. The future was very bright, indeed.

Oct. 12: The *Times* reports today that the Boy Scouts are now accepting girls. I don't think this dooms the group. The Boys Clubs of America continued to thrive after they became the Boys & Girls Clubs of America. The Scouts are trying to adapt, and that is a hard thing to do.

I was never enamored of the organization, even when I was a kid. I was in the Cub Scouts, but I never attained much rank and certainly never tried to become an Eagle Scout like Malcolm Helm. And I never joined the Boy Scouts. When Bryan was a kid, I was a Cub Scout leader for his den for awhile. He was in the group for maybe a year, but it never stuck with him, either.

Oct. 13: Trump has done an end-run on health insurance for the masses. He is dismantling Obamacare piece by piece. We shall see what happens. So far, Big Insurance isn't squawking, so that means there is no problem with the direction he's going as far as they are concerned. And that means they will continue to make Big Money off whatever is in place. You can bet that if that is the case, many Americans will suffer.

Oct. 14: Rachel Maddow, on her show last evening, wondered if it's possible Trump believes that American missile defenses are so absolutely awesome that he can tweak the noses of every nuclear bully on the planet without suffering any consequences. It appears she is right, based on what Trump himself has said to interviewers and in speeches. But, as Ms. Maddow showed, America's success rate on intercepting and killing an incoming missile is about 50-50. So, is it OK that only half the missiles fired at us actually get here?

I have no idea what game Trump is playing when it comes to Iran and his decision to renege on the treaty that required Iran to get rid of its nuclear weapons and machinery to build them. So, here the U.S. had a deal with Iran that everyone signed off on across the world. It was working, according to our own government inspectors. But, Trump calls it off, essentially allowing Iran to renege on its part of the deal, too, to go ahead and produce and deploy nuclear weapons. Where is Israel on all of this? Does Iran love Israel all of a sudden? And what does this episode in lunatic diplomacy mean to the leader of North Korea? Will he want to enter a treaty on nuclear weapons with a country whose president is not going to uphold his end of the bargain?

The *Times* has buried a story this morning about another Trump appointee as an energy advisor. This woman was a Rick Perry person in Texas energy policy-making, and she is a fucking idiot who believes that saturating the atmosphere with carbon dioxide is perfectly OK. Like so many others in this administration, she is part of the energy establishment and will dismantle any programs that would give a leg up to alternative fuels. (How will Elon Musk be affected by the anti-Green policies of this administration? And why isn't he raising holy hell about it?)

Oct. 17: In The *Times* today, Krugman points to his blog, which he says is long, long, about the lies Republicans are telling the public about the tax cut measure that they are pushing. Krugman has always made the point that the bill is a way to reward the rich for being, well, rich. It does nothing for the middle class or the poor. A startling 40 percent of Americans polled on the matter recently said they think the tax cuts will help them out. That's got to be the percentage who watch only Fox News and can't tie the laces on their own shoes. In his op-ed column, Krugman concludes:

"One thing we know for sure, however, is that a great majority of Republican politicians know perfectly well that their party is lying about its tax plan — and every even halfway competent economist aligned with the party definitely

understands what's going on.

"What this means is that everyone who goes along with this plan, or even remains silent in the face of the campaign of mass dissimulation, is complicit — is in effect an accomplice to the most dishonest political selling job in American history."

Oct. 18: The *Times* has a big story today about the liquified natural gas business in this country and the impact of exporting huge surpluses to other countries, mainly in Europe. The U.S. has a glut, which is one reason our monthly royalty checks are so paltry. But, now the country is bracing to export that glut, thus reducing that supply and maybe raising domestic prices. If prices go up a lot, drilling will increase and it might even be possible that our mineral rights in Sterling County could become valuable. That is really pie-in-the-sky dreaming, though.

Every now and then these days there are rumblings about war in Iran or on the Korean peninsula. Neither sounds likely to me. The battles would be proxy fights involving the South Koreans and a few troops from the Second Infantry Division who are located on the DMZ. The shooting would be over before our grandsons could be called up and trained.

Oct. 20: Ken Burns' epic about the Vietnam War is finished. I didn't see any of it, and I didn't hear one single thing about it out in the community. Even though I didn't see it I would bet that it had nothing in it about the poorly prepared leadership in the Army at the small-unit level.

More evidence is surfacing of Monsanto's bad behavior when it comes to testing of its products for their safety in the food chain. The Center for Biological Diversity called on a journal about toxicology to reveal the fact that Monsanto paid for favorable reviews in the journal about the safety of its products. Monsanto is officially too big to fail, and is now owned by an international corporation that has only its stockholders' interests to meet. And like stockholders everywhere, they want profits *uber alles.* I was telling a guy at the library about this the other day because he grew up on a farm in Iowa and watched his family give in to pressure from Monsanto to use their products to control weeds, to increase productivity and ultimately to be peons in servitude to the Monsanto monolith. I saw these things happening in the Panhandle when I was at The *Canyon News*, and I couldn't believe, as I think I have written here before, that farmers were going to become serfs without a fight. But, they did.

Oct. 21: Two items in The *Times* today have to do with climate change. One is a report from the EPA that it is scrubbing its website of any mention of climate change, period. You have to wonder at what point the jerkoffs at the EPA say, No More, and quit when asked to lie about the state of the world. These people would have made good bureaucrats in the machinery of Dachau and Buchenwald, just minding their own business and drawing their paychecks and to hell with the rest of the world.

The second item is out of Santa Fe, N.M., and details how a whole lot of people descended on the State Board of Education to protest changes in science textbooks that would have made climate change seem less a problem or no problem at all.

Four U.S. troopers, three of them Green Berets, were killed a week ago in an ambush in Niger. Today's *Times* has a story that the guys were acting like a bunch of cowboys, chasing Bad Guys here and there with no clear mission in mind. Of course, the Pentagon and the president will try to make it look entirely like an accident or the result of ruthless and cynical Muslims.

Oct. 22: The story of the day in The *Times* is about how it is very hard to replicate studies in psychology and social psychology, and that makes them suspect. Retraction Watch, a daily blog I subscribe to at work, has been on this trail for a couple of years.

The idea that you have all these studies out there about the way human beings react and respond that are probably one-off and can't be replicated must dismay psychologists and researchers in the field, but they have to look at what they're doing and have done that have not been up to scientific standards. Many of the studies' results haven't been validated by replication because the researchers weren't rigorous in applying the standards you'd expect them to apply. For example, many of them misinterpreted probabilities. The focus of the article was on Amy Cuddy, a Harvard psychology professor whose work on body language has been popularized by her TED Talk a couple of years back. In her talk, she cited her own research that she said showed that if you model strength and power in practice body sessions before a job interview, say, you will do better for having done so. So, before a job interview, you're supposed to go into a bathroom stall and raise yourself up like a gorilla or nasty grizzly bear, puff out your chest and imagine yourself prevailing over all opponents. This sounds reasonable to me. It sounds like it would work. But, Cuddy's research couldn't be replicated, so there's concern about the validity of her conclusions.

Oct. 23: The *Times* reports today that the EPA is not allowing several key scientists to attend a conference today on climate change. They were supposed to contribute to the program. No kidding. The Luddites are in control of the ship! Will these scientists walk away out of conscience? Nah.

And on the Business page we learn that the Newseum, the brainchild of the guy who invented USA Today, is in a precarious financial position. Its future is unknown. And it's charging $25 for people to get in; admission is not free.

Holy Moly! I wouldn't pay $25 to go into the Newseum under any circumstances. Maybe if they lowered the price so that people who actually care about newspapers – i.e., old people like me – could go would attract enough interest to offset the deficits. Just as newspaper owners have lacked the kind of creativity required to keep their businesses afloat, so has the Newseum followed that path to what is probably ultimate collapse. I'm not saying that if I stuck around I could have fixed the print-electronic model, but I think I could have done a better job of it than the present owners of all newspapers have done.

First, I would not have insisted that a profit margin of 22 to 25 percent was non-negotiable. Once you got rid of that ridiculous requirement you would have some room to maneuver. You could hire and keep really good writers who would draw a crowd and keep it.

Oct. 24: Senator John McCain, who was a young pilot when he was shot down by the North Vietnamese and was kept prisoner for five years, puts up with only some of Trump's bullshit. Yesterday, he took aim at the fact Trump got several deferments that kept him from serving during the Vietnam War. McCain told The *Times*, obliquely referring to Trump, a rich boy:

"One aspect of the conflict, by the way, that I will never, ever countenance is that we drafted the lowest-income level of America and the highest-income level found a doctor that would say that they had a bone spur," Mr. McCain said. "That is wrong."

John and I weren't poor or from a poor family. We were probably middle class. Still, we were so threatened by the draft that we served anyway. I had to stay in college, whether I wanted to or not.

At Amarillo College I had a chance to hit the reset button on who I was. Nobody knew my history as an under-achiever and hot-rodder. And I really found my niche as a student rather than as a rebel.

Over the summer that year after graduating from high school, I met Neil Hawkins, a young, good-looking English professor. Mr. Hawkins was clearly gay, which didn't affect my relationship with him one bit. He had a great sense of humor and was quick-witted, smart and "with it," in the vernacular of the times. I had him for freshman English and enjoyed every minute. He and Donald Boseman, another of my English professors, seemed to like me and they encouraged me to write and publish in the AC student literary magazine. What a change from secondary school!

Largely on their recommendation and that of Bob Wylie, the journalism adviser and teacher, I won a scholarship from the Amarillo newspaper at the end of my freshman year. The scholarship was for $100 per semester, and it included a provision for me to work as an intern at the *Globe-News* on a part-time basis starting in August 1966. That $100 amounted to almost a full scholarship at A.C.

On August 18, 1966, I showed up at 8 o'clock in the morning for my first day on the job at the *Globe-News*. I reported to Don Williams, who was city editor of the afternoon paper, the *Globe-Times*. Don was in his early 40s, an intense man with reddish hair and angular facial features, chiseled of fine Nordic stock. He was very busy. I found a seat at an empty desk.

Oct. 25: Senator Jeff Flake of Arizona did a most remarkable thing yesterday: He said he will not run for re-election because he does not want to be complicit in the destruction of America's government.

And then there was Harvey Weinstein, about whom Frank Bruni wrote today on the *Times* op-ed pages. Bruni noted that like so many others, Weinstein is blaming some inner demon for his crass behavior toward women.

Later at the Amarillo paper, I occupied a desk right across from Buck Ramsey, my feature-writer hero, and Mary Frances Whittenburg, the daughter of the publisher. I took to Buck right away, and in me he saw an opportunity for mentorship. We became fast friends. When the college term started, Williams moved me more to weekend evenings, and I worked days after classes at A.C. I was working my first Sunday evening shift when I got my first by-line in a daily newspaper as a regular employee, not a Teen Page writer.

At some point not long after I started at the *Globe-News*, we moved to the top floor of a huge cube of a windowless building next door built as a replacement for the 8th Street structure. I kept a desk by Buck Ramsey, some distance from the city desk/copy desk complex. But, I started working nights exclusively, so I was actually a staffer for the *Amarillo Daily News*, the morning paper, and not the *Globe-Times*, the afternoon version. And at that point I was already working full-time. Not long after that, I was made the night police reporter, and I must say that nothing much actually happened on most nights in Amarillo.

Oct. 26: The top story in The *Times* today is how the Trumpistas have hijacked the Republican Party. The old GOP of Richard Nixon and George W. Bush is kaput, gone, done, dead. That's fine. The more they move to the right the more mainstream Americans they lose in the bargain. The Democrats could take advantage of this if they could get their heads out of their collective ass. There is no real Democratic initiative that I can discern. The party is not just in disarray; it's evaporated.

Oct. 27: The CIA and FBI prevailed on Trump not to release some of the Kennedy assassination documents yesterday. He gave them six months to complete another review, after they've had 25 years! This is bullshit. Why he would go along with them is beyond me. He doesn't give two whoops in hell about national security concerns.

Sandy, the rector, got off on how Jesus' death on the cross changed everything. He died for our sins, etc., and that changed everything. Well, I responded, I don't think a group of Syrian refugee children fleeing from Raqqa would think that was the case. What's changed for them? Even if they heard of a Jesus and his death and his kinship with God, what possible difference would it make in their lives and their futures? I told Sandy that I thought that particular group of people, among others, would find the story of Jesus to be inconsequential. For 98 percent of the world, John 3:16 means absolutely nothing, even if they have heard of that verse and know what it means.

Seated across from Buck Ramsey and Mary Frances Whittenburg, the daughter of the publisher, I was in heaven on earth. Hearing the clickety-clack of Royal standards, the ring of the old phones, the hushed voices asking questions, smelling the printer's ink and newsprint, knowing I was going to fit into this adult place and have a shot at making my mark as a writer and reporter – I just fell in love with the whole thing, and when I discovered that you could smoke at your desk and that cursing came as natural to reporters and editors as breathing, I knew this was my world. It was almost just a bonus that I got to write stories that would bear my byline for all of Amarillo and the Texas Panhandle to see and read. I loved the idea of being a journalist and the act of being a journalist among other like-minded folks. I could not believe my good fortune. Very soon after joining the staff, I was no longer a clerk and I was no longer part-time. I was a full-time reporter, first covering night cops on weekends and then covering the region – all of the Panhandles of Texas and Oklahoma, southern Kansas and eastern New Mexico.

Oct. 30: Time magazine, which I just got around to reading yesterday afternoon, had a cover piece on how Trump's appointees are dismantling government in Washington as fast as they can. The number of lobbyists who now have jobs in the agencies they once prodded for benefits is astounding. Trump did not "drain the swamp" as promised. He put alligators in it. Scott Pruitt, the pinhead lawyer from Oklahoma, is a good example. Pruitt is head of EPA and is now turning it into a safe house for Big Oil and Big Chemical. They will be able to do anything they want while Pruitt's people either pave the way by tearing up regulations or by validating their licenses to steal. NPR reported yesterday morning that two EPA scientists had been withdrawn by the agency from speaking engagements on climate change. Why do they stick around? No balls?

Oct. 31: The noose is tightening around Trump's neck. Yesterday, the special counsel investigating the Trump campaign's connections with Russians issued multi-count indictments against two of Trump's campaign buddies. One, Paul Manafort, was his campaign chairman for a while. A third indictment was also issued, but the principle targeted by that legal action had already pleaded guilty to the charges of collusion with the Russians on behalf of the Trumpistas.

The question is whether any of this will make a whit of a difference to Republicans in Congress, and at first blush it appears this will have no impact. They will obviously go as low as they need to give the rich what the rich want, which is all of America, lock, stock and barrel, delivered, if possible, in bundles of small unmarked bills. What the Trumpistas did or did not do makes no difference to them if there is no deleterious economic impact. If the market tanks, we'll see pressure on Congress to get rid of Trump and start over with someone else who can as easily be used by the plutocrats but who doesn't have so much seriously disturbing baggage. The Republicans have been and are abetting criminal behavior, but they couldn't care less. This game is all about who ends up with the most toys, not how those toys were acquired. A more principled electorate would be talking revolution.

Besides colluding with the Russians to ruin this country, the Trumpistas are having trouble simply governing in any venue. One of the easiest things an administration can do, in the wake of the disastrous Bush response to Hurricane Katrina, is send stuff and people to help those who have been hit by natural disasters. Trump can't even get that right. The United Nations sent some observers to Puerto Rico to see how the recovery is going there after the hurricane hit in August.

The company that got the contract to do the electrical grid repair in Puerto Rico, called Whitefish, was based in a small town that just so happens to be the home place of the Trump-appointed secretary of the Interior, or the guy who coordinates emergency assistance. Whitefish had three employees but got a $300 million contract to do the grid work on the island. The Trumpistas said the suggestion that there was a connection between the secretary and the tiny company's contract was ludicrous. Why, the very idea of cronyism in the Trump White House! The company lost the contract this week after it was exposed to the light of day.

Nov. 1: Today the Republicans are supposed to introduce their plan for tax cuts for the rich and famous, provided on the backs of the poor and getting-poor. I'm not sure Democrats have what it takes to do anything but gripe. And they're not even effective gripers. They can't rally anyone to do anything. It's pathetic.

The *Times* has a third-quarter report on its finances: "The sound, if not earth-shattering, financial results were announced as The *Times* fundamentally reshapes itself into a business no longer rooted in newsprint. In the last several months, it has eliminated its copy desk, offered buyouts to employees and reorganized the structure of its newsroom."

As goes the *Times*, so go other newspapers around the country. I would love to know what the finances look like at the *Times Record News* or the *Telegram*. I bet they are absolutely terrifying, especially because those smaller papers depend on retailers right in their communities.

Nov. 3: As promised the Republicans and Trump issued their tax-cut proposal yesterday. From the *Times* James Tankersley: "WASHINGTON — The House Republican tax bill is a clear windfall for corporate America and a roll of the dice for the middle-class families that President Trump promised would be the centerpiece of his economic agenda."

Nov. 4: A group of scientists associated with the government issued a report yesterday asserting that human activities have, in fact, caused the climate to change. This is in direct opposition to what the Trumpistas trumpet and aver. Go figure.

Nov. 5: Nicholas Kristoff speculates in today's *Times* about the likelihood we will go to war with North Korea. We are indeed sliding in that direction, even though such a thing would absolutely ruin South Korea, a long-term ally. (With friends like us, who needs enemies?) From Kristoff's column:

"The Congressional Research Service last month estimated that as many as 300,000 people could die in the first few days of war — and that's if it remains nonnuclear. If there is a nuclear exchange, 'there easily could be a million deaths on the first day,' says Scott Sagan, an international security expert at Stanford."

That seems irrelevant to Trumpistas. These people like to get tough when it requires action by other people, not themselves or their children. Boy, is it easy to be a bully when you have someone else taking the lumps for you.

I covered a great number of other stories that pushed me into new reporting and writing territory, and I felt I was growing. When I had started work as a full-time reporter at the *Globe News* I was making about $75 a week. About two years later, I was making $90, not a bad jump, actually. But, when John Debaun graduated from West Texas, he got a raise from $90 to $95, and I had no reason to believe that two years from that point I would make any more than $95 even with three or four years of experience. Then, they hired Tommy Denton out of Baylor at $95 a week, and that told me that $95 was going to be my salary when I got my degree regardless of my experience. I felt that I was being taken advantage of.

Meanwhile, I had been approached by Troy Martin, publisher of The Canyon News, to come to work as editor. He was launching a Sunday edition to go along with his Thursday number. He offered me $100 to start. I talked it over long and hard with Susan, and she agreed that would be a good move to make. So, I resigned at the Globe News, even after getting warnings from Bob Kerr and Don Boyett that if I went with a nondaily it would be hard if not impossible to get back on the staff of a daily in the future. I should have listened to them and swallowed my pride. Instead, in September of 1968 I went to work at The Canyon News.

Nov. 7: The news is all about the demented shooter in Sutherland Springs, Texas, who killed 26 people and wounded another 20 or so on Sunday. This kind of thing brings out the absolute worst kind of idiotic rhetoric from Republican politicians like Trump, who blamed it all on "psychiatric" problems and not a whit on the ease with which crazy people can buy assault weapons. Ken Paxton, the Texas attorney general who can see no evil when it comes to guns, even suggested that churches have designated shooters themselves! I guess that would go for gambling casinos and movie houses and even elementary schools! Wouldn't America be a better place if all that came to pass? The truth is that absolutely nothing will change.

Which will also be the case when it comes to American corporations acting badly when it comes to hiding their profits so they can't be taxed to benefit American society. Some insider has released a shitload of confidential documents taken from a big law firm in the Caribbean showing how big corporations avoid paying taxes. Chief among them is Apple, your friendly cell phone maker. Apple scurries around the globe looking for ways to hide its profits so they cannot be used to build better schools, better highways and better institutions in this country, their homeland. From The Times: "Apple has accumulated more than $128 billion in profits offshore, and probably much more, that is untaxed by the United States and hardly touched by any other country. Nearly all of that was made over the past decade." This is bad for America, but good for the corporations that are bigger than that, and you can argue all day long that this benefits their shareholders, and I will say to you that there are not very many second-graders in shitty schools who can and do benefit from investments in Apple.

The price for one share of Apple stock this morning is $175.

I took the job at The Canyon News, in part, to get the $100 a week salary, up from $90 I was making at the Globe-News.

I loved Canyon, the college and the proximity to Palo Duro Canyon. At that point, all of the shops on the courthouse square were occupied. There was a men's shop, some ladies shops, a shop for moms outfitting their kids, a print shop, and so on. Canyon was growing, particularly to the north into Hunsley Hills, so new schools were being planned and growth out of Amarillo to the south into Randall County and the Canyon school district was posing particular challenges for county and school officials.

Canyon was a university town, first and foremost, but it was also a county seat and a hub for agriculture. Most of the farmland in Randall County was planted in winter wheat and grain sorghum, all dryland, so the typical yield for a dryland wheat farmer was about 18 bushels per acre. Rainfall was only about 18 inches a year, so there wasn't enough moisture to raise something like corn.

Up north of Canyon a new industry was getting under way: A massive cattle feedyard where up to a million head would be fed out before slaughter in one small area. To the south was a hog farm. Much of the land was not arable, however, and so we had several large ranches that ran cow-calf operations.

Most of the people I ran into were kind and helpful. I was still a kid, but a kid with a pen and pad and access to an unlimited amount of newsprint and ink, so they may have looked at me as something of a benign menace.

In Amarillo, for example, I had never covered a meeting of the City Council and was not familiar with the way home-rule cities operated. After I had covered a couple of Canyon council meetings and published my stories, I got a kind call from Elton Cox, the city attorney, who asked me to have coffee with him at Shell's Pharmacy on the west side of the square. Elton pointed out some pretty glaring errors I had made, errors that were substantial in terms of how cities could operate, but he did so tactfully and nicely and let me know he'd be happy to help me out as I picked my way through municipal law and practice. I came to depend on Elton for a lot of stories, and I often used his law library to try to figure out whether what the commissioners court was doing was, in fact, legal.

Nov. 9: The Tuesday elections turned out to be a pretty resounding rebuke for Republicans and the Trumpistas. From today's front page of The *Times*: "From the tax-obsessed suburbs of New York City to high-tech neighborhoods outside Seattle to the sprawling, polyglot developments of Fairfax and Prince William County, Va., voters shunned Republicans up and down the ballot in off-year elections. Leaders in both parties said the elections were an unmistakable alarm bell for Republicans ahead of the 2018 campaign, when the party's grip on the House of Representatives may hinge on the socially moderate, multiethnic communities near major cities." And so what will the Republicans do? Will they try to dump Trump? Probably not. They still have to get their precious tax cut legislation through Congress and through his office so the 1 percent can accrue even more money to put into offshore accounts.

I have mentioned the Paradise Papers that have been stolen and published out of a Caribbean law office that put together tax shelter deals for the Big Rich. Thousands of rich people are parking their money in offshore accounts so they can avoid paying taxes altogether. Obviously the very idea that they will invest in American enterprise if given a huge tax break as proposed by Trump and the GOP is a joke. They'll just put more money offshore! This includes big guys like Apple. I wonder if Trump won't release his tax documents because they'll give us some insight as to how much money he has in those offshore accounts.

Nov. 10: Yesterday I finished reading the book about WWII called "The Second World Wars: How the First Global Conflict Was Fought and Won" by Victor Davis

Hanson. Hanson did a thorough overview of the causes, the battles and some of the results. I found information I had never heard of before. Here is one conclusion, on page 461:

"Nazi Germany, Italy, and Japan declared war on the largest economy in the world, the one that had the greatest supply of skilled labor, the most abundant fuels and metals, the largest capital reserves, and the most innovative entrepreneurial class – and that had been buoyed by a collective outrage after Pearl Harbor to punish the Axis for attacking the United States and declaring war on a neutral nation. The Third Reich assumed Soviet industrial production would be nullified by the occupation of European Russia, while Britain, if it survived, would lag behind Germany in the 1940s as it had in the 1930s; in truth, both nations soon outproduced both Germany and Japan in most categories of munitions.

"In sum, victory in World War II was a morality tale of production besting killing: those who made more stuff beat those who killed more people."

Rachel Maddow mocked Trump last evening, and rightly so, for humiliating himself in front of the Chinese president on his trip to Asia. Trump's attitude was obsequious. The *Times* was gracious in describing the Trump tactic as "flattery." Trump promised in his campaign to stop China from "raping" the United States. He promised to get tough on China – no holds barred. Now, he goes and faces Xi Jinping and acts like a lapdog.

Meanwhile the South Koreans are in the streets to protest Trump and his promise to go to war with North Korea. The South Koreans understand quite clearly that THE victims of any conflict between the United States and North Korea will be people in South Korea. Shoot, all North Korea has to do is aim a few bazookas toward the south of the DMZ and they'll kill hundreds in no time. A few howitzer rounds could bring down skyscrapers in Seoul. Concentrated fire over the course of a few minutes would kill millions in the south, while leaving the United States completely untouched. This is not a proxy battle; this is suicide by proxy.

Maddow also had a rundown on how depleted the State Department is. They have more positions to fill than they could possibly fill in a few years, and almost nobody in the pipeline. She asks, Why? Why would Rex Tillerson, who made a huge financial pact with Russia before the elections in the private sector, want to take apart the State Department, which helps oversee the Russians' activities worldwide? Why would Trump, whose family has made millions on subterranean deals with Moscow, want to put a muzzle on State?

Clearly, the interests of the United States come in second for this greedy pair and their families and friends. When do we start using the "T" word to describe what's going on between the Trumpistas and Moscow? Why haven't those who have been charged with criminal activities in regards to Russian meddling in our elections actually been charged with treason? What is treason if not working with a hostile foreign government to affect the activities of your own country?

Nov. 11: The *Times* is absolutely filled with crap that Trump has pulled or lied about pulling. He brags about forcing Asians to buy more American stuff, and the *Times* tells us that it's all just window dressing; what he wants them to buy they can't buy outright even if they wanted to do so. Then there's the story about Trump's kinfolks dealing with the Russians. And the story about how his admirers just let him make shit up without consequence. The only thing missing here is something about Mitch McConnell being on the take, which is not as far-fetched as it sounds.

And out of Alabama we have the remarkable story of Roy S. Moore, who is running for the Senate there. Moore is back in the headlines for trying to get teenage girls to go to bed with him. And this may be the story that brings him down, although it should not be. The story that should bring him down is about how when he was justice on the Alabama supreme court he refused to obey state and federal laws and went to jail. This man is a dumbshit pervert of the first order. And Alabamans are too stupid to care.

Meanwhile Tillerson is paying experienced people to leave the State Department, a step worse than just forcing them out. And last night Chris H, on MSNBC, told us about some of the absolutely unbelievable men who are getting onto federal court benches even if they have no prior trial experience and are hostile to the rule of law! It is unfreakingbelievable. We are in the hands of lunatics and guttersnipes with few precedents in history.

I had to be a sponge at The *Canyon News*. I had to learn photography, layout and design. I had to learn about municipal government and county government, how a university operated and how school districts were run. I had to learn the ins and outs of hospital districts, criminal courts, civil courts and dryland farming and ranching. Fortunately, I had a wealth of folks in the Canyon area who were willing to teach me. At the city there was Elton Cox, who was city attorney, and Paul Lindsey, a farmer who was also mayor. At the courthouse there was George Dowlen, who was district attorney. Two county agents helped me understand the cattle business and the challenges of wheat and sorghum farming. I figured out how the university ran by being a student and an observer who was close to members of the political science faculty like Walt Shelley and Pat Stephens. I think I was trusted because I tried to be fair and accurate, and when I didn't know something well enough to write about it I made every effort to get educated.

Nov. 12: I went to the barbecue lunch hosted by the VFW yesterday, and it was a nice affair. The brisket was delicious, although I certainly ate too much. I have no idea how many veterans live in Wimberley and the area, but quite a few were at the VFW hall.

I came home and sent a letter to my grandkids about Trump's preparations for war. I had been thinking about this for some time, and I wanted them to know that any kind of war trumped up by this administration would not be moral or justified. Here is the text of the letter:

Nov. 11, 2017
Dear Lulu,

As your grandfather and a veteran, I am most concerned about your future as well as the future of our country. I believe we are presently led by a tyrant who is willfully ignorant, deeply immoral and adolescent when it comes to his view of how to live sanely in our world. I did not support him as a candidate, and I do not support him now as he tries to bring our nation to its knees and into a war that is not winnable. You are of an age where it is possible you will be asked or required to serve this demigod on a field of battle. I ask you to resist, to say "no," to refuse to serve this man's fits of anger and/or his desires for greater wealth.

I ask you to consider the following paragraphs, which I have taken from a centuries-old document central to the Christian faith: If a nation or a man or woman is to go to war, all of the following criteria must be met at the same time in order for a war to be considered just:
• *the damage inflicted by the aggressor on the nation or community of nations must be lasting, grave, and certain;*
• *all other means of putting an end to it must have been shown to be impractical or ineffective;*
• *there must be serious prospects of success;*
• *the use of arms must not produce evils and disorders graver than the evil to be eliminated. The power of modern means of destruction weighs very heavily in evaluating this condition.*

These requirements are not to be taken lightly. The United States Bishops expanded on these requisites by enumerating the following criteria to which war is a permissible recourse:
• *Just Cause*: to confront "a real and certain danger" to protect innocent life
• *Competent Authority*: declared by those with responsibility for public order
• *Comparative Justice*: Are the values at stake critical enough to override the presumption against war?
• *Right Intention*: War can only be conducted to satisfy the just cause
• *Last Resort*: All peaceful alternatives have already been exhausted
• *Probability of Success*: The outcome cannot be disproportionate or futile
• *Proportionality*: inflicted damage must be proportionate to the good expected

As you can see, one does not go to war or make war for little or no reason or just because one can do so. It is a grave and solemn decision that ought to be made by men and women who are mature and wise, not childish and reactionary.

If you are called upon to pursue war at the behest of the man who would be our king, I ask that you consider the statements above.

I fully recognize there are consequences if you say you will not serve when called. I will do my very best to protect you from harm with legal assistance and whatever financial help I can muster.

I love you dearly.
PaPa Wilson

I don't know how Becca and D'Arcy will take that; I hope in the spirit with which it was sent.

Nov. 14: It seems entirely possible that I will have to retire pretty soon from the library. Lynda's condition is no better day after day, and I'm not sure anyone in the medical field has any clue what's wrong with her. She wakes up every morning with the sweats, and she has a very low energy level all day long. She awoke yesterday feeling nauseated and so bad in general that she called the cleaning lady, Kristen, to come early so she would not be alone. I told Carolyn, my boss, yesterday that I had no plans to leave, but circumstances may dictate that I must.

Trump met with quite a number of world leaders over the course of his tour of Asia, and he gushed and fawned over every dictator he ran into. It was embarrassing. He even gladly embraced Duterte, the tyrant in the Philippines who has his forces just kill suspected drug dealers and users on the spot – to hell with due process. Reports indicate that he made no mention of human rights violations to Duterte or to anyone else. He did emerge at one point to say he believed Putin when Putin said Russians did not hack this country's elections.

The *Times* notes Trump's affections for these dubious characters in an editorial this morning: "Mr. Trump chafes at sharing power with Congress and the courts and invokes the importance of human rights only against governments he despises, like North Korea, Iran and Cuba. Insecure, delusional and frustrated at his inability to act unilaterally, he sees himself as uniquely tough and the only person in his administration capable of achieving foreign policy goals."

Roy Moore, the pathological liar and child abuser, insists he will continue to run for the Senate out of Alabama even as another woman comes forward to testify he tried to rape her when she was 16. The man has no shame, never has. George Will, appearing on a TV show last evening, said he visited Birmingham last week and came back to D.C. believing that Alabamans are smart enough to vote for someone besides Roy Moore. I seriously doubt that. The smart people have left Alabama. The stupid people have stayed and procreated.

The hypocrisy over this situation knows absolutely no bounds in Washington. There, various senators are clucking their tongues and suggesting that Moore should drop out of the race because he will be expelled by the Senate if he tries to take a seat. This embrace of morality comes from men who blindly support a president who himself was a serial sexual abuser, men who don't hesitate to remove health care from the poor, who couldn't care less if our judicial system is decimated by cretins from, well, Alabama!

Nov. 16: Lynda and I were startled to hear on a TV talk show last night that the Senate's tax bill, which now includes cuts to health-care programs nationwide, could end up in cuts to Medicare, Medicaid and Social Security. Wow! We were actually double surprised, first by the fact that the Senate has put into their bill the cut of the individual mandate in the national health-care system. That would essentially gut what's called Obamacare and leave about 13 million people with no insurance. The second surprise was that the framing of the tax measure could lead to cuts in those programs we absolutely depend on: Medicare and Social Security. All of this may just be window-dressing so senators can go home for Christmas and tell their constituents they actually did something this year besides trail along behind Trump with a pooper scooper.

The Roy Moore story out of Alabama is an embarrassing case of an old fool acting like one and not allowing anyone to hold up a mirror so he can see what an ass he's making of himself. One of the things I worry about as I age is that I'll make a fool of myself somehow and somewhere. I've tried to carry some dignity into my senior years. Moore would do well to consider what his grandkids must think about him. I bet they're troubled.

I think maybe the U.S. Constitution should have an amendment that would allow us to force a state to secede, essentially setting it out on the back porch so as not to be tainted by the stench and unnerved by its death rattle. The first candidate for forced secession would be Alabama, home of some of the biggest dumbbasses on Planet Earth, killers of children, haters of women.

Nov. 17: Lynda and I went to the doctor yesterday afternoon, and he said that blood tests discovered that her hormones were screwed up. He put her on Premarin, the "purple football," and gave her some samples because the drug is supposedly pretty expensive. I don't care what it costs if it gets her back to some semblance of normal. She did sleep well last night and got up at 8 o'clock, which is early for her.

The House passed a tax plan yesterday, to the surprise of no one at all. Also to the surprise of no one at all, it will give huge breaks to corporations and raise taxes on the middle class. This is not exactly what Trump had promised when he was campaigning, but he's such a liar you can't hold him to anything he says. The Senate has yet to consider its bill, which now includes a component that would undermine the nation's fragile health-care system. I thought it would be interesting to reprint here some of the headlines in today's *Times* just so you can see what the tenor of our age sounds like:

"G.O.P. in Alabama Endorses Moore Despite Scandal"
"Tax Rewrite Clears House but Faces Senate Obstacles"
"Senate Panel Asks Kushner to Turn Over Documents"
"New F.D.A. Rules Allow for Faster Approval of Gene and Cell Therapies"
"F.C.C. Opens Door to Increased Consolidation in TV Industry"
"Critic of Consumer Watchdog is Expected to Take Its Reins"

Thus, the big get bigger, the rich get richer, the fat and the few get fatter and fewer. Trumpism unbridled after just a year on the job!

Nov. 18: My guess at this point is that Roy Moore will be elected by the dolts in Alabama. My guess is that Al Franken, a Senator from Minnesota who has been accused of groping a woman when he was a working comedian, will get a look from ethicists in the Senate (now, there is a contradiction in terms) and then be cautioned to go and sin no more since his transgression occurred before he was elected.

Nov. 19: *The New Yorker*'s emailed edition today has a summary of what's in the tax bill that the House and Senate want to pass with the lavish praise of corpulent whales who've given birth to a golden egg. It is indeed golden for the rich in this country, but not for the middle class or poor. The liars in both parties supporting this bill continue to say that it will allow corporations to hire more people and pay higher wages, these being the premiums which benefit the lower classes. The image that comes to mind is young Oliver Twist standing, head bowed, before the headmaster of the orphanage, empty bowl in both hands, pleading for more gruel. Most in the Republican leadership admit that the rich will benefit. They are unapologetic.

This is not to be described as a shell game because there are no shells. There is no deception. These assholes just flat-out admit they are screwing everyone and to hell with you if you get in their way. It's breathtaking.

Nov. 20: We are at a critical moment in this country, and not because of Roy Moore. Trump wants to be a dictator, and people are falling in line behind him without much opposition. The rich have bought Congress and are siphoning off as much money as they can to safe havens because they have no faith in the future of our economy or our political system. Our democracy is at stake. And the nation's pastors just continue to rearrange the chairs on the deck of the Titanic. Why do I continue to attend? I'm selfish. I enjoy playing the music on Wednesday evenings with the Halftime Band, and I enjoy the relationships I've developed with people like Tom and Cindy Dawson. I also get paid to do the AV. It's not much, but I do get paid, and that's something I won't easily walk away from.

Nov. 21: The TV news the other night had a clip that showed a bit of back-and-forth between a Democratic senator and a Republican, namely Orrin Hatch, about the tax bill. Hatch retreated into anger when challenged about the bill's effects, primarily its provisions to make the rich richer and the poor poorer. In today's *Times*, Paul Krugman calls out Hatch for the little man's little act. Caught in one of the biggest lies to be told all year, Hatch got all huffy and defensive. Without a doubt all of us ordinary folks will be screwed by this Congress and this president in a myriad of ways that newspapers and television reports can only hope to highlight. There is nothing too niggling and inconsequential that the Trumpistas will not change to their own benefit. What is out there on the other side of outrage?

Nov. 22: One reason I fell in love with newspapering when I was at the *Globe-News* was the very dailiness of it all. I would go to work at 2 or 3 in the afternoon, produce a story or two before leaving at 11 or 12 and see my work the next morning in the paper. I didn't have to carry any baggage home with me. And the payoff was quick, not as quick as in TV, but quick.

At The *Canyon News*, that payoff was delayed somewhat. I would go to work at 8 on Monday, and the paper would not come out until Thursday morning. Meanwhile, I would go to work at 8 o'clock Thursday morning, and the paper would come out on Sunday. For each edition, I had to produce at least six or seven stories that would merit being played on the front page, plus various other stories, such as football game reports and obituaries. The workload was heavy and burdensome, made more so by the fact that on a small semi-weekly newspaper there is no wire material to use as filler or to use in any form or fashion. There is no filler, period. Everything that goes into the paper has to be produced by the staff on the ground there on the square in Canyon, Texas.

Because of the pressure of producing enough stories to fill Page One and all those inside pages, I came to hate holidays that fell in the work week. Holidays like, oh, say, Thanksgiving. Thanksgiving screwed up an entire cycle leading up to a Sunday publication because, a) nothing was open and there was no news to report, thus no stories; and b) you had to be involved out of town with family doings, so even if something happened you wouldn't be in town to cover it. Even all these years after leaving The *Canyon News*, it's hard for me to shake the jitters as we approach Thanksgiving Day, the feeling of panic that the day will not be a net gain but a net loss.

Last September, Trump told a bunch of Haitians who had escaped that island nation after a huge hurricane that he would protect them and take care of them. Yesterday, his folks announced that the Haitians are being kicked out. Meanwhile, only about half of Puerto Rico has power. That's two months after the hurricane. Would Trump let Texas go without power for two months?

Yesterday, Trump announced his endorsement of Roy Moore. Anybody but a Democrat, he said. Of course, he'd say that. After all, 19 women have accused Trump of sexual assault, and he's doing just fine, thank you.

Nov. 23: One of the TV programs we watched last night had an interview with a black author who accused Trump of being racist, which is kind of like accusing Mick Jagger of being a rock star. Trump is literally obsessed with making the U.S. basketball players jailed in China and released at his behest recently and their parents lush and swoon in their thanks and praise for his divine intervention on their behalf. Regardless of what the players and parents say, it's not enough for the exalted Donald. He must have more out of the "thankless Negro," as the commentator put it. It seems he recognizes many of his fans are racists and he must play to their bigotry to keep his job.

Rachel Maddow opened up a very, very interesting story last night on her show. She pointed out that Trump is promising, with fingers crossed behind his back, to pay the legal fees of people who might be called as witnesses in the cases against him. He might. In other words, if they don't promise to back him up and say what he wants, he won't pay their legal fees, all of which will be substantial. Isn't this obstruction of justice? Well, it was when Nixon was the subject of impeachment proceedings.

Nov. 24: The *Times* reports on 1A today that Michael Flynn, the disgraced Army general who used his position to get rich off the Russians, is about to cut a deal to turn state's evidence against the Trumpistas. This could be, in a word, BIG! Flynn apparently did some dirty deeds not only with Russia, but also with Turkey. And he was in the whole Russian thing up to his chin, taking money for information and contacts. At the least I'm guessing that Jared Kushner, the smug little bastard who married Trump's daughter, is not having a good Black Friday.

Nov. 25: The news is filled with stories about shoppers taking advantage of Black Friday specials for the holiday giving season. Retail sales are expected to rise by nearly 5 percent this year over last year, and about half those sales may be online, and most of those may be through Amazon. I actually love shopping malls, not to shop in but to visit like you might a town square – to see people and see what they're wearing and doing. It's too bad that shopping habits are changing so dramatically, but in some cases those habits were never built up and on in the first place. The *Times* reports that more stores are expected to close their doors in 2018 in shopping malls and strip malls across America as retail activity shifts even more to the web. At least part of the damage suffered by retailers has been self-inflicted by not having good sales people and not providing follow-up services.

Nov. 26: Writing in the *New York Times* magazine this morning, a woman describes the experience of flying in this day and age as "humiliating." That's a wonderfully apt way to put it. I hope to never fly again as long as I live, which should not be that hard because I don't have a whole lot of time remaining. What little time I do have I hope not to have to spend a moment of it in a line awaiting a wave-through from a Neanderthal in a TSA uniform.

The idea of actually retiring, fully and finally, is sounding more appealing to me as time goes by. I don't want to get to the point that I dread going in to work, and I don't yet. But, I can see that day coming, and I need to prepare for what happens then, mentally. I think I'd be bored out of my mind after a little while. But, maybe not. I need to go back through and edit this memoir/diary and print off several copies for my grandkids. And I really do need to write a screenplay or a novel, and I think I can get that done now.

Nov. 28: The news out of Washington about the tax bill is so incredible I had to read it two or three times just to make sure I got it right. The news is this: The bill is being held up in the Senate by two members who won't vote for it until it includes even more tax breaks for the rich than are already included. That's right: it's not generous enough to the wealthy! Good Lord. This is like turning down a dish of truffles and gold leaf because it's not expensive enough. And so who is bitching about this, who is crying to the rooftops, who is commiserating with the middle class and poor? Absolutely no one of any consequence.

The feeling of powerlessness that I've been experiencing since Trump's election makes me irritable and, sometimes, angry. Almost all of the news out of Washington is about how the Trumpistas are dismantling government, especially those parts of government built to protect the little guy from the big one. Today's story of the day is about Trump's attempt to hijack a federal agency built to fend off the predations of Wall Street and give consumers a break in marketplace transactions. He wants to install his boy, who hates the consumer agency and wants to tear it apart, as its overseer.

At least the man is consistent. We have a Supreme Court justice he appointed who doesn't believe in justice; we have an education secretary who doesn't believe in public education; we have a housing secretary who doesn't want to help poor people; we have an attorney general who doesn't prosecute Republican or Conservative scofflaws; we have an EPA chief whose goal is to shut the place down; we have a secretary of state who has vowed to do nothing except eliminate positions and tear down the staff; and we have an energy secretary who ran as a presidential candidate on a platform vowing to close that department as well.

Nov. 29: Even the senators who are retiring and can't be hurt in a re-election

240

campaign have folded and now support the tax bill. And, yes, even the senators who said they didn't think the tax cuts were steep enough for the benefit of the rich folks are now on board. I have no idea what happened. But, it's clear that a few senators had a price that was a little steeper than others to buy their support. So much for backbone and moral conduct in the United States Senate. We already know there is a severe lack of both of those in the House, and so the tax cuts will go into effect, and when the shit hits the fan we will have another president and, probably, new congressional leadership who we will be unable to hold accountable.

Nov. 30: The tax bill moves forward, and it will certainly pass despite the fact it screws middle-class and poor people and sends billions into the silk-lined pockets of the rich. As someone noted on TV last night, the Congress is now no longer working for the people. It is working for its real bosses, the big rich. And some even admit that.

Meanwhile, Trump sends three videos via Twitter that show "Muslims" doing some bad things to innocent people, pretending they depict reality when in fact they are part of a propaganda machine out of Great Britain.

Yesterday, Matt Lauer was fired for sexually assaulting some subordinates. He should have been fired a year ago when he embarrassed NBC in his unfortunate performance during the presidential debates. The man was such a lightweight you expected him to float away in a slight breeze like a discarded tissue.

Dec. 1: *The New York Daily News* yesterday called Trump "a madman" who should not be allowed to serve as president. Of course, that's true. And it just keeps getting worse. We learn from *The New York Times* today that Trump has tried to pressure senators not to pursue his family's ties to the Russians. That's called "obstruction of justice." And the president pissed off the British by re-tweeting three photos that he thought were related to Muslim problems in the UK, but which were actually propaganda photos put out by a neo-Nazi group. He is incapable of admitting he's wrong, so he instead blamed the British prime minister for his error in judgment.

The fraud that's called tax reform seems to have been slowed down a bit, not only by those who actually want the rich to get MORE, but also from some Republicans who have suddenly decided they just cannot abide a higher national deficit. A tax committee of congressmen concluded yesterday that the bill that's on the table in the Senate would drastically raise the deficit and nothing in the measure would lower it long-term. Krugman goes after them all with guns a'blazin' on today's NYT op-ed page. Under a headline that reads, "Rot Spreads Wide and Runs Deep," he roasted them for not conducting any hearings on the bill. That's none. Zero. Nada. The whole process, he writes, "involves a level of bad faith we haven't seen in U.S. politics since the days when defenders of slavery physically assaulted their political foes on the Senate floor."

Dec. 2: Nobody on this side of the poor-to-rich spectrum in this country supports the tax bill the Senate passed last night or will pass today. It is chockfull of goodies

241

for rich people, nothing for the rest of us, and most senators have no idea what is in the bill. One senator posted a video last evening saying he had just gotten the bill, and he was expected to read and digest all 490 pages before voting. He showed us a page with handwritten additions and deletions, some of the words indecipherable. This bill represents the hijacking of the American economy by the rich classes, the first big shot fired by the wealthy in the class wars that will soon be upon us.

Michael T. Flynn, disgraced general and fired adviser to Donald Trump, pleaded guilty yesterday to one felony charge of lying to the FBI. He turned state's evidence and will testify against the president and the president's fellow travelers when the time comes. By all reports, this surprised Trump and his boys. Until the man stands in the dock with his ankles in shackles, Trump will be surprised by anything that comes up that pictures him as anything but perfection and wonderful.

Dec. 4: So, not a single Republican in the Senate could find the gumption to do the right thing and vote against the tax bill. Even Corker, who is not running for re-election, signed onto the bill, showing you how deep is the gutter these people bask in.

Now, according to the *Times*, the Republicans are not even waiting to see if the tax bill will result in the economic growth they say and so they are planning to cut Social Security and Medicare next year to make up for the shortfall. This is one of the most deliberately cynical and calculated moves I've ever seen out of a legislative body. It would do no good to write my congressman and senators because my vote doesn't count. They know they have already lost me which is why the gerrymandered the whole of Texas. I am written off, as are all other Democrats in this legislative district, congressional district and the state as a whole.

I checked into my email this morning, and found that 23 and Me had finished my DNA sample. I looked over the report without much depth because I was running out of time. I'll look at it more later. The results show that I am 100 percent European. That breaks down to 99.6 percent Northern European. And that breaks down to 76.1 percent British and Irish; 12.7 percent other Northwest European; and 10 percent German.

I think it's interesting that Mother thought Jim Weatherford, her real father, was half Indian; his mother was reputed by Mom to be Choctaw. It appears very, very unlikely that is the case unless the Choctaw had a clan in Dublin!

Dec. 5: Trump apparently went ballistic yesterday on his Twitter feed about the FBI and the investigation into his Russian collusion. I read about it in The *Times* today. There is no telling what a desperate man will do to assure his weak personality that he is superior to others. Start a war in Korea? I don't think Trump actually understands what a nuclear arsenal can do. And that's just part of the story – he has no idea what a rifle company is capable of in terms of fire power. The fact is that North Korea does not have to target America to make its point. It can just sit 50 miles from Seoul and blow the place up using antique howitzers and hand grenades.

Dec. 5: The argument right now about Trump and his tenure centers on whether he has obstructed justice. His lawyer has taken the curious approach of asserting that a sitting president cannot obstruct justice because, it appears, justice is what he says it is, an odd thing to contend in a democracy. And so The *Times* editorializes about this patently ridiculous claim in today's editions: "This will come as news to Congress, which has passed laws criminalizing the obstruction of justice and decided twice in the last four decades that when a president violates those laws he has committed an impeachable offense."

Trump headed out to Utah yesterday to announce that he's reducing the size of several national parks so that business can go in and drill and mine the properties. People living in New York or Washington and who have only flown over the center of the United States have no idea how much land there is out west. There's plenty of places to drill and mine without reducing the size of scenic and wondrous landscapes, some of which are sacred to Native Americans.

A kind of interesting piece appeared in The *Times* by Michelle Goldberg. It had a headline that pulled me in because it said that young people are ready to move to something beyond capitalism, like, say, socialism. Goldberg cites little evidence of that, but it could be true. After all, today's young people are going to take it in the shorts after the Republicans are finished with them. They won't have good schools because all the taxpayers' money will go to private schools. They won't have good economic mobility because the rich will erect significantly hard barriers for entry into their classes. She writes: "After the fall of Communism, capitalism came to seem like the modern world's natural state, like the absence of ideology rather than an ideology itself. The Trump era is radicalizing because it makes the rotten morality behind our inequalities so manifest. It's not just the occult magic of the market that's enriching Ivanka Trump's children while health insurance premiums soar and public school budgets wither. It's the raw exercise of power by a tiny unaccountable minority that believes in its own superiority. You don't have to want to abolish capitalism to understand why the prospect is tempting to a generation that's being robbed."

Dec. 6: Yesterday was our 36th wedding anniversary, and we both forgot about it on the actual day. We had talked last weekend about how we might celebrate, and then I got sick and that has tended to keep my mind focusing on allergies and coughing and sneezing. I haven't devoted much time to reflection on our marriage, but I can say without having done so that we've generally had a good life together. We raised or helped raise seven children – my three girls and her three girls and a boy. They are all gainfully employed, well-educated and love and are loved by all. We've made some stupid decisions, but not as many as some people I know.

One of my chief regrets is that I drank too much and took too many over-the-counter drugs at the same time, and so was too frequently just sort of out of it. Lynda is not really patient about many things, but she tolerated this behavior, and I'm sorry that she did so. I should have had my ass kicked.

These last couple of years have been hard because she has been in so much pain for so much of the time. Just in the last month or so has she had relief of the pain at the same time as relief from anxiety and depression, thanks to modern pharmaceuticals. I think that overall we've been lucky, and we've been in love.

Dec. 7: Trump held a press conference yesterday to announce that the U.S. would henceforth recognize Jerusalem as the capital of Israel, saying that it was such an obvious fact already that to fail to acknowledge it would be to accept a continuing somehow fatal lie. This from a man who would climb a tree to tell a lie if he could tell the truth standing on the ground. This IS the news: Donald Trump found a lie he didn't love. Everyone else in the world thinks this is a terrible idea, and, in fact, U.S. leaders have refused to give Jerusalem to the Israelis ever since Israel was created in 1948. Did Trump come into office with such insight and policy acumen that he can divine how the U.S. would recognize the capital and then get all the parties in that part of the world to agree to a peace treaty?

Rachel Maddow is piecing together the part of the puzzle regarding Trump and the Russians. The way she has the game board outlined right now, the Russians wanted to get a Trump win, at any cost, because he had promised them he would lift the Obama-era sanctions levied by the free world against the Russians for violating the sovereignty of their neighbors, among other things. It was all quid pro quo. Except, of course, Trump has not lifted the sanctions and won't, even though he will apparently continue to curry favor with Putin and other Third World dictators.

Dec. 9: We watched the Rachel Maddow special last evening on the so-called Russian Dossier, a compendium of facts about the Trumps and their connections with Russians put together by Christopher Steel, a British spymaster. One by one the details Steel put together are proving true as Robert Mueller, the special counsel, digs into how the Trumps and the Russians conspired to steal the 2016 election. What all of this amounts to, as I have said in this space previously, is treason. The Republicans in Congress are fellow-travelers in this whole charade. The question is whether anyone will be punished for selling out the United States and its democracy. Right now it appears that no one will hold anyone in power accountable. I am so disgusted and dismayed I am thinking about not even watching the news anymore. It's too depressing to think of my country being sold out for a few nickels by the rich and powerful.

Dec. 13: Lynda and I stayed up to watch the final results from the Alabama Senate race involving one child molester and serial idiot, Roy Moore, and Doug Jones, a Democrat with an altogether savory and even exemplary record as a federal prosecutor. Jones barely beat Moore, but beat him he did! It was a solid, resounding rebuke of the Trumpistas in general and Trump and Steve Bannon, his shadow Partner in Evil, in particular.

Dec. 14: I am slowly getting better. The allergies are subsiding, but I'm not sure why that is the case. Lynda said yesterday that she doesn't think that cedar trees have even started saturating the air with their pollen yet. If that is true, then this lull in the siege of my sinuses is going to be short-lived.

The *Times* has a good editorial today about the Pentagon appropriation from Congress for the next cycle. The editorial focuses on a recent report. From the editorial:

"The military budget is now $643 billion. The actual and potential threats from Russia, China, North Korea and Islamic extremists are all serious, but giving the Pentagon another huge increase defies common sense. The Pentagon already wastes about one in five of the taxpayer dollars it receives, according to a Pentagon-commissioned study. And the United States, which has plenty of other urgent needs, already spends more on its military than the <u>next seven</u> countries combined."

It's that last sentence that grabbed my attention: the U.S. spends more on its military than the next seven countries combined. Why? Well, because the military has managed to keep key facilities in key congressional districts across the country. That's one reason. Another is that the Republicans traditionally raise the alarm about an unprepared military when they want to rally the dumbest of their constituents to their side. I personally did not see a lot of waste when I was in the Army, but I wasn't in a great spot to see any. I was a lowly lieutenant in a kind of backwater post.

Dec. 15: I left Amarillo and Canyon in summer of '83 after a particularly bad winter. And then shortly after that, Lynda's dad had a physical attack of some sort, perhaps a heart condition, perhaps a stomach condition, and she felt the urge to move to Wichita Falls to be near him and others in her family. I knew nothing about Wichita Falls, so that sounded fine to me as long as I could get a job at the newspaper. In May of 1983 I interviewed at the *Times and Record News* with Billy McGee, the managing editor, and Don James, the editor. Afterwards, they offered me a job as assistant managing editor with an unspecified salary. We packed up, put our Canyon house on the market, and moved to Wichita Falls in late June.

I started work on June 26 or June 28, arriving at the downtown newspaper offices in a dress blue shirt with button-down collar and red-and-blue rep tie, all ready to be an assistant managing editor. When I got there Billy McGee told me that there had been a change of plan in a proposed newsroom reorganization, and instead of being an AME, I was going to be a copy editor on the design desk. This was not even a lateral move for me from TV reporting. It was a step down and monumental fall backwards. I would be making $350 a week, far less than I made at KFDA. I was stuck. There was only one newspaper in town, and it never occurred to me to try to go to one of the TV stations for a job. I was convinced that I was not a TV-type and that if I was going to have a future in journalism it would be in newspapers not television.

My job and my salary were not the only surprises I stepped into when I showed up at the *Times and Record News*. I was actually stepping into newsroom hell.

Dec. 16: My first couple of days at the *Times and Record News* were revelatory. I sensed that the reporters and line editors were, for the most part, completely alienated from the top management, mainly from Don James, the editor. You could feel the animosity in the atmosphere. But, there were also signs of the discontent.

My second or third morning on the job, I noticed for the first time that three big bulletin boards on wheels had been placed facing the copy desk so as to be seen by the line editors and the reporting staff. On the bulletin board the pages of that day's morning paper had been tacked, and the pages were covered with red ink to point out the errors that were in the published product. That was bad enough, but along with the red marks, the critic had also written in big letters things like, "What idiot did this?" and "Why didn't you catch this?" and "What were you thinking about here?" It was a display of utter contempt. It was like seeing your baby, plunged onto a pike, bleeding. I was stunned. I'd never seen anything like it, and everything I'd ever read or heard or learned about good management cautioned against this kind of visceral overkill – this sorry game of "Gotcha" – of poor performance.

All this kind of critique was doing was embarrassing everyone involved and inspiring them to hate the perpetrator, who was Don James, the guy in charge.

I began to realize that I had taken a job in a den of rattlesnakes, a realization reinforced later that week when I attended a rump meeting of editors and reporters conducted in a semi-lit room off the photo department for the purpose of airing staff grievances so as to take a complete list to the publisher in the hopes he would fire Don James. The publisher, Jim Lonergan, did nothing when confronted with evidence of Don's behavior.

Shortly thereafter, the newsroom began to lose reporters and editors. Cindy Rugeley left. The AME for the afternoon paper and his wife, a graphics designer, left. Reporters left. Right after Christmas, with a skeleton staff remaining, I was offered Cindy's job as city editor for the afternoon paper, and I took it. I needed the money, and I needed the move upward because I had no other place to go to work in Wichita Falls.

I just hung in there and eventually made it to be editor in chief, thanks to the untimely death of Don James and other events I had no control over.

Dec. 18: "Star Wars: The Last Jedi" opened over the weekend, and U.S. audiences paid $250 million to see it. Across the world, another $240 million was spent to see it. The *Times* reports today that the film cost a whopping $350 million to make. That is on the far side of incredible. I hope to get to see the movie after the first of the year when it is possible to get a ticket.

The big story on the newspaper's front page today has to do with what spies are doing within and without the EPA to make sure employees toe the line. EPA workers who have criticized Trump or his boy's policies at the top of the agency have had their emails purloined and have been scolded, and worse, for what they wrote. I'm sure this kind of Nazi behavior is not isolated to the EPA. Trump cannot stand criticism, and if you're on his payroll you will agree with whatever he wants, no matter how off the wall or crazy or dangerous that may be, or you will be fired. Remember: For Trump, this gig at the White House is just an extension of his reality TV show, "The Apprentice."

Dec. 19: The Senate and House Republicans are going to pass the tax bill tomorrow, and they will have done so without a single public hearing or a single expert witness's testimony and without any input from Democrats. It will be a remarkable gift for the very, very rich, and a stab in the back for the middle class and poor. And all the while, Trump will claim it is really hurting him and his kids, which is a fucking joke. As The *Times* notes in an editorial today, Trump and fellow real-estate moguls will make out big-time.

Dec. 20: Thomas Friedman has a pretty comprehensive list of the Trump transgressions on the op-ed page of The *Times* this morning. Just one of the paragraphs:

"On norms, we've grown numb to a president who misleads or outright lies every day. Different newspapers measure this differently. The Washington Post says Trump has averaged 5.5 false or misleading claims every day in office, putting him on pace for 1,999 in his first year. According to The Times, Barack Obama told 18 'distinct falsehoods' over his entire eight-year presidency, while Trump, in his first 10 months in office, 'has told 103 separate untruths, many of them repeatedly.'"

Dec. 21: I fully expect Trump to fire Robert Mueller, the special counsel investigating his links to the Russians, this weekend. He is full of himself after the Senate and House passed the tax bill. He will feel emboldened. And he also feels that he can act with absolute impunity. He believes he is accountable to no one. He believes there are no consequences for acting badly, and that has certainly been the case. Republicans in Congress are complicit in treason, but they take comfort in the fact that they are getting richer and richer by the minute.

I am truly so disgusted and dismayed that if Lynda were amenable we would move to Canada as soon as possible and get out of this insane country and this state that's run by cretins and morons.

Dec. 23: Rachel Maddow has focused attention in her last two evening shows on how the Republicans seem to be repositioning themselves to discredit all members of the FBI and then anyone else involved in the Mueller investigation of Trump and the Russians. Without just coming right out and saying so, it is clear that she and some of her guests believe these Republicans are complicit in treason.

It's not clear to her or to me why they would be so quick to embrace the Russians. Are they so beholding to the president that regardless of what he does or who he embraces, they will do so, too? It appears to be the case. History will show, I am convinced, that the Trumps and his friends in the Congress and at Fox News are the 21st century equivalent of Hitler and his Nazi leadership. Piece by piece they are selling us out. At the same time, piece by piece they are dismantling our national government and any programs aimed at helping people.

The longer I was editor of the *Times Record News*, the business side was getting harder and harder to manage. In the fall of 2006, I got a stock option award based on a Scripps stock price of, let's say, $39 a share. In February 2007, the price of the stock had dropped by 33 percent and more. There was no sign of a bottom. In March, the editors and publishers of the Scripps papers in Texas and New Mexico convened in Dallas to talk about what to do. That's the meeting where the Big Boys from Cincinnati suggested that to save money we should cut full-time staff and hire stringers, a laughable and totally unrealistic idea. (That would be the

Wal-Mart business plan: Use only part-time people so you wouldn't have to pay them benefits. Only that kind of operation doesn't work in a newsroom because you can't hire part-time reporters and editors.)

In April, everyone in the Scripps newspaper family who was 60 years old or older got an offer: You could leave and you would receive a full year of pay with a full year of insurance paid up. All around us other newspaper companies were offering buyouts. None of them offered a full year of pay and a full year of insurance, so the Scripps deal was the best. I turned 60 in May of 2007. Lynda and I talked long and hard about taking the offer. I talked at length with my publisher about the future if I stayed on as editor. We all came to the same conclusion: I would never be happy at the *Times Record* News as it was going to be because of staffing and budget cuts. Heck, I was already not very happy with the way things were heading. So, after my birthday in May of 2007, I did take the buyout and landed at home with Lynda and Mom, who at that time lived with us.

Dec. 24: When I left the *Times Record News* in May of 2007, I had no real plan in place for the rest of my life. We were living in a small house on Wenonah Street in Wichita Falls with Mom, so our expenses were pretty low. Just to have something to do, I volunteered to be the executive director of the Zavala Hispanic Cultural Initiative in a cheap office downtown. Several years before this, I had worked to create the Zavala group because I and the other organizers realized after the Year 2000 census count that the future of Wichita Falls belonged largely to the Hispanic population. The Anglo numbers were declining overall, but the fall-off was especially precipitous when you looked at who was aging out of leadership positions in the city and county and school district. New leaders needed to be in place to take over at all levels and in all kinds of organizations, including nonprofits. Through the Zavala initiative, we hoped to train the next generation of Hispanics to be leaders through organized efforts that had been in place for years to train the Anglo population. So, this was something I very much believed in and was happy to donate time to once I had plenty of time to donate.

In August of 2007, I got a letter in the mail from Sue Mayborn, publisher and owner and editor in chief of the *Temple Daily Telegram* in Temple, Texas, asking whether I might be interested in joining that newspaper as managing editor. It would be a huge step down for me, but I didn't have a whole lot of options. I took the job. Unfortunately.

Mrs. Mayborn never had a good word about anything, and I had to meet with the woman every single day at 4 o'clock. She thought my staff was filled with idiots. She thought I was an idiot. Before Lynda and Mom arrived in Temple I was already drinking too much when I would get home. I kept that up after we had a house. The drinking was made worse by the fact that I couldn't get to sleep at night, and so I drank more in an effort to anesthetize myself. Finally, I went to the doctor, and got more pills to help me sleep and then to help me shake off the drowsy effects of sleep in the morning.

Before long I was taking medication to sleep and to wake up, and I was drinking several glasses of wine every single night. The combination was obviously not lethal but it was not conducive to a great home life. I was miserable at work.

Dec. 25: Maybe it's not odd at all, but I have no memory of ever having a Christmas celebration at 914 Bowie Street when I was growing up. Perhaps we had family Christmas tree festivities, but I don't think so. Instead, every Christmas Dad drove us to Greenville, which is about 50 miles northeast of Dallas, to have Christmas with Mama Jo, Ruth and other members of the Wilson family. These were fantastic family affairs mainly because John and I were much loved by everyone there. I would say we were doted upon. My grandmother, in particular, made over us, as did Ruth and my aunt Carolie, who had been in charge of Dad when he was a child.

On Christmas Eve we would all go to services at the Presbyterian church in downtown Greenville, and we would all sit in one pew. Behind the pastor was the rose window the family donated to the church as a memorial to Papa Polk, my grandfather, who died in 1947 before I was born. The feeling I had at those times was of warm inclusion. I had a history. It was admirable, even stellar. I was part of a respected and honorable tribe. And I was well loved. Even strangers loved me because of the family I belonged to.

After three or so years at the Telegram, I wound up with a new doctor at Scott & White whose name was John Walton. He had moved to the hospital medical staff from Idaho or Wyoming, and he was a pretty straight-shooter. When he looked at the list of medications I was taking, he let out a long whistle and asked for some details about my life. I told him about my constant frustration at work, about the disengagement of Lynda. After a few months, Dr. Walton asked me if I was intent on killing myself. He suggested that the alcohol consumption, the medications, the work and Mrs. Mayborn were conspiring to lead me to an early death, perhaps one that was just around the corner. His recommendation: that I retire, the sooner the better.

I talked this over with Lynda, and we decided to check in with Social Security to see what would happen if I did just that. It turned out that we could be OK financially, so in April of 2011 I handed in my resignation as of May 15. Mrs. Mayborn couldn't have cared less. Nor could any of the other poor feckless prisoners I worked with on the senior management side.

All across the country, the Democrats are running multiple candidates for slots now held by Republicans in state legislatures and in Congress. The midyear elections could completely undo the Republicans who have backed Trump and his outrageous dismantling of our federal government.

Dec. 27: After Lynda and I decided it was time for me to retire and after we had figured out that we could make it financially if I did so, she began to look for a place where we could live the rest of our lives. We certainly did not want to live in Temple, and we did not want to return to Wichita Falls or to Amarillo or Canyon. After doing a lot of research online, Lynda found a house in Wimberley that we could afford. That would put us about an hour from Austin and about 30 minutes from Canyon Lake. We would be three and a half hours from Houston, but that was better than the distance we had faced when we were in Temple. So, in May of 2011, we moved to 7 Woodview Court in Wimberley, a town of about 3,000 in the Hill Country southwest of Austin. That's where we live right now, and we do love the location.

A couple of months of complete retirement in Wimberley was about all I could take of inactivity. I was spending a good bit of time at the local library, reading magazines and checking out books. I contacted the Wimberley Village Library folks about becoming a volunteer, and they put me on for a four-hour shift on Fridays.

Dec. 28: The library was a great place to volunteer, because it was a wonderful way to meet people in Wimberley. The library was very much a hub for the literati. By summer's end in 2011, I told Lynda that if I needed to get another job I'd love to work at the library, and I mean not two weeks passed before the woman who was circulation librarian announced she was leaving her job to move to Chattanooga, Tennessee.

I applied for the job, which was 20 hours a week for $12 an hour. And after interviewing, I got it. I started work around the first of September, and I have been working at the library ever since, so that is six years now. During that time, I have made innumerable friends and acquaintances, and I have added some significant programs, including an annual film festival (the 2018 version is on Jan. 13) and an adult spelling bee, conducted every year in the fall. I also update the library website and present a few programs of my own every year (last year, I presented a program on the possibility of humans colonizing Mars, an interest of mine). The library director, Carolyn Manning, is easy to work for, and I enjoy my colleagues on the staff.

Only recently in Wimberley have I gotten involved in volunteer work again. I am a member of the board for the Citizens Alliance for Responsible Development and also a member of the board of the Wimberley Valley Dark Sky Alliance. I'm also on the vestry at St. Stephen's Episcopal Church and I play in the little band for Wednesday night services. The latter was just a continuation of sorts of my desire to volunteer as a musician at church. I began playing in the choir at Our Lady of Guadalupe Catholic Church in Wichita Falls. I loved the people in the choir and in that church and much enjoyed playing and singing in both English and Spanish at a variety of services, including the ones conducted on Christmas Eve.

I should mention that I helped produce a book about the Memorial Day flooding in Wimberley along the Blanco River in 2015. The book is mainly interviews with a few photos.

Dec. 29: The story of the day in The *Times* is at the top of the Business Day section and bears this striking headline: "Bookstore Chain Succumbs, as E-commerce devours retailing." That's an interesting choice of verbs. The story by David Streitfeld focuses on Book World, a small chain, and its demise this year. It could not compete against Amazon and other online retailers. Nobody else in the book business can, either. In one paragraph, Streitfeld talks briefly about the death of Hastings, a regional chain.

The *Times* story makes it clear that bookstores cannot survive in today's marketplace. I'm not too worried about the future of libraries, because we're not competing in the world of retail. We're loaning things out. A couple of years ago, we worried about inroads that might be made by e-readers like the Kindle. But, I have been approached by very few people about downloading books, even library books. I think a handful of people, like Lynda, love their e-readers. Other people want books in their hands.

Streitfeld, among many, many other writers, focuses on the very tip end of the supply and production chain in publishing. I have never seen a really good book-length explanation of how technological advances in publishing over the past 50 years affected the labor market and, more importantly, the quality of the work produced for people to buy and consume.

As I wrap up this year of reflection (my last entry will be on Sunday, Dec. 31), I want to address these changes as I saw them occur first-hand. It's important to be aware of the fact that a newspaper that arrives on your front porch or in your mailbox online is a product that is made through a factory-like process.

When I started work as a young reporter at the *Amarillo Globe-News* in 1966, many skill sets were required to get a newspaper out of the conceptual stage and onto a front porch, and many steps were involved as well. At the front end of the factory was the editorial department where I worked as a reporter. Sixty or 70 of us gathered news in our notebooks, turned those notes into stories typed onto flimsy paper and gave the stories to line editors who fixed the stories and then sent them in paper form to the backshop in a vacuum tube.

This system was designed not only to produce a finished print product but also to assure that it was correct and complete. That changed with high-tech progress in editing software and hardware.

The savings in materials at the back end of the printing process were also substantial. So, where did that money go?

Well, I can tell you where it did not go. It did not go into vastly better salaries for the reporters and editors. When I started as a reporter at the Amarillo paper, the staffers with experience could expect to make at least as much money a year as did public school teachers if not a little more. When I left the business in 2011, our reporters never made anywhere near what teachers made with similar years of experience. They were better off doing just about anything other than being journalists.

Dec. 30: The technological changes that took place in the newspaper industry from 1966 through 2011 vastly reduced the number of people involved in production and put an increasing burden on people in the editorial department, especially people on the copy desks. Dozens of jobs were eliminated at the *Times Record News* thanks to computerization.

But, I don't think the changes made us a better paper. In some ways we were measurably worse, although we were better than we were in the '70s, when newspapers outside the major cities looked like they had been put together by 7th-graders. The savings that came from the technological changes went to publishers. They did not flow back into the newsroom to produce a better newspaper. In fact, after the advent of the internet, the opposite was the case, as I have noted elsewhere.

Dec. 31: This is the final entry in this project. I am pretty proud of myself. I have written something for every single day of 2017. As time has run out, I have realized how many things I failed to address. The year has gone by quickly.

I want to end by underscoring the factors that I believe turned a small-town kid from the most conservative part of the most conservative state in America into a liberal. Those factors are simply these: I had parents, especially a father, who encouraged me to think and to discuss politics at any time (until later in his life); I read widely, and was especially intrigued early on by the logic and humor of William F. Buckley Jr. (I did not want to be like him politically, but only rhetorically); I was befriended and mentored by Buck Ramsey, a rational and angry liberal who taught me about how politics really works; I grew up Presbyterian and took seriously the teachings of Jesus Christ and Paul, encouraged to do so by the Rev. Baldwin Stribling and a number of my college political science professors; the teachings of those professors themselves; the deplorable racial disparities I saw in Amarillo, in person, and across America, on TV; the eye-opening experiences I had before and during my military service during the war in Vietnam; and the abuses visited upon me and other workers by the people with big money, the people who actually ran the country and still do, the American Oligarchs.

CPSIA information can be obtained
at www.ICGtesting.com
Printed in the USA
FSHW011222100519
58021FS